MW01194586

After Collapse

After Collapse

The Regeneration of Complex Societies

edited by Glenn M. Schwartz and John J. Nichols

The University of Arizona Press
Tucson

The University of Arizona Press
© 2006 The Arizona Board of Regents
All rights reserved
∞ This book is printed on acid-free, archival-quality paper.
Manufactured in the United States of America

11 10 09 08 07 06   6 5 4 3 2 1

Library of Congress Cataloging-in-Publication Data
After collapse : the regeneration of complex societies / edited by
Glenn M. Schwartz and John J. Nichols.
    p. cm.
  Papers presented at a symposium held during the Annual
Meeting of the Society for American Archaeology in
Milwaukee, April 2003.
  Includes bibliographical references and index.
  ISBN-13: 978-0-8165-2509-6 (hardcover : alk. paper)
  ISBN-10: 0-8165-2509-9 (hardcover : alk. paper)
  1. Civilization, Ancient—Congresses. 2. Social evolution—
Congresses. 3. Social archaeology—Congresses. I. Schwartz,
Glenn M. II. Nichols, John J. (John Jackson), 1963– III. Society
for American Archaeology. Meeting (68th : 2003 : Milwaukee,
Wis.)
  CB311.A35 2006
  303.4093'091732—dc22
                        2005028813

Contents

1 From Collapse to Regeneration 3
Glenn M. Schwartz

2 The Demise and Regeneration of Bronze Age Urban Centers in the Euphrates Valley of Syria 18
Lisa Cooper

3 Amorites, Onagers, and Social Reorganization in Middle Bronze Age Syria 38
John J. Nichols and Jill A. Weber

4 "Lo, Nobles Lament, the Poor Rejoice": State Formation in the Wake of Social Flux 58
Ellen Morris

5 The Collapse and Regeneration of Complex Society in Greece, 1500–500 BC 72
Ian Morris

6 Inca State Origins: Collapse and Regeneration in the Southern Peruvian Andes 85
Gordon F. McEwan

7 Regeneration as Transformation: Postcollapse Society in Nasca, Peru 99
Christina A. Conlee

8 After State Collapse: How Tumilaca Communities Developed in the Upper Moquegua Valley, Peru 114
Kenny Sims

9 Patterns of Political Regeneration in Southeast and East Asia 137
Bennet Bronson

10 From Funan to Angkor: Collapse and Regeneration in Ancient Cambodia   144
Miriam T. Stark

11 Framing the Maya Collapse: Continuity, Discontinuity, Method, and Practice in the Classic to Postclassic Southern Maya Lowlands   168
Diane Z. Chase and Arlen F. Chase

12 Postclassic Maya Society Regenerated at Mayapán   188
Marilyn A. Masson, Timothy S. Hare, and Carlos Peraza Lope

13 Before and After Collapse: Reflections on the Regeneration of Social Complexity   208
Alan L. Kolata

14 Notes on Regeneration   222
Norman Yoffee

References   229
About the Editors   277
About the Contributors   279
Index   283

After Collapse

From Collapse to Regeneration

Glenn M. Schwartz

In the 1960s and 1970s, comparative studies of early complex societies in anthropological archaeology focused overwhelmingly on the emergence of the first states and urban societies.[1] Prime movers, primary states, and the earliest urban systems were the subject of intensive investigation and theorizing. An investigation of the origins of civilization is certainly an appropriate task for archaeology, since the formation of the new institutions, technologies, and modes of thought inherent in that process represents one of the most important transformations in human history. Moreover, archaeology can preside in near-total isolation over the topic, since textual evidence is likely to be minimal or absent until states are well ensconced.

But by at least the 1980s, dissatisfaction with the emphasis on civilization's rise had emerged. On the one hand was the critique levelled against processual archaeology and its reliance on the band-tribe-chiefdom-state evolutionary model. On the other was the problem that a focus on origins assumed that there was little else to learn about complex societies once they appear; it implied that social evolution was complete when cities and states emerged. But the more the workings of early complex societies were exposed, the more apparent it became that these were not smoothly functioning machines that ran perfectly once their engines were turned on. Complex societies could be unstable phenomena, prone to episodes of fragility and collapse.

As a result, the study of collapse in early complex societies has become a research focus of considerable significance. Among the studies devoted to collapse are Yoffee and Cowgill 1988 and Tainter 1988, not to mention discussions of specific episodes of collapse such as that of the Classic Maya (Culbert 1973a, 1988; Webster 2002), the Indus civilization (Kenoyer 2005; Possehl 1997), and Near Eastern urban systems of the late third millennium BC (Courty and Weiss 1997; Wilkinson 1997).

The recognition that early complex societies were prone to episodes of falling and rising has led to the advancement of a cyclical model in which societies oscillate from periods of urbanism and sociopolitical centralization to intervals of ruralism and local autonomy (Yoffee 1979). Such a model departs from traditional neo-evolutionist assumptions of linear progression, allowing for the possibility of decreasing as well as increasing sociopolitical complexity.

The goal of this book is to push the investigation one step further. A focus on rise and collapse still leaves the consideration of social evolution unfinished; what happens *after* collapse? In this volume, our emphasis is on the reappearance of societal complexity after periods of disintegration. How do "second generation" states form in regions that experienced political disintegration? How do they differ from or resemble the states that preceded them? And why are urban systems and states reestablished in some regions but not in others?

Compared to the interest in the emergence and collapse of civilizations, the regeneration of societal complexity is a relatively neglected topic. Models of societal birth, growth, and death—well known from the ideas of scholars such as Edward Gibbon, Oswald Spengler (1918–22), and Arnold Toynbee (1933–54)—have been echoed in more recent work in archaeology and elsewhere, but revival and resurrection are largely excluded from attention. As Joyce Marcus (1989:201) has commented, "most scholars have devoted more attention to the 'rise and fall' of civilizations than to the processes that subsequently led to a reorganization of the population remaining in their territories. And relatively few archaeologists have studied the processes of dissolution, recovery, and reorganization, preferring instead to study the 'golden ages' of ancient civilizations, when those societies were 'in full flower.'" Despite this neglect, the study of the regeneration of complex societies is an especially appropriate subject for archaeology as opposed to text-based history, since written texts are likely to be meager or totally lacking in "dark ages" after collapse, in the absence of central authorities, bureaucratic administrations, and scribal installations. While narratives of the collapse period might have been produced in subsequent eras, their frequently propagandist character and chronological remove from the period in question renders their utility limited (Renfrew 1979).[2]

I became interested in the question of regeneration as a consequence of my fieldwork at Tell Umm el-Marra in Syria (Curvers and Schwartz 1997; Schwartz, Curvers, Gerritsen et al. 2000; Schwartz et al. 2003), where excavations have yielded a sequence of occupations spanning periods of early urbanism, collapse, and regeneration (see Nichols and Weber, chapter 3). It was my expectation that a cross-cultural examination would not only assist in comprehending regeneration at Umm el-Marra, but would also contribute to a general understanding of the phenomenon. A comprehensive, cross-cultural investigation of regeneration might also be expected to broaden and strengthen theoretical frameworks on the character and workings of early complex societies (Trigger 2003). As a result, John Nichols and I organized a symposium on regeneration considered from a cross-cultural perspective at the Society for American Archaeology annual meeting in Milwaukee in April 2003. The chapters in this volume derive from that meeting, with the addition of Ian Morris's contribution (chapter 5) on Archaic Greece, solicited so as to include that well-documented and extremely influential case.

It might be observed (or objected) that in recent years—largely due to the postprocessual critique—comparative, diachronic studies of the sort we are attempting, with a focus on developmental issues, have frequently been avoided in favor of synchronic analyses of individual societies and their historical specificities. But a total abandonment of the comparative and diachronic would be misguided (DeMarrais 2002; Trigger 2003:3–4, 25–39; Yoffee 2005:194). While each society is historically unique, societies nevertheless display common patterns whose recognition allows for a better understanding both of individual societies and of human society in general. An appropriate analogy might be supplied by the human individual: each person is unique, with his or her own unique history, but the behavior of an individual usually can be better understood given an awareness of broader-scale phenomena such as the individual's gender, nationality, and economic status. I concur with Gil Stein (1998:25–26) that "the challenge is to develop a new synthesis that can incorporate the historically unique developmental pathways of specific polities within a more general approach that elucidates cross-cultural regularities in the processes of social evolutionary change."

Collapse

Regeneration presupposes collapse. Consequently, it is necessary to define collapse before investigating and explaining regeneration. In the archaeological literature, collapse usually entails some or all of the following: the fragmentation of states into smaller political entities; the partial abandonment or complete desertion of urban centers, along with the loss or depletion of their centralizing functions; the breakdown of regional economic systems; and the failure of civilizational ideologies. As the contributors in Yoffee and Cowgill 1988 concluded, rarely does collapse involve the complete disappearance of a group of people or of a "great tradition."

Suggested causes for collapse are manifold and have been much debated. Scholars do not refer to invasions as much as they used to, but they frequently consider other external variables such as climate change, particularly episodes of desiccation that weaken the agricultural base of urban societies dependent on agricultural surpluses (Dalfes, Kukla, and Weiss 1997; Gill 2000; Hodell et al. 2001). Other approaches emphasize internal variables, noting the tendency of complex societies to impose heavy demands on their physical environments, rendering agricultural systems vulnerable to crisis (Abrams and Rue 1988; Shaw 2003; Tainter 1988; Wilkinson 1997). Ideological failures may occur as a consequence of other failures of the central authority (Lucero 2002): if the economy suffers or the government neglects to perform its expected tasks in other ways, the populace may lose its faith in the governing ideologies and abandon its allegiance to the system. Another perspective focuses on the tension between traditional kinship systems and the centralizing, socially stratifying activities of the elite (Iannone 2002; McAnany 1995). In this view, elites may have found it difficult to maintain "large-scale inegalitarian structures for long periods of time" (Marcus 1998:94).

An additional problem when considering collapse lies in assessing the sociopolitical organization of postcollapse societies. Do states and complex societies that have experienced collapse "devolve" to chiefly or tribal societies? If such ideas of reversion are rejected, what are the ways in which sociopolitical and economic organization are structured in periods of collapse?

In Norman Yoffee and George Cowgill's edited volume on collapse (1988), many if not most of the contributors agreed that collapse is almost never total or complete. As Shmuel Eisenstadt asserts (1988:242), "Ancient states and civilizations do not collapse at all, if by *collapse* is meant the complete end of those political systems and their accompanying civilizational frameworks. Thus, the investigation of collapse in ancient states and civilizations really entails identifying the various kinds of social reorganization in these types of societies and so viewing collapse as part of the continuous process of boundary reconstruction."

Regeneration

One such manifestation of boundary reconstruction is regeneration of societal complexity. If collapse entails, at least in part, the disintegration of states, urban systems, economic systems, or ideologies, then regeneration should consist of the reconstruction of the same kinds of institutions and phenomena. It is important to emphasize that by regeneration we mean the reappearance of societal complexity (states, cities, etc.) after periods of decentralization, not the reappearance of *specific* complex societies.

Although previous considerations of the reasons for, and mechanisms of, regeneration have been minimal, several case studies can provide information on the range of ideas on the subject previously advanced. One of the first well-known considerations of historical decline and regeneration is found in ibn Khaldun's fourteenth-century AD work the *Muqaddimah*, which conceives of history in terms of cycles of ruling dynasties or states. States disintegrate and are replaced by new entities headed by former lower-level administrators or rebels, who emulate the institutions of the preceding dynasties. But perhaps the best-known example of regeneration in recent historical scholarship is that of the reemergence of cities and states in western Europe after the collapse of the western Roman empire. By the middle of the first millennium AD, cities were largely abandoned except for ritual purposes, the infrastructure of the Roman empire had been dismantled, and most of the institutions of classical civilization had disappeared. How did the states and complex societies of medieval Europe emerge out of this prototypical Dark Age?

An extremely influential perspective on this issue is that of Henri Pirenne (1925, 1939). In his view, the key factor for understanding both the decline and the reemergence of western European complex society was long-distance trade. According to Pirenne, the barbarian invasions were not responsible for the collapse of Roman institutions and urban systems, since the barbarians preserved what they could. Instead, the crucial factor was the detachment of western Europe from Mediterranean trade networks by the Muslim Arab conquests of the seventh century AD. With the disappearance of the commercial classes and the wealth derived from Mediterranean trade, urban life collapsed and political institutions disintegrated. Only with the establishment of new trade networks in northern Europe and the Mediterranean in the late first/early second millennium AD did cities and centralized states revive. The static, closed economy of the Dark Ages was opened up, and regeneration began.

Subsequent revisions and critiques of Pirenne's thesis have continued to emphasize the importance of trade in the regeneration of European complex society, while modifying the details (Havighurst 1976). Richard Hodges and David Whitehouse (1983), reviewing archaeological data, concluded that demographic and urban decline was observable in western Europe several centuries before the emergence of Islam. Although they maintained that Europe's disconnection from Mediterranean trade was not critical in the formation of early medieval Europe, they concurred with Pirenne that regeneration entailed the opening up of new trade networks in northern Europe in the late first millennium AD. Rejecting Pirenne's insistence on the isolation of Europe from the Islamic world, Michael McCormick (2001) has advanced a model in which Europe, a periphery, offered a raw material—slaves—to the Muslim core in exchange for specialized goods: "the voracious appetite [of the Muslim world] for northern slaves provided the first great impetus to the development of the European commercial economy" (McCormick 2001:768). In all these discussions, the importance of long-distance trade networks for the maintenance and regeneration of urban systems and states is repeatedly underlined.

Within archaeology, perhaps the most extensive discussion of regeneration has been offered by Joyce Marcus (1989, 1992, 1993, 1998; see also Iannone 2002). Considering the cyclical patterns exhibited by Mesoamerican states such as Teotihuacán and Monte Albán, Marcus observes that urban-based states typically exerted control over vast territories early in their life-spans, but they fragmented as provincial centers broke away. A secondary center would eclipse its former overlord to become the capital of a new and more powerful state. Despite this change in fortunes, the original centers grew even larger after their political power began to wane.

In this cyclical pattern of peaks and troughs, which Marcus terms the "dynamic model," regeneration is powered by the rise of ambitious elites in provincial contexts forging alliances and re-creating large-scale political entities. While Marcus's observation of cyclical patterns of centralization and decentralization is significant, some details of her model may not always be applicable beyond Mesoamerica. In Bronze Age Syria, for example, there is much continuity in the centers of power before and after the collapse circa 2000 BC, rather than a scenario of provincial elites establishing new capitals (see Cooper, chapter 2; and Nichols and Weber, chapter 3). It is also questionable whether the earliest states were uniformly large-scale, unitary, territorial monoliths, as is asserted in the dynamic model (cf. Uruk period Mesopotamia, which is more likely to have consisted of an array of city-states [Algaze 2001:55]).

Nobles and Commoners

A frequent emphasis in discussions of regeneration (and collapse) is on elites, leaving the impression that regeneration relied primarily on the ambitions and aspirations of would-be rulers and that collapse mainly involved a failure of elite policies. In contrast to such "top-down" views of collapse and regeneration, some scholars have stressed the importance of rural or non-elite resilience (cf. Adams 1978) in the reconstruction of complex societies. Gray Graffam (1992) maintained that in the period after the collapse of Tiwanaku in the southern Andes, raised field farming—thought to be a state-associated, labor-intensive practice—continued to be practiced by rural populations. Such a retention of precollapse institutions in rural contexts may have served later as a foundation for the reconstruction of complex societies.[3] Mary Van Buren (2000) suggests that non-elites played a crucial role in the transmission of Andean "high culture" in periods of collapse; the derivation of the Inca cult of the sun god from pre-Inca non-elite populations is cited as an example of this phenomenon.

How much do either regeneration or collapse affect the peasant, and what part do the non-elite sectors of society play in those processes (Freter 1994; Joyce et al. 2001)? In this volume, Lisa Cooper (chapter 2) suggests that the resilience of extrastate kin-based social structures in the Bronze Age middle Euphrates was significant in the region's recovery after urban decline. Diane Chase and Arlen Chase (chapter 11) posit that symbolic egalitarianism was crucial in the reestablishment of societal complexity under the Classic Maya. Similarly, Ellen Morris (chapter 4) observes that the social mobility characteristic of the First Intermediate period in Egypt influenced the strategies of the rulers of the regenerated Middle Kingdom, who represented themselves as attentive to the needs of the common people. Perhaps the most blatant example of the role of non-elites is provided by Archaic Greece (Ian Morris, chapter 5), where city-states (*poleis*) are characterized by a "middling" ideology centered on the male citizenry that culminates in the formation of democracy.

With the disintegration of traditional sociopolitical and ideological structures, new opportunities for social mobility and individual agency may emerge during periods of collapse. Ambitious non-elite individuals may find new avenues for the acquisition of power, with less hindrance from traditional hierarchical structures. As Ellen Morris (chapter 4) points out, social class may have mattered less in situations of severe crisis than did a talent for making things work.

Survival of Preexisting Institutions

It is likely that a crucial factor in regeneration is the survival of institutions or ideas from the era before collapse, supplying a base for the eventual re-creation of complex societies: the chances are good that regenerated complex societies did not have to totally "reinvent the wheel," literally or otherwise. In such a scenario, one might imagine that lower-level administrative units or personnel from collapsed states survived in local contexts, or that ideologies and values of earlier complex societies provided reference points for second-generation states.[4] The contributors to this volume repeatedly emphasize the importance of sociopolitical, economic, ideological, and other models from precollapse periods in the processes of regeneration.

If building blocks left over from the collapse of complex societies were available to the survivors, it is necessary to explain how they were used to reconstruct societal complexity, by whom, and why. Ostensibly, one may envision ambitious local leaders or groups intensifying their power through competition and warfare (Brumfiel and Fox 1994; Rees 2001), accumulation of dependents, and alliances, resulting in the reconstruction of large-scale polities. A model of peer polity interaction enacted in a secondary context may also be applicable (Renfrew and Cherry 1986). If trade is identified as a decisive variable, leaders may have participated in long-distance exchange networks, acquiring exotic goods with which to gain and reward followers; alternatively, mobilization of foodstuffs from agricultural surpluses in a staple finance system may have been significant (D'Altroy and Earle 1985). The use of ideology, ritual, and privileged access to the spirit world by nascent leaders is also likely to have been important (Chang 1983; DeMarrais et al. 1996; McAnany 2001).

Such strategies are already familiar from studies of how the first complex societies emerged. It would be useful to ask, therefore, if the regeneration of urban and state societies can be understood as a "replay" of the processes from earlier developmental episodes, or whether the formation of second- or third-generation states involved new trajectories and strategies for the acquisition of power not seen in primary or pristine cases. In some cases discussed in this volume, the formation of regenerated complex societies appears to entail totally new strategies of power acquisition (Conlee, chapter 7). In others, such as Middle Kingdom Egypt (Ellen Morris, chapter 4), we see a partial reappearance of processes familiar from the formation of the first state, but these are accompanied by innovations resulting from changes that occurred during the period of collapse.

The deliberate rejection of previous ideologies and institutions may also have played a significant part in the process of regeneration (see Ian Morris, chapter 5; Conlee, chapter 7; Sims, chapter 8; Chase and Chase, chapter 11; and Masson, Hare, and Peraza Lope, chapter 12).

Other Variables

Additional factors that may have been instrumental in the regeneration of complex societies can also be proposed. One is the role of external societies: economic, ideological, technological or political stimuli from foreign complex societies, and/or emulation of those societies might result in a "repeat" of secondary state formation (Price 1977; Thurston 2001). As Bennet Bronson (chapter 9) notes, regenerating states often emulate neighboring complex societies even while claiming to derive their primary inspiration from ancestral groups. Trade with external societies, identified as a crucial variable in the revival of complex societies in medieval Europe, also figures prominently in Bronze Age Syria (Cooper, chapter 2; Nichols and Weber, chapter 3), Archaic Greece (Ian Morris, chapter 5), and Postclassic Mesoamerica (Masson, Hare, and Peraza Lope, chapter 12).

If climatic deterioration is implicated in societal collapse, then enhanced climatic conditions might be correspondingly influential in regenerative processes. In such circumstances, climate amelioration could facilitate agricultural surpluses and the regeneration of elite power based on those surpluses (see Ian Morris, chapter 5). Alternatively, if anthropogenic environmental degradation was a causal factor in collapse, then environmental recovery during periods of decentralization could also be instrumental to regeneration, given the reappearance of natural resources important for the reestablishment of societal complexity.

Technological changes may also facilitate new hierarchies of power. For example, Lynn White (1962) proposed that a decisive variable in the revival of urban society after the collapse of Roman civilization in northern Europe consisted of innovations in agricultural technology, particularly the introduction of the heavy plow.

Complex societies are often characterized by overcentralization and organizational rigidity (Kolata, chapter 13), which may render them vulnerable in times of social or environmental stress. Lisa Cooper (chapter 2) and John Nichols and Jill Weber (chapter 3) argue that strategies of flexibility may allow for survival and adaptation during periods of decentralization and may be crucial in the reconstruction of complexity. Such strategies entail diversity in subsistence activities or in social organization, as in the tribal or heterarchical structures described for Bronze Age Syria in chapters 2 and 3. Cooper suggests that regions with corporate or heterarchical political organizations are more likely to experience a revival of societal complexity after collapse.

It might be argued, as in the case of the Amorites of Middle Bronze Age Syria (Nichols and Weber, chapter 3), that newly successful ethnic groups previously on the margins of power may have been motivated to restore the institutions and symbols of earlier centralized authority to legitimize their power and confirm that they "belonged" (Renfrew 1979:484; see also Marcus 1998 on the role of peripheral elites). A similar process is described by ibn Khaldun (1969): in weakening polities, rebels from outside the core of power sweep in and assume political control, all the while emulating earlier institutions and concepts of those polities.

Finally, the influence of extraordinary leaders and other agents (Flannery 1999) in the implementation of new institutions and ideologies should not be overlooked. As Ellen Morris points out (chapter 4), such individual actors are likely to have been consistently important in the process of regeneration.

As is the case with the formation of the first complex societies, it will be imperative to consider large-scale spatial contexts when investigating cases of regeneration: societies tend not to be closed, discrete units but are usually better understood as tapestries of interconnected and interweaving entities, each influencing and transforming the other (Stein 2002). Approaches such as world-systems theory have emphasized that developments in one society cannot be understood without reference to others, and it is likely that individual episodes of regeneration will be better understood within larger "international" contexts.

Also important is the consideration of cases in which regeneration does not take place. In the Tumilaca example (chapter 8), Kenny Sims concludes that the exclusion of local elites from imperial administrations that existed prior to collapse was responsible for the absence of regeneration. Regeneration may be likely to fail in regions without vigorous and long-lasting traditions of complex political structures (Bronson, chapter 9) or long-held hegemonic worldviews (Kolata, chapter 13).

Organization of the Volume

In this volume, specialists from a wide range of geographical areas are represented—including Southwest Asia, Egypt, the Aegean, East Asia, Mesoamerica, and the Andes—controlling different varieties of data and with different theoretical orientations. An even broader geographical range would have been desirable, but constraints of space require a certain selectivity. When considering the problem of regeneration, the participants were asked to consider such questions as the following: Why does regeneration occur in some areas but not in others, and with different schedules of emergence? Which institutions survived collapse, and which proved instrumental in regeneration? Did collapse and regeneration entail changes to a "bundle" of institutions (Yoffee 1993:64), or, as is perhaps more probable, did some institutions or phenomena fail while others did not?

Recognition of cross-cultural patterns should not obscure the likelihood of significant variability in our data: regenerated states are likely to occur with a diversity of organizational styles (e.g., Blanton et al. 1996), and the trajectory of regeneration is likely to exhibit different patterns in each case and in each region. Such variability is well illustrated by the results detailed in this volume's chapters.

Chapters 2–4 consider the effects of collapse and processes of regeneration in the Near East in the transition from the Early to Middle Bronze Age, late third to early second millennium BC. Lisa Cooper (chapter 2), discussing the middle Euphrates Valley in Syria, postulates that the relatively marginal environment of the region gave its inhabitants an edge over people in "core" areas in times of collapse, because the region's diversified subsistence economy allowed for flexibility and resilience. The relatively autonomous character of local settlements may also help to explain their success at regeneration: not tied to the fate of a higher, more centralized power, they could adapt to crisis more successfully than regions more tightly integrated into large, powerful states.

In chapter 3, John Nichols and Jill Weber document collapse and regeneration in the Jabbul Plain of western Syria and its regional center, Tell Umm el-Marra. They observe that regeneration involved both the retention of precollapse phenomena (e.g., economic specialization, traditions of public ritual, resilient subsistence strategies) and important innovations such as the hunting of onagers for leather production in the context of an expanded commodities sphere. Nichols and Weber also underline the importance of ethnic changes and possible reasons for such a development; the newly powerful Amorite group's flexible subsistence practices (see also Cooper, chapter 2) may have provided an advantage in periods of environmental stress.

Although pharaonic Egypt was relatively stable, it experienced several "intermediate periods" of decentralization, as discussed by Ellen Morris in chapter 4. Morris emphasizes the importance of ideology in the regeneration of states and urban life, proposing that a strong template for regeneration existed in the ideology of *maat*, or order in the universe, which was possible only when one divine king ruled over a unified Nile Valley. But competing leaders aiming to reestablish the kingship also had to take new social developments into account: when social mobility became common in the First Intermediate period (ca. 2200–2000 BC), the rulers of the reconstructed Middle Kingdom state were compelled to amend royal ideologies by representing themselves as responsible shepherds responding to the needs of their people.

In chapter 5, Ian Morris reviews the well-known case of late second/early first millennium BC Greece, when Mycenaean palace-based states disintegrated and collapse was followed by the emergence of the *polis* and Classical civilization. In this case, regeneration is associated with the revival of trade with the Near East and with demographic growth partly correlated with climatic improvement.

Chapters 6–8 focus on the Andes in the periods following the collapse of the Tiwanaku and Wari states in the early second millennium AD. Particular attention is devoted to the effect of Tiwanaku and Wari on the societies that flourished in their wake. Gordon McEwan (chapter 6) discusses the results of archaeological fieldwork in the Cuzco Valley, Peru, the heartland of the Inca empire. Because of their unique position on the periphery of the Wari and Tiwanaku empires, the peoples of the Cuzco area inherited agricultural infrastructure, ideology, and practical statecraft information from the two empires. McEwan argues that the Inca state was built using those surviving elements—together with invented traditions of the empire's origins. In contrast, Christina Conlee's (chapter 7) evidence from the Nasca region of coastal southern Peru reveals that local elites rejected Wari institutions and ideology after the Wari collapse. Instead, regeneration was effected by an expanded network of elites exploiting new avenues of power acquisition (e.g., craft production and feasting) in new contexts of production and exchange. The Nasca data indicate that the relationship a region has with a conquering state affects how the area is impacted by both conquest and collapse.

Kenny Sims's data (chapter 8) provide a case of a region in which collapse occurred but regeneration did *not* take place. Sims argues that the Wari and Tiwanaku empires inhibited the development of political and economic complexity by subsequent Tumilaca groups in the Moquegua Valley of southern Peru. Members of local elites were not appointed to administrative positions within either of the two imperial regimes, so their descendants were poorly prepared to fill the power vacuum after collapse. Sims maintains that such cases of "negative" regeneration are more common than those of secondary state regeneration in the post-Wari and post-Tiwanaku Andes, and their study is critical for understanding why some regions regenerate while others fail to do so.

Chapters 9–10 examine cases of collapse and regeneration in East Asia that occurred over extensive geographical areas and spans of time. Most broadly, Bennet Bronson (chapter 9) proposes a typology of regeneration for East Asia that may prove applicable to other parts of the world. Two kinds of "false" regeneration are defined, in which (1) a new phase of complexity appears in the same location as an earlier one but as the result of an intrusive external political unit, or (2) complex nodes in a system shift from place to place, but regional structure remains relatively constant. Stimulus regeneration involves revival through historical memories, which may or may not be accurate; inspired by these memories, leaders come to believe that a higher degree of centralization is possible and make that centralization more palatable by harking back to an illustrious past. In contrast, template regeneration adheres closely to a fully understood, well-recorded model.

Concentrating on first and early second millennium AD Southeast Asia, Miriam Stark (chapter 10) discusses cycles of integration and disintegration manifested by the succession of Khmer polities. Although power centers, upper-level elites, trade networks, and political structures changed, regeneration was facilitated through continuity in variables such as subsistence economy, ideology, ethnicity, and lower-level administrative structures. The Khmer case suggests an example of Bronson's "template regeneration."

Chapters 11 and 12 focus on the Classic Maya collapse and the Postclassic developments that succeeded it. Avoiding traditional explanations for regeneration in the Postclassic Maya period, Diane Chase and Arlen Chase (chapter 11) employ frame analysis to provide a more dynamic view, with particular reference to data from the site of Caracol. Postclassic regeneration is observed to have entailed the restoration of Classic Maya models and institutions including symbolic egalitarianism and shared rule. Terminal Classic strategies such as dynastic rule, graded status distinctions, and monumentality were abandoned along with the Terminal Classic centers themselves.

In their consideration of data from the large Postclassic center of Mayapán, Marilyn Masson, Timothy Hare, and Carlos Peraza Lope (chapter

12) observe regeneration to have entailed both the reproduction and the rejection of institutions from Chichén Itzá and other preceding complex societies, with both replication and rejection the result of deliberate selection informed by historical memory. Important new innovations were also brought into play, including an increased importance of long-distance exchange and the development of political and economic power sharing among lords, priests, and merchants.

The concluding chapters (13 and 14) provide a commentary on the preceding chapters, revealing commonalities, differences, flaws, and areas for future research. In chapter 13, Alan Kolata observes that regeneration is not a uniform process: in some cases there is a local focus on autonomy and resilience; in others there is an international orientation that leads to regeneration. Nor does regeneration necessarily entail the duplication of the precollapse state—new and different institutions often emerge, with different ideologies and strategies. But these patterns of variability should not be allowed to disguise regularities and commonalities. Kolata argues that the character of the precollapse society is directly correlated with the character (or likelihood) of regeneration. Two varieties of precollapse political entities are recognized, each associated with different worldviews: (1) hegemony with sovereignty, which is associated with orthodoxy, or the mental internalization of state values by subjects of the state, and (2) hegemony without sovereignty, which is associated with orthopraxy, or the practice of state values without their mental internalization. Kolata suggests that precollapse states of the first type are more likely to regenerate, since their citizens have accepted hierarchical institutions as natural phenomena. His emphasis on ideology is an important reminder of the importance of that variable in regeneration.

In his review of the volume's chapters (chapter 14), Norman Yoffee notes that regeneration often tends to involve secondary elites' and marginal regions' taking advantage of opportunities in the wake of collapse. Considering why regeneration sometimes fails to occur, Yoffee reviews the evidence from Assyria and Babylonia after the collapse of the Neo-Assyrian and Neo-Babylonian empires in the seventh and sixth centuries BC, respectively. He observes that the Neo-Assyrian kings had undermined the power of the traditional Assyrian nobility, relying instead on the large non-Assyrian population that had been resettled in the Assyrian heartland. When the Assyrian state was defeated by external enemies, the non-Assyrian elites remaining in Assyria had little investment in traditional models of Assyrian statecraft. In the Babylonian case, we find that the Babylonian kingship was assumed by foreign Persian rulers who affected Babylonian royal titles and culture but nevertheless converted the region into an imperial province, subverting its political and cultural autonomy. Like Kolata, Yoffee emphasizes the importance of ideology in the consideration of regeneration: why are some aspects of the precollapse period remembered and utilized and others discarded or forgotten? And who benefits from the remembering and/or forgetting?

Future Directions

This book is intended to stimulate scholars of complex societies to think more seriously about what happens after collapse. Is regeneration a useful analytical concept, and if so, how do we go about identifying and studying it in greater depth? The editors and contributors to this volume hope that the approaches and data offered here will supply a foundation for future work and that the consideration of historical specifics as well as cross-cultural regularities will yield new insights on this important aspect of sociopolitical evolution.

Acknowledgments

I would like to thank Jerrold Cooper, Irad Malkin, David Nierenberg, and Miriam Stark for their comments on preliminary drafts of this chapter. I am also grateful to Lisa de Leonardis for her recommendations in organizing the SAA session and to the two anonymous reviewers for their thoughtful and extensive comments on the book manuscript. Much of my work on this book was conducted while I held a visiting professorship at the Università degli Studi di Roma "La Sapienza," and I wish to thank Paolo Matthiae and Maria Giovanna Biga for their great generosity and assistance during my stay in Rome.

Notes

1. In this volume, the term *complex societies* refers to societies with extensive populations, large-scale and often multilevel political organizations (states), large and hierarchical settlement patterns (urban systems), and (usually) socially stratified populations.

2. In some cases, "collapse" may even be a construct promulgated by elites or their agents, acting to legitimize or idealize their own state at the expense of preceding eras said to be chaotic and troubled.

3. Note, however, that more recent work in the Tiwanaku region has suggested that raised field agriculture was not used on a large scale following the Tiwanaku collapse (Kolata 2003).

4. Thomas Charlton and Deborah Nichols (1997) observe that the existence of the Teotihuacán state created a reference point and precondition for later state development. See also Wattenmaker 1994:203 on the survival of economic specialization during collapse and its relevance to regeneration.

2 The Demise and Regeneration of Bronze Age Urban Centers in the Euphrates Valley of Syria
Lisa Cooper

In the Near East, the end of the third millennium BC was a tumultuous time characterized in many regions by the demise of state society or, at the very least, the increased fragmentation of urban polities that had once controlled large tracts of land and had prospered under stable, productive economies. This demise is observable in southern Mesopotamia, for example, where two great empires fell in succession in the last centuries of the third millennium BC. The house of Akkad, the first imperial power in southern Mesopotamia to consolidate political control over a mosaic of competing city-states and to establish trading opportunities over a vast area of the Near East, came to a dramatic end around 2150 BC (Yoffee 1988a:46–49). The Akkadian empire was replaced shortly afterward by the Third Dynasty of Ur, although this state too, characterized as it was by an extremely centralized bureaucracy and over-stretched economy, rapidly crumbled around 2000 BC (Yoffee 1988a:49–50). The once-great capital city of Ur was overrun by foreigners, and the whole empire was thrown into a state of internal chaos and political fragmentation.

North of the Tigris-Euphrates floodplain, the region of the Jezireh of Upper Mesopotamia, essentially comprising the Khabur Plains of north-eastern Syria and the Sinjar Plain of northern Iraq, also underwent a crisis toward the end of the third millennium BC. Up to this point, the area had been pursuing a regime of agricultural maximization, no doubt precipitated by the growth of large urban settlements. Extensive manuring (evidenced by widespread sherd scatters) and a multitude of linear hollows, which are interpreted as roadways radiating out from settlements to the fields, are believed to reflect the intensity of agricultural production that took place during this period (Wilkinson 1994:492–93). Around 2200 BC, however, the area experienced a dramatic reduction in this intensified dry-farming agricultural regime, about the same time that Akkadian imperial control in this region began to weaken (Weiss and Courty 1993). While recent archaeological evidence at sites such as Tell Brak and Tell Mozan indicates that some urban settlements in the region survived after this period (Oates et al. 2001:393), an appreciable reduction in the number of occupied sites and a pattern of contracting settlement appear as the prevailing trend in the Jezireh between 2200 and 1900 BC (Peltenburg 2000:164–65; Weiss and Courty 1993:141). This change may have been brought about by a large-scale population emigration, in which human groups moved toward southern Mesopotamia via the Euphrates River valley in their quest for reliable food and pasturage (Weiss and Courty 1993:144). Alternatively, it is possible that many of the inhabitants adapted successfully to pastoralism within the region and that such a transformation left sparse remains in the archaeological record (Peltenburg 2000:165).

Still other regions of the Near East were affected by collapse at the end of the third millennium BC. In Egypt, this period is marked by the end of the prosperous Old Kingdom and its replacement by the First Intermediate period, a time of political fragmentation and decentralization (E. Morris, chapter 4). In most areas to the west of the Jordan River in Palestine, as early as 2300 BC, the Early Bronze III urban centers were destroyed or abandoned, and the stable productive subsistence system, based on intensified agriculture, industry and trade, ceased to operate (Dever 1989:228; Richard 1987:34). In the Early Bronze IV period that followed, the region experienced a kind of "ruralization," in which a diversified subsistence economy based on small-scale farming and pastoral nomadism prevailed for several centuries (Palumbo 2001:237).

Climate change is frequently posited as an important factor that brought about the widespread collapses that were witnessed in many parts of the Near East and even beyond (Bell 1971; Weiss 1997). However, whether climate change was the principal catalyst by which change was effected or whether it simply exacerbated existing political, social, and economic stresses that urban societies were already experiencing remains uncertain (Dever 1989:232–33; Peltenburg 2000:178–80). Despite the indeterminate nature of the cause of collapse, however, its consequences frequently had pronounced effects. Noteworthy is the considerable length of time that elapsed before areas saw the return of urban societies and a stabilized agricultural economy in some areas. In much of Palestine, for example, nearly four centuries passed before the reestablishment (at the beginning of the Middle Bronze Age) of city-states, characterized by settlement hierarchy, the presence of monumental public works, long-distance trade, and agricultural specialization (Ilan 1995). Similarly, in the Khabur Plains, roughly three hundred years passed before that region witnessed a similar reestablishment of permanent settlements and the reintensification of agriculture (Weiss and Courty 1993:146).

Decline in the Euphrates River Valley of Northern Syria

Without question, the demise in urban society that was experienced in several regions of the Near East also affected the northern Euphrates Valley of Syria, the principal focus of this study (fig. 2.1). Toward the end of the Early Bronze IV (EB IV) period, dating to the last centuries of the third millennium BC, several large towns or cities along the river, which had once supported sizeable populations and were frequently characterized by fortification systems, public buildings, funerary monuments, and densely inhabited domestic quarters, were abandoned (fig. 2.2). The site of Jerablus Tahtani, for example, which in the mid Early Bronze Age had a city wall and protective glacis, textile and metal manufacturing installations, and grain processing and storage facilities, as well as a prominent burial monument in the form of a tomb enclosed by a tumulus, was abandoned. The tell was not reoccupied again until the Late Iron Age (Peltenburg 1999:103; Peltenburg et al. 1995:14–15). While the excavators of Jerablus Tahtani do not posit a precise date for this abandonment, a comparison of the late Early Bronze Age pottery from this site and other Euphrates sites whose relative dates are reasonably secure suggests that its final occupation did not extend beyond around 2200 BC.

Another instance of abandonment is the great mortuary center of Tell Banat on the eastern bank of the Euphrates River. Even as early as 2300 BC, this site, which had once supported several large tombs, a related public building, and associated pottery manufactory, was deserted. Around the same time, the nearby monolithic tumulus known as the White Monument ceased to be maintained (Porter 2002a:12, table 1; Porter and McClellan 1998).

The site of Selenkahiye, which possessed an elite residence as well as housing, workshops, and a city wall, was also deserted some time around 2100–2000 BC, judging by its latest pottery (van Loon 2001).

Significantly, an even greater number of sites along the Euphrates River that were not abandoned also appear to have been affected by the widespread tide of collapse. Such sites are characterized by a considerable diminution of their settlement size and/or the disuse of public buildings and

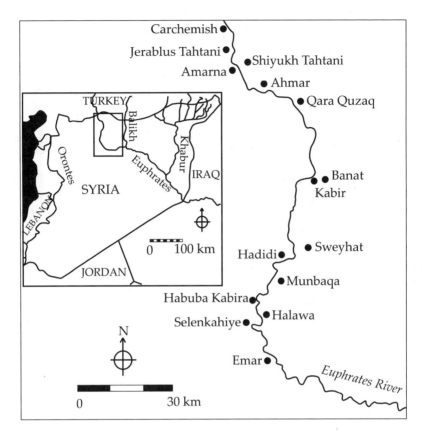

Figure 2.1 Map of Syria, indicating Early and Middle Bronze Age settlements in the northern Euphrates Valley.

fortifications, accompanied in some cases by destruction by fire (fig. 2.2). At the site of Tell Kabir, for example, the Early Bronze Age long-roomed "temple-in-antis" fell out of use, and after a time its walls collapsed (Porter 1995a:130). Dug into this bricky collapse were four large storage pits in which were found good examples of late third millennium (late EB IV) pottery (Porter 1995a:139–43). Following this phase and dating to the earliest phase of the Middle Bronze Age (MB), only domestic architecture characterized this sector of the settlement (Porter 1995a:143–52).

At the site of Halawa, the EB IVA phases (3c and 3b) were characterized by a sizeable residential district, a city wall, gates, and a long-roomed

	EB IVA (2500–2300 BC)	EB IVB (2300–2000 BC)	MB I (2000–1900 BC)	MB IIA (1900–1800 BC)
Jerablus Tahtani	city wall, glacis, craft work— shops, storage facilities, housing, elite tomb	‡		
Amarna	tombs———	housing		———housing
Shiyukh Tahtani	housing, tombs———	housing		———housing
Ahmar	elite tomb, elite building——?—	?		———housing
Qara Quzaq	"temple-in-antis"———	housing———hiatus?———housing		"temple-in-antis," housing, silos
Banat	housing, craft workshops, elite public building, elite tomb, funerary tumulus	—‡		
Kabir	"temple-in-antis"———	pits—	housing———	‡
es-Sweyhat	housing, tombs, elite building with wall paintings	housing, craft workshops, — housing city walls and gate, large-scale storage and cooking facilities, elite building		‡
Hadidi	monumental tombs, housing, shrine (?)	———housing———	housing———	———housing, glacis, ditch, gate, tower, craft activities

el-'Abd   elite building (?), ——————————————— ‡
           housing, city wall, glacis,
           tower

Munbaqa   housing ———————— city wall, fortified gates, ——————— "temples-in-antis,"
                             housing, temple   housing, city wall, elite
                                                                  building, public building
                                                                  (temple?)

Halawa   housing, "temple- ———————————————— silos, working ——————— planned housing,
           in-antis," city wall,   surfaces, fire pits   streets
           glacis, city gate, tower

Habuba Kabira   city wall, housing ——————— city wall, housing, gatehouse, ——————— housing, silos
                                           tower, working surfaces,
                                           potter's kiln

Selenkahiye   housing, city wall (?) ——————— housing, city wall, gate, ——————— ‡
                                             tower, ditch, workshops,
                                             elite residence

Emar   housing, glacis ————————————————————————————————————— housing, city wall

Figure 2.2 Euphrates settlements of the late Early Bronze Age (EB IVA, EB IVB) and Middle Bronze Age (MB I, MB IIA). The end of occupation is indicated by the symbol ‡.

"temple-in-antis" (Orthmann 1989:35–44, 65–66). In contrast, the succeeding phase 3a, which dates to the very end of the Early Bronze Age and the beginning of the Middle Bronze Age, was characterized by the absence of fortifications and monumental architecture. The remains of flimsy walls or reused older walls define the nature of occupation (Orthmann 1989:19, 54). In association with these modest architectural features were storage silos, small fireplaces, *tannours* (round clay bread ovens), and irregular working surfaces made of clay, pebbles, and plastered material (Orthmann 1989:55).

The settlement history of Tell es-Sweyhat presents a similar picture of decline. The site had enjoyed its florescence late in the third millennium BC, when it was composed of a fortified citadel on the central mound and a large lower town enclosed by a wall (Zettler et al. 1997:4). Sweyhat may have reached a size as large as forty hectares (Danti and Zettler 1998:213). Consequently, however, this settlement shrank dramatically in size, continuing to exist only on the central mound while the important public function of the citadel buildings appears to have been discontinued after they were abandoned or destroyed by fire (Holland 1976:51; Zettler et al. 1997:27). The last phases of the third millennium BC at Sweyhat are characterized by layers of ash and flimsy architectural remains, largely the remnants of domestic dwellings (Zettler et al. 1997:27–28).

Last, there is evidence that the settlement at Tell Hadidi underwent a diminution in size and importance at the very end of the Early Bronze Age. In the late third millennium, the settlement had included an extensive lower town composed of tightly spaced houses along a long street, and a central acropolis mound (Dornemann 1979:116). Elite individuals at the settlement were buried in monumental chamber tombs located in various sectors of the lower town (Dornemann 1979:117–18). During its floruit in the Early Bronze Age, Tell Hadidi had grown to some fifty-six hectares, making it one of the largest known settlements in the northern Euphrates Valley of Syria (Dornemann 1979:116; McClellan 1999:413). The presence of smaller EB satellite sites in the vicinity of Hadidi, as well as several roadways radiating out from the site and even crossing to the other side of the Euphrates, testifies further to Hadidi's prominence in the third millennium (Wilkinson 2004:fig. 7.5). Around 2000 BC, however, the settlement appears to have undergone a dramatic diminishment in size after a major destruction. The lower town was abandoned altogether, and occupation became limited to the area of the main acropolis mound (Dornemann 1985:50–51). There is no evidence that Tell Hadidi was characterized by anything other than simple domestic housing during this period of "collapse."

In sum, archaeological evidence testifies to a regionwide collapse of settlements at the end of the Early Bronze period marked by the complete abandonment of sites or a dramatic reduction in site size and settlement complexity. In association with these observed developments we may posit a disintegration of the city-states that typified the Early Bronze northern Euphrates settlement system. No longer were urban centers and their dependencies of farming and pastoral communities bound together into tightly integrated political polities, flourishing from economic exchanges with one another and through the intensive agricultural and pastoral exploitation of their hinterlands. By the end of the third millennium, the northern Euphrates region had become a ruralized landscape of small self-sufficient village-sized settlements. Each community, no longer under the control of an urban center and not having to meet the demands of the city-states' elites, functioned at a very simple political and economic level of organization. Settlements were composed chiefly of domestic housing, and simple food-producing and food-processing activities served to meet the needs of those small communities only.

While the decline in settlement in the northern Euphrates Valley in Syria at the end of the third millennium BC cannot be overlooked, one must also take note of this region's successful regeneration at the beginning of the Middle Bronze Age in the early second millennium BC. After only a short period of time, perhaps no more than a century, the region once again featured large settlements strung along the banks of the river, each growing in prosperity through the exploitation of the natural resources of the surrounding territory and taking part in the brisk commercial trade that had resumed along the river from north to south and overland from east to west. What is even more striking is that considerable cultural continuity appears to have existed throughout, with many aspects of the material culture from the Early Bronze Age developing smoothly into the subsequent Middle Bronze period, despite the interval of collapse that separated these two periods. Furthermore, archaeological and textual evidence suggest that the same fundamental aspects of Euphrates urban government and economic structures resurfaced after the period of collapse. Despite the widespread turmoil and weakness that gripped many parts of the Near East at the end of the Early Bronze Age, the culture of the northern Euphrates Valley shows itself to have been remarkably resilient, able to withstand considerable stresses to its political fabric and subsistence economy, regenerating smoothly and changing little in its essential core over an extended period of time.

Resiliency and Cultural Continuity

The following observations provide details of the evidence that supports an overall trend of resiliency and cultural continuity from the Early to the Middle Bronze Age. As mentioned above, several sites, although experiencing some diminishment in size and the discontinuation of public buildings, elite tombs, industrial manufactories, and fortifications at the very end of the Early Bronze Age, show no signs of having been completely destroyed or abandoned. On the contrary, these sites appear to be characterized by a continuous and unbroken sequence of occupational phases that carry through from the end of the Early Bronze Age into the Middle Bronze Age. Sites with such settlement continuity (see fig. 2.2) include Tell Amarna (Pons 2001:41–42; Tunca 1999:130–31),[1] Shiyukh Tahtani (Falsone 1998:25, 1999:138), Tell Ahmar (Roobaert and Bunnens 1999:164–66), Qara Quzaq (Valdés Pereiro 1999:118–19, 2001:120), Tell Kabir (Porter 1995a), Tell es-Sweyhat (Cooper 1997:24–26; Holland 1976:49–63, 1977a:37–43, 1977b; Zettler et al. 1997:19–28), Tell Hadidi (Dornemann 1979, 1985:50–56), Munbaqa (Werner 1998:38–48), Halawa (Orthmann 1981, 1989), Habuba Kabira (Heusch 1980:168–77), and Emar (Finkbeiner 1999–2000, 2001:11–16).[2]

The time between the demise of the urban polities of the EB IV period and their regenerated forms in the Middle Bronze Age appears to have been very short, perhaps no more than a hundred years. This is evinced, for the most part, by the fact that many of the new foundations of MB structures were set directly on top of the remnants of earlier EB buildings. One can note this phenomenon at Halawa, for example, where the MB inhabitants even reused the foundations of the earlier EB buildings, integrating the remains into the foundations of new houses (Orthmann 1989:23). It is also interesting to note that at Halawa, in the case of at least one sector of the city, the function of that quarter remained the same. Quadrant Q, which in the Early Bronze Age was the principal domestic area of the settlement, continued in that capacity into the Middle Bronze Age, implying that the later inhabitants were well aware of the configuration of the earlier settlement and retained that layout (Orthmann 1989:22).

At Habuba Kabira, the continued existence and use of several mud-brick walls through occupational phases attributed to both the end of the Early Bronze Age and the early Middle Bronze Age have been noted, indicating that only a short interval had passed between these periods (Heinrich et al. 1969:48). Continuity in architecture can also be observed in the form of part of Habuba Kabira's fortification walls, which feature a distinctive inset-offset pattern of buttresses and recesses in the latest EB levels (Heusch 1980:174–75). This type of wall construction may also have existed along the northern fortification walls of the EB settlement of Selenkahiye, where short bastions or small buttresslike jumps have been observed (van Loon 2001:3.87). Interestingly, this architectural feature is manifested again in the regenerated settlement of Munbaqa, where the long, well-preserved stretch of the MB town wall features a strikingly similar pattern of alternating buttresses and recesses (Machule et al. 1993:76–77).

Finally, we may consider the long-roomed "temple-in-antis" structure (Steinbau 1) at the site of Munbaqa, excavated on the summit of the mound. Its original foundations appear to have been constructed in the Early Bronze Age, when the building featured a small cult room with a stepped podium (Orthmann and Kühne 1974:59–65). Consequently, the temple remained as an important religious center through the Middle and Late Bronze Age, indicated by the number of alterations and restorations performed in subsequent building phases (Heinrich et al. 1974:11–45). Again, such evidence highlights the degree of occupational and architectural continuity, not to mention an unbroken sequence of religious-cultural traditions.

Cultural continuity is readily observable in the pottery assemblages from the Early to the Middle Bronze Age. Rather than revealing a sharp and abrupt break in stylistic traditions and technology between these two periods, the Euphrates ceramic sequence indicates a smooth, unbroken development of vessel types from one cultural phase to the next. To be sure, there is evidence that the frequency of many of the finer, thin-walled and highly fired wares of the assemblage, such as caliciform cups, dropped dramatically in the last centuries of the third millennium BC, concurrent with the last phase of the Early Bronze Age (Cooper 1999:324). Still other fine or decorated wares, such as plain and painted Orange Spiral Burnish wares and Grey Spiral Burnish wares, ceased to exist altogether in the latest phase of the Early Bronze Age. Such wares are absent, for example, in the assemblage of the Area IV "Burned Building" at Tell es-Sweyhat, which can be dated later than 2150 BC (Holland 1976, 1977a; Zettler et al. 1997:25). They are also absent in the Period II "pit" phase at Tell Kabir, which is contemporary with or slightly later than the Area IV occupation at Tell es-Sweyhat (Porter 1995a:139–43). One can also observe that MB vessels are somewhat thicker walled and coarser than EB pots and that the MB assemblage possesses fewer ware categories and fewer varieties of surface decoration.

Despite these changes, however, it is apparent that several EB vessel forms continued throughout the last years of the collapse at the end of the

Early Bronze Age and persisted or evolved gradually into the subsequent regenerated occupation phases of the Middle Bronze Age (Cooper 1998: figs. 1–2). Some technological aspects of the Euphrates pottery also exhibit considerable continuity. Cooking pots—which by the last phase of the EB IV period were carefully finished on the wheel and characterized by simple out-turned rounded rims and a calcite tempered fabric—continued to be produced with the same technological and morphological characteristics well into the Middle Bronze Age, persisting as the standard northern Euphrates cooking vessel (Cooper 1999:324). We see, therefore, that the developments observed in the pottery assemblage of the northern Euphrates Valley demonstrate the same degree of change, whether by evolution or by transformation, that would characterize any ceramic tradition of a continuously occupied region over an extended period of time.

A growing amount of archaeological data shows that the political configuration of settlements in the Euphrates Valley was quite similar before and after the period of collapse that separated the Early Bronze and Middle Bronze Age. In the Early Bronze Age, the region comprised autonomous cities characterized by densely populated centers that were surrounded by tracts of agricultural fields and grazing land and sometimes featured smaller satellite communities. That each of these urban polities was politically and economically independent of one another is suggested by the fairly even nature of their size and complexity and the redundancy of key administrative and ideological features within each settlement (storage facilities, craft workshops, temples, and public buildings that may have served in some capacity related to the city's administration). It may also be noteworthy to report that few of these sites have yielded more than a small number of administrative trappings and other material evidence suggesting any significant authority or influence from the important yet distant urban centers of Ebla and Mari, which according to inscriptions were constantly vying for control of this particular stretch of the river (Astour 1992:26–51). Indeed, the dearth of archaeological evidence for control from Ebla and Mari should caution us against making too many historical reconstructions through textual sources alone. What may have been claimed as real military and economic successes in this region among the authorities of these two great centers may have actually been regarded as something quite different in the region in question.

During the Middle Bronze Age, the same configuration of urban settlements appears to have reemerged, each settlement having its own control over land and other resources. To date, no archaeological evidence suggests that any one settlement had political and economic authority or control over the others. Again, contemporaneous textual sources from Mari may distort this picture somewhat, suggesting that this stretch of the Euphrates River was near or formed the border between the states of Mari, Yamkhad, and Carchemish and that settlements and populations along the river's banks were firmly under the control of one of these polities. Nonetheless, archaeological investigations of these sites have not yet produced any tangible evidence for such political configurations (for a full discussion, see Cooper 1997:332–47, 2001).

Thus, while some Euphrates urban settlements were abandoned or contracted in size and diminished in complexity at the end of the Early Bronze Age, the region did not collapse and wither altogether. On the contrary, several features testify to a strong, unbroken cultural continuity and the persistence of social and political structures across several centuries of urban florescence, decline, and regeneration. This phenomenon becomes especially striking when it is compared to the developments that have been documented from the same time period in other regions of the ancient Near East, such as Palestine and the Khabur Plains of northeastern Syria, where severe and long-lasting settlement disruptions and cultural discontinuities occurred. What, then, accounts for this high degree of continuity and resiliency in the Euphrates Valley of Syria? What factors existing within this region and among its inhabitants could have prompted these trends, setting the region apart from other areas of the Near East? While almost certainly a multitude of factors bear on this issue, three key and somewhat interrelated features can best account for this unique situation.

First, the environment played an important role in the way in which the settlements developed in the northern Euphrates Valley. Studies indicate that this region is located at the southern limit of the semiarid transitional zone between the desert steppe and the better-watered lands of northern and western Syria (Lewis 1987:1–2). This stretch of the Euphrates Valley was, therefore, a relatively marginal territory in which dry farming, although possible, was precarious and where pastoralism as well as other forms of food production constituted critical parts of the subsistence economy (Zettler et al. 1997:2). Thus, for successful survival in this marginal environment, a diversified subsistence economy was necessary.

Recent paleobotanical and faunal analyses confirm this assumption. In and around the site of Tell es-Sweyhat, for example, there is ample evidence for the herding of sheep and goats in the steppe behind the river valley, even during the floruit of Sweyhat's urban phase in the twenty-second century

BC (Zettler et al. 1997:141). Moreover, the percentage of wild animal remains, particularly onager and gazelle, reaches a maximum when the population of the city is at its highest (Zettler et al. 1997:141–42). Both types of evidence, therefore, underline the varied subsistence base that existed in this region, even in times of stability and relative prosperity. As a result of this varied, flexible economy, when the Euphrates Valley was faced with the disintegration of a centralized urban authority or climatic deterioration, the diversity of its subsistence base enabled the remnant population to adapt accordingly. Consequently, the return to a more prosperous economy and stable political system would have occurred swiftly and smoothly. This situation appears in marked contrast to the agricultural regimes that appear to have characterized western Palestine in the EB III and the Khabur Plains of Upper Mesopotamia. Because these areas had concentrated intensively on one form of subsistence—agriculture—over any others, when negative forces came into play in the form of either climate change or political instability, these regimes lacked the flexibility to withstand such stresses and rapidly withered. This lack of flexibility might thus explain why these regions experienced long "dark ages" in the last centuries of the Early Bronze Age, before their eventual rejuvenation in the Middle Bronze Age.

Second, the very fact that the settlements of the Euphrates Valley were largely autonomous and never under the rigid control of a greater political authority during the Early and the Middle Bronze Age may also help to explain their high degree of resilience and cultural continuity. Individual settlements or city-states were not intimately tied to the fate, successful or otherwise, of a higher, centralized power. Again, the Khabur Plains region provides an interesting counterpoint to this situation. Because this region had come under the control of the expanding Akkadian empire, it enjoyed increased prosperity and grew in complexity (Weiss and Courty 1993:139–41), but this very dependence may have been what led to its downfall. When the Akkadian empire broke apart, settlement in the Khabur Plains crumbled along with it. In contrast, in the environment found in the Euphrates Valley, where settlements were largely autonomous and economically self-sufficient, their ability to both withstand stresses and encourage growth was much greater. They depended heavily on the abilities of their individual inhabitants. This point may go far to explain the varying local responses to the problems of the late third millennium BC in the northern Euphrates Valley, in which some settlements were abandoned while others bore the hardships of the period and adapted accordingly.

A third important feature of these settlements is their persistent tribal character throughout the Early and the Middle Bronze Age. While Euphrates settlements expanded into large centers at times of stability and prosperity, they never adopted what can be considered fully hierarchical political systems, typically characterized by the presence of a dominant ruling class in opposition to commoner strata within a closed, urban environment. On the contrary, the population appears to have been continuously defined by loosely organized confederacies of both agrarian and pastoral nomadic kin groups whose membership often transcended the boundaries of individual centers or specific places of residence. The political relationships of such groups did not preclude the dissemination of power and decision making across the community rather than being solely concentrated in the hands of a few elite individuals. Given the region's subsistence strategy of long-range herding of sheep and goats, perhaps this tradition of collective power can be attributed in part to "the tendency of pastoralists to manage access to grazing land at the collective level, for whole communities" (Fleming 2004:218).

The type of political organization posited here conforms to the model formulated by Richard Blanton and his colleagues, who have observed that the political systems of some complex societies are not entirely and rigidly hierarchical in their structure. While "exclusionary" strategies are centered on individual leadership and the monopolistic control of sources of power, the "corporate" political strategy is more group oriented, with power shared across different groups and sectors of society (Blanton et al. 1996:2; Fleming 2004:177). Within this system, constant tension exists between the two political actions, one striving to concentrate power in the hands of one individual or a single authoritative group or class within the society, while the other attempts to offset the attainment of absolute power by maintaining an emphasis on collective political authority (Blanton et al. 1996:2; Fleming 2004:180; Porter 2002b:167).

While Blanton and his colleagues used their model to better elucidate patterns of political action in ancient Mesoamerica (Blanton et al. 1996), its application to other complex societies around the world, including the ancient Near East, is highly tenable. Most recently, this so-called dual-processual model has been applied by Daniel Fleming to the political world of the Mari archives of ancient Syria during the early second millennium BC, the Middle Bronze Age (Fleming 2004). Fleming cogently observes that although Syrian cities and states were controlled by leaders or kings who ruled from well-demarcated urban centers and who expressed their status and sovereignty by building palaces and other impressive monumental structures, a collective decision-making tradition also existed. There is frequent mention in contemporaneous textual sources of "elders," for example, whose collective authority was distinct from that of a king (Fleming 2004:190–91). Such assemblies of elders are known to have engaged in diplomacy, acted as witnesses in legal affairs, and played important roles in religious rituals (Fleming 2004:191–92). Abundant reference to collective assemblies in the textual sources suggests that a "corporate" political strategy was prevalent during this period and existed alongside more "exclusionary" forms of political authority.

The presence in the letters of the Mari archives of a collective decision-making group called the *tahtamum* stands out as a particularly significant form of assembly of elders, since it is known especially from Tuttul and Emar, two cities situated along the Euphrates River of Syria at the southeastern end of the region considered in this chapter (Durand 1989; Fleming 2004:212–16). Fleming suggests that the towns' distance from the shadow of major kingdoms may have allowed this distinctly collective political tradition to thrive with relatively little interference from outside powers (Fleming 2004:213). Besides the fact that the *tahtamum* has its origins in the Early Bronze Age, as attested by the term's occurrence at third-millennium Ebla (Fleming 2004:214), both Tuttul and Emar were known to have been prominent Early Bronze Age towns, suggesting that this institution of elders may well be rooted in this earlier period (Fleming 2004:214). In light of this evidence, it seems highly plausible that neighboring third-millennium Euphrates cities such as the ones under examination here also shared the same collective political traditions.

Turning now to the archaeological record, we see convincing evidence among Euphrates settlements of Syria during both the Early and the Middle Bronze Age to reflect a tribal social-political configuration in which "exclusionary" power coexisted with "corporate" types of authority and collective ideological traditions. The third-millennium monumental stone tombs and tumuli of Jerablus Tahtani, Tell Ahmar, and Tell Banat surely testify to the presence of elites, whose wealth and labor resources no doubt assisted in the construction and accommodation of these lavish funerary monuments. But as Anne Porter has observed among the graves and mortuary mounds of Tell Banat, many interments contained disarticulated human bones in secondary burials, and the lack of differentiation between burials and groups of burials does not "express the individuation of specific members of the groups, their status or position, but rather highlight[s] the corporate nature of the deceased" (Porter 2002b:166).

Although archaeological investigations at Euphrates sites have un-covered considerable architectural evidence for the Early and the Middle Bronze Age, few excavations have uncovered large buildings that can be considered true "royal" residences. In the Early Bronze Age, perhaps only three sites have revealed the presence of secular elite buildings of any kind: Public Building 7 at Tell Banat, the Southern Mansion at Selenkahiye (van Loon 2001:3.35–3.42), and the "Burned Building" and the newly discovered "building complex" on the central mound at Tell es-Sweyhat (Danti and Zettler 2002:39; Holland 1977a:36–43). However, Building 7 at Tell Banat is open of access and does not dominate the site (Porter 2002b:167), and nei-ther of the elite structures at Selenkahiye and Tell es-Sweyhat is especially monumental or palatial in plan (van Loon 2001:3.110). At Tell es-Sweyhat, the layout and furniture of the recently excavated building complex on the high mound suggest that the structure may have served as a gathering place for the elders of the city, not the residence of a royal individual (Danti and Zettler 2002:39).

Excavations in Middle Bronze Age contexts have failed to uncover any elite structures that might be connected with a centralized authority or king. Although evidence of substantial fortifications (Tell Hadidi, Munbaqa, and Emar), quarters of domestic housing (Halawa, Habuba Kabira, and Emar), and storage facilities (Qara Quzaq) has been identified at these regener-ated Middle Bronze Age sites, no palatial-style residences have yet been un-earthed.

There is, therefore, compelling textual and archaeological evidence for the persistence of a tribal, corporate sociopolitical structure among the Euphrates communities of the Early and Middle Bronze Age. This form of political organization may have had the effect of curbing or hindering the growth of highly centralized urban polities characterized by ruling dy-nasties and rigid social hierarchies. Although the existence of such strong decentralizing forces meant that this region never enjoyed the heights of political power and economic prosperity, it probably also meant that the Euphrates region would never experience the kinds of precipitous or vio-lent collapses to which tightly structured and rigidly organized state sys-tems are highly susceptible.

This phenomenon may be both analogous and somewhat related to the region's adaptation to its environment as described above. The subsistence economy of the Euphrates was flexible and varied and enabled the region's communities to adapt successfully to prevailing environmental conditions in difficult times. The same can also be said for the sociopolitical structure of such communities, whose loosely organized and heterarchical political relationships gave them a highly elastic character, thus enabling them to modify their social and political structures to suit the conditions in which they found themselves. At the end of the third millennium BC, therefore, the local communities of the Euphrates Valley, despite experiencing forces that threatened to bring an end to their economies and way of life, were able to devise strategies that ensured their continued existence and carried them through to more stable times, making the task of rebuilding and revitalizing their communities a relatively straightforward process.

Comparable Data from Jordan

The findings and conclusions for the Euphrates Valley of Syria seem to parallel closely those recently proposed for the trans-Jordan region during the EB IV period (ca. 2350–2000 BC). Like the Euphrates Valley, the trans-Jordan area did not experience a dramatic shift from an urban landscape with an intensified agricultural economy to a complete absence of cities and few sedentary, farming communities, as has sometimes been posited for western Palestine (Dever 1995:291). On the contrary, EB IV trans-Jordan comprised a myriad of small sedentary sites and at least one fortified "town" (Palumbo 2001:240–46). Furthermore, technological and provenience studies of the material culture assemblages from several sites have highlighted the degree of specialized production and technological innovations that developed at the village level during this time, despite the absence of large towns or cities and the complex production processes and exchange nodes that large settlements might be expected to facilitate (Falconer 1994; Palumbo 2001:253–57).

What is highlighted in Bronze Age Jordan is the persistence and resilience of human settlement at the village level, which is seen as the strongest and most enduring socioeconomic entity in the region. In this ruralized landscape of autonomous villages, a diversified, flexible economy was prevalent, giving the population the adaptive ability to shift from one type of productive strategy to another as deemed necessary by the circumstances (Marfoe 1979:8; Palumbo 2001:260). As for cities, in this "heartland of villages" (Falconer 1987), they are to be viewed as superimpositions on a fundamentally rural system. While economic complexity and social stratification became more pronounced during periods of urbanism, the underlying village core, with its kin-based structure and diversified, flexible economy, remained essentially stable and intact.

Overall, the conclusions reached for the trans-Jordan region parallel those suggested for the Syrian Euphrates, especially when one considers the strong continuity that is manifested in the Syrian Euphrates throughout the periods of urban florescence, decline, and regeneration. This phenomenon of continuity reflects the stable, adaptive capabilities of a largely rural-based economic system. Such a model also fits very well with the posited tribal character of the Euphrates communities, since such a social structure would have been more likely to have resulted from a landscape of smaller, loosely organized confederacies of kinship groups spread out across village communities than from a landscape perennially characterized by urban polities and their hierarchically structured socioeconomic systems.

Regeneration in the Middle Bronze Age

Even if we accept that the Euphrates landscape was like its Levantine neighbors in that it was essentially rural and tribal at its base, we must still search for an explanation of why this region experienced a transformation toward larger, more densely populated settlements, some characterized by considerable defenses and other public works, at the beginning of the Middle Bronze Age (ca. 2000–1900 BC). Of course, one has to keep in mind that most of these Middle Bronze Age settlements were founded directly upon earlier EB IV settlements and display considerable cultural continuity from the earlier periods. Furthermore, many of the same basic social structures appear to have remained intact, and the basic subsistence economy, although intensified, was never radically altered. Thus, this transformation cannot easily be credited to an influx of new people who implanted their radically different urban ways on the region. Rather, the growth in size and scale of the Euphrates settlements at the beginning of the Middle Bronze Age appears to have been a phenomenon that took place within the existing communities.

Nevertheless, it is not altogether impossible to look for the cause of growth from the outside. At the start of the second millennium, there was a consolidation of power by a number of powerful Amorite groups in Mesopotamia, some of the most influential locating themselves along the Euphrates River at sites such as Mari (Kuhrt 1995:1:95–98) or in southern cities such as Larsa and Babylon (Kuhrt 1995:1:78–80, 108–9; see also Nichols and Weber, chapter 3). These new centers, eager to validate and to enhance their power and prestige, energetically pursued their quest for valuable materials such as precious metals, stone, and timber and, in so doing, revitalized trade routes that led to such materials. The Euphrates was one of the most profitable of these routes, providing access to the rich resources of the Taurus to the north and the active ports of the Mediterranean to the west (Klengel 1983). In this light, therefore, perhaps the regeneration of settlements along the northern Euphrates River can be attributed to this resumption of trade and exchange. Such settlements would have benefited economically from the establishment of commercial relationships with foreign merchants and caravans. They could have intensified their own levels of production to participate in this active commerce and may also have received tariffs from shipments of goods passing through their territories (e.g., Burke 1964; Durand 1990:81). In all, this growing prosperity and increased contact with the wider world may explain in large part the growth in size and complexity of their settlements.

Admittedly, this proposition is only conjecture at this point. For it to be verified, archaeological and textual evidence will have to prove that the growth of urban life and the resumption of long-distance trade began earlier in the Middle Bronze Age at other settlements such as Mari and then spread to points farther northwest along the Euphrates. Although this will require further archaeological investigations and especially a fine-tuning of the relative chronologies of Middle Bronze Age sites in Syria, such valuable information could provide the critical key to unlocking this very intriguing period of urban decline and consolidation.

Minimizing Collapse, Maximizing Regeneration

The example of the Bronze Age Euphrates Valley settlements provides information that can aid in understanding the process of the collapse and regeneration of complex societies in antiquity. Factors such as the environment, a subsistence economy, and the sociopolitical character of a region's population greatly affect the degree to which such processes are experienced. In the Euphrates Valley, adaptations and responses to a marginal natural environment, combined with a decentralized political arrangement, greatly reduced the extent to which the area suffered from periods of dramatic decline. The same factors enabled its communities to recover with success and rapidity.

Notes

1. While it is difficult to verify from the published reports of the architectural re-mains that Tell Amarna has an uninterrupted stratigraphic sequence from the Early to the Middle Bronze Age, this is clearly borne out by the pottery from the site, which has been carefully studied by Nina Pons (2001). In particular, the pottery of Phase III in Area A possesses some of the same "transitional EB-MB" forms as exist at other Euphrates sites. Moreover, the author's research on Middle Bronze Age tombs at the site has confirmed the existence of a well-developed MB assemblage at Amarna. In summary, Tell Amarna's pottery assemblage comprises all periods under scrutiny in this investigation (EB IV, EB-MB, MB) and thus supports the premise of settlement continuity.

2. The absence of fine-tuning of the relative ceramic chronology and still-incomplete or not-altogether-certain stratigraphic sequences at some of these sites (namely, Tell Ahmar, Qara Quzaq, and possibly Munbaqa) leave open the possibility that they ex-perienced occupational hiatuses at the very end of the Early Bronze Age or beginning of the Middle Bronze Age (e.g., Valdés Pereiro 2001:120; Werner 1998:45). Nonetheless, these disruptions do not appear to have been very long in duration.

3 Amorites, Onagers, and Social Reorganization in Middle Bronze Age Syria

John J. Nichols and Jill A. Weber

If societal collapse and regeneration occur as a result of the failure and reorganization of regional systems that structure networks of people and places, how are these processes manifested at individual communities within those systems? In this chapter, we address this question using evidence from Tell Umm el-Marra, the largest settlement in northern Syria's Jabbul Plain (fig. 3.1) during much of the Bronze Age (ca. 2700–1200 BC).

In the Jabbul region and elsewhere in Syria, collapse at the end of the third millennium BC entailed failure of regional economic and political networks, resulting in the disintegration of states into smaller political entities (Schwartz, chapter 1). Because integration of institutions and social groupings in complex societies is largely provided by political structures (Kaufman 1988:220), their dissolution compels local settlements to stabilize at lower levels of differentiation, a process Shmuel Eisenstadt (1964:379) terms "regression." After the loss of integrative coherence afforded by a political superstructure, the constituent institutions underlying urban complexity may survive independently, with varying degrees of independence and cohesion (Eisenstadt 1964:378; Yoffee 1988b:15). Such regression into locally stable societies (the "nearly decomposable systems" described by Herbert Simon [1965:70]) may provide a basis for the revitalization of complexity (Eisenstadt 1964:379). The evidence from Umm el-Marra suggests that while local regression follows regional collapse, continuity combined with flexibility in local economic institutions enhances the stability of the reorganized polities and provides a framework for a return to regional complexity.

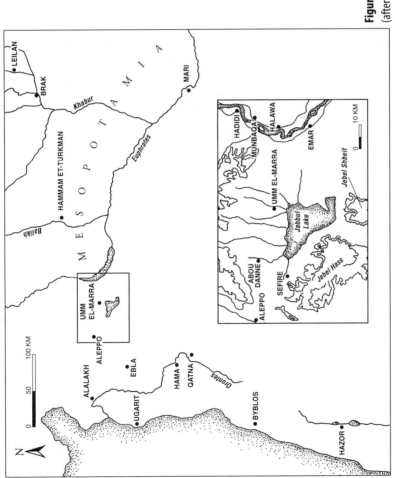

Figure 3.1 Map of Syria with Jabbul Plain inset (after Schwartz et al. 2003, fig. 1).

Historical Context: Centralization and Decentralization in Syria in the Third and Second Millennia BC

In the ancient Near East, virtually all complex social systems experienced cycles of centralization and decentralization (Adams 1978; Kohl 1978; Yoffee 1995). Only rarely were Syro-Mesopotamian regions unified under a single hegemon. Rather, competition among multiple urban centers resulted in the rise and fall of given polities, similar to the situation Miriam Stark describes for the lower Mekong basin (chapter 10). Much of the final period of Early Bronze Age Syria, or EB IV (ca. 2500–2000 BC), is characterized by urban nucleation and state building. A few powerful regional polities emerged as virtual hegemons in northern Syria, from Mari (modern Hariri) in the south, to Ebla (modern Mardikh) in the west, to Nagar (modern Brak) in the east. Within this nexus of powerful urban centers, weaker cities were integrated into a network of economic and political exchange. In the process, these second-tier cities—such as Umm el-Marra—augmented their own internal cohesion and complexity. Ebla was the dominant power in western Syria; competition between Ebla and Mari resulted in the shifting allegiances of those weaker polities, as reflected in administrative texts from Ebla and elsewhere (Archi 1998; Archi and Biga 2003). Loyalty to one or another hegemon, however, often benefited client polities with status and wealth (Pearson 1997).

Umm el-Marra, provisionally identified as ancient Tuba (Catagnoti 1992; Matthiae 1980), became the largest community in the Jabbul Plain by virtue of its strategic location along major routes of communication and commerce (Curvers and Schwartz 1997:203–4; Tefnin 1980:91–92). Both the presence of a ruling elite at Tuba and its subservient position vis-à-vis Ebla are indicated by Eblaite textual evidence. Despite such political asymmetry, diplomatic ties and interdynastic marriages cemented links between cities while establishing filial networks among polities of differing rank. Competition among cities was continual, as were changes in alliances prompted by military conquest (Astour 1992).

One of the most disruptive of such conquests was that by the Akkadian empire from its center in Mesopotamia circa 2300 BC. This conquest resulted in the disruption or termination of the ruling dynasty at Ebla and the presence of Akkadian rulers in the Khabur Valley of eastern Syria at Brak and perhaps at Shekhna (modern Leilan), and at Urkesh (modern Mozan), to name a few important cities. The Akkadian empire collapsed about a century later, coincident with a reduction in dense populations in parts of northeastern Syria (Meijer 1986; Weiss and Courty 1993), though some centers, such as Urkesh and Nagar, persisted. In western Syria, urbanism continued unabated for a century or two following the dissolution of the Akkadian empire, but by the end of the third millennium BC, many Euphrates Valley sites were deserted or partially abandoned (Cooper, chapter 2), while large cities in inland Syria (e.g., Ebla) decreased in size and significance. The causes of this collapse have been vigorously debated, particularly with respect to the timing and potential impact of climatic desiccation and environmental degradation (Courty 2001; Nichols 2004; Weiss et al. 1993; Wilkinson 1997). Evidence from across Syria indicates that human responses to this changing social and physical environment varied widely.

Following the collapse of urbanism in Syria at the end of the Early Bronze Age, the beginning of the Middle Bronze Age in Syria (MB I, ca. 2000–1800 BC) was an era of relatively few cities and numerous small, dispersed settlements (Peltenburg 2000). Many areas lack evidence for regional settlement hierarchy and appear to consist of rural settlements without urban centers or dominant state polities (Cooper, chapter 2).

Reurbanization in the Second Millennium BC

Existing evidence shows that by the nineteenth century BC, urban centers with literate bureaucracies reappeared in force across the Syrian landscape. Many of these cities arose atop the *tells* of EB IV polities. There is no evidence linking this secondary urbanization to technological innovation or transference, such as the metallurgical advances that Philip Kohl (1996) sees behind the resurgence of complexity in southern Turkmenistan in the early second millennium BC. Nor is obvious influence detectable in imported items or material culture styles from other complex societies such as Egypt or Mesopotamia. Neither faunal nor botanical data show indisputable evidence of climatic change; fundamental patterns of natural resource exploitation continue in the choice of environmental niches and spectra of species (Schwartz, Curvers, Gerritsen et al. 2000).

One relevant factor is the widespread acquisition of power by a newly significant ethnic group. According to textual evidence, most of the new cities and larger political entities were ruled by Amorites or individuals who claimed membership in the Amorite ethnic group, a group that largely had been stigmatized and marginalized in the official records of the preceding millennium. Vast areas of Syro-Mesopotamia coalesced under trade networks ostensibly based on Amorite ethnic relations (Cooper, chapter 2;

Kuhrt 1995:1:74–75). Local Amorite rulers politically influenced their pu-
tative hinterlands while vying for position within interregional networks
of exchange. Such Amorite rulers included Shamshi-Adad of Shubat-
Enlil (modern Leilan), Yakhdun-Lim of Mari, Yarim-Lim of Halab (modern Aleppo), Ishkhi-Adad of Qatna (modern Mishrifeh), Yibbit-Lim of
Ebla, and numerous others. While ancestral lines of succession appear to
have been severed between the Early and the Middle Bronze Age, elites'
strategies of diplomacy and governance remained virtually the same. As
in EB IV Syria, the Middle Bronze Age rulers were connected not only by
commercial contacts but also by marriage alliances and treaties governing
mutual defense and use-rights of pasturelands. Amorite ancestry became
an important means of legitimation for dynastic rulers. Though no historical evidence of Amorite rule is extant for Umm el-Marra specifically, archaeological evidence from Umm el-Marra—in conjunction with historical evidence for Syria at large—suggests that Amorites contributed to the
city's reorganization in the early second millennium BC.

Evidence from Umm el-Marra

Tell Umm el-Marra (fig. 3.2) is located in the Jabbul Plain of western Syria,
midway between the Euphrates River and Aleppo. At approximately twenty-
five hectares, Umm el-Marra is the largest Bronze Age site in the Jabbul,
historically an important conduit between western Syria and Mesopotamia
(Curvers and Schwartz 1997:203–4). Umm el-Marra also is located at the
frontier between the rainfall farming zone to the north and west and a drier
steppe zone to the south and east, traditionally associated with pastoralism
(Lewis 1987). Since the inception in 1994 of the joint Johns Hopkins and University of Amsterdam Umm el-Marra Project under the direction of Glenn
Schwartz and Hans Curvers, the site has been the focal point for investigation of the developmental trajectory of Syrian complex societies in the Early,
Middle, and Late Bronze periods (Curvers and Schwartz 1997; Schwartz et al.
2003; Schwartz, Curvers, Gerritsen et al. 2000). One aim of the project is to
try to clarify the nature of urban coalescence in the Jabbul Plain in the early
to middle second millennium BC, as Umm el-Marra was absorbed into the
Amorite-ruled regional state of Yamkhad, centered at Aleppo.

   In considering the evidence from Umm el-Marra in its Early to Middle
Bronze Age transition, we will discuss architectural and ceramic data as well
as the results of ecofactual analysis, particularly faunal analysis. The faunal
data reveal changes in concentrations and spatial distributions of animal

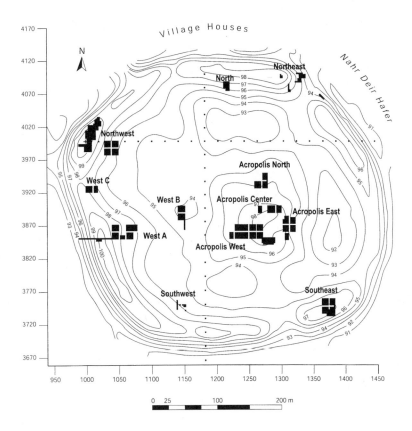

Figure 3.2 Tell Umm el-Marra (after Schwartz et al. 2003, fig. 2).

bones from the relevant Early and Middle Bronze Age periods, most notably with respect to bones of the onager (table 3.1). These data suggest that the onager—a wild equid akin to the ass—was a primary source of leather at Umm el-Marra. Changes in the character of onager exploitation and leather production reveal significant aspects of Umm el-Marra's transition from collapse to regeneration. Local increases in the scale and uniformity of onager-carcass processing, as well as diversification in the types of production activities, coincide with the regeneration of regional economic and political networks. It must be emphasized, however, that while the ecofactual and artifactual data are suggestive, many of the ideas advanced here are based on excavations limited to the site's acropolis and may require revision as excavation broadens.

Table 3.1 Equid bones from Umm el-Marra's Acropolis dating to the Early and Middle Bronze Age

	Acropolis			
Period	West	East	North	Center
Pre–EB IV B		22 (46)	22 (42)	
EB IV B	22 (55)	11 (35)	7 (19)	
MB I	31 (56)			
Early MB II	34 (68)			
Late MB II	37 (64)	28 (68)	36 (61)	36 (63)

Note: The first number in each pair is the percentage of equid bones within the total number of bones of identified species; the number within parentheses is the percentage of equid bones within the total weight of faunal specimens.

EB IVA–B at Umm el-Marra (ca. 2500–2000 BC)

As the largest settlement in the Jabbul Plain during EB IV, Umm el-Marra occupied the apex of a multitier site-size hierarchy and ostensibly asserted authority over its densely settled hinterland (Schwartz, Curvers, Gerritsen et al. 2000:450–51). Umm el-Marra appears to have been the center of a client-kingdom of the more powerful Ebla polity. In EB IVA (ca. 2500–2300 BC), Umm el-Marra was enclosed by a substantial mud rampart. Excavations have exposed segments of domestic architecture on the eastern and northern portions of the Acropolis, a relatively low, broad mound near the center of the site.

The presence of high-status elites at Umm el-Marra in this period is demonstrated by the richly provisioned tombs of the burial complex in the Acropolis Center (Schwartz et al. 2003). This complex includes conspicuous, freestanding mortuary structures built of stone and brick. Elite inhumations and ostentatious mortuary complexes dating to this period have been discovered throughout the Near East; as in Umm el-Marra's case, non-looted tombs commonly are replete with luxury items of precious metals and stone (Porter 1995b; Woolley 1934). Interments of equids with human burials also are a common mortuary feature of this period (Zarins 1986). In keeping with this tradition, equids or equid skeletons were installed in structures ancillary to the tombs excavated in Umm el-Marra's mortuary complex. Similarities in the types of human burials found and in their contents suggest a shared sensibility governing the treatment of deceased members of the elite in EB IV cities. The local importance of this complex is signified not only by its conspicuous consumption of wealth in its provisioning and monumentality, but also by its high visibility at an elevated location at the settlement's center. With the demise or conquest of many of this period's powerful dynasts—including those of Ebla—at the end of EB IVA, Umm el-Marra's elite burial complex fell into disuse.

In EB IVB (ca. 2300–2000 BC), newly segregated economic activity is seen in the Acropolis West. This area has yielded concentrated deposits of discarded equid bones. While, overall, the relative abundance of equid bones did not increase in EB IVB (equaling roughly 14 percent of the number of identified specimens of all bones recovered from both the EB IVA and EB IVB strata of the Acropolis), differences between the relative proportion of disposed equid bones recovered from the newly occupied Acropolis West (22 percent) and from the continued occupations on the Acropolis East and North (11 percent and 7 percent, respectively) are substantial. The frequency of discarded bones is significantly higher in the Acropolis West than in the Acropolis East and Acropolis North combined. Moreover, domestic (Schwartz, Curvers, Gerritsen et al. 2000:425) and industrial (Schwartz et al. 2003:329–30) use of space in the Acropolis West differs fundamentally from that seen in the phases of domestic architecture of the Acropolis East and North excavation areas. There is substantial similarity between the eco- and artifactual discard associated with the domestic structures on the Acropolis East and Acropolis North, but the lack of uniformity between assemblages from these areas argues against specialized or specialist processing.

The Acropolis West's concentrated equid-bone discard and its spatial and functional architectural disparities together point to reorganization of economic activities involving equid carcasses. Inhabitants or workers in the Acropolis West may have had preferential access to equid carcasses, which were processed primarily in this area. In the absence of broad excavation of EB IVB deposits outside the Acropolis, we cannot conclude that the equid-bone concentrations on the Acropolis West are unique. However, the transformation and transfer of equid processing from a dispersed domestic activity to a more integrated activity occurring in the newly occupied Acropolis West is compelling evidence for labor reorganization, including the increased differentiation of manufacturing activities. Moreover, while currently there is no evidence linking the specialized treatment of equids on the Acropolis West to a central authority, the central location of this segregated activity and its proximity to the EB IVA elite mortuary complex may indicate such an association, as is more clearly demonstrated in evidence from later periods (see below).

The data discussed here, in conjunction with more comprehensive evidence from later periods, indicate that onager hides were sought for exchange. While texts from the third millennium BC reveal that both donkey and onager hides were valuable (van Lerberghe 1996:113), onager specimens were especially prized (Postgate 1986:194). Corresponding botanical evidence indicates that as the scale of onager exploitation increased dramatically in the Middle Bronze Age, the pasturing of sheep and goats in the steppe declined, evidently in conjunction with the preferential use of the steppe for onager exploitation (Schwartz, Curvers, Gerritsen et al. 2000:447).

MB I at Umm el-Marra (ca. 2000–1800 BC)

The collapse of regional political networks at the end of the Early Bronze Age resulted in regional settlement disruption, including site diminution or abandonment at and around Umm el-Marra. Survey data from the Jabbul Plain indicate that twenty-five of forty-seven EB sites were deserted by MB I (Schwartz, Curvers, Gerritsen et al. 2000:451), and ceramic evidence raises the possibility that Umm el-Marra was completely abandoned for a short time in early MB I (Schwartz et al. 2003). In later MB I, occupation is evident in the Acropolis West and North, but other excavated areas have little or no evidence for this period. The present evidentiary emphasis on the Acropolis, however, may color this observation. Further excavation outside the Acropolis may reveal additional MB I occupation.

Regardless of these developments, the scope of economic activity at the Acropolis West clearly intensified in the MB I period. The relative proportion of bones from equids—predominantly onagers—discarded in this area increased from 22 percent to some 30 percent of the total, suggesting an increased scale of activity.

In conjunction with these changes, Umm el-Marra's MB I inhabitants established a link with past occupants of the site. A monumental platform constructed of large stones and cobbles, evidently used for ceremonial purposes, was erected near or directly above the EB IV burial complex (Schwartz et al. 2003:345). Although this monument's precise date has not been ascertained, associated pottery has been dated preliminarily to later MB I (G. Schwartz, personal communication 2005). As a result of a contraction of the limits of occupation in this period, all activities at the site came to occur in close proximity to this visibly demarcated and tradition-ally sacred precinct. Public focus on the sacred central space at a time when equid exploitation intensified on the Acropolis may signify efforts by an emergent elite to identify this industry with sacred space and ancestral rul-ers. We posit that this appeal to a common ancestry and ideology was made to integrate the society and sanction its economic production.

MB II at Umm el-Marra (ca. 1800–1600 BC)

By the eighteenth century BC, the Amorite-ruled regional polity of Yam-khad emerged with its center at Aleppo, fifty-five kilometers west of Umm el-Marra. Dominating much of northwestern Syria, Yamkhad putatively controlled the Jabbul region. This regeneration of regional complexity is correlated with increased settlement in the Jabbul Plain, where Umm el-Marra, still the largest settlement, once again occupied the apex of a settle-ment hierarchy (Schwartz, Curvers, Gerritsen et al. 2000:451). Many sites that had been abandoned following regional collapse at the end of the third millennium BC were resettled; in MB II, Umm el-Marra was completely re-occupied, attaining the same size as its Early Bronze Age predecessor. Glacis fortifications, most convincingly dated to MB II, were built around the site, and a mud-brick city wall was erected on top of them.

Changes in the economy of Umm el-Marra accompany changes in the spatial organization of the site from MB I to MB II. Building on the animal-processing economy already evident in EB IVB and MB I, Umm el-Marra's MB II inhabitants further intensified the processing of equid carcasses at the Acropolis West. Equid bones are found there in unprecedentedly high concentrations, representing about 34 percent of the total number of ani-mal bones found and about 68 percent of the faunal samples' total weight.

Butchering practices also were modified and standardized in MB II; the discarded bones indicate a heightened focus on skinning the animals. Most of these bones come from an enormous ash deposit reaching as deep as 1.9 meters (Schwartz, Curvers, Gerritsen et al. 2000:425); its full areal extent has not been determined. To the north of this ash deposit, a series of ovens were excavated (some with clay andirons in situ [Schwartz et al. 2003:345]), which may be the source of this ash. Ovens with clay andirons also were excavated on the Acropolis North (Schwartz, Curvers, Gerritsen et al. 2000:429). The presence of these ovens and their characteristic andirons in the Acropolis West and North may reflect growth in the scale and scope of equid-processing activities such as curing or dyeing, though this is not currently demonstrated via the faunal remains. Together with these distinctive installations, altered but uniform bone-modification patterns suggest greater segmentation—and thus complexity—in the processing of equid carcasses. The centralized context and locus of production in the Acropolis West remained constant from MB I to MB II, and such centralization was underlined early in this period by the construction of a wall enclosing the Acropolis (Schwartz et al. 2003:341). The locus of equid processing in the Acropolis West thus was enclosed together with the apparently sacred area of the Acropolis Center.

The character of the Acropolis was modified in later MB II. The enclosure wall no longer was in use, and domestic architecture was constructed atop its ruins in the Acropolis East and North (Schwartz et al. 2003:342). These and other new buildings underwent extensive modifications and additions in later MB II. Similarly, new architecture above the pyrotechnic facilities of the Acropolis West is characterized by rebuilding and agglomeration (Curvers and Schwartz 1997:211–12). A common peculiarity of this new architecture on the Acropolis is the inclusion of large numbers of equid-bone fragments within the walls' substructures and the placement of complete equid bones between their sub- and superstructures, evidently a new practice at Umm el-Marra. In addition, a complete donkey skeleton was found within the blocked doorway of a contemporaneous building in the Acropolis East. At the same time, the monumental stone platform remained intact, and the Acropolis gate remained standing, which suggests continuing demarcation of the Acropolis.

Umm el-Marra's MB II architectural and cultic changes accompanied profound economic growth. While the Acropolis West was the sole locus of a production focus on equid hides in MB I, this production had spread throughout the Acropolis by late MB II. As the scale of the operation increased, so too did its intensity; equid bone remains for this period amount to nearly 40 percent of the total count and over 60 percent of the weight of all bones excavated on the Acropolis. The bone waste discarded on the Acropolis, particularly the profusion of extremities (Serjeantson 1989a:5; Stol 1983:529 §5) and the preponderance of juvenile and wild animals (Reed 1972:36–37; Serjeantson 1989b:131), represents the by-products of hide production. In addition, bones of twenty complete "paws" (also extremities) from a minimum of eleven dogs were recovered from the Acropolis. Individuals and "workshops" on the Acropolis received or systematically segregated select portions of uniformly butchered and dismembered equid carcasses. From these carcass portions, metapodial bones were removed and manufactured into awls. Worked-bone debitage, unfinished tools, and used and broken tools dating to later MB II were uncovered only on the Acropolis, despite exposure of diverse Middle Bronze Age phases outside the Acropolis, suggesting that the tools were made, used, and discarded on the Acropolis exclusively. The presence of the used and discarded tools is evidence for the sewing and finishing of leather products. Data from southern Mesopotamian texts reveal that upon receiving skins, leather workshops may have sent the skins elsewhere to be cured, retrieving them for finishing (Sigrist 1981:172–73). No definitive evidence of tanning facilities has been found on the Acropolis; one might interpret this as evidence *ex silentio* for tanning elsewhere and, accordingly, for segmentation of the leather production process.

Evidence for discrete economic activities involving animal products by late MB II also has been obtained from Umm el-Marra's Northwest Area, far removed from the Acropolis, where gazelle bone remains, including manufactured tools, are uniquely concentrated in an architectural complex built against the city wall (Schwartz et al. 2003:342–44). Among the animal bone remains found there, the proportion of gazelle bones is 26 percent, a high concentration with no parallel in preceding periods or contemporary contexts (e.g., contemporary Acropolis contexts yielded only 4–7 percent gazelle remains). In addition, botanical evidence suggests a decline in the pasturing of sheep and goat herds in the steppe and an increase in the agricultural production of fodder (Miller in Schwartz, Curvers, Gerritsen et al. 2000:446). Sheep and goats provide competition to onager and gazelle herds for steppic pasturage, which may have been reduced by this period as a result of an increase in the number of settlements (Schwartz, Curvers, Gerritsen et al. 2000:451).

A Local Response to Regional Collapse

How did Umm el-Marra adapt and reorganize in the face of regional collapse? Disruption of regional political structures and exchange networks, together with landscape degradation, precluded urbanism based on agricultural surpluses alone. In MB I, the diminished population of Umm el-Marra responded to this crisis by emphasizing and capitalizing on the equid-hunting and -processing economy observed in the preceding period. Exploitation of the products of the steppe formed the basis of Umm el-Marra's animal economy, in contrast to the small fraction of the site's late EB IV economy based on steppe exploitation. We posit that this was the economic engine for the reemergence of sociopolitical stratification at the site. We suggest that emerging "innovative" elites (after Eisenstadt 1964:384–85) in MB I used the economic benefits of a successful equid-processing industry to solidify local control. We further hypothesize that these ambitious and opportunistic individuals cultivated their economic success and furthered the prestige basis of this industry by adopting local EB IVA elite ancestry as a legitimizing tool at home and to imbue themselves with standing in interacting commercially, politically, and socially with contemporary regional and interregional elites. Umm el-Marra's nascent elites may have accomplished this in part by erecting the ceremonial platform in the Acropolis Center, thus claiming a link to the revered elites interred in Umm el-Marra's EB IV mortuary complex.

As a regional network of authority and exchange reemerged in early MB II, specialized equid processing was associated with the sacred space in the Acropolis Center, perhaps to link this economic activity to the ostensibly fictive elite ancestors of Umm el-Marra's Middle Bronze Age elites. The locus of this consecrated industry was physically bounded and separated from the rest of the settlement by the Acropolis enclosure wall. Later, as regional systems continued to strengthen and powerful polities such as Yamkhad reemerged, equid processing further intensified and expanded in scale into a commercial enterprise. This activity entailed greater segmentation of production and a higher degree of labor differentiation. Such markers of complexity are indicated by the increase in the number and type of goods manufactured on the Acropolis and the restricted access to, and use of, gazelle carcasses at the site's Northwest Area.

These economic changes are suggestive of Umm el-Marra's active participation in an expanding sphere of commodities exchange. By late MB II, Umm el-Marra's standardized leather production and the increase in quantity and types of manufactured leather goods at the site seem to indicate a shift from prestige production to commoditization (Kopytoff 1986:73; P. Rice 1989:204). Increasingly dispersed settlements, larger urban centers, and a growing commercial trade network spurred a demand for utilitarian goods such as finished leather, the use of which for outfitting trade and military expeditions is attested in Syro-Mesopotamian texts dating to the eighteenth and seventeenth centuries BC. For instance, in the eighteenth century BC, the northern Mesopotamian ruler Shamshi-Adad instructed his son, the king of Mari, to prepare "52 water-skins, 64 sandals, 1 big leather sack, (and) 10 leather straps of 9 meters" for an expedition of 32 men and 10 donkeys (Dossin 1950, no. 17, cited in Postgate 1992:148, text 7.6). Umm el-Marra's economic transformation occurred at a time in the Middle Bronze Age when the route between Aleppo and the Euphrates was subject to unprecedented traffic, which, as the text above suggests, would have been equipped with leather tackle and water-skins. Umm el-Marra was geographically and economically positioned to benefit from this traffic.

The evidence for regional commercialization coincides with an increase in historical evidence for ethnic Amorite populations in the Syrian plains in the first half of the second millennium BC (Heimpel 2003:14; Streck 2000:40–41). Such Amorite communities coupled intensive foddering with seasonal transhumance (e.g., Nichols 2004:45). These integrated strategies of resilience gave Amorite groups an adaptive edge over their counterparts. Amorite populations took advantage of geopolitical changes by pasturing their livestock along riverbanks and in other choice areas traditionally dominated by urban centers such as Mari (see Klengel 1992:42–43; Luke 1965), and by reducing their need for extensive transhumance by cultivating newly available land for fodder (Buccellati 1997; Luke 1965:244–45). The Mari archive includes agreements between Amorite communities and Mari for such land use (e.g., Durand 1988:426–29). Middle Bronze Age Umm el-Marra may have followed a similar pattern as steps were taken—including more intensive foddering—to facilitate the compatibility of activities stemming from both animal herding and harvesting (Schwartz, Curvers, Gerritsen et al. 2000:447). Such actions probably resulted in an increased division of labor.

Segregated production activities in differentiated contexts (components of specialization) in late MB II thus were spread across the city and no longer were confined to the Acropolis, the city's symbolic center. A logical inference is that greater numbers of people and institutions were involved in coordinating these various economic activities. Such citywide integration would explain why the Acropolis wall was eliminated in favor of the reconstructed fortifications around the entire city.

Although Umm el-Marra's Middle Bronze Age economic growth was profound, we cannot yet, given available evidence, conclude whether those who orchestrated that growth were endogenous occupants of the EB IV city or whether they were outsiders. They shared with their Early Bronze Age predecessors an economic and ritual focus on equids, and both populations used the ideological import of the Acropolis to further their administrative aims. Continuity is also evident in the persistence and intensification of pottery specialization and standardization from the Early Bronze Age to the Middle Bronze Age, as is demonstrated by a reduction in the number of vessel forms and by more cursory surface decoration, such as comb-incision. Umm el-Marra's Middle Bronze Age ceramics generally have fewer ware categories and are thicker walled and coarser tempered than are its Early Bronze Age ceramics. This local trend follows a regional emphasis on ceramic mass production in the Middle Bronze Age (Akkermans and Schwartz 2003:291).

The discontinuities in material culture may reflect a newly conspicuous presence of the Amorite ethnic group (Emberling 1997), whose significance as administrative elites at this time is documented across Syro-Mesopotamia. For instance, there are formal and superficial differences between the site's Early and Middle Bronze Age pottery. Innovations in Umm el-Marra's Middle Bronze Age pottery repertoires include the introduction of sharply carinated pots and bowls resembling metal vessel forms, pottery with rims having a multiple-groove profile, and painted vessels of the Syro-Cilician pottery group (Nichols 2004:156–58; Schwartz, Curvers, Gerritsen et al. 2000:425–26). Although the production of wheel-made pottery spanned the Early and Middle Bronze periods, cooking vessels were manufactured on the wheel in the Middle Bronze Age for the first time. In a regional light, the site's new Middle Bronze Age ceramic forms share numerous characteristics with Middle Bronze Age pottery assemblages from elsewhere in western Syria, particularly Ebla (Akkermans and Schwartz 2003:342n70; Schwartz, Curvers, Gerritsen et al. 2000:425n23).

Other behaviors of the MB I occupants of Umm el-Marra's Acropolis differ from those of their urban predecessors in a way that suggests new social influences, if not the dominance of a different social order. One potentially significant difference is seen in burial practices. At EB IVA Umm el-Marra, infants were buried with or near elite adults in the central burial complex on the Acropolis, possibly indicating their inclusion in hereditary dynastic reckoning. No such infant burials—and no adult human burials of any kind—have been found among the Middle Bronze Age Acropolis contexts. In contrast, domestic subfloor infant burials inside pottery vessels are prevalent among Umm el-Marra's Middle Bronze Age contexts, which may indicate the primacy of one's family consanguinity as opposed to that of an elite dynastic lineage. This infant burial type is typical for Syria's Middle Bronze Age sites (e.g., Dornemann 1979:138; Mallet 1989:52; al-Maqdissi et al. 2002:83; Meijer 1996:184; Warmenbol 1980). While this infant-burial type is by no means unique to Middle Bronze Age Syria, there is only one attestation at Early Bronze Age Umm el-Marra. MB I is the period in which the intrahousehold burial of infants supersedes public burial of the city's ruling elite.

This apparent Middle Bronze Age shift to a focus on the household co-incides with the abandonment of Umm el-Marra's Early Bronze Age elite burial complex and the rejection of that space for burials in this and later periods. While the sanctity of this mortuary complex is appropriated for use by Umm el-Marra's Middle Bronze Age inhabitants, there is no com-pelling evidence that these inhabitants shared kin-group affiliation with the individuals interred there. One might interpret this as an attempt at legitimization by tapping into Umm el-Marra's "ancestral" ruling lineage, though possibly by unrelated administrators seeking affiliation with fictive elite ancestors from the preceding era of prosperity.

Other archaeological evidence dating to the Middle Bronze Age suggests that individuals and groups with a different ethnicity or kin-group affili-ation—most likely Amorite—were newly significant. One is the organic planning and agglomeration typical of the site's Middle Bronze Age dwell-ings. This may reflect the organization of households as corporate groups composed of extended families (Stone 1977), a form of social organization postulated for patrilocal Amorite kin groups (Schloen 2001). Another is the proliferation of the ritual use of equids at Umm el-Marra in the Middle Bronze Age. While equids commonly are associated with human burials in EB IV Syria (Zarins 1986), including inhumations at Umm el-Marra (as dis-cussed above), new types of equid ritual activity appear in MB II contexts.

Deposits of equid bones at Middle Bronze Age Umm el-Marra in ar-chitectural foundations across the Acropolis (see above), together with the profound upsurge in industrial equid refuse, demonstrate an increased significance of equids in the site's ritual and economic activity. The ritual significance of equids among heads of Amorite clans and cities in Middle Bronze Age Syria is well documented in texts from Mari (Durand 1988:119–22), which include reference to the slaughter of equid foals (usually inter-preted as donkeys) to solemnize treaties between Amorite rulers. The ritual use of equids at Umm el-Marra was not new to the site's Middle Bronze Age occupants, but it was adapted for peculiarly Middle Bronze Age rites. In the face of such changes, however, the symbolic importance of the Acropolis was preserved.

Theories of Regeneration

We offer the following working hypothesis to explain the regeneration of complexity at Middle Bronze Age Umm el-Marra following collapse at the end of the Early Bronze Age. The inhabitants of MB I Umm el-Marra who reoccupied the largely deserted ruins of a formerly flourishing Early

Bronze Age center were Amorite agro-pastoralists possessing an intimate knowledge of the steppe and the hunting, trapping, and other technologies relevant to that environmental zone. The ethnic Amorite kin-based organization and flexible agricultural and pastoral economy of this population lent them greater adaptability to the stresses induced by environmental deterioration and the collapse of regional political systems. This is especially important at this arid-steppe boundary, where economically tenable cultivation is sensitive to sociopolitical conditions (e.g., de Vogüé 1865:23–24; Lewis 1987). The economic resilience enjoyed by groups with the ability to use diverse economic strategies and exploitation niches underlay this MB I population's adaptability. Ethnic affinity with other Amorite kin groups would have provided entry into the social infrastructure of communication and exchange that presupposed the larger political networks resulting in the privileged ascendancy of Amorite-administered cities in MB II Syria. At Umm el-Marra, it may have been Amorites who introduced or turned to hunting practices, perhaps to meet a new or newly lucrative demand for useful commodities. Such demand appears to have been generated, at least in part, by the dominant Amorite populations. Cured hides and meat as well as finished leather goods replaced cereals and traditional pastoral surplus as the currency of local and regional commercial finance. Textual evidence for extensive leather craft working and workshops in southern Mesopotamia (Loding 1974; Van De Mieroop 1987) and northern Syria (Gadd 1940; al-Jadir 1967:197) underscores the potential importance of leather in the exchange network among Amorite settlements in the Middle Bronze Age.

This hypothesis parallels Lisa Cooper's observations (see chapter 2) of the resilience of polities in the Euphrates Valley. In the Jabbul region, a principal means of diversification was an increase in the exploitation and manufacture of products of the steppe; greater reliance was placed on harvested, in contrast to husbanded, resources. In addition, hunting forays in the steppe may have facilitated increased contact between far-flung populations, particularly those frequenting the steppe and semiarid environments. Umm el-Marra profited from its frontier location in terms of communication with other polities and access to resources. In addition to its frontier status, Umm el-Marra's position on a longstanding transport route (Hallo 1964:57, 81) provided "locational stability" (Horne 1993:43), encouraging the reestablishment of complexity. The importance of "place" is further emphasized by the continuous use of the centrally situated Acropolis for the integration of economic and symbolic power. The significance of "place" in regeneration and the adoption of (modified) EB IV economic and symbolic capital by the Middle Bronze Age inhabitants suggests a "template regeneration" as described by Bennet Bronson (chapter 9).

Syro-Mesopotamia experienced the same types of cyclical centralization and decentralization as did many of the major states of East Asia and Southeast Asia (Stark, chapter 10), all of which may be considered examples of template regeneration. While the regeneration of the state in northern Syria may have followed a template regeneration pattern, whether that concept can be applied generally to the local settlement systems of regenerated states in Syro-Mesopotamia is unclear. Local-level revitalization usually was a response to, or an element of, regional regeneration. The particular characteristics of Umm el-Marra's physical landscape in part dictated the circumstances under which urban regeneration and prosperity were possible. Success in this location was driven by a much larger system of commercial and informational exchange in which Umm el-Marra functioned as a nexus for people and goods from diverse geographic and social environments. It is not coincidental that Umm el-Marra's periods of urbanization occurred during the suzerainty of regional hegemons to the west, whose status depended on reliable transport routes to and from the Euphrates River, toward the east. Regeneration of urban complexity at Umm el-Marra thus was fostered by regional powers whose resource requirements encouraged widespread economic and diplomatic networks that included elites at Umm el-Marra.

This differs markedly from the situation that Kenny Sims describes for the Moquegua Valley (chapter 8), where regeneration did not occur following the collapse of the surrounding Wari and Tiwanaku empires. An important distinction between the Jabbul Plain and the Moquegua Valley lies in behaviors of given social groups relative to dominant polities as well as in the degree of inclusiveness or exclusiveness of their respective ruling polities. Whereas Tumilaca villagers were ill prepared to structure new, postcollapse power relationships, Amorite kin-group affiliations formed a new social idiom through which newly or formerly powerful individuals could ascend the political hierarchy. Amorites were not necessarily political intruders, though the appeal to Amorite ethnicity was new.

Similarly, the rise of the Inca state occurred within the vacuum left by the collapse of Wari and Tiwanaku, accomplished in part through kin-group identification with the previous hegemons and the adoption of "imperial ideology" (McEwan, chapter 6). Regeneration at Umm el-Marra accompanied the regeneration of larger territorial states through the use of real or feigned—but nonetheless vital—ethnic affiliations. Amorite kin-group affiliations would have provided local and regional cohesion by eliminating potential tensions between urban and rural kin-group components and central authorities, thus increasing the local and regional prestige of Umm el-Marra's emergent elites.

This did not necessarily represent an inversion of the social order from the period of statehood in EB IV, as Ellen Morris demonstrates for the First Intermediate Period in Egypt (chapter 4). Rather, the example of Umm el-Marra seems to have more in common with that of post-Wari Nasca (Conlee, chapter 7), where the emergence of a new power structure allowed individuals of diverse backgrounds to achieve positions of social and political influence. Thus, while "kingship" remained a legitimate form of authority in the Middle Bronze Age, an ideological shift in the calculation of succession occurred: in the Early Bronze Age, each city-state dynasty had only limited familial connections to rulers elsewhere, but Amorite rulers of diverse polities in the Middle Bronze Age claimed descent from common ethnic ancestors (Finkelstein 1966).

Economic Flexibility and Administrative Adaptation

The economic resilience of Umm el-Marra in its Middle Bronze Age reorganization was coupled with a persistent belief in and reliance on the core institutions that structured governance and economics, but with significant changes in the social composition of the accepted personnel within those structures. Economic flexibility was crucial to the local population's success in exploiting its marginal environment, but such success also must be attributed to Umm el-Marra's location in the geographically diverse Jabbul Plain and on the major east–west route connecting Mesopotamia with Aleppo and the Mediterranean.

Though the exploitation of equids was important in both the Early and the Middle Bronze Age at Umm el-Marra, the Middle Bronze inhabitants returned the site to urban complexity in part by modifying traditional agro-pastoralism to emphasize hunting—particularly the acquisition of onagers—in adapting to their changing social and physical environment. Ethnic kin-group ties facilitated the establishment and maintenance of commercial and informational links in the absence of an overarching, state-operated political and economic network. Emerging elites at Middle Bronze Age Umm el-Marra solidified and signaled their status by co-opting for their legitimation the necropolis in which rulers of the powerful Early Bronze Age city were entombed. Umm el-Marra's Middle Bronze Age elites maintained their prestige through the exploitation of equids, including the processing of equid hides and the cultic use of equids. Their initially tenuous administrative authority increased as they transformed small-scale production of leather luxury goods into a regionally important, multitier leather-processing industry.

Acknowledgments

The Umm el-Marra Project is grateful for the support of the Directorate-General of Antiquities of Syria and for funding provided by the National Science Foundation (BCS-0137513, SBR-9818205) and the National Geographic Society, among other sources.

4 "Lo, Nobles Lament, the Poor Rejoice"

State Formation in the Wake of Social Flux

Ellen Morris

Within a comparative framework of early state societies, pharaonic Egypt stands out as one of the most stable, integrated, and long-lasting political entities of which we have record. Indeed, in the two millennia or so that constituted Egypt's journey from the institution of a pharaonic state in the First Dynasty to the onset of terminally troubled times at the end of the Twentieth Dynasty, Egypt experienced only two intermediate periods, each of which lasted for roughly a century or so.

The term "intermediate period" is used by Egyptologists to designate those times during which weakness in Egypt's core—aggravated or provoked in each case by circumstances beyond governmental control—prompted the breakdown of political unity throughout the Nile Valley. During the First and Second Intermediate Periods, the patterns of collapse and regeneration followed a broadly similar pattern. Owing to the failure of strong centralized rule, the peripheries first fragmented to the level of local communities, each of which was forced then to look inward or to its nearest neighbors to cope with problems and to meet its basic needs.

Throughout the duration of these intermediate periods, however, the Egyptians maintained a strong template for political reconstruction. For centuries upon centuries, Egyptian elites had actively promoted an ideology that held that the achievement of *maat*—or order in the universe—was possible only when one sacred king ruled over a unified Nile Valley. Thus, within a few generations, local aggrandizers invariably set themselves to the task of reasserting this lost order. In the process, the best positioned and most determined of them carved out larger and larger polities, until in the end one man was able to assume the long-coveted mantle of the Good God, the king of Upper and Lower Egypt, and to reward his followers with important (and lucrative) positions in the newly reestablished governmental infrastructure.

Despite the fact that Egypt's eras of political disintegration were fewer, shorter, and milder than those experienced by any of the other civilizations discussed in this volume, the aftermath of governmental collapse in the Nile Valley was nonetheless both traumatic and transformative for those who experienced it. Within this chapter I explore, utilizing both archaeological and textual lines of evidence, the ramifications of the radical reshaping of social order that occurred during the First Intermediate Period. I argue that although numerous parallels can be drawn between the processes of state formation and those of state re-formation in Egypt, it is misleading to re-gard the latter as a simple replay of the former.

Although Menes and Mentuhotep II—the founders of the First Dynasty and the Middle Kingdom, respectively—were both held in special reverence by the Egyptians for their respective roles in unifying the country, the char-acters of the monarchies that the two men established were fundamentally different from each other. The First Dynasty, for instance, was distinguished by the sacrificial deaths of hundreds of retainers at royal funerals and by the establishment of a rigid class system. What the Middle Kingdom is known for, however, is a blurring of class boundaries and an ethos that held the king to be the concerned caretaker of his people. The differences in these outlooks had everything to do with the fact that on the eve of the First Dynasty the concept of the state remained a complete unknown, whereas throughout the First Intermediate Period the memory of pharaonic rule lingered, still relatively fresh.

While some of the reminiscences of life under the state were no doubt nostalgic, others surely were not. In the century following the collapse of the Old Kingdom government, non-elites for the first time experienced numerous social and religious freedoms that had formerly been denied to them. Rights, once tasted, are difficult to revoke, and the populace of Egypt—though they helped position the Eleventh Dynasty pharaohs in power—apparently had no intention of quietly resettling into the old social order. Cognizant of this fact, Middle Kingdom pharaohs found themselves compelled to develop an entirely new vocabulary to legitimize their rule to subjects with heightened expectations.

The First Intermediate Period

The First Intermediate Period lasted from roughly 2160 to 2055 BC. Thus, at the point that it began, Upper and Lower Egypt had been unified for 850 years or so, a truly astounding breadth of time for a coherent state system to persist without significant interruption. This longevity must be viewed, in some respects at least, as a testament to the success of both its dominant ideology and the flexibility of its administrative infrastructure. Eventually, however, the state faltered. This is not the place to delve deeply into the multitude of reasons behind the collapse of the Old Kingdom at the end of the Sixth Dynasty, but increasing governmental corruption and lassitude as the 94-year reign of King Pepi II progressed has often been cited as a powerful contributing factor (e.g., Malek 2000:116–17; Redford 1992:57–63).

Far more damaging to any state, but especially to a sacred kingship, however, are extended bouts of ecological disasters. These came at the end of the Sixth Dynasty in the form of an unremitting series of low floods (Bell 1971; Butzer 1976:32–33, 53–55; O'Connor 1972:94). The resulting famines over a number of years expended Egypt's reserve supplies of grain and then effectively prevented the accumulation of new surpluses. Moreover, each new substandard flood exposed Pepi II and the ineffective kinglets who came after him as manifest failures in their ability either to intercede with the gods or to alleviate the suffering of their subjects.

A dimly optimistic proverb quoted in a First Intermediate Period letter states, "Being half alive is better than being dead" (trans. Kemp 1990:10). But other texts talk more soberly of people (especially Upper Egyptians) dying of hunger—a factor possibly explaining what seems to be a sharp spike in the death rate evinced in cemeteries from this period (O'Connor 1972:94). Such an evident rise in mortality may also, however, have been a symptom of increasing civil unrest and regional warfare. Contemporary texts describe the amassing of local militias and make frequent reference to "terror." Likewise, according to retrospective texts, the dangers posed by marauding bandits and foreigners prompted the prudent farmer to carry a shield when venturing out to tend his crops (for a selection of these texts, see Bell 1971; Breasted 1988:180–91; Lichtheim 1973:85–107, 139–69). Indeed, such an increased reliance on weaponry as a fact of survival almost surely accounts for the unusual prevalence in graves at this time of both functional and model weapons (Podzorski 1999:553).

What, then, can one point to as the predominant archaeological symptoms of the First Intermediate Period? A higher-than-average death rate and evidence for a greater attention to martial themes in the mortuary record are indeed witnessed. Likewise, elite monuments of any commanding size virtually disappear with the death of Pepi II. Additionally, as one might expect, ceramic forms become sharply regionalized—with the traditional high shoulders on jars prevailing in the north and with newfangled scrapped and droopy bases all the rage in the south. Further, an even more heterogeneous regionalization is exhibited in artistic style and paleography (see Seidlmayer 1990, 2000 for summaries of the material culture of this period). Without a recognized center to dictate appropriate fashions, to educate youth, to monitor quality, and to restrict access to their services, scribes and artists were in effect left to their own devices—much to the horror of latter-day art historians.

So, indeed, the norm within Egyptology has been for studies of this period to lay their emphasis on degeneration and death. Yet the archaeological record is much more interesting than this, for hand in hand with a so-called decline in artistic standards came a whole new affordability in personal monuments and an entirely new set of consumers eager to take advantage of products that formerly had been the exclusive perquisite of the old guard elite (Richards 2000). Consequently, for the first time in nearly a millennium, Egypt's mortuary cult was infused with a new vigor. As will be discussed in greater detail below, graves of the non-elite in the First Intermediate Period are noticeably larger and better equipped than had been the case throughout the entirety of the Old Kingdom. How or why commoners should have experienced such evident prosperity at a time when the dual scourges of famine and civil distress ran rampant is not immediately intuitive.

Mortuary Elaboration and Social Flux

Two possible explanations for this phenomenon are especially interesting to consider. The first is that a strong state is buoyed by high taxes, which tend to depress levels of personal wealth among the general populace. Certainly, under the Third and Fourth Dynasties especially, we know that a great portion of the country's material and human resources must have been funneled into projects connected with the building of massive stone pyramids and their associated mortuary temples. These endeavors, designed to aid the royal soul's transition from the defunct casing of its earthly incarnation to the more communal realm of potent ancestral spirits (*akhw*), thus represented a tangible investment in the future prosperity of the nation. The cult of the sacred king, which formed the centerpiece of Egyptian ideology, did not come cheap.

If the duty of all good Egyptian citizens was indeed to regularly contribute to supporting this god-king in life and in death, then the removal of such a burden in the First Intermediate Period might very well account for why non-elites seem suddenly to have had access to significant "extra" income. Likewise, the apparent impoverishment of the nobles could be easily explained by the fact that the shattered remnant of the royal court no longer found itself in a position to subsidize the construction of elite burial monuments. Both the tidiness and the logic of this theory lend it a great appeal, and there is undoubtedly much truth in it.

I confess, however, to being intrigued by an alternative (or perhaps complementary) explanation for why non-elites in the First Intermediate Period would invest so much more in the construction and provisioning of their graves than their forefathers had done at the height of the Old Kingdom. This theory draws upon the work of Michael Parker Pearson (1982) and Aubrey Cannon (1989) in arguing that it is precisely at times when personal advancement within a society is feasible that mortuary rites become a vibrant arena for social competition. Not only does this explanatory framework reveal why the mortuary cult should have become a focus of energy during the Sturm und Drang that surrounded the regeneration of the state in the First Intermediate Period, but it also can be employed to demonstrate why this cult had largely lain dormant among non-elites since the period of primary state formation.

Intrigued by the possibility of problematizing the notion that elaborate burials must necessarily reflect the high social standing of the deceased, both Parker Pearson and Cannon examined a series of case studies and concluded that mortuary practices tend to become highly elaborated during times of socioeconomic foment and status uncertainty. Rites of passage—such as weddings, christenings, bar mitzvahs, and funerals—offer families and other corporate units a unique opportunity to present themselves as they would wish to be viewed before their own community. At such times when a rigid social order breaks down or is perceived as permeable, a family with resources to spare can emulate rituals typical of a "higher" social stratum and hope thereby to be perceived as having moved up in the world. The success of this strategy is witnessed in the archaeological record by a great onslaught of similarly inspired conspicuous displays of wealth.

Interestingly, the results of the studies by both Parker Pearson and Cannon suggest that this trend toward competitive display will generally continue until such persistent and aggressive outlay leads to a point of diminishing returns. When virtually all members of society are devoting so much of their corporate resources toward elevating their position by way of flashy rites of passage, "true" elites have progressively more difficulty distinguishing their own displays from those of ambitious social climbers. When matters reach such a head, the upper stratum generally initiates a movement toward restraint in burial practice. If amply empowered, this movement may even include the issuance of rules and regulations to help enforce such temperance in society at large.

The Evolution of Egypt's Mortuary Cult over the Longue Durée

Both Parker Pearson (1982:112) and Cannon (1989:437) emphasize the need to contextualize mortuary studies within an evolutionary trajectory in order to fully grasp the significance of findings from any given time period. With regard to Egypt, happily, this task is not difficult. When such a long view is taken, the trends conform to those observed by Parker Pearson and Cannon elsewhere, and it is thus worthwhile, in order to understand the First Intermediate Period, to first sketch out what preceded that period.

It is no exaggeration to state that the last time such an intense society-wide preoccupation with provisioning the dead was evidenced in the Nile Valley, the processes of state formation had only just begun to percolate in earnest. During the Nagada II period (ca. 3500–3200 BC), independent farming villages in Upper Egypt seem to have first come under the sway of a variety of burgeoning regional centers. Ambitious elites at Hierakonpolis, Nagada, Thinis, and Qustul occupied themselves at this time in aggressively jockeying for primacy over Upper Egypt and the adjacent resource-rich region of Lower Nubia.

As if in sympathy with the political struggles occurring throughout the upper Nile Valley, inhabitants of discrete communities also appear to have become caught up in the fervor of vying for status, at least insofar as mortuary rites were concerned. Excavations of Egyptian cemeteries demonstrate that funerary ritual at this time typically involved lavish feasting and the interment of the dead—even children—with a whole "kit" of specially manufactured funerary goods. In-depth studies of particular cemeteries betray the presence of as many as four or five social strata in the major centers (Bard 1989:241). Further, at cemetery N7000 at Naga ed-Deir, at least, the distribution in space and time of various ritual indicators (such as animal offerings and ash-filled pots) suggests to Stephen Savage (1997:255–56; see also Bard 1989:242) that certain high-status funerary rituals were being very deliberately imitated by others in the community. Such competitive emulation, he posits, must have fueled the progressive elaboration of the mortuary cult at this site and others throughout the Nagada II period.

Following the unification of Upper Egypt under a single ruler in the

Nagada III period (ca. 3200–3000 BC), however, a dramatic division be-tween elite and non-elite segments of society becomes observable. Among the elites, expenditures for mortuary investment rose at this time, while non-elites seem no longer to have aspired to elaborate burials. This distinct drop-off in attention to the funerary cult and/or in prosperity among the non-elites is manifested in an increased percentage of individuals buried in small tombs with only a modest accompaniment of grave goods (Wilkin-son 1996:75, 81, 86).

After the jostling for power in the Nagada II period had been largely resolved—first for Upper Egypt in the Nagada III period and then for Egypt as a whole with the advent of the First Dynasty—it may have been that the new ruling elite actively attempted to discourage such status displays among the populace. Or perhaps the move to abandon competitive display came from the bottom up. After all, the state's strict compartmentalization of society into categories of nobles, bureaucrats, and commoners may sim-ply have convinced ordinary Egyptians that expensive attempts at boosting their social standing would come to naught. Certainly, a hallmark of the ideology typically propagated by early state societies is that economic and political inequality is not only perfectly natural, but indeed is essential to the proper functioning of the cosmos. Thus, according to these worldviews, the duty of the lower classes is to embrace their position in society, not to contest it.

Perhaps not surprisingly, then, this decline in mortuary differentiation among non-elites seems only to have intensified with the solidification of the state. From the First through Fourth Dynasties (ca. 3000–2494 BC) espe-cially, archaeological remains demonstrate that outside of expenses lavished upon the king's funerary monument and upon those of his immediate fam-ily members, Egypt's mortuary cult was muted. While elites possessed far larger tombs than commoners did, the vast majority of the most impressive mastabas appear to have been commissioned, positioned, and constructed by the king (Baines and Yoffee 1998:245). The assumption of such responsi-bility by the state, although expensive, assured the pharaoh that his nobles would remain indebted to him and, hence, fully aware of their place both in this world and in the next.

As for non-elites of the early Old Kingdom, while theoretically an ab-sence of state interest in regulating their burials could have resulted in the type of mortuary elaboration present in prehistory, it evidently did not. Ordinary people were most often interred in small tombs or pit graves to-gether with only a spartan assemblage of grave goods. Indeed, according to a common wisdom shared by many premodern Egyptologists and ancient tomb robbers alike, interments dating from this era simply did not repay the costs of excavation (Bard 1989:225; Seidlmayer 2000:122).

According to the theories of Parker Pearson (1982:107) and Cannon (1989:447), a strong class system renders obsolete many of the strategies otherwise employed by the non-elite to better their own status. All indications are that in the Old Kingdom, social stratification was relatively rigid. According to official dogma, human beings were divided into two groups: the *rekhyet* (who were commoners) and the *iry-p't* (who were members of the elite). In this society, the estimated 1–5 percent of the population that made up the *iry-p't* distinguished themselves from the masses by way of formal education, the wearing of clean linen, the ownership of valuable resources, the occupation of villas and (then) elaborate tombs, and the virtual monopoly that they held over prestigious civil and sacerdotal offices. According to this class system, other Egyptians either served the elite and the institutions they administered or eked out a living as "orphans," that is, individuals who owned their own limited plots of land or herds of animals and paid taxes directly to the state (Faulkner 1962:133; Gardiner 1933:21).

The archaeological remains do little to add nuance to this picture. Individuals who possessed large tombs in the salad days of the Old Kingdom were almost uniformly members of the nobility who served in the court of the king. Moreover, at the time when the pyramids at Giza were built, a large proportion of this inner core of elites appears to have been drawn from the pharaoh's family. Settlement archaeology, unfortunately, cannot challenge this portrait, as the vast majority of preserved towns from this period had been built for the express purpose of housing state workers. In such a society—where one's status in life seems to have been ascribed, cradle to grave—elaborate and expensive display activities undoubtedly offered little payoff.

Only with the gradual transfer of the balance of power from the capital of Egypt to its peripheries in the Fifth and especially the Sixth Dynasties (ca. 2494–2181 BC) did the mortuary cult in Egypt again begin to exhibit signs of enlivenment. Despite these harbingers, full-blown, society-wide investment in the mortuary cult did not come into fruition until the First Intermediate Period—when the central state had for all intents and purposes collapsed. With no single power administering a unified Nile Valley but with numerous small polities actively involved in the formation of ever-larger political blocks, a situation came into being that was analogous to that which had existed just prior to the first formation of the state.

In First Intermediate Period cemeteries (such as Akhmim, Abydos, Elephantine, Edfu, and Cusae), non-elite graves begin once again to exhibit signs stereotypically associated with elevated prosperity. Ordinary tombs increased in size and came to be far better equipped with grave goods and amenities such as coffins than had been the case for centuries past under the supposed benefits of pharaonic rule. Indeed, Guy Brunton (who excavated many hundreds of Upper Egyptian graves in the regions of Qau and Badari) observed that "the tombs with the most objects are precisely those of the vii–viiith dyn. period. Here we find the greatest profusion of beads and amulets; no diminution in the number of alabaster vases, and all the alabaster headrests; the greatest number of mirrors of any period; and the least number of simple, shallow graves" (Brunton 1927:76). With the sole exception of imported goods, then, non-elite interments exhibited more trappings of wealth in the First Intermediate Period than did or would their counterparts at any time when the state was strong.

A World Turned Upside Down

Within stratified societies, little seems to be more threatening to the former elite stratum than to witness a reorganization of the status quo. The abandonment or rejection of a system that had jealously restricted the perks of power and prestige to one small segment of society demonstrates to all that there had been nothing natural or god-given about the system. During the First Intermediate Period and the very early years of the Middle Kingdom, the remnants of Egypt's literati produced a genre of writings that Egyptologists term "pessimistic" but that Mesopotamian scholars might well dub "lamentation literature."

Some of these ruminations, especially those penned under the patronage of the early Middle Kingdom pharaohs, are certainly political documents. In these, the disorder and chaos of the First Intermediate Period become the foil that highlights the benefits attendant upon the reinstallation of the monarchy. Yet despite the tendentiousness of some of these sources and the inevitable indulgence in hyperbole, there is in these purported eyewitness accounts very little that one would not *expect* to observe in a society—ancient or modern—that had suffered the effects of both environmental catastrophe and political anarchy.

A document known as the "Admonitions of Ipuwer," for example, bemoans ravages caused by famine, civil war, pestilence, incursions of hostile foreigners, and the breakdown of law and order amid a long litany of evils that supposedly befell Egypt during this time of upheaval. What is fascinating, however, is that the vast majority of space in the text is in fact given over to a series of strident and repetitive complaints about the inversion of social order. Commoners, the text charges, have become owners of wealth. Lo, the nobles lament, the poor rejoice. The man of rank can no longer be distinguished from he who is a nobody. Noblewomen suffer like maidservants. All female servants are free with their tongues. He who was a great man now performs his own errands. He who could not make a sarcophagus for himself is now the possessor of a tomb. Precious stones adorn the necks of maidservants, and men who used to wear fine linen are beaten, et cetera, et cetera, ad nauseam (cf. Lichtheim 1973:150–63).

Critiques of this work have long ridiculed the notion that the admonitions bear any relevance to the First Intermediate Period whatsoever, as the idea that commoners would have access to wealth during a time of social upheaval and want was met with scorn (e.g., Lichtheim 1973:150). Yet, this is precisely what we observe in the archaeological record. Although most items interred with the dead had been specially purchased as grave goods, jewelry made of hard stone, gold, or other highly valued materials seems to have been culled from the personal possessions of the deceased (Seidlmayer 2000:122). Just as Ipuwer describes, then, precious stones may indeed have adorned the necks of maidservants.

Moreover, not only did the inhabitants of non-elite cemeteries equip their graves during this period with a far greater quantity and variety of grave goods than they ever had before, but they also took the liberty of adopting for themselves tickets to an afterlife previously denied them. It is a well-deserved Egyptological cliché to speak of the First Intermediate Period as initiating a "democratization" of religion. Prior to this time, excavations suggest that only the elite had access to certain charged amuletic symbols associated with eternity, regeneration, or even kingship. Likewise, kings appear to have held the exclusive right to commission religious texts to help them navigate the perilous passage between death and eternal life. By the end of the First Intermediate Period, however, not only would individuals who could afford it be inscribing such texts on their coffins, but even humble mercenaries and people without any titles whatsoever would claim the right to directly address the most powerful of gods on their funeral stele (Richards 2000).

State Formation and State Re-formation: Variations on the Theme

Thus, with regard to both the Nagada II period and the First Intermediate Period, a situation of status uncertainty evolved in which boundaries between elites and commoners were somewhat fluid. In this highly charged atmosphere, members of society at large competed with one another for status and focused great attention on the mortuary cult as a platform for social advancement. Likewise, in both instances, competition among numerous aggrandizers appears to have eventually resulted in the consolidation of power in the hands of a very few individuals.

This process, arrived at through inference with regard to the period of state formation, can be fleshed out in detail for the First Intermediate Period. Certainly, in the first few generations following the dissolution of the Old Kingdom, testaments of individuals who claimed to have worked their way up in society from modest beginnings to a position of leadership are common. These men attributed this increase in power to their own resourcefulness, which had allowed them to augment their flocks and to intensify agricultural production in a time of suffering and want. Not only their own dependents, but also members of their entire community, these men claimed, benefited from their largess (cf. the texts quoted in Bell 1971).

Archaeology has the power to reveal such bootstrap rhetoric to be just that—more bluster than autobiography—and at least one such "self-made" man of the late Old Kingdom has recently been unmasked as none other than the son of a vizier (Richards 2002). With respect to the First Intermediate Period, however, one is tempted to view such narratives of self-reliance with a little less jaundiced an eye. In a time of famine, hallowed connections to a long-gone court life would presumably do little to bolster one's status. Likewise, at a time when no great divide separated the elite from the non-elite materially, what one did may well have counted for far more than who one was.

As the First Intermediate Period wore on, both the presence of capable providers in specific districts and the danger posed to dispersed settlers in a time of societal unrest may have contributed to the observed nucleation of settlement around particular centers (Seidlmayer 2000:122). This too parallels the situation documented archaeologically in the Nagada II period (Bard 1989:242). In both eras, the concentration of people in discrete locales, the emergence of strong leaders, and—as voiced repeatedly in the First Intermediate Period—a very real need for the acquisition of additional arable land led to the formation of alliances and the fomenting of hostilities among various regional elites.

The ultimate victor in the struggle for political and economic control of the Nile Valley in the First Intermediate Period—as in the period of state formation—hailed from Upper Egypt. Because Thebes has been extremely well excavated and studied, the emergence of this polity as a political power can be traced step by step, from its rocky start (at which time as many as seven local leaders succeeded one other in the lifespan of a single official) to the conclusion of an important political alliance with the nearby polity of Coptos. Although Thebes and Coptos were at first defeated in battle by the army of a very powerful local leader at Hierakonpolis, the Thebans and their allies would later succeed in their efforts and extend their sovereignty all the way south to Nubia (for a history of the rise of the Eleventh Dynasty, see Hayes 1971:472–88). Owing to its status as the gateway to a vast wealth of prestige goods, Nubia had also been a primary target of aggression in the earliest days of the Egyptian state.

The Regeneration of a Divine King

In light of all of the parallels cited above, is it viable to view the activities of the Eleventh Dynasty Thebans more or less as a replay of politics at the time of the state's first formation? In broad outline, yes. However, some very important differences are evident between the second time the state was formed and the first. As Egypt represents one of the relatively rare examples of pristine state formation, no paradigms originally existed for the methods whereby a powerful regional leader might transform himself into the king of a nation-state. The second time the state was formed, however, numerous blueprints for the fashioning of a properly functioning national government existed.

Because the First Intermediate Period lasted for only a century or so, during much of this time the state persisted in living memory. Furthermore, to supplement old tales, monuments erected by Old Kingdom rulers served as tangible signs that powerful and pious men had indeed once reigned over a prosperous Nile Valley. While chances of southerners having witnessed firsthand such awe-inspiring monuments as the Giza pyramids are very slight, Fifth and Sixth Dynasty pharaohs had made sure to lavish significant attention on regional temples. As a result of this practice, beautifully carved scenes of kings communing with divinities and their own divine ancestors would have littered the Nile Valley.

To borrow the terminology employed by Bennet Bronson (chapter 9), Mentuhotep II's unification of Egypt in the Eleventh Dynasty can aptly be categorized as a template regeneration, for the footprints of the Old Kingdom state were still everywhere evident. Thus, when Mentuhotep set out to the north to conquer Middle and Lower Egypt by force, he must have known that the battles ahead were not to be solely military. If his legacy was to last, battles would also have to be fought on ideological ground. Therefore, in addition to claiming responsibility in a priestly function for the major temples in his territory, Mentuhotep went several steps further. At Abydos, Dendera, possibly Thebes, and in all likelihood numerous other temples throughout his realm, he dedicated statues of himself so that they might become objects of worship in their own right. Furthermore, on the walls of numerous temples he had himself depicted—in an archaizing style consciously borrowed from Old Kingdom rulers—as physically interacting with the gods (that is, holding their hands, suckling from their breasts, and receiving from them caresses and gifts of eternal life).

To reinforce the point that in his unification of Egypt and his ascension to the throne he had been transformed from a powerful mortal into a god, Mentuhotep also had himself portrayed on monuments wearing the tall, feathered crown peculiar to the god Amun. Moreover, on at least one temple, he not only sported this same crown, but also portrayed himself masturbating with his left hand while holding his right hand aloft. This pose scrupulously mimicked that of the deity Min, caught in the act of cosmic creation. Other poses adopted by Mentuhotep II as visual confirmation of his new status—such as the "smiting enemies" pose—were those traditionally adopted by Egyptian kings since the dawn of the state (for a study of the monuments of Mentuhotep II, see Habachi 1963).

Re-formation and Reformation

If we view Mentuhotep and his successors as stepping into the shoes of the first pharaohs, then we must accept that the fit was not perfect—for the nature and expectations of the people governed had undergone a radical shift during the First Intermediate Period. At the time when the first kings united Egypt, the creation of the state was a completely new venture, and those with power were free to break new ground in terms of ideology and the creation of perquisites of which they were the sole recipients. Hand in hand with the creation of the state, therefore, also came the creation of inflexible and divisive social categories.

The Middle Kingdom pharaohs who assumed control of Egypt following the First Intermediate Period, however, aspired to win the loyalty of a populace that had experienced previously unknown freedoms in the wake of the Old Kingdom's collapse. In the course of this crucial century, the class system had for the first time become permeable. Individuals who had formerly relied on the court for power and prestige found their position precarious, while others who managed to amass provisions and dispense them wisely in a time of want rose to positions of power. At this time, as archaeology and narrative demonstrate, the non-elite were able without hindrance to assume for themselves many of the markers of status and sanctity formerly denied to them.

It is important to emphasize that the reinstitution of the state in the Middle Kingdom should not with hindsight be interpreted as inevitable, for the 99 percent or so of the people who had not and would not become part of the ruler's inner circle could simply have refused to participate in the state system. This majority must have made clear to the new leaders that they assisted to power that not everything was to be returned to the status quo. Trends such as the "democratization" of religion and the blurring of boundaries between elites and wealthy or influential commoners only intensified following reunification. Indeed, the Middle Kingdom is widely known for tremendous numbers of personal votive stelae and for the emergence in the funerary record and administrative archives of what some have interpreted as a "middle class" (cf. Richards 1997).

The Middle Kingdom is, moreover, perhaps equally famous for the state-sponsored propaganda that touted these monarchs as "good shepherds," men whose very legitimacy was embedded in the care that they took to provide for their subjects (see Richards 2000:44). Not content simply to inscribe this message upon monuments and to broadcast it aurally in public assembly, Middle Kingdom rulers also commissioned statues of themselves to communicate it visually. Once secure enough in their throne to abandon the bland archaizing styles of the Old Kingdom, the Middle Kingdom rulers adopted a mode of representation all their own that more fittingly conveyed the image of themselves that they were concerned with promoting.

Careworn brows, in combination with serious expressions and even bags under the eyes, effectively communicated to the viewer that these were men upon whom responsibility weighed heavily. Yet a visual sense of capability and strength was also expressed in the extremely large hands and strong bodies of the rulers. Perhaps most poignantly of all, however, these Middle Kingdom pharaohs seem to have sacrificed a certain amount of dignity in order to be portrayed with uncommonly large ears. These ears—like those frequently depicted upon Egyptian stelae—needed to be capacious enough to inspire confidence among all who saw them that it was the king's earnest intention to pay heed to the prayers and entreaties of his subjects (see Bourriau 1988).

5 The Collapse and Regeneration of Complex Society in Greece, 1500–500 BC

Ian Morris

Greece between 1500 and 500 BC is one of the best-known cases of the collapse and regeneration of complex society. In the 1870s, Heinrich Schliemann showed that a Mycenaean (Late Bronze Age; see table 5.1) culture had preceded Greece's Classical civilization, and in 1890 Flinders Petrie published examples of Mycenaean pottery from Egypt correlating the destruction of the Mycenaean palaces with the Egyptian Nineteenth Dynasty, around 1200 BC. Their work created a wholly new framework for early Greek history. After three generations of fieldwork and analysis, Anthony Snodgrass systematized a new consensus in his magisterial *Dark Age of Greece* (1971): a period of sophisticated palaces (ca. 2000–1200 BC) gave way to a depressed Dark Age (ca. 1200–750), only to be replaced by new and brilliant Archaic (ca. 750–480) and Classical (ca. 480–323) civilizations.

As Glenn Schwartz (chapter 1) and Bennet Bronson (chapter 9) point out in this volume, one of the main problems facing a comparative study of collapse and regeneration is the sheer variety of phenomena that could be included under this heading. To clarify matters, I will begin by stating six important characteristics of the period 1500–500 BC in Greece:

1. Throughout this period, "Greece" was a cultural system, not a political unit. Political unity came only with the Roman conquest in the second century BC.
2. Greece was an example of what Bronson calls "genuine" regeneration: it was a case not of a political and economic center shifting but of the transformation of the entire system.
3. The end of the Dark Age was, on the whole, an example of endogenous regeneration.
4. The "second generation" (post-750) complex society did not much resemble the "first generation" (pre-1200) one. Networks of city-

Table 5.1 Standard periodization of Greek history

Time period	Date range
Late Bronze Age/Mycenaean period	c. 1600–1200 BC
Early Iron Age/Dark Age	c. 1200–750 BC
Archaic period	c. 750–480 BC
Classical period	480–323 BC

states characterized both periods, but their social, economic, and political structures differed strongly.

5. The second-generation society had only distorted memories of the first, but these notions of a lost heroic age were central to second-generation culture.

6. The second-generation system was larger and more complex than the first, extending geographically around the shores of the western Mediterranean and the Black Sea.

Ten Dimensions of Collapse and Regeneration in Greece

Progress in analyzing the collapse and regeneration of complex society requires explicit criteria for measuring "collapse" and "regeneration," which in turn imply shared definitions of "complex society." Trait-list approaches are open to well-known objections (e.g., Trigger 2003:43–46), but nevertheless they provide a good framework for organizing data that can be used to develop broader theories. In this section, I group the evidence from Greece into ten categories, based on Gordon Childe's famous (1950) discussion of the rise of urban society but modified to fit the particulars of the Greek case. These indices for measuring social complexity are (1) urban centers, (2) peasants paying taxes and rent, (3) monuments, (4) ruling classes, (5) information-recording systems, (6) long-distance trade, (7) craft specialization and advanced art, (8) military power, (9) scale, and (10) standards of living.

Urban Centers

Late Bronze Age cities were relatively small: just eight hectares at Tiryns (fig. 5.1), twenty to thirty at Pylos, Thebes, and Troy, and not much more at My-

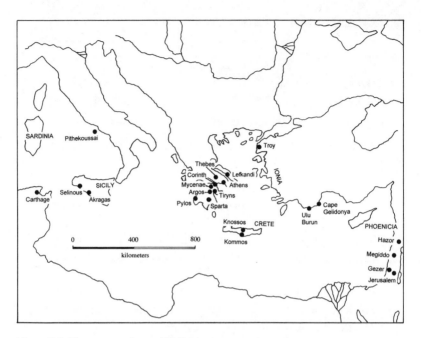

Figure 5.1 The eastern and central Mediterranean.

cenae itself. The largest site, Knossos on Crete, covered seventy-five hectares. The mainland sites had perhaps five thousand to ten thousand residents, and Knossos about fifteen thousand. These cities were of roughly the same size as contemporary Anatolian and Levantine centers (Whitelaw 2001a).

After 1200 BC, the largest settlements contracted sharply. Most people lived in hamlets of a few dozen souls (Whitley 1991), and parts of Greece were virtually abandoned. Finds at the biggest site, Athens, spread across two hundred hectares, but this seems to have been a group of villages, its population probably never surpassing twenty-five hundred to five thousand. Other large communities, such as Argos and Knossos, probably had one thousand to two thousand residents (Morris 1991:29–34).

City size increased in Archaic times. By 700 BC, Athens, Argos, and Knossos must have had five thousand to ten thousand people, and dozens of towns were in the one thousand to five thousand range. Pithekoussai in the far west, a new foundation around 770 BC, expanded in two generations to about four thousand people. Urban growth continued unabated across Archaic times, and in 480 BC Athens's urban population must have numbered twenty thousand. Most sixth-century Greeks lived in settlements of a few thousand people (Morris 2005a).

Peasants Paying Taxes and Rent

The best evidence for Mycenaean taxation comes from Linear B tablets, bureaucratic records of palace transactions, but these are partial and selective. The rulers apparently procured staples (cereals, olives, wool) directly but left many nonstaples to private producers. There were variations between palaces and complex patterns within each sector of production. The palaces sometimes provided capital (land, seed, animals), with peasants providing labor; other times, palaces taxed flocks and land owned by nonpalace personnel (Halstead 2001; Killen 1985). Statist models emphasizing centralization and redistribution were once popular, but recent studies have shown that while redistribution was a major economic strategy, many people remained outside palatial control (Galaty and Parkinson 1999).

Mycenaean bureaucracies and Linear B tablets disappeared after 1200, and elite abilities to tax declined. Homer's poetry, written down around 700 BC, is set in a vanished heroic age but probably reflects contemporary and recent institutions (Morris 2001). Homeric rulers collected "gifts" from their people, but taxation was unsystematic. Homer says nothing explicitly about rents but implies that dependent agricultural laborers and client craft workers were common, while ostentatious elite spending was much lower than in Mycenaean times (Donlan 1997).

Some Archaic communities (notably Sparta) practiced serfdom, with state-owned laborers supporting small warrior elites, but in most city-states, most free citizens owned and farmed small plots of land. Richer citizens used imported chattel slaves to work larger plots or rented land out through the market. Direct taxes were virtually nonexistent. Communities normally met state expenses through revenues from state property or through indirect taxes, particularly harbor and market dues (Andreades 1933 remains the best review). State finance was largely a function of taxable trade, and some city-states saw a sharp increase in revenues after 550 BC.

Monuments

The main Bronze Age monuments were elaborate palaces, combining political, religious, and economic functions. The first appeared around 2000 BC, on Crete, and by 1600 BC the largest, at Knossos, covered one hectare

(Driessen et al. 2002). Cretans also built elaborate sanctuaries at the peaks of the highest mountains. Palaces appeared on the mainland around 1600 BC. They were smaller than the Cretan structures and organized differently (Galaty and Parkinson 1999). Mainlanders built no peak sanctuaries, but the elite favored much more elaborate tombs than the Cretans.

No Dark Age monument begins to compare with the palaces of the Bronze Age. The largest known structure, an apsidal mud-brick building of circa 950 BC from Lefkandi, was forty-five meters long and would fit easily into the central court of the palace at Knossos. The building may have been a chief's house or a monument to two people buried within it; either way, it was deliberately filled in and converted into a tumulus (Popham et al. 1993). Other Dark Age grave mounds survive, mostly on the northern fringes of the Greek world.

All across Greece, people started building temples around 750 BC. A few were *hekatompeda*, "hundred-footers," and by 675 the richest cities invested in stone temples. Thousands were built across the next two centuries. Temple building peaked around 550–525, with some cities (particularly Akragas and Selinous in Sicily) erecting avenues of towering marble temples up to eighty meters long, ringed with columns and decorated with sculptures and paintings. Nonreligious public buildings never competed with temples. Some graves had mounds or statues as markers, but there was little private display (Morris 1998).

Ruling Classes

Mycenaean palaces had rulers called *wanakes* surrounded by lesser officials, and rich aristocrats' mansions dotted the landscape (Laffineur and Niemeyer 1995; Rehak 1995). In Dark Age Greece, the most important men were called *basileis*, a corruption of the Mycenaean term *pa-si-re-u*. The *pa-si-re-u* had been a minor official in the palaces, but after 1200 BC this was apparently the highest rank that still had meaning. In Homer, *basileis* functioned as informal councils of warrior chiefs. They recognized Agamemnon as their leader, but he was merely *primus inter pares,* constantly open to challenges.

Dark Age burials are very homogeneous, but I have argued (Morris 1987) that there was a hidden exclusivity, with a wealthier stratum of farmers monopolizing archaeologically visible displays. There is evidence of similar restrictions on worship of the gods, with only a limited few having access to rituals in chiefs' houses (Mazarakis Ainian 1997). These ritual distinctions may correspond to a social distinction between free and dependent peasants.

The *basileis* disappeared across the eighth and seventh centuries, being replaced by aristocratic colleges. By Near Eastern standards, Greek aristocrats were poor, weak, and divided, but they were often willing to close ranks to prevent any one of their number emerging as sole ruler (*tyrannos*). The earliest law codes (ca. 620 BC) focus on procedural rules to block conversion of state offices into tyranny (Gagarin 1986). From the eighth century on, a powerful "middling ideology" set limits on the powers of aristocrats, who always depended heavily on popular backing. By 525, the poorer citizens in some states decided that they did not need aristocrats to make decisions for them and increasingly took over political activity in mass assemblies of all adult males (Morris 2000:155–91).

Information-recording Systems

Mycenaean Linear B was a syllabic script, and all known examples come from palatial administration. Writing was probably restricted to a small scribal class. It disappeared after 1200, and the only example of writing from the next four centuries is a Semitic inscription on a bronze bowl in a tomb at Knossos, dating to circa 900 (Sznycer 1979).

Writing reappeared around 750, with a brand-new alphabet derived from Phoenician prototypes. Some Semiticists argue that the Greek script owes more to eleventh-century Phoenician inscriptions than to eighth-century writing (Naveh 1973) and that Greeks were writing on perishable materials throughout the Dark Age, shifting to potsherds around 750. However, the corpus of Phoenician texts is very small, and few scholars accept this theory.

From the outset, alphabetic Greek had many functions and clearly was not controlled by scribes. The earliest texts are mostly poetic, scratched on pottery and stone (Powell 1991), but Archaic legal, economic, and religious inscriptions also survive. As many as 10 percent of fifth-century Athenian citizens may have been functionally literate (Harris 1989:65–115).

Long-distance Trade

Bronze Age *wanakes* exchanged luxury gifts with Near Eastern kings, and shipwrecks at Ulu Burun and Cape Gelidonya document bulk trade in metals (Cline 1994; Cline and Harris-Cline 1998). The excavated ships are small, but Aegean metallurgy depended on imported copper and tin. The total volume and economic importance of traded metal must have been high. Some Mycenaean pottery is known from Sardinia, Sicily, and southern Italy, which may also be related to the metal trade (Vagnetti 1999). Interannual variability in rainfall always made crop yields unpredictable and probably required bulk shipments of cereals in all periods of high population (Garnsey 1988:8–16). The silence of the Linear B tablets on these details suggests that such trade was largely in private hands.

The new settlements that grew up in the shadow of the ruined palaces in the twelfth century retained attenuated contacts with the Near East, but trade declined sharply after a second wave of destruction circa 1100. Very few Near Eastern objects are known from Greece, or Greek objects from the Near East, between 1050 and 950. Phoenician traders returned to the Aegean by 925 and even set up a typically Levantine shrine at Kommos in the ninth century (Shaw 1989), but extra-Aegean contacts only really took off after 800. Settlement of the coasts of Sicily and southern Italy, beginning in the 730s, doubled the amount of arable land in Greek hands. Cereal exports were probably important from the beginning (De Angelis 2000, 2002) and were essential for the growth of Greek cities by 500. By the late sixth century, Greece had become the center of an unprecedented network of international trade in bulk commodities, and gains from trade were significantly improving living standards.

Craft Specialization and Advanced Art

Mycenaean craft production reached remarkable levels. Palaces maintained their own workshops for items such as metalwork and perfumed oil but left pottery to outside contractors (Laffineur and Betancourt 1997; Whitelaw 2001b). After 1200, many advanced skills (e.g., fresco painting, gem carving) quickly disappeared. The best vase painters retained high technical standards in the tenth and ninth centuries but simplified their repertoire, and the large, highly standardized workshops of the Late Bronze Age almost certainly gave way to household-level artisans (Crielaard 1999; van Wijngaarden 1999). Homer describes *basileis* retaining craftsmen among their clients and also mentions *demioergoi*, "public workers" who might travel from town to town hawking their wares.

At their best, the Geometric pottery styles of the Dark Age were pleasing and carefully made, but skills advanced rapidly after 750. There is no evidence for concentration of production or state-owned workshops, but small, probably family firms proliferated. Pottery shops in Corinth, Ionia, and Athens produced millions of painted vessels, which were exported and imitated all around the Mediterranean (Stissi 1999). Sculptors and architects learned from Near Eastern and Egyptian artists and then surpassed them, reaching extraordinary levels of skill in the sixth century (Osborne 1998). There is some evidence of individual craftsmen working in several media, which diffused innovations quickly. Artists developed a sophisticated theoretical literature, although little of this survives. Craft production was market driven, and there are signs that potters carried out research on outlets (Osborne 1996). By 500, Aegean Greece had emerged as the most dynamic cultural center in the Mediterranean.

Military Power

Bronze Age Crete is famous for its lack of fortifications and the peaceful themes of its art, but military symbolism dominated Mycenaean elite burials, and many sites were fortified, especially in the thirteenth century. The Linear B tablets show that palaces maintained standing armies and at least some ships, as well as significant (and expensive) chariot forces, although heavy infantry probably dominated Mycenaean battlefields (Laffineur 1999).

Grave goods suggest a shift from thrusting spears toward javelins after 1200, which probably reflects the introduction of lighter infantry and skirmishing tactics. Fortifications were rare in the Dark Age, probably meaning that raids, rather than sieges and sustained campaigns, were normal. Homer's battle accounts are notoriously hard to interpret, but they most likely elaborate eighth-century practices, as bronze armor and massed infantry once more took on a serious role (van Wees 1997).

By 650 many city-states could field hundreds of bronze-armored hoplites, developing phalanx tactics that could be devastating on the right terrain. Greek hoplite mercenaries were in high demand in the Near East throughout Archaic and Classical times. Hoplites normally provided their own arms and armor and volunteered their time for war and training. Hoplite warfare was capital intensive, but the costs were privately borne. The main exception was Sparta, where serfdom supported a permanent hoplite army whose discipline and ferocity were incomparable. Sparta suffered no major defeats until 371 BC.

Greek warfare started changing rapidly around 550, as state income from taxes on trade took off. Greeks had adopted the triple-decked warships called triremes from Phoenicia around 700, and the first naval battle was fought around 664; but only after 550 could states afford proper navies (Wallinga 1993). In 483 the Athenians invested revenues from a rich silver strike into a fleet of two hundred triremes (requiring between thirty-five thousand and forty thousand crewmen) and dominated the eastern

Mediterranean throughout the fifth century. The increase in state spending power also transformed hoplite battle and fortifications in these years (van Wees 2004).

Scale

Mycenaean material culture dominated about 100,000 square kilometers, covering the modern nation-state of Greece (except its northern part) with enclaves on the west coast of Turkey. The population of this area was perhaps a million people (cf. Branigan 2001:46, tables 4.1, 10.2; Renfrew 1972: table 14.IX), averaging ten people per square kilometer, although in the core areas around Mycenae and Pylos, population densities must have been two or three times as high. Only at Pylos can we estimate the territory controlled by a single state. Here, the Linear B tablets imply a territory of 2,000 square kilometers, with a population of perhaps 50,000 (i.e., 25 persons per square kilometer; Bennet 1998).

Dark Age material culture has more regional variability, but by most definitions of "Greek," the geographical scale of the system contracted slightly, to perhaps 75,000 square kilometers. Population fell by one-half to two-thirds (Morris 2006), giving an average density of just 3–4 people per square kilometer. There is no reliable way to reconstruct the size of political units.

Colonization extended Greek settlement to some 150,000 square kilometers between the 730s and 500 BC, and total population rose to more than 2,000,000, giving an average density of 12–15 people per square kilometer. The largest polity, Sparta, controlled about 8,500 square kilometers after the eighth-century conquest of Messenia, with perhaps 150,000 people (17 per square kilometer). Sparta was a freakishly large state, but Athens and Akragas both had areas around 2,400 square kilometers. By 500 BC, Athens's territory had probably 200,000 residents, with a very high density of 85 people per square kilometer (rising to 130 per square kilometer in the fifth century). Akragas's population and density are harder to estimate but were probably about half of Athens's. Most city-states, however, had just a few hundred square kilometers of land and populations in four figures.

Standards of Living

In the 1980s, economic historians shifted from measuring living standards through real wages toward direct measures of bodily experience, such as mortality, morbidity, age-specific stature, housing, leisure, and education (e.g., Fogel 1993). Some of these are archaeologically visible (Morris 2005b; Steckel and Rose 2002).

Skeletal data collected by Lawrence Angel ($n = 727$) suggest that men's average age at death fell from 39.6 years in the Late Bronze Age to 39.0 years in the Dark Age, before improving to 44.1 years in Classical times. Women's ages at death declined from 32.6 to 30.9 years across the Late Bronze and Iron Ages, rising to 36.8 years in Classical Greece (Bisel and Angel 1985). Physical anthropologists have made many advances since the 1970s, and data collected in the 1990s ($n = 773$) produce lower ages at death but preserve the same pattern of lower Dark Age scores compared to Mycenaean and a Classical peak (Morris 2004:fig. 2, 2006:table 9.3).

Health and nutrition produce messier patterns (Morris 2004:715–19), but house sizes show the same trends as ages at death. The area of roofed space in the ground plan of the median house in thirteenth-century Greece was 70 square meters. This fell to 45 square meters in the ninth century, climbed slowly to 50 square meters across the eighth and seventh centuries, and then returned to 70 square meters in the sixth century. Most of the improvement came after 550 BC, and the fifth-century median rose to 149 square meters (Morris 2006:table 9.8). Quality of construction and the richness of domestic finds also declined in the Dark Age before rebounding in Archaic times.

Evaluation of the Pattern

The data are very consistent across all ten categories reviewed in the preceding section: Greece saw the collapse of complex society between 1200 and 1000 BC, stagnation between 1000 and 800, and regeneration after 800, with the pace of change accelerating after 550.

Gradualist Models

Snodgrass's systematic (1971) survey of the evidence made the collapse-depression-regeneration model unchallenged by 1980, but in the 1990s several critics suggested that "Dark Age" is in fact an inappropriate label for the period 1000–800. In various ways, they argued for stronger continuities from Bronze Age to Archaic Greece, with more gradual changes in the twelfth and eighth centuries (e.g., de Polignac 1995; Foxhall 1995; S. Morris 1992a; Papadopoulos 1993).

New finds have certainly made the patterns less stark than they seemed when Snodgrass was writing *The Dark Age of Greece*. We now have some unambiguous evidence for religious activity between 1050 and 850, a handful of Greek artifacts from Syria and Italy between 1050 and 950, and remarkable finds from Lefkandi in the years 950–850. However, the critics—who consistently avoid quantitative analysis—have not made much effort to contextualize the new finds within the mass of previously accumulated data. The most influential gradualist treatment holds that "Recent archaeology [at Lefkandi] has dispelled Greece's 'Dark Age'" (S. Morris 1992a:140). Yet the finds of the 1980s barely alter the statistics underpinning the collapse-depression-regeneration model and can also be accommodated comfortably within more qualitative treatments of the traditional model (I. Morris 2000:195–306).

Gradualist critics also suggest that placing Greece in a broader geographical context that includes the Near East dispels illusions of a Dark Age depression (e.g., S. Morris 1992b). They are right that no part of the Near East or Egypt seems to have suffered such an abrupt collapse as the Aegean after 1200, but the most recent surveys of Near Eastern history nevertheless reveal that by all the criteria discussed above, the entire area from western Iran to Anatolia experienced decline in the twelfth and eleventh centuries and recovery from the ninth or eighth century on (e.g., Kitchen 1986; Kuhrt 1995:385–646; Van De Mieroop 2004:161–252).

The major possible exception is Israel, where the Hebrew Bible says Solomon concentrated power as early as the 960s, waged expansionist wars, traded far and wide, and filled his kingdom with monuments (1 Kings 1–11). However, archaeologists have not found these monuments in Jerusalem, and Israel Finkelstein has recently proposed downdating the supposedly Solomonic levels at Hazor, Megiddo, and Gezer to the ninth century (Finkelstein 1996, 1999, 2004; Finkelstein and Piasetzky 2003; cf. Franklin 2004; Gilboa and Sharon 2001). This remains controversial (e.g., Ben-Tor 2000; Bruins et al. 2003a, b; Mazar 1997), but Finkelstein's low chronology makes the data more consistent with the general eastern Mediterranean pattern, with post–Dark Age regeneration beginning in Israel in the ninth century but coming to Judah only in the eighth (Finkelstein and Silberman 2001:130–225).

Explanations of Regeneration

Snodgrass (1980:15–48) emphasized population decline between 1200 and 1000 BC and subsequent growth after 800 as the motors of collapse and regeneration. In the decline phase, Greece was the extreme case of a broader eastern Mediterranean and western Asian collapse; in the growth phase, it was part of a Mediterranean-wide pattern (experienced as regeneration in the eastern Mediterranean). To explain such broad patterns, we should perhaps seek equally broad explanations. The shift from the warm, dry sub-Boreal climate phase toward the cool, wet sub-Atlantic phase in the ninth and eighth century (Bradley 1999:15; Fagan 2004:196–202) must be relevant. Cooler, wetter weather after 900 would have relieved some of the problems of interannual variability in rainfall, with more dependable winter rains making farmers' lives easier. Such weather also would have improved the disease regime, since textual records from a range of premodern Mediterranean societies show that most deaths came in the hot summer months from gastric complaints (Scheidel 2001:1–118, 2006). The sub-Boreal to sub-Atlantic shift might also explain the fact that population trends in temperate Europe are the opposite of those in the Mediterranean, with growth in the eleventh and tenth centuries and decline in the eighth and seventh: cooler, wetter weather would have made farming the potentially fertile but heavy soils of valley bottoms more difficult, while exacerbating the lung diseases of the cold winter months that are the main killers north of the Alps (Bouzek 1982; Kristiansen 1998:28–31, 408–10).

Some archaeologists have emphasized political rather than climatic factors, suggesting that as Assyrian military power revived in the late tenth century, Assyrian demands for tribute drove Phoenician merchants to travel farther afield, partially converting the Mediterranean basin into a periphery to an Assyrian core (Aubet 1993:50–76; Bierling 2002; Frankenstein 1997:35–64; Gitin 1997, 2001; Sherratt and Sherratt 1993). In the ninth century, the Aegean was part of this periphery, but in the eighth and seventh centuries it emerged as a semiperiphery, before establishing itself as a core region in its own right in the sixth and fifth centuries.

These perspectives are mutually compatible: the improved climate and disease pool fueled population growth after 800 BC, which increased competition all across western Asia and the Mediterranean, driving Assyrian military predation, Phoenician commercial expansion, and the regeneration of complex society in Greece. Most scholars have described the process in the language of world-systems theory, but there are, in fact, few signs that the development of an eastern Mediterranean core was linked to the underdevelopment of western Mediterranean peripheries, as world-systems models require (Wallerstein 1974:1:87–100, 310–24; cf. Frank 1993). I have proposed describing the accelerating economic and social integration after 800 as "Mediterraneanization," analogous to modern globalization, similarly producing new winners and losers within a context of generally rising standards of living (Morris 2003).

These macrolevel theories may account for the material bases of regeneration, but they do not explain why the second-generation societies of the eighth century and later took such different forms around the Mediterranean basin. Egypt and western Asia saw the revival of older, centralized kingdoms, but often with new levels of militarism; the Aegean saw new types of city-state, founded on egalitarian male citizenship; and the western Mediterranean, which shared in growth from the eighth century onward but had not experienced collapse in the twelfth and eleventh centuries, saw the rise of its first really powerful chiefs and cities. I have suggested (Morris 1998:69–70) that differences in local histories explain these varied responses. In each of the three regions, previously existing class structures and cultures limited the range of responses available to the changing environment. In Assyrian western Asia, rising population triggered conflicts between the royal palace and local governors, decisively resolved in the monarchy's favor by Tiglath-Pileser III after 744 BC. In the Aegean, there were no royal palaces or local governors in 800 BC; instead, the main struggle was between aristocrats who wished to centralize powers in their own hands and those who wished to preserve the broader dispersal of powers typical of the Dark Age. The main outcome was very weak oligarchies dependent on popular support ruling small city-states. In the western Mediterranean, would-be chiefs and kings seem to have more easily defeated their rivals to establish one-man rule.

The Regeneration of the Greek City-state

The Greek world saw the collapse of complex society between 1200 and 1000 BC, a long depression between 1000 and 800, and rapid regeneration after 800. Climate, improved health conditions, and demography were probably the ultimate causes of regeneration; but the Greeks' geopolitical situation was also critical, and very localized cultural and political factors determined the details of second-generation Greek complex societies. The Greek city-states developed peculiar forms of state power that are difficult to accommodate within standard evolutionary typologies (Morris 1997). However, despite the diffusion of political power through broadly defined male citizen communities and the general weakness of state offices, the regenerated Greek city-states mustered the military force to inflict shattering defeats on Carthage in the west and the mighty Persian empire in the east in 480 BC and emerged as centers of cultural innovation far outstripping their first-generation predecessors.

Inca State Origins
Collapse and Regeneration in the Southern Peruvian Andes
Gordon F. McEwan

As a result of archaeological fieldwork of the past two decades in Cuzco, Peru, Inca origins can now be viewed from a perspective significantly different from the traditional ethnohistoric analyses of the postconquest Spanish chronicles. It now appears that the formation of the Inca polity resulted from a uniquely fortuitous set of conditions that resulted in what Bennet Bronson (chapter 9) terms "template regeneration." The Inca heartland was strategically located midway between two extraordinarily long-lived and powerful early empires. Both the Wari and the Tiwanaku empire exerted great influence on the Cuzco region and continued to do so even in the period after their collapse. Elements of Wari statecraft are reflected in the material culture—especially the architecture and ceramics—of the succeeding culture and seem to have survived in situ in the Cuzco Valley. Influence from the Tiwanaku empire probably came indirectly before the Wari conquest of Cuzco and later with a migration of elites from the Titicaca basin to Cuzco after the fall of both Tiwanaku and Wari. This post-Tiwanaku influence is manifested in the intrusion of a new elite burial tradition and its accompanying architecture and ceramics. The subsequent Inca state was the product of peoples able to use and build upon the social tools and techniques of these earlier empires for their own purposes, employing surviving elements of statecraft and social organization that persisted throughout the Late Intermediate period.

Traditional Ethnohistoric Accounts of Inca Origins

The Spanish written sources give two basic versions of Inca origins based on interviews of surviving Incas conducted by the Spanish after the European conquest (see Rowe 1946 and Urton 1990 for a complete discussion of these myths). Most accounts gave the story that the first Inca emperor, Manco

Capac, was created by the sun god Inti and emerged with his brothers and sisters from a site with three caves called Tambo Tocco near a place called Pacariqtambo not too far from Cuzco. After a series of adventures, Manco Capac led his followers into the valley of Cuzco, conquered the local inhabitants, and set up the Inca state. In Spanish colonial times, a small town about thirty kilometers south of Cuzco became identified as Pacariqtambo, the official origin place of the Inca dynasty. Recent scholarship has shown that this identification came about largely because of political maneuverings among surviving Incas in the Colonial period (Urton 1990).

The second version of the origin story states that the Inca were created by the sun god Inti on an island in Lake Titicaca in modern Bolivia. The Incas migrated northward to Cuzco, conquered the local peoples, and set up their state. The thrust of these stories is that the Incas were basically supermen chosen by the gods to rule the earth. They essentially invented ancient Peruvian culture and civilized the barbarian tribes that had existed until then. All of the marvelous things that the Spanish conquerors encountered, with very few exceptions, were attributed to the Incas.

Archaeological Evidence for Inca Origins

In the past few decades, archaeological research has provided a wealth of new data illuminating the pre-Inca culture history of the valley of Cuzco. Studies by Karen Mohr Chavez (1980) at the Marcavalle site in Cuzco have revealed cultural links to the altiplano to the south during the Early Horizon (ca. 1400–400 BC) and the Early Intermediate period (400 BC–AD 540). Intensive studies at the Wari sites of Pikillacta (McEwan 1991, 1996, 1998) and Huaro (Glowacki 2002; Zapata 1990, 1992) have helped to define the nature of the Middle Horizon (AD 540–900) occupations in Cuzco. Finally, thirteen field seasons of extensive excavation at the Chokepukio site in Cuzco have revealed a stratigraphic sequence encompassing Early Intermediate period through Late Horizon (AD 1476–1532) occupations and have provided an especially rich database on the Late Intermediate period (AD 900–1476) that immediately precedes the rise of the Incas (McEwan et al. 2002).

Cuzco before the Wari Invasion

Although the valley of Cuzco was to play an important role during the expansions of the Middle Horizon and Late Horizon states, its early cultural history is not well known. The earliest cultural tradition noted by

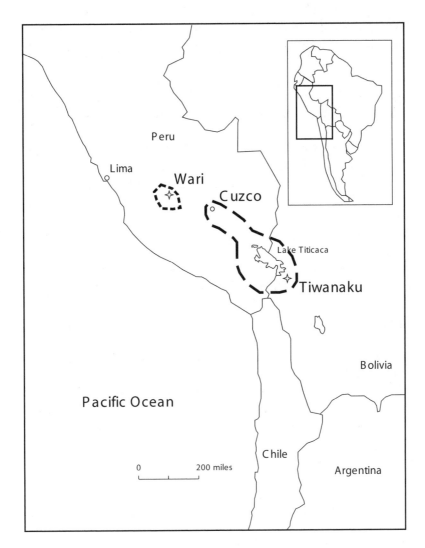

Figure 6.1 Wari and Tiwanaku spheres of influence prior to the imperial expansions of the Middle Horizon.

archaeologists is marked by a ceramic style called Marcavalle. Excavations by Karen Mohr Chavez recovered radiocarbon samples placing the Marcavalle style in time between 1400 and 650 BC (Chavez 1980:204; Valencia and Gibaja 1991:21). She has further demonstrated a wide distribution of Marcavalle-related styles as far south as Puno in the Peruvian Andes and has suggested that the center of origin for the style lies to the south of Cuzco near Lake Titicaca (Chavez 1980:205). The settlements associated with the Marcavalle style appear to be villages inhabited by farmers, ceramic specialists, and producers of salt and preserved camelid meat, as well as other specialists. These settlements participated in a south highland region of interaction and exchange without a complex state-level political organization (fig. 6.1).

This cultural pattern appears to have been very stable and long lived. By about 650 BC, the Marcavalle ceramic style had transitioned into a new style called Chanapata (Rowe 1944). The pattern of involvement with the south highland interaction sphere continued, and there is no evidence of any great social complexity. The earliest stratum encountered in recent excavations at the Cuzco Valley site of Chokepukio has revealed a Chanapata occupation dating from approximately 350 BC to AD 600. A village of small houses was the home of peoples who made their living through farming and exploiting the lacustrine resources at nearby Lake Muina. Social and stylistic change seems to have been very gradual over this long period of time, and social and political complexity appears to have continued at a low level. Near the end of the Chanapata occupation at Chokepukio, Tiwanaku-related ceramics and artifacts appear in modest quantities. This suggests that the focus of exchange was still on the southern interaction sphere. Further evidence of Tiwanaku influence is found at the town of Huaro, about fifteen kilometers to the east of Chokepukio. Here, pure Tiwanaku ceramics have been recovered in burials at the prehistoric cemetery of Batan Urqo (Julinho Zapata, personal communication 1995).

In summary, prior to the Middle Horizon, the cultures of the Cuzco Valley appear to have participated in the sociocultural interaction sphere centered at Lake Titicaca to the south. With the development of social complexity at Tiwanaku there is some evidence of interaction, probably through trade, but the local political level of organization in Cuzco does not appear to have changed. Although the Cuzco sites contain Tiwanaku-related artifacts, the region does not appear to have been conquered or incorporated into the larger state.

Cuzco during the Wari Occupation

The Middle Horizon (ca. AD 540–900) is a time of imperial expansion, with the polities at Tiwanaku (to the south of Cuzco) and Wari (to the north of Cuzco) both encompassing vast territories (fig. 6.2; see Isbell and McEwan

1991; Schreiber 1992). Although traditionally in the orbit of the Lake Titicaca interaction sphere where Tiwanaku arose, with the construction of the largest of the Wari provincial centers at its heart, the Cuzco region ended up being tightly incorporated into the Wari empire, centered at Ayacucho to the north. The province of Cuzco, and especially the areas of the Huatanay and Vilcanota drainages between the modern cities of Cuzco and Urcos, became some of the most heavily occupied real estate in the Wari realm (Glowacki 2002; McEwan 1991, 1996, 1998). Beginning about AD 600, the Wari empire took control of the region and built an enormous infrastructure. Large centers with monumental architecture, believed to be related to imperial administration and ceremony, were constructed at Chokepukio, Pikillacta, and about fifteen kilometers farther east at Huaro (Glowacki 2002; McEwan 1987; McEwan et al. 2002). The labor investment at Pikillacta alone approaches five million man-days, and construction of Huaro would probably have exceeded this (McEwan 2005). Associated with these large imperial centers are a great number of smaller sites, including the site of Araway that lies beneath Inca Cuzco, and a site at Andahuaylillas between Cuzco and Huaro. Many small sites are clustered around the larger installations at Pikillacta and Huaro and seem to represent an imposed settlement pattern peculiar to the Wari that Richard Schaedel (1966) has described as the "Middle Horizon hillside town." This town plan consists of a large segmented settlement nucleated around strategic features and extending for more than one kilometer in one of its dimensions. It consists of formally and functionally distinct components systematically interrelated by elements of the infrastructure including huge aqueducts, terracing, extensive canals, and a highway system. The need for the construction of this massive infrastructure indicates that the level of political organization of the conquered Cuzco peoples was not very complex at the moment of conquest. As Dorothy Menzel (1959:141–42) observed in the case of the Inca empire, the largest investments in infrastructure by ancient Peruvian empires occurs where social complexity of the conquered group is low, resulting in the absence of infrastructural features that can be co-opted and reused. Katharina Schreiber's (1992) study of the Wari empire makes clear that the Wari also invested most heavily in infrastructure in conquered areas that lacked previous large-scale social complexity. In what she terms the "mosaic of control," the extent of the reorganization of settlement systems is directly correlated with the preexisting situation encountered by the conquerors.

There are several reasons for this huge investment on the part of the Wari. The agricultural potential in this area is enormous. With the construction

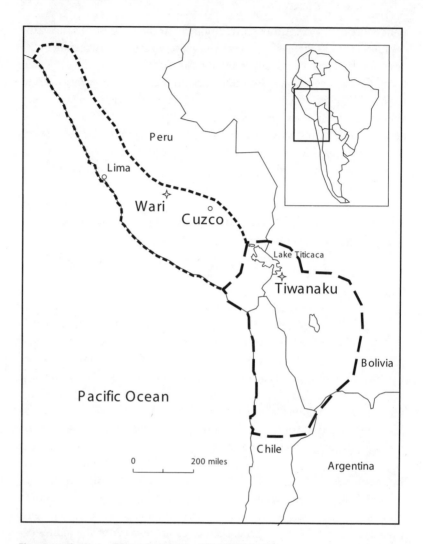

Figure 6.2 The Wari and Tiwanaku empires of the Middle Horizon.

of hydraulic works, more lands could be opened for water-intensive crops such as maize, which was a principal fuel of later Inca ceremony and expansion. The main traffic corridor for travel between the Titicaca basin and the central Peruvian highlands passes through the Huatanay and Vilcanota drainages in which these sites lie. The Wari site clusters in the Lucre basin of the Cuzco Valley and farther east at Huaro and Urcos are both located at narrow natural topographic choke points that permit strategic control of movement along the north–south highway. Finally, the intense occupation was no doubt related to the fact that the frontier between the Wari and Tiwanaku states lay only a relatively short distance to the southeast. Tiwanaku was the only polity of the Middle Horizon large enough to threaten the Wari empire from the south. The scale of the occupation suggests that the Pikillacta and Huaro complexes comprised a regional subcapital of the larger Wari state that was charged with controlling this frontier.

In addition to the administrative nodes that were taken over, there is also a pattern of Wari occupation of and incorporation of the religious sites that are called *huacas*. Throughout the empire, ceramic offerings of polychrome vessels decorated with religious iconography were placed into preexisting shrines and temples to co-opt these into the imperial ideology. Examples of this practice can be seen in offerings found in the north coast shrines of Huaca del Sol and the huaca of Pañamarca and at the shrine of Pachacamac, near Lima on the central coast (Lumbreras 1974:173–74; Schaedel 1951:150; Schreiber 1992:105–6). In the city of Cuzco, fragments of an elaborate Wari polychrome offering vessel have recently been excavated at the huaca of Sacsayhuaman (Arminda Gibaja, personal communication 2002). At Chokepukio, also a major huaca, a temple with Wari associations was excavated by my team in 2001. At the huaca of Mama Qolla, at the opposite side of the Lucre basin from Chokepukio, Wari ceramics have also been found by me and others. Farther to the east at Huaro, the Wari occupied the sacred mountain of Cerro Wiracochan and the huaca and cemetery of Batan Urqo (Glowacki 2002; Zapata 1990, 1992). The Wari seemingly went to great pains to incorporate the conquered territory both physically and ideologically.

Not only was the Wari occupation extensive, but it was also remarkably long lived. Radiocarbon assays and ceramic stylistic evidence indicate that construction of the infrastructure began around the year AD 600, and the occupation persisted until as late as AD 1000–1100 (Glowacki 1996; McEwan 1996). Throughout this period the cultural impact on the Cuzco locality would have been enormous.

Imperial Collapse

By the year AD 1000, both the Tiwanaku and the Wari empire seem to have collapsed. The reasons for the collapse are poorly understood, but a climatic fluctuation entailing significant desiccation probably contributed substantially to the demise of these states. Alan Kolata (1993:284) argues persuasively that the climatic shift was of massive proportions and undermined the agro-economic base of the state. This change is documented in the ice cores taken from the Quelccaya glacier (located in southern Peru approximately midway between Cuzco and Lake Titicaca) and sediment cores taken from Lake Titicaca indicating that a great drought ensued after AD 1000 (Kolata 1993:285).

Both Wari and Tiwanaku had built their wealth and expanded their power through systems of hydraulic agriculture. A major long-term disruption in water availability would have been catastrophic and would have seriously weakened the rulers of these states by undermining their power. The wealth of a ruler consisted of the stored surplus from each year's production. Andean administrative as well as ritual activity involved ritual generosity on the part of the ruler, usually in the form of large quantities of corn beer called *chicha,* but also in distributions of food and clothing as pay to retainers and bureaucrats as well as to the people in times of need. The rulers were generally believed to rule by divine right and to have the power to intercede with the supernatural. The perceived inability of the ruler to maintain the food supply and conditions necessary to produce it (such as adequate water) would have seriously undermined the power of the central government.

In the Tiwanaku heartland, the empire fragmented into multiple smaller kingdoms. Over the following centuries, these contesting polities gradually evolved toward reconstitution of a state until they were overrun by the Inca (Kolata 1993:300).

In the Wari heartland, a similar fate was probably encountered. The capital city of Wari in Ayacucho was depopulated and abandoned by AD 1000 if not slightly earlier. Although Wari stylistic influence persisted in many regions of the empire, production of pure Wari-style artifacts ceased. The unity of the state had disappeared, and many principal Wari sites were abandoned.

In the Cuzco region, construction dates for the final phase of the Wari site of Pikillacta suggest abandonment between AD 1000 and 1100. After centuries of use, there was a late effort to greatly expand the site of Pikillacta. This construction effort was halted relatively abruptly, leaving three of the four sectors of the site in an uncompleted state. The site was carefully closed down, the contents of the occupied portion of the buildings were removed, and many of the doorways in the completed section were closed with stone. Efforts seem to have been made toward mothballing the complex with an eye to resuming its construction at a later date. Construction efforts on state projects seem to have ceased, indicating a loss of direct control from the capital.

At Huaro the change is not as abruptly marked as in the architecture at Pikillacta, but the ceramic evidence indicates a tapering off of traditional Wari-style ceramic usage, and a new style called the Lucre style began to evolve (Glowacki 2002). During the Middle Horizon in the Andes, the rituals of administration and religious ceremonialism required certain distinctive sets of ceramic vessels used in feasting and ritual drinking. These are quite different from those in everyday use. These vessels were decorated in a highly uniform, elaborate style of iconography that is found throughout the empire and constitutes the Wari horizon style defining the Middle Horizon (Rowe 1962). Some of these vessels seem to have actually been imported from the capital city of Wari in the central highlands. After the collapse of the empire, locally made variations of these vessels began to appear in former Wari territories, and in some areas their use ceased altogether. This new ceramic style echoed many common Wari decorative themes and vessel forms but utilized a new and different ceramic technology. Its makers clearly intended for it to recall the prestigious Wari style, but they were free to express its iconography in their own idiom.

Regeneration after the Collapse

The standardized and uniform high-quality Lucre ceramic style provides a clue to what happened politically in the Cuzco region with the collapse of the Wari empire. The polychrome component of this style is, as with the Wari, composed of ceremonial feasting wares. The primary distribution of this style essentially encompasses the eastern end of the valley of Cuzco where Chokepukio and Pikillacta are located, extending to the southeast to include the modern towns of Andahuaylillas, Huaro, and Urcos. Since this distribution corresponds to that of the principal Wari sites in the Cuzco region, and the Lucre style has strong echoes of the old Wari decorative patterns, it probably represents a surviving subunit of the old Wari administrative organization. As a regional administrative capital of the Wari empire, this particular territory would have been the center of the most intense Wari influence. The people using the Lucre styles are imitating the remembered practices of the Wari.

In the western end of the valley of Cuzco and in the area to the north and west of the valley, there seems to be much less unity (based on what can be seen of Wari influence on material culture). In these areas, a series of ceramic styles unrelated to the Lucre style extends from Cuzco toward Paruro and also down the Urubamba Valley (Bauer 1990, 1992; Bauer and Covey 2002). These styles are all related to the K'illke style defined by John Rowe (1946) at the type site in the Cuzco basin. Although related, these styles are distinctive enough to be regionally identifiable and are technologically much different from the Lucre style (Chatfield 1998). Ceremonial behavior and feasting like that of the Wari do not seem to be reflected in these assemblages, and they lack the uniformity that would suggest centralized control of production. This variation in styles may be reflective of a more fragmented political situation in this area. Inca accounts recorded by the Spanish speak of a number of small competing ethnic groups in this region at the time of the first Inca entrance into Cuzco. Apparently the old Wari imperial organizational structure was not preserved in the region marked by the distribution of K'illke-related styles. This is possibly a reflection of their location on the margins of the imposed Wari centers, where they may have been less integrated into the empire. Unlike those who adopted the Lucre style (for whom we have monumental and domestic architecture as well as a wide variety of material culture), these groups using the K'illke style are unfortunately known only from ceramic remains. Therefore, any conclusions about their character are tenuous.

At Chokepukio in the Lucre basin of the valley of Cuzco, there appears strong evidence for some continuity of Wari ideology and statecraft reflected in both architecture and ceramics. Radiocarbon dates from structures on this site indicate that a new construction phase of monumental architecture began between AD 1000 and 1100. The buildings constructed during this phase replaced the Middle Horizon architecture on the site but still echoed ceremonial behavior reflected in the Wari structures at Pikillacta.

In a structural form at Pikillacta called the niched hall, the Wari interred human remains in the walls and placed elaborate offerings beneath the floors. These buildings have been interpreted as temples used in ancestor worship and feasting ceremonies. They are believed to represent a behavioral pattern related to Wari statecraft (McEwan 1998). This statecraft technique involved co-opting local lineages by means of establishing fictive kin ties. This in turn engendered an asymmetrical reciprocal relationship through which the rulers exercised power through kinship obligations. Alan Kolata (1993:280) has suggested something similar as a statecraft technique used by the Tiwanaku.

At Chokepukio during the Late Intermediate period, a number of very large niched halls were built. Like their Wari counterparts, these niched halls contain human wall burials, offerings, and evidence of ritual feasting using Lucre-style ceramic vessels derived from the earlier Wari ceramic tradition. Ruling lineages probably were celebrated, and their ancestral ties to the prestige of the Wari empire publicly displayed. A local expression of Wari ritual behavior provided legitimacy for the local lords, whose presence is reflected by finds of gold and silver ornaments and jewelry made of turquoise and shell. In pre-Columbian Andean societies, only the nobility were allowed to possess gold and silver and other fine objects of adornment and clothing.

A few centuries later, circa AD 1300, a second building phase was initiated at Chokepukio, resulting in the construction of additional niched halls. Up to this point, the predominant postcollapse cultural influence had been derived from the Wari. The second building phase seems to represent the arrival of an elite group from the old Tiwanaku sphere of influence. A northern Bolivian ceramic style called Mollo appeared on the site at this time and was used in ritual feasting in the niched halls. Another southern trait, *chullpas* or burial towers in the altiplano style, appeared at Chokepukio and other sites throughout the eastern end of the valley of Cuzco at this time. These elements seem to indicate the migration to Cuzco of people from the old Tiwanaku core area. Seeming to confirm this are human remains found at Chokepukio in the niched halls, the remains of individuals who have been identified as genetically Aymara, matching the modern inhabitants of Bolivia and different from the Quechuas of Peru in terms of their mitochondrial DNA. Interestingly, the appearance of these traits is associated not with a large-scale population shift but rather with an influx of a small, elite group that took up residence in the monumental structures at Chokepukio. This perhaps indicates a usurpation of the local kingdom or a regal vacancy filled by a member of a foreign lineage viewed to be more legitimate than anyone locally available. In a recent study, Juha Hiltunen (1999) has proposed a scenario based on the chronicle of the Spanish cleric Fernando de Montesinos, written around AD 1642, in which power in the Cuzco region was usurped not once but twice during this period by elite groups from the old Tiwanaku heartland. In a collaborative effort, Hiltunen and I (Hiltunen and McEwan 2004) have compared the archaeological evidence with the history given by Montesinos and suggest that descendants of the elite personages involved in the first migration to Cuzco later went on to found the Hanan (or upper moiety) of the Inca dynasty and united the various ethnic groups using K'illke ceramics, who were organized into the Hurin (or lower moiety).

Factors Contributing to Regeneration in Cuzco

Because of its unique position on the periphery of two empires, the strategic Cuzco area was well situated to be the seat of an imperial regeneration. Peoples in Cuzco were heavily influenced over long periods of time by the two great empires of Wari and Tiwanaku. The people of Cuzco probably inherited not only imperial ideology but also a great deal of practical statecraft information. This influence can be seen in many of the most important aspects of Inca life. The Spanish chroniclers report that the Inca were quite aware of the ruined site of Tiwanaku, the seat of the former empire. They revered it as a major shrine or huaca and even incorporated it into one version of their origin myths (Hiltunen and McEwan 2004). Inca royalty dressed in tunics that derived their form and patterning of small rectangular designs from both Wari and Tiwanaku elite textiles. Surviving examples show that Inca nobles had ceramic vessels painted with copies of Tiwanaku polychrome motifs for use at Inca shrines such as Sacsayhuaman. More significant for the argument of regeneration, the Spanish recorded certain elements of statecraft and ideological behavior that seem to have had their roots in the Wari culture. These specifically have to do with the control of populations through holding their ancestral mummies and huacas hostage, the practice of feasting and drinking with ancestors, and administrative rituals involving feasting and drinking in niched halls with special sets of vessels. These patterns of behavior can be traced through time from the Middle Horizon occupation at Pikillacta through the Lucre culture's temples at Chokepukio and finally to the imperial Inca capital at Cuzco (see McEwan 2005; McEwan et al. 2002).

Equally important was the Inca inheritance of infrastructure. The hydraulic systems and highway systems would have provided the basis for rapid expansion of the early Inca state. Since all of the major Wari administrative centers are located on the later Inca highway, there can be little doubt that the highway was originally built by the Wari and for the express purpose of managing an empire, which would have required the efficient movement of troops and goods over long distances. The vast hydraulic systems put in place in the Cuzco region by the Wari are directly physically connected to the sites of Huaro and Pikillacta. Their capacity exceeded the needs of the local population, and these systems probably had, during the Late Intermediate period, unused capacity left over from the former empire that could easily have been brought on line to supply the food resources to feed the armies needed to begin the Inca expansion.

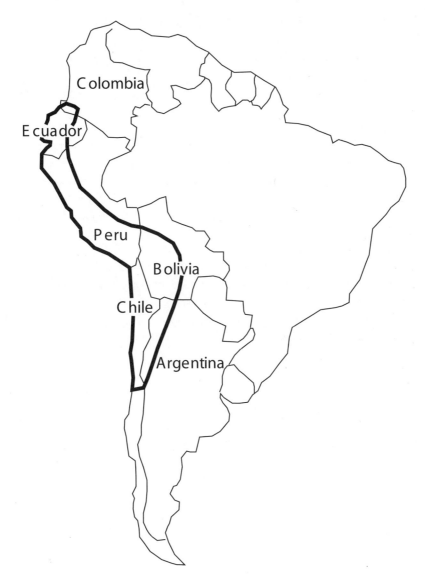

Figure 6.3 The Inca empire.

Knowledge of large-scale building with stone was retained by the direct descendants of the Tiwanaku, and later Inca emperors imported labor from the Tiwanaku heartland to build some of their greatest monuments (Gasparini and Margolies 1980). The ground plan of the basic Inca architectural form called the *cancha* is also likely to have been directly derived from the architectural plan of Pikillacta (McEwan 2005).

A further advantage to the Inca was the fact that their closest neighbors, those that they conquered first, had also been heavily exposed to the prior imperial states. As in Cuzco, there were probably many other territorial fragments of the old empires that could be relatively easily grafted onto the new Inca state. The earliest and closest in terms of geography were simply incorporated as adopted Incas and joined the imperial nobility. Many of the later additions to the empire were already complexly enough structured that the Incas left the local administration in place with only a governor for oversight (Rostworowski 1999). With these advantages, the Inca rapidly expanded in the short span of only fifty to eighty years into the largest of the pre-Columbian Andean empires (fig. 6.3). Their unique history provided them with a large store of knowledge from which they could pick and choose the techniques most suited to their ambitions.

Acknowledgments

Fieldwork at Chokepukio has been made possible by generous grants from the Bernard Selz Foundation, supplemented by the Curtiss T. and Mary G. Brennan Foundation, the J. M. Heinz Foundation, the National Science Foundation, the National Geographic Society, and numerous small donations. Archaeological studies at Chokepukio were co-directed by Gordon McEwan and Arminda Gibaja, assisted by Melissa Chatfield, Sheldon Baker, Valerie Andrushko, Alana Cordy Collins, Froilan Iturriaga, and the men and women of the village of Huacarpay, Cuzco, Peru. Advice and assistance were provided by Dr. Alfredo Valencia, Dr. Luis Barreda, and Dr. Jorge Flores.

7 Regeneration as Transformation
Postcollapse Society in Nasca, Peru
Christina A. Conlee

The Wari empire was probably the first true imperial power in the Andes, and its expansion, consolidation, and ultimate collapse profoundly changed the nature of power and political organization in many areas that were part of its dominion. In the eighth century AD, the Nasca region of south coastal Peru became part of the Wari state. By AD 1000, the empire had completely collapsed, and Nasca experienced a period of disruption followed by an intense era of regeneration that resulted in a new type of regional integration and sociopolitical organization. These transformations were facilitated by the development of new types of elites created when the Wari empire ruled the region, by opportunities in the postcollapse period for people outside of the traditional political hierarchy, and by an expansion in the economic base and the material resources used to obtain power.

Collapse and Regeneration

The cyclical nature of collapse, reorganization, and expansion is widely recognized, and the collapse of complex societies is viewed as a process and not a singular event (e.g., Marcus 1998; Schwartz, chapter 1; Yoffee and Cowgill 1988). Although collapse has often been perceived as the complete destruction of a society, many scholars have emphasized that collapse is not an end to "civilization" but rather the dissolution of the political system (Yoffee 1988b:18). Collapse can be identified as that process in which the political system breaks down and societies become organized on a less complex scale. Despite the awareness that the processes of collapse and recovery are intertwined and the recognition of the dynamic nature of postcollapse periods, regeneration has been the focus of few archaeological studies. Instead, most investigations concentrate on collapse itself and not on the specific effects of collapse and the restructuring of society.

The collapse of empires is a particularly complex process, bringing an end to the political domination and integration of vast regions. The timing, progression, and effects of state disintegration will vary throughout the provinces that were once under imperial control. After collapse, areas on the periphery may become new nodes of control and the focus of postcollapse development (Bowersock 1988; Marcus 1998). Therefore, regeneration will take many different forms throughout the regions that were incorporated into the empire. Scholars often focus on the dissolution of the central political system, and there has been less study on areas that were once integrated into this system. The period after collapse entails a restructuring of provincial areas; through recuperation and reorganization, new forms of political, economic, and social organization develop. Often, local groups are able to reassert the power that they lost and are able to thrive in the wake of collapse. During this time, traditional ways of life may strengthen or reemerge to provide security and a foundation on which to build the new political system. However, local groups do not necessarily return to a simpler way of life after collapse but may use much of the technology and other ways of life that the conquering state had imposed in a process of restructuring (e.g., Graffam 1992). In some situations, a provincial society is irreversibly changed with the fall of the empire.

Several views of collapse, while not specifically focused on the postcollapse period, provide useful models for studying regeneration. The general systems theory approach is based on the organization of biological organisms. Within systems theory, Herbert Simon's (1965, 1973) perspective views complex systems as comprised of many stable lower- and intermediate-level controls that manage short-term and local goals, while higher-level controls provide decision making for the entire system. The implications for postcollapse periods are that the intermediate and lower-level units remain and can be used once again to build a hierarchical system. To study the collapse of systems, therefore, one must first identify the intermediate- and lower-level controls. These are the levels of organization that local people were involved in; consequently, gaining an understanding of local society under imperial control becomes critical.

Joseph Tainter's (1988) view of collapse builds on ideas of adaptation and economics. He sees societies as problem-solving organizations in which sociopolitical complexity is developed to meet energy needs. At a certain point, however, complexity will no longer be the best response and will have "declining marginal returns" (Tainter 1988:194). Tainter concludes that collapse is an "economizing process" necessary for a society's survival. Rather than the result of a society's failure to adapt, collapse is an adaptive response to stress. This perspective stresses that collapse is a positive response to failures in a system and is essential for the survival of human societies.

The level of integration among different parts of a society has implications for collapse. Integration can be defined as the degree to which a person is a member of more than one subgroup in a society (McGuire 1983). For a society to be more resistant to collapse as its population grows and individuals become part of different subgroups, the boundaries between groups need to weaken and the interconnectedness needs to be increased. "Furthermore, differential emphasis on these mechanisms of integration affects what happens to civilizations when they do collapse" (McGuire 1983:121). Therefore, how and to what degree a society is integrated will have an effect on collapse and the regeneration of society.

Another approach that has been used in the study of prehistoric collapse is chaos theory, which also stresses the interrelatedness of all parts of a society; however, in this view, societies are vulnerable to collapse despite integration. In general, chaos theory considers the unique history of a system and the beliefs and actions of individuals: "chaos theory results in a non-linear model of culture change which states that small perturbations to certain parts of the system can result in the disruption of the structure of the entire system, resulting in instability" (Stone 1999:111).

Shmuel Eisenstadt's (1969, 1988) view of collapse is particularly useful in studying postcollapse regeneration. He sees collapse as the dramatic reconstruction of social and political system boundaries. Boundaries are part of all spheres of a social system (political, economic, etc.), and they are open and continually being constructed. The trajectory of collapse depends on the kinds of boundaries that are failing and how these relate to other boundaries, especially those of the political system. The effects of state dissolution will depend on the internal specifics of a system, such as the coalitions of elites, division of labor, international setting, and ecological setting (Eisenstadt 1988:242). This perspective addresses the variability among societies in dealing with collapse, and it emphasizes that collapse is only an extreme example of boundary restructuring. Most important, it stresses that collapse is also the beginning of new social institutions. One idea that many of these different perspectives share is that collapse is variable throughout a system. "The degree of instability produced by the collapse in any part of the former system is dependent on the area's level of participation, own particular history and the participants' perception of the remaining relationships" (Stone 1999:112).

The view of collapse employed here incorporates these various perspectives to examine the effects of the fall of the Wari empire and subsequent regeneration in the Nasca region. One critical element in studying collapse and regeneration is to understand how local societies functioned under imperial control and not just how the external state governed its territories. The strategies that local people employed to work with or against an intrusive state help set the stage for the kinds of responses they will exhibit upon the disintegration of external control. Similarly, the degree to which a local community was integrated into the imperial state and the ways in which that integration was accomplished will have an impact on how collapse affects that particular region. In this context, it is important to examine the unique history of a province and, if possible, the beliefs and actions of individuals under imperial rule. It is also necessary to specify what has collapsed and to view the regeneration process as the creation of new types of sociopolitical organization, not as the end of society. I attempt to consider these issues in the following analysis of postcollapse regeneration in Nasca.

Wari Conquest and Collapse in the Nasca Region

Located on the south coast of Peru in a very arid desert environment, the Nasca drainage is situated between the Pacific coast and the foothills of the Andes (fig. 7.1). The drainage consists of several river valleys that flow into one outlet to the Pacific Ocean and contain intermittent water and limited arable land. The first permanent settlement of the region occurred after 800 BC, when irrigation agriculture was introduced (table 7.1). In the Early Intermediate period, the era before Wari expansion, societies identified as chiefdoms developed in the drainage (Carmichael 1988; Schreiber 1999; Silverman 1993; Silverman and Proulx 2002; Vaughn 2000). The Nasca culture of this period is known for fine polychrome ceramics and textiles containing elaborate iconography, the ceremonial center of Cahuachi with its large pyramidal mounds, and the construction of the geoglyphs (the Nasca lines). The latter features, which were important loci of ritual practices during this period, consist of large images and lines created by sweeping away the dark stones on the desert floor. Most people of this time lived in small villages (between 0.5 and 2 ha), although sites grew in size (with the largest around 15 ha) by the end of the period (Schreiber 1999; Schreiber and Lancho 1995; Silverman 1993, 2002). Elites of the Early Intermediate period were based at Cahuachi, where they presided over large ritual gatherings and feasts (Silverman 1993; Silverman and Proulx 2002; Valdez 1994). The power of these elites was founded primarily on ritual knowledge and

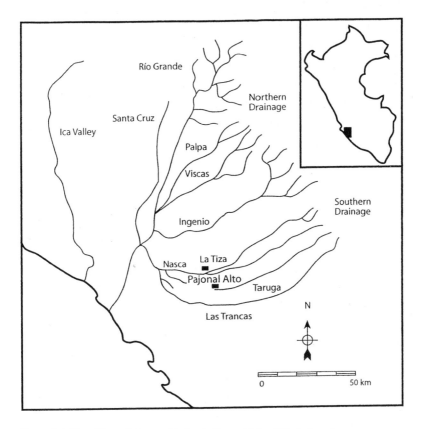

Figure 7.1 Map of Nasca drainage with sites La Tiza and Pajonal Alto indicated.

was probably noncoercive in nature (Silverman 1993; Vaughn 2002). Poly-chrome ceramics contained images of natural and supernatural beings and were the principal medium that expressed religious ideology and solidified elite power (Carmichael 1998; Vaughn 2005).

The subsequent Middle Horizon (AD 600–1000) was a time of state expansion in the Andes. Two states—Wari, based in the central highlands, and Tiwanaku to the south near Lake Titicaca—impacted and transformed many societies throughout the region during this period. Of the two states, Wari was the most expansive, encompassing an area of Peru that was not surpassed in size until the Inca empire in the fifteenth century. The most visible remains of the Wari empire are intrusive administrative sites with a homogeneous style of architecture consisting of large rectangular enclosures containing interior patio groups (Isbell and McEwan 1991; Isbell and Schreiber 1978;

Table 7.1 Chronology of the south coast of Peru

Time period	Culture name	Approximate date range
Late Horizon	Inca	AD 1476–1532
Late Intermediate period	Tiza	AD 1000–1476
Middle Horizon	Wari, Loro	AD 750–1000
Early Intermediate period	Late Nasca	AD 550–750
	Middle Nasca	AD 450–550
	Early Nasca	AD 1–450
Early Horizon	Proto Nasca	100 BC–AD 1
	Paracas	800–100 BC
Initial period		1800–800 BC
Archaic		9000–1800 BC

Schreiber 1992; Spickard 1983). These administrative sites are found all over the highland areas of the empire, while few are found in the coastal regions. Distinctive imperial ceramics are associated with these administrative sites and are also found at local settlements throughout the empire.

There was a close connection between Nasca and the Wari heartland during the time of state development, a phenomenon particularly evident in shared aspects of the ceramic styles of both areas. In the Ayacucho region, where the Wari capital was located, both the pre-Wari ceramic style and the imperial style borrowed considerably from the iconography and technology of Nasca (Benavides 1971; Cook 1984–85; Knobloch 1976; Menzel 1964). A degree of shared religious ideology is also indicated (Conlee 2000; Menzel 1964). Dorothy Menzel, who worked extensively with Nasca and Wari ceramics, categorized the relationship between the two societies as very close. According to Menzel, Nasca held a privileged position in the Wari empire and shared in the prestige of that empire in a manner comparable to the relationship between Greece and Rome (Menzel 1964:68). The strong connection and syncretism that developed between the two areas influenced the effect of the later Wari collapse on Nasca.

Some scholars have argued that Wari did not actually conquer areas of the Peruvian coast, but several varieties of data from Nasca indicate that a Wari conquest did occur there in the eighth century AD. A major Wari offering deposit at Pacheco in the lower Nasca Valley has been understood to imply the existence of a colony of highland Wari people or an intrusive administrative center at that site (Menzel 1964; Schreiber 2001). The small Wari administrative site of Pataraya, consisting of typical imperial architecture (a rectangular compound with interior patio groups), is associated with a small village of local highland architecture and agricultural terraces in the upper elevations of the southern drainage (Schreiber 1999:169). Furthermore, a major road connected the highland Wari capital with the coastal Nasca valley by way of the Sondondo Valley and the administrative site of Jincamocco (Schreiber 1984:89). In addition, Wari imperial ceramics are commonly found in Nasca burial contexts and habitation sites, suggesting frequent interactions (directly or indirectly) with the state.

One of the most persuasive lines of evidence supporting Wari imperial expansion into the Nasca region is the dramatic change in local settlement patterns during the period of Wari expansion. At that time, the number of sites decreased and the populace moved to the southernmost part of the drainage, a considerable distance from the Wari-related settlements (Schreiber 2001). This trend suggests some resistance to the empire that was probably initiated by local leaders (Conlee and Schreiber 2006).

Despite the Wari occupation of the region, the state probably did not rule Nasca directly but governed indirectly through local elites. This can be understood as a case of hegemony without sovereignty (Kolata, chapter 13) but with the addition of strong religious integration. The Wari presence led to the establishment of intermediate elites who obtained power through their association with or opposition to the Wari state (Conlee and Schreiber 2006). For the first time, the people of Nasca became part of a state-level society and were exposed to power and political organization on a grand scale. In addition, the political hierarchy was changed to include a new type of elites, who acquired power in different ways than had previously been the case.

The collapse of Wari led to a period of disruption and balkanization in Nasca that provided the opportunity for dramatic change. In Nasca, the collapse occurred in phase 2 (in the middle of the Middle Horizon), somewhat before it occurred in the Wari core area. This pattern of the early dissolution of Wari control and influence on the coast is repeated elsewhere. A similar trend is associated with the collapse of Tiwanaku, where state control was absent in the Moquegua valley long before it disappeared in the highlands (Bermann et al. 1989; Goldstein 1993b; Sims, chapter 8). Because of the highland base of Wari, it was probably difficult for this state to maintain control of coastal regions; when things began to get difficult, these would have been the first areas to be relinquished.

Various ideas have been proposed to explain the Wari collapse, although little research has been directed at collecting data to address this issue. Edward Lanning (1967) has suggested that competition between Wari and Tiwanaku may have contributed to the dissolution of both states. While contact between the two states is documented at a Wari site on Cerro Baúl inside Tiwanaku territory, no other archaeological evidence suggests that intense competition or warfare led to the collapse of either system. In addition, as Tainter (1988:61) has pointed out, conflict between two powers usually leads to the expansion of one, not the fall of both. Another theory is that internal peasant revolt caused the fall of Wari (Katz 1972; Lanning 1967). Maria Rostworowski (1999:24, 152) proposes that collapse resulted from conflicts between the Wari state and the Chancas, an ethnic group from the central highlands that had entered the Wari heartland.

Climatic change, which appears to have been an important factor in the breakdown of the Tiwanaku state (Binford et al. 1997; Ortloff and Kolata 1993), might also have impacted Wari. Ice core data reveal that there were climatic changes before and after the Middle Horizon, including periods of greater precipitation and periods of drought that may have affected the rise and fall of the Wari state (Thompson et al. 1985). In the case of Tiwanaku, a period of drier conditions with less rain and snowfall may have lowered the water level of Lake Titicaca and put a stress on agricultural production, leading to the fall of the Tiwanaku state. This research also shows that the post-Wari period began during a pluvial interval of improved coastal climate, and societies once again grew in the coastal regions (Ortloff and Kolata 1993). Gordon McEwan (chapter 6) notes that Wari, like Tiwanaku, obtained wealth and expanded its power base by establishing large systems of hydraulic agriculture. He believes that serious long-term disruption in water availability would have been disastrous and weakened the power of the rulers. Tainter (1988:205) suggests that the Wari empire invested so heavily in changing and controlling the people and land under its rule that the economic costs eventually outweighed the benefits. Whatever the precise explanation for the Wari collapse, the Wari state ceased to exist by AD 1000.

In Nasca, the collapse of Wari was followed by severe disruption characterized by a long period of site abandonment, population movement, and resettlement (Conlee 2000; Reindel and Isla 1998; Schreiber 2001). During this period, almost all existing settlements were abandoned. While new sites were established in different locations, fewer existed than had previously been the case (Reindel and Isla 1998; Schreiber 2001). This suggests that long-term adversity occurred when Wari collapsed, the effects of which might have included the abandonment of villages, irrigation systems, and fields (Gordon 1979). Like collapse, abandonment is a process and not an event, often inducing cultural change (e.g., Cameron 1993; Pauketat 2003; Tomka and Stevenson 1993). "Abandonment is a process of transformation from one way of using the landscape to another, within sites, locales, and regions" (Nelson 2000:54). Movement of people and resettlement causes everyday routines to change and may correspondingly alter traditional practices (Nelson 2000; Pauketat 2003). Options for moving and resettling vary by individual and household (Nelson 2000:59), a variability resulting in new behaviors and relationships.

After a period of long-term adversity, a region may recover, but new power structures will have developed (Gordon 1979). Situations of upheaval provide the opportunity for both elites and commoners to overcome the restrictions and oppression of the political system (Joyce et al. 2001; Love 2002; E. Morris, chapter 4). Elites of this period probably comprised both people who had held positions of power during the Wari empire and were able to successfully maintain power (probably through new means), and those who were not part of the traditional political hierarchy and were able to use the situation to their advantage. Modifications in the activities of elites in this period would have been particularly significant, since they would have been most able to transform society through their actions. Shifts in elite activities were facilitated by changes in the social/political environment (Wari influence was no longer a factor) and in the physical environment (people abandoned their homes and moved to new settlements). The activities of non-elites were also altered, and the social environment would have provided an opportunity for them to express resistance and become agents of social change (Joyce et al. 2001). However, commoners would also have been affected by changes in elite activities and the jockeying for power that occurred during this period.

The disintegration of the intrusive Wari power structure permitted and required the emergence of new types of political organization. The postcollapse period was a time when local elites struggled to maintain power positions they had achieved during the Wari occupation and a time when they were forced to obtain power through new realms (Conlee and Schreiber 2006). While collapse may lead to the loss of power for some, it can also provide new opportunities for people not previously part of the political hierarchy. The specific reconfigurations that occurred through the actions of both elites and non-elites in the postcollapse period led to the unique society that developed in the subsequent Late Intermediate period.

Nasca Regeneration

The Late Intermediate period (AD 1000–1476, see table 7.1) was a time of postcollapse regional development throughout much of the central Andean region. Collapse in the Wari center led to decentralization and the development of a much less complex society; however, in other areas of the empire, opportunities were created for local groups to strengthen and, in the case of the Cuzco region, to reestablish an empire (McEwan, chapter 6). By the end of this period, large regional polities developed in many areas that were characterized by high levels of competition, new types of political organization, and expanded economic and trade networks.

In Nasca, postcollapse restructuring consisted of a regeneration of local society facilitated by the changes that the Wari empire brought to the region. Although an empire was not reborn in Nasca, a new society developed that was more complex than Nasca had been in pre-Wari times. Settlement patterns indicate the existence of a high population density and two to three levels of settlement hierarchy above the village level. Information from settlement patterns and the sites of Pajonal Alto and La Tiza (see fig. 7.1) help to illustrate the new type of sociopolitical organization that developed during this period.

The village of Pajonal Alto was abandoned when Wari collapsed but was fully reoccupied by the middle of the Late Intermediate period (ca. AD 1350), when the region had recovered and new forms of social, political, and economic organization had developed. Pajonal Alto provides data on village life after regeneration occurred and on the nature of the new society flourishing in the region. La Tiza was a large town that may have served as the regional capital and was occupied for most of the postcollapse period. This settlement reveals the significant differences between a regional power center of the Late Intermediate period and those of the preceding era, reflecting the restructured nature of sociopolitical organization.

Before I describe the dramatic changes that occurred in postcollapse Nasca, I think it appropriate to note the elements of continuity that can be identified in the region. For example, there was general stability on the subsistence level and little change in the agricultural base, an unsurprising situation given the environmental conditions limiting the types of crops grown in the region and the degree of intensification possible (Conlee 2000). People probably did their best to maintain agricultural practices that had been successful in the past, including changes that had been implemented under Wari control (Conlee and Schreiber 2006). The use of animal resources also exhibited much continuity, although there is evidence for an increase in domesticated camelids (llamas and alpacas) and in the consumption of shellfish (Conlee 2000). In Nasca, one can observe the continuation of some pan-Andean religious practices that were not associated specifically with the previous Nasca or Wari cultures but were practiced throughout the Andes in many periods and cultures. These include mountain and water worship, animal and plant sacrifices/offerings, and the use of *chicha* (maize beer), *Spondylus* (spiny oyster), and panpipes in rituals.

Despite the continuity in these areas, regeneration resulted in striking transformations in most other realms. On the regional level, the location, size, layout, and type of sites changed considerably. Throughout the drainage, there was an increase in the number of settlements, with population reaching its pre-Columbian peak. Domestic sites were much larger than in earlier periods, with several between eight and twenty hectares located throughout the drainage (Alfaro de Lanzone 1978; Browne 1992; Browne and Baraybar 1988; Schreiber and Lancho 2003; Silverman 2002). There were major centers and secondary centers in both the northern and the southern drainage. Many settlements were located in defensive locations, especially in the north. Sites were more aggregated and contained new types of architecture. The most common type of settlement was built on a steep hillside with rectangular terraces containing square or rectangular agglutinated structures.

At the town of La Tiza (28 ha), one of the largest habitation sites in the drainage, there was substantial variability in domestic architecture. This plurality of domestic architecture may reflect an expanded social hierarchy and/or the development of different ethnic groups (Conlee 2005; Conlee and Rodriguez 2002).

One of the most dramatic areas of change in postcollapse Nasca was in religion and ritual, observable at the regional and site level. After the disintegration of Wari, ritual resources that were closely associated with the Nasca and Wari cultures were abandoned. Throughout the drainage, the elaborate iconography that began with the Nasca culture and was later adopted by the Wari empire was rejected. Nasca/Wari iconography, characterized by polychrome representations of complex images of supernatural beings, was replaced by simpler, nonrepresentative and geometric designs executed in three-color combinations of red, black, and white. There is little evidence that the geoglyphs continued to be constructed or used, and existing large ceremonial sites were abandoned, with new ones no longer built (Reindel and Isla 1998; Silverman 1993).

The type and location of ritual activities changed, a development that can be seen at a variety of sites. At the village of Pajonal Alto, ritual activities were conducted in a small mound and plaza area. This development suggests a focus on community-based ritual activities and a shift away from the regionally based gatherings of earlier time periods. Since the small plaza and mound at the village were adjacent to the elite habitation area, one may infer that elites had privileged access and probable control of this area (Conlee 2003).

However, ritual was just one of many avenues through which elites were able to obtain power. Even at the large town of La Tiza, there is little evidence for large gatherings or a focus on ritual activities. Rather than large plazas and mounds, La Tiza has small lookout areas and ridge tops with smashed, decorated ceramics that may have been the focus of restricted ritual activities. Elites appear to have abandoned religious resources as the primary means to build power, possibly because such resources were seen as unstable and too intertwined with the failing Wari political system (Conlee 2005).

It is likely that the syncretism between Wari and Nasca resulted in a severe disruption to the Nasca ideological system when Wari collapsed. This situation probably led future populations in the Nasca region to restructure the relationship between religious beliefs and the political system, a development that may explain why collective ritual such as that practiced previously at Cahuachi was no longer used for integrating the population. In the postcollapse period, religious resources no longer had the prominence they once had, and other types of material resources were employed to obtain and maintain political power (Conlee 2005).

Economic activities and exchange were also restructured when the Nasca region recovered from the Wari collapse. At the village of Pajonal Alto, the context and organization of production changed, a development especially evident in ceramic manufacture. There was apparently less self-sufficiency among households in the manufacture of utilitarian goods, and prestige items do not appear to have been a focus of manufacture (Conlee 2000). Instead, there is evidence that elites were involved in utilitarian ceramic production at Pajonal Alto. In the elite-associated habitation area, pottery production is indicated by the presence of unfired ceramics, polishing stones, and worked pieces of clay. Members of an elite family appear to have been producing utilitarian pottery, perhaps for use in regional exchange and/or community feasting activities. The number of ceramic paste types found in the assemblage in both utilitarian and decorated wares is far greater than is manifested at sites of earlier periods, suggesting an increase in regional exchange at small villages (Vaughn et al. 2002). Evidently, a greater number of communities were involved in ceramic production than had previously been the case, with frequent exchange among communities. Elites may have been involved in the regional exchange of utilitarian pottery and other items partly to establish and maintain alliances with other settlements throughout the drainage. Elite individuals were likely to have also been involved in feasting, and their participation in the production of utilitarian pottery, especially large cooking pots, may have been related to the provision of food and drink for large gatherings. Of particular note is the fact that the elite residential area at Pajonal Alto was adjacent to the plaza, a probable locus for feasting activities. In sum, the manufacture and exchange of pottery was probably one area in which elites obtained and wielded power throughout this period (Conlee 2003).

Both regional and long-distance exchange appear to have increased at villages in this period. In addition to pottery, regional goods such as marine resources and cotton yarn apparently were also more frequently exchanged (Conlee 2000). Long-distance exchange items included obsidian from the central highlands and the marine shell *Spondylus* that originated in southern Ecuador. These goods were almost exclusively associated with the elite habitation area at Pajonal Alto. *Spondylus* is a well-documented long-distance prestige item in the Andes, and it played an important role in ritual and the political economy (Murra 1975; Pillsbury 1996). Since *Spondylus* shells have not been identified at small villages of earlier time periods in Nasca—only at large sites and ceremonial centers—postcollapse village elites appear to have been able to obtain prestige goods that their counterparts in earlier villages had not been able to.

Political organization was also radically transformed in Late Intermediate Nasca. At Pajonal Alto, elites were identified through intrasite differences in the quality of architecture, length of occupation, diversity of food remains, and access to long-distance exchange goods (Conlee 2003). Since villages of earlier time periods have little evidence of social differentiation (Vaughn 2000), the presence of elites at Pajonal Alto indicates a shift in the nature of inequality. There was an increase in the overall number of elite individuals in the region and an expanded sociopolitical hierarchy. These individuals participated in a broad range of activities such as the production of utilitarian items, exchange, feasting, community/exclusive ritual, and probably warfare and defense (Conlee 2003). The changing nature of sociopolitical organization is also evinced by the diversity of domestic architecture at the large center of La Tiza. At this site, the distinct clusters of different types of domestic structures probably reflect a town where people of many different statuses resided. These statuses were likely the result of people who had a variety of social identities and economic positions and belonged to different ethnic groups. During this period, the resources of power were more variable than had previously been the case, resulting in a more heterarchical society with diverse ways of ranking and classifying people (Conlee 2005).

The creation of a society with complex types of power relationships that were segmented and hierarchical had its roots in the fall of the Wari empire. The collapse of Wari probably facilitated the development of factions and ethnic groups in the Late Intermediate period (Conlee 2005). State collapse often leads to the establishment of wealth and power outside of strict political control (Brumfiel 1994:10). This development may include the creation of organizations based on craft production or trade and the establishment of religious power in new institutions such as the priesthood (Blanton 1983; Brumfiel 1994). These new groups would compete for power or form alliances with established elites and factions, helping to transform political structure by emphasizing functionally different interest groups (Brumfiel 1994:10). With the development of factions and new interest groups, a more complex type of sociopolitical organization would be created as new kinds of groups are incorporated into society.

Conquest, Collapse, and Social Transfomation

In Nasca, postcollapse regeneration included resettlement and aggregation, the rejection of the previous religious ideology, an expanded network of elites, an increase in the means by which individuals could obtain power, and new contexts of production and exchange. The evidence from Nasca reveals that the relationship a region has with a conquering state will make a difference in how the area is impacted by both conquest and collapse. A shared religious ideology may lead to greater disruption in a province when an empire collapses, in part because the perceived instability is great. When collapse results in the abandonment and resettlement of sites, there is the possibility of major transformation because of the changes in everyday activities and traditional practices. A period of long-term adversity facilitates

the development of new types of power structures, and different varieties of social and economic organization also emerge. Collapse can lead to
the establishment of wealth and power outside of the political hierarchy.
This creates factions and the development of new interest groups that compete with traditional elites for political power. Regeneration can take many
forms; in Nasca it consisted of new types of religious, economic, and political organization that resulted in the wholesale transformation of society.

Acknowledgments

I would like to thank Glenn Schwartz for helping to organize this volume and for his insightful editorial comments. Funding for research at La Tiza was provided by the National Science Foundation (BCS-0314273) and by the H. John Heinz III Fund Grant Program
for Latin American Archaeology. The work at Pajonal Alto was supported by a National
Science Foundation dissertation improvement grant (#9616637).

8 After State Collapse
How Tumilaca Communities Developed in the Upper Moquegua Valley, Peru
Kenny Sims

The peak of centralization and political power in the Moquegua Valley occurred circa AD 800, when the Wari state controlled the upper valley and
the Tiwanaku state, the middle valley. Following the withdrawal of Tiwanaku
(ca. AD 950) and Wari (ca. AD 1050), the remaining Tiwanaku communities underwent social, political, and economic transformations that led to a
culture that archaeologists call "Tumilaca" (Bermann et al. 1989; Goldstein
1989a; Moseley et al. 1991). With the collapse of Tiwanaku and Wari, Tumilaca
communities settled along the coast and in the lower, middle, and upper valleys of the Moquegua River drainage (fig. 8.1). In contrast to the other cases
discussed in this volume, the Tumilaca provide an instance in which regeneration or second-generation state formation did *not* occur after collapse. It
will be important to consider how and why this is the case.

The Tumilaca communities that I discuss in this chapter occupied the
upper Moquegua Valley for 250 years, from AD 950 to 1200 (Moseley 1992;
Stanish 1992). The development of these upper-valley Tumilaca communities—in contrast to those in the middle, lower, and coastal areas—was
a complex and unique process initiated more than a century before Tiwanaku lost control of the middle Moquegua Valley. In the upper valley, an area
controlled by the opposing Wari state, Tumilaca communities developed
from two sets of Tiwanaku migrants: those who moved into the upper valley
at AD 800 and lived alongside and within the Wari state for 250 years, and
those who left the middle valley at AD 950, after the dissolution of the Tiwanaku state in Moquegua (Owen 1996; Williams 2002). Thus, from AD 950 to
1050, the upper valley was occupied by members of the Wari state, Tiwanaku
migrants (from AD 800), and poststate Tiwanaku groups that were in the
process of transforming into the first Tumilaca communities. One hundred
years after this, by AD 1050, the upper valley was solely occupied by Tumilaca
communities, which presumably incorporated and recombined the tradi-

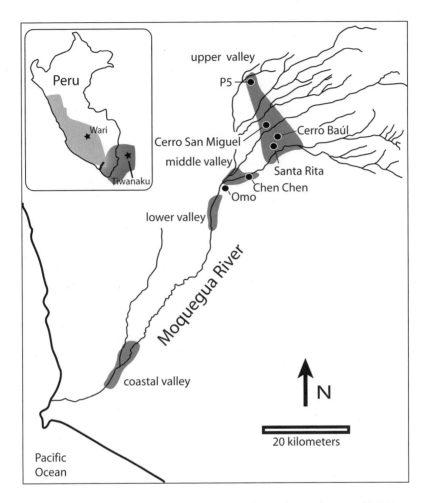

Figure 8.1 Moquegua Valley. Shaded areas indicate Tumilaca settlement clusters ca. AD 1000. Inset shows extent of Tiwanaku and Wari states ca. AD 800.

tions of the earlier groups into this poststate culture (Bermann et al. 1989; Goldstein 1989a; Moseley et al. 1991; Owen 1993).

   Although Tumilaca is generally discussed only as a cultural development that followed Tiwanaku state collapse (Bermann et al. 1989; Goldstein 1989b; Moseley et al. 1991; Owen and Goldstein 2001; cf. Lozada and Buikstra 2002), I advance from this traditional model for the upper Moquegua Valley and consider that the Wari state, which survived for approximately one hundred years after Tiwanaku lost control in Moquegua, was a critical component in the sociopolitical development of the upper-valley Tumilaca. The abandonment at AD 1050 of the Wari complex at Cerro Baúl was accompanied by changes in upper-valley settlement patterns, internal site organization, and deintensification of agricultural practices (Williams 1997, 2001), all of which affected upper-valley cultural developments. The role of Wari state involvement in subsequent Tumilaca developments can be addressed only by examining data that extend from the period of the Tiwanaku state to the era following the abandonment of Wari state settlements.

The upper-valley Tumilaca groups constitute an important case study because they emerged during the decline of Wari and Tiwanaku control in the valley and are the first of a series of groups that occupied the Moquegua Valley during a four-hundred-year period of regional decentralization, AD 1050–1450 (fig. 8.2). During this period, neither the Tumilaca nor the subsequent Estuquiña group unified the upper valley or administered it from a single capital. A new peak of political centralization did not recur until the Inca (ca. AD 1450) incorporated Estuquiña communities of the Moquegua Valley into their expansionist state.

Many regions in Peru and Bolivia were affected by Wari and Tiwanaku expansion between AD 550 and 1100, but few became a staging ground for second-generation state formation (Marcus 1998). Such complex societies that did not regenerate are more abundant than formerly thought, and they are crucial for understanding long-term trends in the political history of any area (Marcus 1989).

Political Collapse and Lack of Regeneration

The collapse of centralized states can lead to a landscape of multiple polities; new social, political, and economic networks; and the formation or transformation of rival polities on the periphery of what had been a centralized state (Marcus 1989, 1992). Such political transformations can be accompanied by a rapid change in archaeological markers (e.g., ceramic styles, architecture, and settlement patterns), suggesting to some researchers that little population continuity occurred. Archaeologists who emphasize such apparent discontinuity often regard collapse as a single catastrophic or "enigmatic" event that affects the entire region.

Recent work, however, suggests that collapse was a regional dynamic process that might be more accurately called "transformation." With the "death of a civilization," argues Joseph Tainter (1988:40), certain forms of cultural behavior continue to organize societies, making collapse a unique

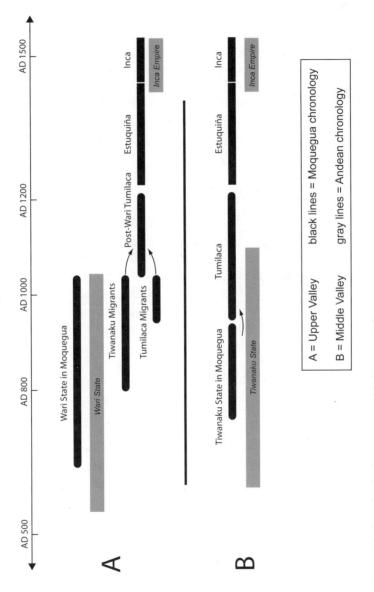

Figure 8.2 Chronology for the upper and middle Moquegua Valley.

political and economic experience across regions and between sites. Such changes affect each site differently—disrupting some traditions but not all (Marcus 2001; Yoffee 1988b; Yoffee and Cowgill 1988). Political transformation creates new opportunities for local groups, and local elites as well as non-elites can experiment with different forms of economic and political organization while retaining some traditional values and styles. A new polity can rise to prominence and reincorporate areas that had been under the political umbrella of the earlier state. At other times, state collapse can result in the development of less hierarchical, less centralized political institutions with little control over other regions. In both cases, the "new" cultural traditions and political institutions are contingent upon antecedent forms of organization; new administrators modify, reject, or maintain past strategies, previous institutions, and earlier cultural values (Eisenstadt 1988; Hastorf 1993).

Alternating cycles of state formation and state collapse can create a series of peaks and valleys: that is, periods of political centralization alternating with periods of decentralization (Marcus 1992, 1998). Most archaeologists have focused on the peaks of centralization, but Glenn Schwartz (chapter 1) persuasively argues that the process of collapse, regeneration, and the nongeneration of subsequent states should be studied in greater detail. We need to know why some areas stay in a "political valley" or "trough" (Marcus 1998), never again reaching a peak of recentralization.

Most chapters in this volume address recovery and recentralization, but data for the Tumilaca period in the Moquegua Valley suggest that state institutions did not reemerge there. I argue that the Tiwanaku and Wari states inhibited such development. It is my contention that the first wave of Tiwanaku migrants who settled within the upper-valley Wari domain (AD 800) and the first set of Tumilaca groups—displaced Tiwanaku groups from the middle valley—who entered the upper valley while Wari still controlled this territory (AD 950) were never permitted to hold top-ranking administrative positions within the Wari state. By the time the Wari state retreated (AD 1050), the upper-valley Tiwanaku groups and the recently migrated Tumilaca groups had established competing villages and households whose administrative practices were, to different degrees, dependent on the existence of the Wari state. Both groups were involved in the Wari political economy, but with important differences: the post–AD 800 Tiwanaku migrants had a domestic economy completely embedded within the Wari state economy, while Tumilaca villagers appear to have been more politically and economically self-sufficient.

The economic stability of each set of villages (i.e., Tiwanaku and Tumilaca) and the relationship between village leaders and commoners in each group was defined by the Wari political system that administered all levels of the political economy in the upper valley from AD 950 to 1050. Tiwanaku and Tumilaca administrative practices that developed under the Wari state could not be maintained in the absence of a state. Opportunities for Tiwanaku and Tumilaca elites to advance in the hierarchy were evidently missing from the Wari system; it was a system that did not promote village leaders into positions of authority that extended their domain beyond their native village constituencies. For Tiwanaku and Tumilaca elites, the lack of political experience in higher-level administrative posts would pose historically determined constraints on the symbolic and practical-administrative resources that could be marshaled to create a centralized polity after state collapse. Thus, the Tumilaca communities in the upper Moquegua Valley were poorly prepared to fill the power vacuum after Tiwanaku and Wari collapsed.

Administrative Underdevelopment

To explain why Tumilaca groups were unable to reestablish centralized governments following state retreat, I utilize the concept of "administrative underdevelopment," a strategy of keeping local village leaders in low-level administrative posts. Such a strategy prevented local leaders from acquiring administrative knowledge, experience, and skill, impeding their ability to reestablish hierarchical administration after state collapse.

Anthropologists have long been interested in the relationship between states and local communities. In his "Law of Evolutionary Potential," Elman Service (1960) suggests that long-term domination of smaller, less developed groups by a larger, more developed group has a direct bearing on the smaller groups' ability to rise to political prominence later. To paraphrase Service (1960:96–97), the dominance that a more complex polity may exert over less developed groups is an effective inhibitor of any potential that the underdeveloped group may possess to centralize its political system at a later date. As a corollary, I suggest the following: the intensity and duration of a state's control may limit the number of choices that populations have for reorganizing or reconstituting their government and economy. For provincial contexts, the trajectory of political recovery after state collapse is inescapably tethered to the degree and nature of interaction between the state and local communities.

After a state retreats from a province, the overarching administrative institutions and hierarchies disappear. The sociopolitical landscape will consist of an array of petty managers and midlevel administrators whose authority to conduct specific administrative tasks is no longer state directed or state sanctioned. These local managers can find themselves out of a job after state collapse, and those who seek to reestablish some form of institutionalized authority must develop new forms of legitimization and management. Peaceful reorganization of local administration may be difficult to effect, especially in a context of competing village leaders, with each group possessing a subset of necessary administrative skills and having limited authority.

Aspiring village elites who attempt to reinstitute a hierarchical organization are faced with the challenge of reestablishing what Shmuel Eisenstadt (1988:240) terms the three dimensions of social order: (1) trust and solidarity; (2) the chains of authority that construe elite management as legitimate; and (3) organizational activity. Legitimate administration must be reestablished, reorganized, and revalued under new regimes with new agendas. During and after state dissolution, new rules of interaction between local elites and local commoners must be defined. Competing managerial strategies, as in the case of Tiwanaku migrant versus Tumilaca village leaders in the upper Moquegua Valley, must meet Eisenstadt's three dimensions so that the local leaders' imposed authority over lower-ranking elites and commoners is accepted and ratified in the poststate period.

After a region is incorporated into a state, the roles of local leaders are redefined; they must obey commands coming from higher levels and thwart resistance from lower levels (Murra 1964). According to John Murra (1962), as the Inca empire expanded, traditional leaders (*kurakas*) were subject to novel constraints and demands as they (re)organized community activity to satisfy a new battery of imposed duties. The relationship between kuraka elites and non-elites was also critical, because these local/imperial managers were "still amenable to the pressures of kinship and local tradition" (Murra 1962:2) while having to satisfy foreign economic and political obligations. Under the aegis of the state, these local elites/managers acquired sufficient legitimacy and resources to demand increased labor from their subordinates, but this demand was, in part, contingent on the state's regional control. At the same time, states could decentralize indigenous structures of authority by allowing lower-ranking elites and commoners access to more rights and goods, sidestepping established and higher-ranked elites within the new administration (Costin and Earle 1989).

When a state incorporates a community, new positions of authority may emerge or be transformed, but these will persist only as long as the socio-political context in which they operate. After states collapse, communities are not governed by precollapse politico-economic logic. The rapid loss in sociopolitical complexity during collapse (Tainter 1988:4) will have greater disruptive effects on the local organization of those communities that were more directly embedded in the state. The greater the separation between failing state political systems and local systems (and the greater the autonomy of the latter), the more the consequences of collapse will be attenuated and the easier reestablishing some degree of local political and economic stability will be.

The concept of administrative underdevelopment allows us to explore cases in which states never reemerge. Administrative underdevelopment is the long-term result of local elite leaders' being allowed marginal administrative positions within the state, affording them short-term privileges and wealth. States reduce their administrative costs by co-opting local administrators and granting them new responsibilities and privileges. Such co-option of indigenous elites can cause long-term organizational problems when state control declines. The concept of administrative underdevelopment is particularly useful in interpreting the trajectory of the Tumilaca communities that appeared in the upper reaches of the Moquegua Valley.

Tiwanaku Colonialism in Moquegua (AD 750–950)

The archaeological identification of colonies in the Andes has been a topic of interest since Murra (1972) first proposed his "vertical archipelago" model, in which the state resettled people in complementary ecological zones to exploit resources. The dispersal of community groups throughout the variable and noncontiguous ecological zones that characterize the Andean mountain chain permitted states such as the Inca and Tiwanaku direct access to multiple resources over short and medium distances (Aldenderfer 1993; Rice et al. 1989; Van Buren 1996). Previously, the presence of Tiwanaku material culture—even without evidence of Tiwanaku households, cemeteries, and administrative or corporate architecture—was considered sufficient for concluding that Tiwanaku's influence was colonial in nature (Berenguer and Dauelsberg 1989; Mujica 1985). However, such interpretations have been criticized (Dillehay and Nuñez 1988; Stanish 1989).

At present, only the middle Moquegua Valley can be considered a well-documented instance of Tiwanaku colonialism (Goldstein 1989a, 1989b,

1993b; Moseley et al. 1991). Circa AD 750 to 800, the Tiwanaku state established control over the most productive maize-growing zone of the Moquegua Valley (1,000–2,000 meters above sea level [masl]) in a form that can be interpreted as colonial administration. Settlement evidence supporting a colonial interpretation includes twenty-eight sites with a wide range of Tiwanaku material culture and associated cemeteries (Goldstein 1989a); elite-ceremonial architecture constructed to replicate the architectural canons of the Tiwanaku capital (Goldstein 1993b); and development of large-scale irrigated fields adjacent to the Tiwanaku site of Chen Chen (Moseley et al. 1991; Williams 1997). In addition, biometric cranial data and nonmetric dental trait analyses conducted on altiplano and Moquegua skeletons from Tiwanaku cemeteries confirm that the Tiwanaku population in the Moquegua Valley migrated from the altiplano during this period (Blom et al. 1998; Sutter 2000). The recovery of Tiwanaku exotic materials (e.g., snuff tablets, textiles, llama wool) as well as fine- and blackware ceramics from household, mortuary, and temple contexts buttresses the settlement and genetic data and suggests that the Moquegua and altiplano populations were in continuous communication (Goldstein 1989a, 1993b).

The Tiwanaku state orchestrated its administration of the middle valley from two key sites (fig. 8.1): Chen Chen, the economic center; and Omo, the political and ritual site (Moseley et al. 1991). The advent of Tiwanaku colonialism in Moquegua initiated the development of extensive agricultural fields adjacent to Chen Chen (24.3 ha total), a site that included a small ritual structure and multiple Tiwanaku-affiliated cemeteries (Goldstein and Owen 2001:153). The size of the irrigated fields and the large quantities of food processing tools at Chen Chen suggest that the residents harvested and processed crops that could have been exported to the altiplano (Bandy et al. 1996; Goldstein 1989a; Williams 1997). The Tiwanaku state was interested in the Moquegua Valley for obtaining necessary components for altiplano rituals, including maize and coca, which could not be grown in the high altiplano, at an elevation of 3,800–4,000 masl (Kolata 2003b). In return, the Moquegua Valley received wool, freeze-dried potatoes, and freeze-dried llama meat—goods not available at low elevations. These highland items, along with imported prestige items (ritual drinking and eating vessels, textiles, snuff tablets, jewelry), are the material evidence of interaction between the Tiwanaku state and the local elite of Chen Chen in the Moquegua Valley (Goldstein 1989a, 1993b).

Omo is located seven kilometers downriver from Chen Chen, away from the extensive agricultural fields. A large, three-tiered platform temple, bearing a strong resemblance to the sacred Akapana platform at the Tiwanaku capital (Goldstein 1993b), was built at Omo. To explain why Tiwanaku was more interested in funding large-scale monumental architecture in the Moquegua Valley than in Arequipa, Cochabamba, and northern Chile, Michael Moseley and colleagues (1991) cite the presence of the Wari state's defensible site Cerro Baúl twenty kilometers upriver from Chen Chen. In addition to investing in terraces and canals, Tiwanaku elites built ritual structures that replicated the sacred landscape of the capital to reinforce ideological and social control over the population. Monumental architecture and ritual sites are not only "measures and reflections of power and authority" (Sinopoli and Morrison 1995:85) but are also elite investments into the legitimization of the sociopolitical structures that frame their authority. Imitating or replicating the buildings and monuments of Tiwanaku's sacred landscape was an effective mechanism for extending the ideological, social, and political tenets of the state into areas beyond the capital (Janusek 2002). Tiwanaku symbols of power were commonly incorporated into the domestic, corporate, and ritual domains of both elites and commoners in Tiwanaku society (Albarracin-Jordan 1996; Moseley et al. 1991). At Chen Chen, the ceramic style also bears sacred motifs such as the Front Face Deity and Puma Head (see fig. 8.3: B), two icons whose political message conveyed the central authority of the state (Goldstein 1989b; Moseley et al. 1991). The ubiquity of these political motifs in all contexts of activity—from ritual to domestic, high status to low status—is the materialization of the Tiwanaku political hierarchy in the valley colony.

Wari Colonialism in Moquegua (AD 650–1050)

The principal Wari administrative center in the upper Moquegua Valley (2,000–2,500 masl) was founded circa AD 650 on the flat mountaintop called Cerro Baúl (Williams 2001). Cerro Baúl (fig. 8.1) was the southernmost colony of the Wari state, with the Wari capital, Ayacucho, located 525 kilometers to the north (Schreiber 2001). Cerro Baúl, only 20 kilometers upriver from the Tiwanaku settlements in the middle valley, lies in an arid zone between the Moquegua River's Tumilaca and Torata tributaries (Moseley et al. 1991; Watanabe 1989).

Wari entered the Moquegua Valley with a centralized political system designed to suit the needs of an expanding state. During the seventh century AD, the Ayacucho-based polity quickly expanded beyond its local borders and incorporated many regions of Peru and in some cases converted the indigenous groups into subjects of the Wari state (Isbell and McEwan 1991; Schreiber 1992; Williams 2001). In cases where Wari could not co-opt local administration, the expanding state annexed a territory and imposed an administrative center (Schreiber 1992).

The installation of the Wari colony in the upper Moquegua Valley (AD 650) preceded the Tiwanaku state's expansion to the middle valley by about a century (fig. 8.2). The upper valley was either sparsely occupied or completely vacant when the Wari arrived (Owen 1996). The success of Cerro Baúl, therefore, depended on the complete and rapid imposition of Wari governmental and administrative institutions, the typical modus operandi of Wari expansion into unoccupied areas (Schreiber 2001).

Wari colonists constructed Cerro Baúl, Cerro Mejía (a secondary center), and several other sites to form a multitiered settlement hierarchy (Nash 1996, 2002). Wari colonists transformed the mountains and arid terrain of the upper valley into a highly productive agricultural zone by constructing terraces and an extensive canal, thirteen kilometers long (Williams 1997). Because of the steep slopes of the upper valley, development of large-scale agriculture relying on canals and terraces would have been a necessity for any centralized polity in the area.

Unlike the Tiwanaku state, whose agricultural technologies and water management techniques were well suited to flat lands or *pampas* (Goldstein 1989b; Kolata 1985, 1986), Wari had refined steep-slope terrace and canal technologies to make previously barren zones very productive. Katharina Schreiber (1992) documents an example of Wari expansion in which local agriculture was augmented by state-directed terracing and canal systems at Jincamocco in the Sondondo Valley. The surplus produced at Jincamocco was probably used to maintain the rapidly growing political economy at the Wari capital, four days' walk to the north (Schreiber 2001). This investment in terraces and canals doubtless gave Wari an advantage in its quest to expand its domain across Peru and into the Moquegua Valley.

The desire for subsistence crops, however, cannot account for the presence of the Wari state in the Moquegua Valley. Not only is the distance from Cerro Baúl to the Wari capital in Ayacucho close to the upper limits (600 km) for the transport of bulk staple foods (Stein 1999:58), the maximum yield of the Wari agricultural fields was only enough to support the Cerro Baúl complex (Williams and Sims 1998). Rather than procuring crops, Wari was probably acting preemptively by establishing a defensible southern presence that might hamper the regional growth of the developing Tiwanaku state, as well as extracting precious stones (azurite and chrysocolla) and securing control of obsidian exchange routes in southern Peru (Burger et al. 2000:338–39; Moseley et al. 1991; Watanabe 1989).

Wari hegemony in the upper Moquegua Valley (fig. 8.2) lasted some four centuries (AD 650–1050). In this region, as with the Tiwanaku colony at Omo and Chen Chen, elite authority was displayed and legitimized through the construction of buildings that replicated architecture developed and sanctioned by the state capital, in this case two ceremonial (D-shaped) structures and multiple patio-group palaces (Cook 2001; Isbell et al. 1991; Williams 2001). Once the Cerro Baúl settlement was in place, the political economy was highly centralized, extremely productive, and complex; the upper-valley landscape was transformed into a state economic system.

The Wari colonial center at Cerro Baúl underwent massive architectural remodeling circa AD 900, resulting in the enlargement of elite administrative space. Wari administrative architecture tended to emphasize large plazas and reception halls (Isbell et al. 1991; Williams 2001), and Wari provincial administrators probably remodeled administrative buildings and reception halls in response to the well-established Tiwanaku colonial administration in the middle valley (Williams and Nash 2002). Both the Wari and the Tiwanaku state invested in administrative structures, perhaps competing with each other over labor at a time when river water was becoming more abundant and larger investments into each state's colonial project were becoming feasible (Williams 2002).

Prior to the remodeling of the Cerro Baúl center, a drastic restructuring of the Wari administration in the upper valley had occurred. The abandonment circa AD 800 of the secondary administrative center at Cerro Mejía resulted in a net downsizing of the total Wari administrative apparatus in the Moquegua Valley (Nash 2002). Abandonment of Cerro Mejía would have required the reallocation of administrative tasks both up and down the hierarchy. Expansion of the administrative space on top of Cerro Baúl would have met the growing administrative needs of the Wari center, which was beginning to attract non-Wari clients (i.e., Tiwanaku migrants) as agricultural laborers into the upper-valley political economy.

Evidence of Wari and Tiwanaku Interaction (AD 800)

Despite their proximity, the middle valley Tiwanaku administrators appear to have had limited interaction with their Wari counterparts. Minor quantities of exotic obsidian artifacts from Wari-controlled quarries in the Arequipa area and some twenty Wari ceramic vessels (Qosqopa style)—out

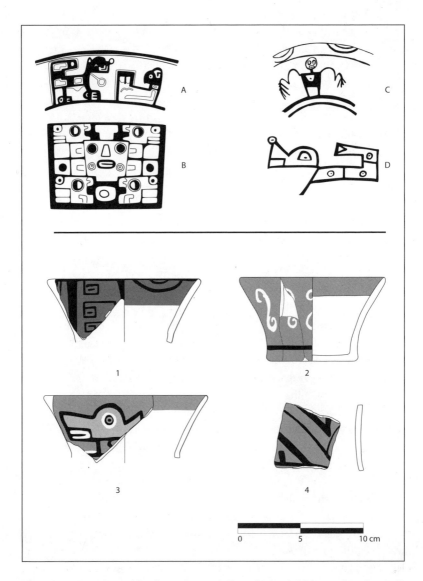

Figure 8.3 Tiwanaku and Tumilaca ceramics. A: Tiwanaku L-tailed feline and condor motifs (redrawn from Moseley et al. 1991:fig. 10-C); B: Tiwanaku Front Faced Deity with four surrounding box-head puma motifs (redrawn from Moseley et al. 1991:fig. 7-E); C: unusual anthropomorphic motif found in Tiwanaku context but not conforming to known Tiwanaku styles; 1, 2, 4: Tiwanaku motifs and ceramics from the upper Moquegua Valley; D: Tumilaca motif from Site P5 (redrawn from Bermann et al. 1989:fig. 4); 3: Tumilaca cup and motif from Santa Rita. (Unless otherwise noted, images are from my excavation and lab work, derived from field drawings by Adan Umire.)

of the thousands of excavated Chen Chen Tiwanaku tombs—account for the majority of evidence of Tiwanaku-Wari interaction in the Moquegua middle valley (Burger et al. 2000; García 1990). Since Arequipa is the source of this obsidian and the Qosqopa style is prevalent in Wari contexts there (and rare at Cerro Baúl), local Tiwanaku elite relationships with the Wari state might not have been mediated through Cerro Baúl. Given the paucity of direct evidence, Bruce Owen and Paul Goldstein (2001) can only suggest that interstate administrative interaction between the upper and middle valley was limited.

The first well-documented interaction of Wari and Tiwanaku occurred circa AD 800 with the arrival of Tiwanaku migrants into Wari territory in the upper Moquegua Valley. This migration must have been viewed as an advantage by Wari administrators interested in increasing the size of their labor force at a time when water availability was at an all-time high in the valley. Previously, each state had developed its political economy to maximize agricultural output, taking advantage of the end of a one-hundred-year drought between AD 650 and 750 (Williams 1997). With an abundance of water, labor was the limiting factor for the increase in possible agricultural and/or mining output in either region. By AD 900, what was initially the resettlement of a few Tiwanaku households from the Chen Chen and Omo settlements into Wari-controlled territories had grown into neighborhood enclaves of multiethnic Tiwanaku groups (fig. 8.1; Goldstein and Owen 2001; Owen 1999; Williams and Nash 2002).

The Effects of Tiwanaku Settlements in the Upper Moquegua Valley (AD 800–1050)

Tiwanaku migration from the middle valley to the upper valley suggests a political and social disruption of Tiwanaku authority in Moquegua. The loss of some Tiwanaku laborers to the Wari state might not have debilitated the state's political economy, but this rebellious relocation occurred at a time when the Tiwanaku capital's interests in Moquegua were leading to the intensification of agricultural production. The fact that Chen Chen elites were trying to consolidate Tiwanaku control through the propagation of artifacts bearing state motifs and investments in large-scale elite architecture throughout the middle valley settlements did little to stop the resettlement of a subset of the Tiwanaku population. The Tiwanaku settlers entered the upper valley as individual families and lived alongside Wari laborers in commoner complexes adjacent to the Wari agricultural canal.

The earliest Tiwanaku occupation on the flanks of Cerro Baúl dates to the first half of the ninth century. However, the preponderance of dates for other Tiwanaku household and temple contexts in the upper valley suggests that many Tiwanaku migrants arrived later, between AD 850 and 900 (Williams and Nash 2002). While the exact number of Tiwanaku settlers is uncertain, the excavation of four Tiwanaku households and two temples as well as visible surface ceramic scatters along the northern flanks of Cerro Baúl support the idea that Chen Chen and other Tiwanaku ethnic groups eventually settled in large numbers. The largest surface scatters of Chen Chen ceramics are concentrated in settlements below the Wari canal, away from the earlier households of Tiwanaku and Wari occupations in areas that had been agricultural fields. The excavated Chen Chen ceramics from the flanks of Cerro Baúl incorporated the motifs and forms associated with contemporary Tiwanaku assemblages found in the middle valley (fig. 8.3:1, 2, 4); a few examples that do not conform to Tiwanaku styles were also recovered (fig. 8.3:C). Common decorative themes include the interlocking L-bar design, continuous volutes (fig. 8.3:4), S-shaped designs (fig. 8.3:2), and multicolored birds, most of which were painted on red-slipped backgrounds. The use of polychromes (i.e., black, cream, orange) and the quality of manufacture are consistent with Chen Chen traditions, unlike later Tumilaca wares whose ceramic motifs use fewer colors and are poorly executed. Notably absent from the excavated assemblages are vessels with state emblems (i.e., Front Face Deity or Puma Head; fig. 8.3:B) and highly decorated serving or ritual wares (i.e., *incensarios* and portrait head vessels), which would have suggested ideological/political connections with the middle-valley Tiwanaku institutions.

Situated one hundred to four hundred meters downhill from the Tiwanaku households on former Wari agricultural fields are two rudimentary temple structures (one of which has been interpreted as the upper valley's version of the Omo ritual platform and temple; Owen 1999) that are assumed to have been constructed by Tiwanaku migrants. Construction of this building was apparently not state sponsored, since its architectural layout, quality, and mode of construction are very different from its larger and well-constructed middle-valley counterpart. That the two temples are located within Wari agricultural fields is significant, suggesting that the Wari administration approved or tolerated their construction and use.

In addition to the temples, nondomestic architecture has been found at a small Tiwanaku administrative site built on the end of a prominent ridge off the northern base of the Cerro Baúl mountain. This site (Site 308;

Owen 1996) was located downhill from the domestic areas, at the northern edge of the Wari terrace-field systems. Site 308 had a dozen or so small terrace platforms recorded by the author that were strategically placed to observe activities on the Wari terraces and the Torata River floodplain. The site's surface was scattered with numerous stone hoes and decorated Tiwanaku drinking cups and bowls. The absence of domestic architecture and utilitarian household artifacts and the high incidence of painted cups and bowls suggest that the site functioned as an administrative locale for local Tiwanaku populations working in the Wari fields and in the Torata River floodplain.

For more than two hundred years, Tiwanaku migrants resided in the upper valley and contributed to the Wari political economy. The fact that very little evidence of Wari material culture has been recovered from the middle-valley Tiwanaku sites (Burger et al. 2000; Garcia 1990; Goldstein and Owen 2001), together with the absence of Tiwanaku political motifs on ceramics from the upper valley, minimizes the likelihood that these groups were either delegates or part of a trade diaspora (Stein 1999) from the Tiwanaku state in the middle valley. Their political allegiance and economic obligations to the Tiwanaku state are not evident; rather, these settlers appear as emigrants who chose to pursue their interests in what may have been a more stable economy (Williams 2002).

Current data suggest that Tiwanaku clients initially entered the Wari political economy as small independent family clusters that lived and worked alongside Wari laborers. Eventually the number of Tiwanaku settlers located within the Wari complex increased and became spatially removed from neighboring Wari families. Tiwanaku families settled on agricultural lands below the Wari canal line, where they constructed their two small temples and a specialized administrative site. I suggest that the impressive growth of Tiwanaku settlement in the upper valley, along with the construction of nondomestic buildings, represents the gradual development of a Tiwanaku elite authority under Wari rule. Tiwanaku elite authority within the Wari political economy was probably specific to agricultural tasks, since there is no evidence for this group's participation in state mining or craft production activities.

The development of an embedded Tiwanaku administrative group that directly managed the agricultural fields would have been a sensible policy for the Wari elite. The progressive reduction in the total size of the Wari administrative apparatus (i.e., the abandonment of Cerro Mejía) could have been compensated for by allowing Tiwanaku clients to develop specialized manager/leaders who could organize laborers and serve as intermediaries between upper-level Wari elites and Tiwanaku commoner groups. From AD 850 to 1050, the management of Tiwanaku households in the upper valley gradually became part of the political purview of emerging Tiwanaku leaders who, through the use of specialized administrative sites and temples, were able to extend their authority beyond the household, but only as far as the Wari state sanctioned.

With the abandonment of the Wari center at Cerro Baúl (ca. AD 1050), reorganizing these Tiwanaku communities would have been difficult for aspiring leaders. First, they would have had to reestablish their authority outside of the Wari political economy; and second, they would have had to face the fact that the legitimacy of Tiwanaku social and religious practices had been devalued for over a century (AD 950–1050), following the abandonment and destruction of the Tiwanaku state colony in the middle valley (Goldstein 1989a; Moseley et al. 1991).

Tiwanaku State Collapse as the Origins of Tumilaca Communities (AD 950)

The collapse of Tiwanaku state rule in the middle Moquegua Valley occurred circa AD 950 (Goldstein 1989a; Moseley et al. 1991; Owen and Goldstein 2001). Archaeologically, postcollapse Tiwanaku populations in Moquegua were labeled Tumilaca and initially were defined through seriation analysis of pottery described as poorly executed versions of earlier state wares (Goldstein 1985). One drawback of this classification was that the Tumilaca phase was defined by an event, the collapse of Tiwanaku state control in the valley, and not by a systematic shift in attributes between assemblages. As a result, identifying Tumilaca ceramics rested on the assumption that poorly crafted materials were the result of poststate economic recession. Biologically, Tumilaca populations are discussed as the descendants of Tiwanaku populations, with little acknowledgement that local Huaracane (prestate indigenous people) and Wari settlers could also be involved (cf. Lozada and Buikstra 2002 for an alternative interpretation of Tumilaca ceramics and biogenetic communities for the coast). As a result, "Tumilaca" has come to stand for a time period (Goldstein and Owen 2001; Owen and Goldstein 2001; Stanish 1992), a ceramic phase (Goldstein 1985), a settlement pattern (Owen 1993, 1996), a community of people (Bawden 1993), and political processes associated with state collapse and the degradation of a cultural tradition (Bermann et al. 1989; Goldstein 1989b; Moseley et al. 1991). Here, the name Tumilaca will refer to post-Tiwanaku and/or post-Wari communities that existed in the Moquegua Valley from AD 950 until 1200, as well as their material culture.

While Tumilaca ceramic styles are derived from Tiwanaku themes, Tumilaca potters eliminated all symbols associated with the Tiwanaku state and classic Tiwanaku culture (fig. 8.3:A; Goldstein 1985), particularly the Tiwanaku Front Face Deity and Puma Head (fig. 8.3:B), which are elite markers of the Tiwanaku state. The absence of these motifs implies the rejection of state ideology by Tumilaca elites and commoners, as had been the case with the Tiwanaku migrants discussed above (Bermann et al. 1989; Moseley et al. 1991).

Archaeologists have also documented widespread and systematic destruction of many Tiwanaku households and temples, as well as the digging up of Tiwanaku cemeteries (Goldstein 1989a; Moseley et al. 1991). Presumably, the sudden emergence of the new ceramic tradition and the regional destruction of Tiwanaku sites indicate that the end of the Tiwanaku regime was accompanied by a large-scale transformation in rituals and belief systems. Collapse appears as the transformation of local Tiwanaku groups into an assertive and independent set of Tumilaca communities whose ethnic identity—although derived from Tiwanaku—was founded in a new and independent political organization.

Tumilaca populations expanded well beyond the territories previously under the aegis of Tiwanaku, settling between the coastal and highland regions of the Moquegua Valley (Owen 1993, 1996; Owen and Menaut 2002). The four groups of Tumilaca settlements—coastal, lower valley, middle valley, and upper valley—occupied areas adjacent to the most productive floodplains (fig. 8.1). The dispersal of these middle-valley populations decentralized the system of agricultural production that had developed under the Tiwanaku state. Any attempt to reconstitute a centralized agricultural system in the middle valley would have had to reconcentrate labor in this depopulated area. But that task would have been difficult under the direction of a Tumilaca polity; regional settlement patterns supply no evidence of a centralized Tumilaca administration (Bermann et al. 1989; Goldstein 1989b; Moseley et al. 1991), and Tumilaca sites lacked the administrative and religious installations that might have served to integrate multiple households and communities under a single manager.

Tumilaca and Wari State Interaction in the Upper Moquegua Valley (AD 950–1050)

In contrast to the Tumilaca migrants who settled on the coast and along the lower valleys or remained in the middle valley, the Tumilaca who migrated to the upper valley circa AD 950 were faced with the continued presence of the Wari state at Cerro Baúl. A recently excavated household with Tumilaca ceramics located near the Cerro Baúl administrative sector suggests that Cerro Baúl became a refuge for some Tumilaca families (Williams and Nash 2002), while a second group of Tumilaca migrants from the middle valley founded small communities (1.0–1.5 ha) south of Cerro Baúl. Santa Rita, excavated by the writer, and other Tumilaca sites along the Tumilaca River were founded along the floodplains, distant from Wari agricultural activity.

Tumilaca farmers exploiting the Tumilaca River floodplain had only half the area (50–70 ha) of what was available to Tiwanaku settlers from the AD 800 migration living along the Torata River (>150 ha). These Tumilaca populations did not benefit from the extensive Wari agricultural system, making them more susceptible to the fluctuations in highland rainfall patterns and loss of topsoils during infrequent high-energy river floods. The Tumilaca villages had a more restricted economy unaccompanied by state-run canals and terraces, and their participation in the Wari political economy was less pronounced than that of the AD 800 Tiwanaku migrants.

Excavated household data from Santa Rita further support the idea that the Tumilaca communities operated independently of Wari administration. The village appears to have been managed by local families and to have lacked specialized administrative and religious structures. Unlike the northern Tiwanaku migrants, who constructed administrative and religious structures adjacent to the Torata River, the Tumilaca groups were developing administrative practices that were not dependent on an overarching Wari political system.

A multiroom elite residential compound at Santa Rita included a specialized cooking area, a storage shed for agricultural and hunting tools, and a reception hall/domestic unit. The latter room contained an assortment of highly decorated serving, drinking, and eating vessels as well as spindle whorls and storage and cooking vessels. The presence of ritual and domestic artifacts on the floor indicates that this locale doubled as a venue for ritual and domestic activities. The kitchen was presumably devoted to the preparation of large quantities of food and beverages prepared for elite individuals of the village. In the past, as today, the sponsorship of ritual feasts was a common practice for Andean elites who wanted to secure labor obligations and tribute commitments from their constituencies. In addition, elites who could recruit a troop of workers to perform a task also assumed the cost of provisioning food and drink for the laborers while they were at work on a project (Abercrombie 1998; Isbell 1977; Moseley 1992). In these cases, elites were bound by kinship and local tradition (Murra 1962:2), and their failure to supply provisions could result in challenges to their authority (Saignes 1986). Tumilaca villages thus appear to have had a new type of political organization focused on elite households rather than specialized nondomestic venues.

Wari State Collapse and Two Alternatives for Upper-valley Political Practice (AD 1050)

Up to the time of Wari collapse, at least two different administrative systems existed in the upper Moquegua Valley. One was that used by the Tiwanaku migrants who had settled in Wari territory circa AD 800; they developed a system of administration that required special-purpose locales above the household level, integrating elite households under a single centralized political order. This strategy is consistent with the administrative practices that had been introduced by Tiwanaku and Wari.

One might suggest that Tiwanaku elites in the northern territory of the Cerro Baúl complex could have used this strategy of specialized administration to reconstitute a system of authority during the post-Tiwanaku, post-Wari Tumilaca period in the upper valley (AD 1050–1200). To accomplish this, the leaders of the Tiwanaku migrants would have had to develop the economic and political means of implementing institutional frameworks from the Wari political economy. However, Gil Stein notes (1999:57, following P. Kohl) that tools and techniques are more readily exchanged between regions than are organizational forms, which are "so embedded in cultural value systems, they are often difficult to assimilate into the preexisting social and cultural schemata of the borrowing polity." I would argue that similar constraints were at work for the upper-valley Tiwanaku who were attached to the Wari political economy, even though the transmission occurred over time rather than between regions. The Tiwanaku migrants who had settled within the Wari complex since AD 800 were able to assimilate the tools and techniques for canal and terrace irrigation but would have faced a greater challenge in reestablishing a sustainable specialized administration in the poststate period. Because of their position in the Wari political economy, the Tiwanaku migrants enjoyed economic stability and the ability to engage in Tiwanaku religious and cultural practices that had been violently rejected by Tumilaca groups elsewhere. According to the principle of administrative underdevelopment, however, the marginal and specialized nature of the occupational roles that the Tiwanaku migrants occupied within the Wari political economy would have inhibited them from maintaining or re-creating equivalent administrative institutions after state collapse.

In contrast, Tumilaca residents in the upper valley settled at a greater distance from the Wari domain and developed a system of suprahousehold management by elite residential compounds where domestic economies were, in Marshall Sahlins's (1972:130) terms, "mobilized in a larger social cause." The ideological foundations of household organization were expanded to encompass the political and economic needs of village-level organization, and the domestic economy was intensified through ritual events linking elites and commoners in a reciprocal labor system. In these cases, general household practices became specialized activities to intensify the production of surplus goods, critical for labor exchange systems that maintained social networks beyond the immediate family (Costin 1998:10). This system offered an alternative to the Tiwanaku migrant strategy; local politics and labor were reorganized without being embedded in a state administrative apparatus. In this way, Tumilaca domestic/village administration was less susceptible to the structural disadvantages of communities for which organizational strategies were developed and legitimized within an overarching state political economy.

Postcollapse Upper-valley Tumilaca (AD 1050–1200)

After Wari retreated from the upper Moquegua Valley, the largest occupation was situated at the Tumilaca site of Cerro San Miguel. This site lies north of the Cerro Baúl complex, adjacent to the Torata River floodplain previously exploited by Wari and by Tiwanaku migrants. Tumilaca and Tiwanaku migrant communities were probably aggregated at Cerro San Miguel. As is usual with Tumilaca sites, there is no evidence of specialized administrative architecture (Owen 1999). In the wake of Wari retreat, the founders of Cerro San Miguel seem to have abandoned political practices grounded in state administration strategies and instead opted for household-based administration. The administrative limits of the

household-based system of earlier Tumilaca villages were overcome, however, through the incorporation of four times as many households than had
previously been organized in a single Tumilaca village.

Post-Tumilaca Organization (AD 1200–1450)

The Moquegua Valley did not experience political recentralization in the
Tumilaca period, which is best described as a village system of balkanized
political units with little or no supravillage authority (Bermann et al. 1989).
All the Tumilaca sites were abandoned by the end of the twelfth century AD,
and the valley was occupied by the Estuquiña culture between AD 1200 and
1300 (Bawden 1993; Stanish 1992).

The shift from Tumilaca to Estuquiña is abrupt and represents a cultural
replacement with absolutely no continuity of Tumilaca cultural traditions.
As with Tumilaca, Estuquiña regional settlement patterns show no evidence
of a centralized political system (Stanish 1992), nor are there identifiable
administrative or religious structures above the level of the household. Not
until the Inca invaded Moquegua circa AD 1450 was the valley recentralized
(Bürgi 1993; Covey 2000).

Implications of the Data

The development of Tumilaca administrative systems appears to have been
directly affected by the relationship between Wari administrators on the
one hand and Tiwanaku migrants and Tumilaca communities on the other.
Tiwanaku migrants in the upper valley from the AD 800 influx remained
in midlevel agricultural administrative positions within the Wari political
economy. Neither Tiwanaku migrants nor Tumilaca groups ever occupied
top-level administrative posts within the Wari administration; instead, they
were state clients with limited occupational roles or had indirect ties to the
political and economic apparatus at Cerro Baúl. Once the Wari state dis-
solved, the remaining Tumilaca and Tiwanaku elites—an amalgam of petty
leaders and midlevel managers—were confronted by social constraints that
limited their ability to establish a centralized polity. For the upper Moquegua Valley, the Tumilaca system of household politics was a more viable and less socially challenging option for the foundations of a poststate
system.

The concept of administrative underdevelopment helps to isolate the
underlying social constraints that would-be leaders would have had to con-

tend with after Tiwanaku and Wari collapsed in Moquegua. By focusing on the detailed interaction between communities and between their elites, we can analyze collapse and regeneration as events for which the trajectories are, in part, determined by the specific relationships between local and state administrators. After collapse, the potential to reestablish authority and administrative control would be tied to the parameters of elite authority as it existed before collapse.

The implication of these data is that regional systems must be understood over long time spans, allowing us to see both the political peaks and the troughs. Just as large regional studies and long time spans are essential in documenting the processes of collapse, regeneration, and the absence of regeneration, so is understanding the microlevel negotiations of authority between states and subject communities. After Wari and Tiwanaku retreated from the regions they had incorporated, some of those areas did not form secondary states. Regions such as these, where states do not regenerate, are just as critical for understanding political history as are those areas that go on to form state after state.

Acknowledgments

I am deeply grateful to the persistent support of my mentors, colleagues, and peers who have contributed to this chapter from start to finish. Most of all, I would like to thank Joyce Marcus, Glenn Schwartz, Norman Yoffee, and Alan Covey for their insightful comments of earlier (unsightly) drafts of the manuscript. My inability to do justice to all of their suggestions is entirely my own limitation; any errors in the text are, as always, entirely my own as well.

9 Patterns of Political Regeneration in Southeast and East Asia

Bennet Bronson

In the archaeologically visible history of Asia, there are numerous declines, apparent and real, and several patterns of regeneration. These may be divided into patterns of the false, stimulus, and template type.

There would seem to be two kinds of false regeneration, both of which may be hard for the archaeologist to recognize. The first is a situation in which a new complexly organized society appears in the same place as an earlier one but no historical connection between the two exists. One can imagine that this applies to any environment where settlements or larger units tend to recur in the same places owing to unusually favorable environmental conditions, access to a key resource, locations on the nodes of major trade routes, et cetera. In the dry lands of the ancient Levant through western India, for instance, settlements are remarkably persistent on given spots. As in the case of Jericho or any of tens of thousands of other mud-brick mounds or tells, all mounds composed of the debris of former settlements, whether abandoned or not, were consistently preferred as locations for new settlements. The same was true in ancient central Thailand, where there are very few settlements of the early historic period that do not rest on top of Metal Age settlements, even though the latter may have been deserted many hundreds of years before the former were built.

In Southwest Asia, already-built-up mounds may have been preferred for defensive reasons, but no one knows why low, indefensible mounds in Thailand show an almost equal persistence of settlement through major changes in artifacts and phases of apparent abandonment. In both Thailand and Southwest Asia, each incident of resettlement at a site could be interpreted as evidence of regeneration. However, documentary evidence in Southwest Asia shows that in many cases—for instance, the Persian levels at Gordion in Turkey—the resettlement represents an intrusive political unit from outside rather than a regenerated version of an earlier local polity.

In Thailand, similar conclusions may be drawn from the drastic nature of artifact changes that occurred every few hundred years from the early Metal Age in the late third millennium BC down through the protohistoric period in the first millennium AD. Site unit intrusion often seems a more plausible explanation than does regeneration.

A second type of false regeneration can occur where regional political structures are organized in such a way that complex nodes in the system are intrinsically evanescent, shifting from place to place every few decades, while the overall regional structure remains more or less constant. Insular-peninsular Southeast Asia provides a prime example. The region that stretches from 6 degrees south latitude to about 10 degrees north—including Sumatra, the Riau archipelago, East and West Malaysia, Kalimantan, and the southern Philippines—seems in the period 600–1500 AD to have been characterized by intense competition between similar trade-oriented political units, more or less statelike, variable in size, and all speaking Malay as a lingua franca, that appear, disappear, and reappear elsewhere with disconcerting rapidity. The fact that one among several such interchangeable units has declined may have been of significance only to the leaders of that particular unit. The populace, maritime in orientation and highly mobile, could easily move to another unit, and such outsiders as foreign traders were equally mobile and perhaps even less loyal to the endangered current polity. The point is that individual nodes may have reappeared in the same or different places and with the same or different names, but they were relatively unimportant within the regional system, and the system itself (acephalous, prosperous, and resilient) was not a candidate for regeneration in any ordinary sense. A rather similar situation is described by Lisa Cooper (chapter 2) in the northern Euphrates Valley, where a system of numerous autonomous, heterarchically organized sociopolitical units exhibited much greater resilience and continuity in the late third millennium BC than did the great kingdoms of central and southern Mesopotamia.

Stimulus regeneration, by contrast, is a real process though sometimes based on false facts. All historical reconstruction or revival involves an element of guesswork. It follows that all attempts at political regeneration are motivated partly by the stimulus of diachronic hearsay, an unsubstantiated rumor that something used to be done in a particular fashion. This hearsay, composed of hazy historical memories that may or may not be accurate, serves to convince leaders that a higher degree of centralization is possible and to make that centralization more palatable by wrapping it in the mantle of a glorious past. However, the connection between the past model and the present reconstruction, however much emphasized, is bound to be somewhat exiguous if not actually fictional. The Holy Roman Empire is an example: in reality it was holy and imperial enough but, even when it controlled central Italy, not at all Roman. The United States of the 1780s is another example. It adopted much of the terminology of the Roman republic in spite of having vastly different social, cultural, and environmental circumstances and in spite of the fact that surviving records of the Roman republic were far too scanty for that political system to serve as a usable model for the government of a village, much less that of a nation.

Neither the Holy Roman Empire nor the early United States is a pure case of stimulus regeneration, and in fact, pure cases may not exist. Such cases would have to represent the ab ovo creation of a full-blown state in a geographical and social setting where no immediately antecedent complex society had existed and where a historical stimulus—the abstract knowledge that states had once existed among that people or in that place—was a prime cause of political re-formation. The Zulu empire of Shaka might constitute such a case if, as has sometimes been claimed, he was aware of the example of Great Zimbabwe or other early South African kingdoms. However, Shaka's empire, if indeed it represents regeneration of some kind, is one of the very rare pure cases, whereas partial cases are very common. As noted below, most instances of regeneration contain an element of fantasy or at least unrealism about the past that has been deliberately introduced to legitimize institutions that are actually brand-new borrowings or innovations. In spite of what the regenerators say, the real models must usually be contemporary polities, perhaps belonging to enemies, rather than the polities said to have belonged to the regenerators' own ethnic group at some point in the distant, poorly recorded past.

An interesting case of a newly invented state that claimed to be a revival rather than a new invention is that of the Jurchen or Manchus of Northeast Asia, who began the process of state formation in the 1580s and by the 1640s were ready to attack and conquer China. They succeeded in their conquest and went on to rule China as the Qing dynasty from 1647 to 1911. The original founders of the Manchu state, Nurhaci (active from 1583 to 1626) and Hongtaiji (ruler from 1626 to 1643), consistently sought to present their government as a revival of hazily remembered "barbarian" empires ruled by the dynasties of the Khitan Liao (907–1125), the Jurchen Jin (1115–1234) and the Mongol Yuan (1271–1368). This pedigree was not entirely fictional, as Nurhaci and Hongtaiji may have had Mongol blood and were themselves members of the ethnic congeries still known at that time as the Jurchen.

However, they had little information about any of those historical empires and showed no real interest in getting it.

In reality, Nurhaci and Hongtaiji built their state partly from scratch and partly by liberal borrowing from their traditional enemy, the Ming empire, on the periphery of which they lived. Both leaders, with Hongtaiji's talented half-brother Dorgon, were brilliant innovators: among the most talented social engineers in the history of any region. In only several decades, they worked out not only a formidable multiethnic military and political system but also a comprehensive ideology of mission that would put most modern corporations to shame. The ideology, while in fact newly cut from whole cloth, was claimed to be a revival of the ideology of the Jurchen Jin empire of five hundred years before. The military and political system too was a newly minted creation, a hybrid of diffusion and innovation from scratch described by the innovators as a regenerated version of the Mongol and Jin empires. The new system enabled Dorgon in 1644 to overthrow the Ming dynasty with relative ease.

The opposite of stimulus regeneration is template regeneration, whereby the revival process adheres closely to a fully understood, well-recorded model. Although Egypt under the Old and Middle Kingdoms presents interesting parallels (however, see E. Morris, chapter 4), China offers the classic, extreme case of repeated template regeneration. In the last 2,200 years, China's periods of cohesion were regularly separated by lengthy periods of marked decentralization and loss of complexity, yet each of those periods of "decline" was followed with seeming inevitability by a regenerated empire that was very similar to the one that had preceded it a century or two before. The similarity extended to details of government organization, institutions, language, cultural manifestations, and style. The key was widespread literacy and the existence of accessible historical records that provided a sufficiently detailed blueprint for the preexisting system to be more or less fully reconstructed. One could perhaps argue that the regenerated Sui-Tang state (AD 581–906) that grew from the chaos of the first dark age in Chinese dynastic history, the Three Kingdoms and Six Dynasties period (220–581), did not fully replicate the preceding Han state (206 BC–AD 220). However, later regenerated states—the Song (960–1279) and Ming (1368–1644)—were faithful copies of their pre–dark age predecessors, the Tang and Song. So faithful were those copies that Chinese historians have traditionally maintained that China constituted a single political and cultural entity throughout the imperial period of its history, from 221 BC to AD 1911. The fact that ordinary Chinese have traditionally maintained this as well has helped and still helps in resisting fissiparous tendencies and maintaining territorial integrity.

Similar patterns characterize the other major states of East Asia: Korea, Vietnam, and Japan. The first two have experienced the same kind of periodic dissolution and have come together again as readily as China. The last, Japan, may not have suffered an equivalent level of dissolution during its various times of troubles, perhaps because, as a result of its isolation, there were no near neighbors waiting to take advantage of the troubles and deepen the dissolution. Yet all three countries have experienced similar cycles and have had little trouble in regenerating states that were in most essentials very much like the states that preceded them. As in the case of China, the explanation lies in the quality of written records. Enough details of institutions and procedures survived for the task of regeneration to be relatively straightforward.

A somewhat similar case is provided by the western Roman empire in the three and half centuries from Augustus through Diocletian and Constantine, and by the eastern Roman or Byzantine empire from the reign of Justinian in the sixth century through that of Basil II in the eleventh century. Although neither empire suffered actual dissolution of its full political structure during those time spans, both showed exceptional capacity for revitalization after sharp declines. As in East Asia, their resilience had much to do with good records and strong traditions of continuity.

In contrast, the decline of the western Roman empire after the fourth century was too complete for anything like simple revitalization to be possible. The only hopes for a revived Roman empire in the West had been reconquest by the Eastern Empire or thoroughgoing regeneration. The first proved to be impossible, in spite of the efforts of a series of talented Byzantine military leaders. The second turned out to be equally impossible, at least partly because so much—the former bureaucracy, fiscal and legal systems, much of the population, most of the records, and even the skills in reading and writing needed to make use of whatever records survived—had been irretrievably lost (Schwartz, chapter 1). Hence, the would-be regenerators—the Merovingians, Carolingians, Ottonians, and their ilk—not only had very limited resources, as one would expect in the early stages of most regeneration situations, but also had much less information about how Rome in the days of its success had actually been run. It is even possible that their information was sometimes deliberately distorted by religious advisors, who had a near-monopoly on literacy as well as agendas of their own. The result was that the regenerators had to do a great deal of improvising. Some such improvisations, as in the case of Charlemagne's many reforms, were ingenious and successful. Some, like the Frankish legal system, were straightforward copies of genuine Roman institutions. But in spite of

Charlemagne's own claims to the contrary, his Roman empire was more of a new invention than a regenerated version of classical Rome.

One of Charlemagne's problems was that there were no highly organized political units near enough to northwestern Europe for him to observe them in operation. In many regeneration situations, the would-be regenerator has available not only a template based on written or oral records of varying quality, but also observations of neighboring, currently more-centralized societies. In a sense, the organization of these societies also constitutes a kind of historical template.

The borrowing of organizational models from one's neighbors is exceedingly common in ethnopolitical history. Though not ordinarily considered a mode of regeneration, borrowing can play a central part in the maintaining of the regional models, detailed enough to count as templates, that have been applied and reapplied repeatedly by societies within a given region over periods of many centuries. Examples include kingdoms in the Burma-Thailand-Laos-Cambodia-Assam region, the historical states of South Asia, and indeed states and statelike units in most other regions with enduring political patterns, such as northwestern Europe, the northern Mediterranean, the Middle East, and Mesoamerica. At a given time, any such region is likely to contain a number of individual political units that rise and fall in an unsynchronized fashion, with some reaching an apogee of success while their neighbors, quite possibly because of competition from successful units, fall into deep decay or dissolution. In such regional systems, regeneration and new generation are normal events, both based on the use of currently successful units as models. The currently successful units, however, are themselves modeled on past successful units, and those in turn have used models even further in the past. In this way, political units themselves serve as historical records, transcribed afresh with the rise of each new or regenerated kingdom. Although the transcription is undoubtedly imperfect, the models—being actual functioning polities—are not only highly detailed but also convincingly workable. One could argue that chains of overlapping political units are as effective a device for maintaining regenerative continuity as are the detailed written records kept by East Asian and to a lesser extent Middle Eastern, Mediterranean, and northwestern European societies.

It is not always true that complexly organized polities will be regenerated after a decline (see, for example, the case of Tumilaca in ancient Peru; Sims, chapter 8). In regions with traditions of state organization and more or less widely accepted organizational models, regeneration may be a predictable process, aborted only by large-scale disasters like the demographic decline and political turmoil that occurred in western Europe between the fourth and seventh centuries. In other regions, however, declines may be permanent, without a subsequent regeneration. Most possible cases of this kind have occurred in regions without a tradition of complex political organization, such as eastern North America, southern Africa, and perhaps Oceania or prehistoric northern Eurasia. Both the Hopewell culture of southern Ohio and the Zimbabwe culture of Africa have long seemed anomalously highly organized for their regions and periods. Both were eventually replaced by markedly less complex polities and did not regenerate. Perhaps we may hazard the generalization that such abortive efforts at increasing political complexity were commonplace in earlier periods of centralization and intensification, before usable models had been developed and before methods of documenting continuity, such as writing, had come into being.

10

From Funan to Angkor
Collapse and Regeneration in Ancient Cambodia
Miriam T. Stark

The cyclical quality of ancient states (Adams 1988; Feinman 1998; Marcus 1998; Yoffee 1988b) is abundantly evident in mainland Southeast Asia, where multiple and overlapping histories of collapse and regeneration characterized the region from the first millennium AD onward (Hutterer 1982:562; Stark and Allen 1998). Many areas experienced this first pulse of state formation, from the Irawaddy River valley of Myanmar and the Chao Phraya delta of Thailand to the Bac Bo region of northern Vietnam. The archaeological record of early Southeast Asia involves nucleated settlements and religious monuments that suggest a close articulation of religious ideology and sociopolitical organization (see also Hagesteijn 1996:187).

The very monumentality of the ninth–fourteenth century Angkorian empire may explain why scholarship on ancient Cambodia continues to focus on the latter period of ancient Khmer civilization rather than on its earlier periods. Yet the Angkorian state represents the endpoint in a 1,500-year developmental sequence, the beginnings of which lie in the late prehistoric period. From the mid first millennium AD onward, Khmers constructed brick, stone, and laterite monuments with dedicatory stelae bearing Khmer, Sanskrit, or Khmer and Sanskrit inscriptions; these constitute the primary indigenous documentary source. Conventional historiography (e.g., Briggs 1951; Coedès 1968; Wheatley 1983) depends inordinately on Chinese documentary evidence rather than on indigenous inscriptions to reconstruct ancient Khmer history. Resultant reconstructions are problematic (Jacques 1979:371; Stark 1998), as Chinese dynastic annals describe "kingdoms" that emissaries encountered, while most indigenous inscriptions record the beneficence of aspiring elite individuals.

While the Chinese documentary record focuses on periods of political consolidation and dissolution through time, indigenous documents emphasize long-term political unity and continuity. Beginning no later than the mid first millennium AD, individual Khmer states rose and fell for more than nine centuries. External documentary sources misrepresent the region's actual history, which counterpoised conflict and power struggles of individual rulers against persistent social and ideological institutions for many centuries (Vickery 1998; Wolters 1979).

If Khmer states were inherently fragile, then what accounts for the persistence of the Khmer civilization for more than a thousand years? And, following George Cowgill (1988:275), how closely was the Angkorian longevity connected to degrees and kinds of economic, political, and social integration?

This chapter examines the nature of collapse and regeneration in ancient Cambodia by identifying points of continuity and discontinuity in the sequence. Sociopolitical change in ancient Khmer civilization appears to have assumed two primary forms: (1) collapse and regeneration of economic and social institutions that mark the life spans of individual "states" (some of which the Chinese described), and (2) some continuity in elites' practice of Indic religious ideologies to legitimate their claims to power, which ordered the political organization of the first- and second-millennium Khmer states.[1]

That continuity in the "cultural matrix" (Wolters 1999) characterizes the ancient Khmer civilization through time is becomingly increasingly clear as research on ancient Cambodia accelerates. This syncretism melded aspects of Indic ideology with an emergent Khmer cultural identity and was embodied in elite practice and temple construction. It proved instrumental in regenerating Khmer states during the turbulence that characterized Cambodia's early history.

Historical Sequence

Cambodia's ancient history is among the least known in Southeast Asia, owing to decades of civil war and a parochial, colonialist tradition of historiography that has only recently been challenged. Most scholars have relied on external documentary sources such as Chinese annals, contemporary inscriptions (in Sanskrit and Khmer), and retrospective Angkorian period allusions to the pre-Angkorian period to reconstruct a dynastic history of Khmer civilization. Problems are inherent in taking either the inscriptions or the Chinese sources literally or privileging one source over the other (Jacques 1979, 1995; Vickery 1994, 1998). Both sources probably sought to elevate existing polities to kingdom status: the former out of self-aggrandizement and legitimation, and the latter out of self-promotion.

Archaeological research has played a secondary role in studying the Cambodian historical sequence, for political as well as historical reasons. Yet archaeological research in neighboring Thailand documents a continuous trend toward increasing complexity in the first millennium BC and the emergence of relatively stratified societies by the time of contact with South Asia (Higham 2002:193–212).

The name "Funan" was applied to the earliest state in the Mekong delta (fig. 10.1), which emissaries visited during the third and sixth centuries AD (Coedès 1968; Pelliot 1903). Chinese annals and indigenous inscriptions (in Khmer and in Sanskrit) also document a successor state to Funan in the lower Mekong basin that materialized in the seventh century AD along the banks of the Mekong River in central Cambodia. The third polity appeared two centuries later in the northwestern region of the country and is known as Angkor. Its florescence after the ninth century AD and collapse six centuries later created the Khmer empire, the largest territorial entity in mainland Southeast Asia. A growing body of archaeological and historical research on these polities is forcing scholars to revise their conventional models of political structure and process.

Cultural Chronology

The following periods demarcate the political history of ancient Cambodia (table 10.1): (1) the early historic period, which straddles the boundary between the Iron Age and the historic period; (2) the pre-Angkorian period, a term that Cambodian scholars have used for nearly a century; (3) the early Angkorian period, to designate the period during which the Angkorian polity was established and developed; and (4) the mature Angkorian period, to identify the period of the Khmer empire's greatest expansion. The Khmer empire did not collapse until some point during the mid fifteenth century, but the period after AD 1250 is excluded because this era involved a gradual decline in the political and economic prominence of the region from which the Khmer state never recovered.

The term "state" is used here to refer to a polity characterized by at least two classes of social strata, in which the government is centralized and specialized (following Feinman 1998). Determining scalar differences between successive Cambodian states is essential to understanding their structure, where scale refers to the extent of territorial integration (follow-

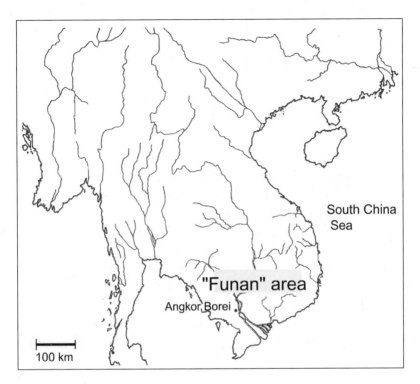

Figure 10.1 Mainland Southeast Asia during the early first millennium AD (after Hall 1985).

Table 10.1 Temporal framework for Southeast Asia

Time period	Date range	Cultural development
Early Historic	~500 BC–~AD 500	Origin of earliest state and development of international maritime trade
Pre-Angkorian	AD 500–~800	Adoption of indigenous writing and expansion of early states
Early Angkorian	AD 802–1000	Founding and expansion of the Khmer empire
Mature Angkorian	AD 1001–1250	Florescence of the Khmer empire

ing Adams 1988:23). Lack of systematic archaeological survey precludes the construction of standard site distributional maps. The following maps instead combine well-documented sites with dated inscriptions to indicate the geographic extent (but not the precise configuration) of each of these periods of time.[2]

The Early Historic Period and the Rise of "Funan"

One of the earliest and most important polities in this process emerged in the rich alluvial lowlands of the Mekong delta of southern Cambodia and Vietnam. Described in detail by visiting Chinese emissaries (Pelliot 1903) and linked intimately to the international maritime trade network that circulated goods from China to Rome, the Mekong delta formed an economic and administrative hub in the region from the early to the mid first millennium AD. This was a time of international maritime trade, with overland and ocean routes that linked Han China with the Roman empire through South and Southeast Asia (Ray 1989, 1994; Smith 1999).

South Asian religious and political ideas also diffused eastward into Southeast Asia during this period. Indic statuary, Sanskrit-derived scripts, and brick monuments are materializations of this trend that vary in form from one region to the next. As one example, pre-eighth-century Vishnu sculptures have been recovered from a broad geographic region that begins in the Mekong delta, extends south along peninsular Thailand and Malaysia, and ends in western Java (Dalsheimer and Manguin 1998:106–7; Lavy 2003). Despite regional variation in Vishnu sculptures, the shared iconography partly resembles fourth-century Pallava styles from the Andhra coast of eastern India (Ray 1989:53) and reflects a widespread economic and ideological network.

South and Southeast Asia formed critical interstitial zones for this interaction. Archaeological evidence suggests that complex polities that might be described as early states emerged by the early first millennium AD, after a protracted period of internal political development that involved intra-regional trade networks (Christie 1990, 1995; Higham 2002:168–227). These early states appeared during a time when economic relations between South and Southeast Asia seem to have become regularized (Bellina 1998, 2003; Glover 1996).

After a six-decade research hiatus caused by the Indochinese conflict and subsequent civil war, archaeological research in both Cambodia and Vietnam has begun to document occupational sequences between circa 500

BC and AD 500, or the early historic period (Stark 1998). Since 1975, archaeologists have documented a substantial number of archaeological sites dating to this period throughout the Mekong delta (Dao Lin Côn 1998; Ha Van Tan 1986; Trinh Thi Hoà 1996). The indigenous documentary record for this period is thin; only three to four inscriptions, all in Sanskrit, predate the seventh century in southern Cambodia and southern Vietnam (Vickery 1998:37).

Figure 10.2 uses well-dated archaeological sites and inscriptions to provide the approximate boundaries of these early historic polities, which extended east into Vietnam and perhaps as far west as the Chao Phraya river basin (Thailand): the area traditionally known as Funan is hatched. Knowledge of "Funan" derives almost exclusively from Chinese dynastic histories that were written during the early to mid first millennium AD (Ishizawa 1995; Pelliot 1903).[3]

The only reliable histories for Funan date from the third and sixth centuries, when Chinese records describe Funan as a polity with protourban centers (Pelliot 1903; Wheatley 1983:123). Chinese emissaries described multiple and competing capitals that housed substantial populations, arable lands, large walled and moated settlements that housed elites in their wooden palaces, and libraries that were filled with documents. The annals recorded the existence of sculptors and scribes who worked in stone as well as the presence of sumptuary goods such as precious metals and pearls (Coedès 1968:40–42, 46–47; Malleret 1959, 1962; Pelliot 1903).

Evidence from archaeology and art history suggests that these early historic polities were centered in southern Cambodia and Vietnam (Ha Van Tan 1986; Stark 1998; Trinh Thi Hoà 1996). At least ninety "Oc Eo" period complexes have been recorded throughout southern Vietnam's Mekong delta (Vo Si Khai 2003); contemporary sites have been reported along the coasts of peninsular Siam with similar material culture. This peninsular region served as an important point in the Asian maritime route as early as the fourth century AD, and many trading settlements were established along its eastern shores, which faced the Mekong delta (Manguin 2004:296).

The Mekong delta's inland settlements, which today lie in Cambodia, are found along the edge of floodplains whose inundation each year lasted approximately six months and formed a natural irrigated agricultural system. Over several centuries, populations reaped great yields from the land (Pelliot 1903). Canal networks cut across the delta to link settlements and facilitate the movement of goods have now been documented in both Cambodia and Vietnam (Bishop et al. 2003; Bourdonneau 2003).

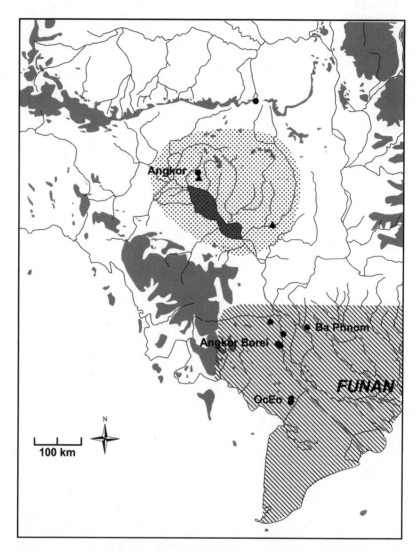

Figure 10.2 Proposed minimal geographic extent, based on extant distributional information on archaeological sites and inscriptions, of the Funan polity (marked with hatching) and a possible Tonle Sap polity (marked with dot pattern), early historic period. Gray areas indicate mountain ranges or islands, except for the area southwest of Angkor, which demarcates the Tonle Sap lake. Circles mark sites; triangles mark inscriptions.

To the south were probable coastal centers (ports) that negotiated maritime trade with foreigners, funneled sumptuary goods to the north, and received agricultural goods in exchange to feed traders and coastal populations whose local environment was not amenable to agriculture. Indian sources from the first millennium AD reported the Roman empire's demand for Southeast Asia's aromatic woods, camphor, and cloves (Ray 1989:47). China also sought these goods—among others—as well as western products that were transshipped through Southeast Asia (Hall 1992). With the collapse of the Han empire in the third century AD, Asia's maritime trade route via Southeast Asia became even more important (Manguin 2004:292).

The recovery of watercraft dated to the first millennium AD suggests that Southeast Asians had the maritime technology and seafaring knowledge to participate in the international maritime trade network. They may have even controlled commercial traffic in the South China Sea at this time. Remains of at least four traditional Southeast Asian sewn-plank watercraft have been recovered that yield radiocarbon dates from the first millennium AD (Manguin 1996:186).

Funan rulers were diplomats, warriors, and privileged trading partners with the Chinese. At least twenty-six embassies were sent from Funan to the imperial Chinese courts of the third century Wu and sixth century Sui dynasties (Ishizawa 1995:17). Each brought tribute or quasi-tribute with them.[4] Chinese annals also describe the battles that Funan rulers fought and the conquests that they made. These included expansion of their territories in the third century AD to include coastal trading settlements along the Gulf of Thailand and peninsular Malaysia, ensuring direct access to the Chinese markets (Pelliot 1903; see also Manguin 2004:297).

Most Funan rulers' names are lost to history, but one name that the Chinese recorded was the first (Kaundinya) Jayavarman, who ruled by or before AD 478 (Coedès 1968:57–58; Vickery 1998:70) and began what was to become a thousand-year Khmer rule of the region. Rudravarman, the last king of Funan, declared Angkor Borei his capital in AD 514 (Coedès 1968:60–61; Vickery 1998:45). Archaeological field investigations at Angkor Borei suggest that this settlement had already been occupied nearly a thousand years before Rudravarman came to power (Stark 2003; Stark and Bong 2001; Stark et al. 1999).

Chinese documentary evidence, indigenous inscriptions, and an emerging archaeological record suggest that the Mekong delta in the early first millennium AD comprised multiple competing polities rather than a single unified kingdom (e.g., Jacques 1979:376–77, 1990:257; Vickery 1998; Wheatley 1983:125–27). In frequent comparisons to a mandala structure, scholars argue that each polity was headed by a charismatic leader or "man of prowess" (following Wolters 1999) whose entourage constituted the core of a sociopolitical unit (Bentley 1986:292–93; Higham 1989; Tambiah 1976, 1977). This multicentric political configuration may represent an extension of heterarchical dynamics that structured polities of the mid to late first millennium BC throughout much of mainland Southeast Asia (Bronson 1979:320; Dalsheimer and Manguin 1998:104–5; Manguin 2002; White 1995; White and Pigott 1996). While such "polycentricity" characterizes many early states worldwide (Adams 2001:350), more systematic archaeological survey is needed in both Cambodia and Vietnam to find its signature in the delta's archaeological record.

From Funan to Chenla and the Pre-Angkorian Period

Chinese dynastic descriptions of the Funan state disappear in the mid sixth century AD, Tang dynastic records report the conquest of Funan by "Chenla" in the early seventh century AD (Ma Tuan-lin 1883), and archaeological evidence from the Funan port town of Oc Eo suggests that the settlement was abandoned by the mid seventh century (Manguin 2004:300). Population settlement, however, persisted throughout the Mekong delta: religious shrines in the hills above Oc Eo were probably used for five or six more centuries, and substantial settlement associated with brick shrines continued in the Angkor Borei region to the north (Stark and Bong 2004). This reported conquest of Funan may merely have been a dynastic dispute (Coedès 1968:68), and perhaps the "collapse" the Chinese describe was instead a geographic shift by Funan rulers to the north in response to declining trade returns as they sought to capitalize on newly opened trade routes to central Vietnam (Vickery 1998). The "end" of Funan corresponds closely with a southward shift in maritime trade networks to Sumatra and the rise of the trading empire of Srivijaya. The termination of Funan is also contemporaneous with a shift in overland trade networks that occurred when the Chinese gained control of trade routes across central Asia (Hall 1982, 1985); dating to this period as well is the first well-documented appearance of Indic statuary and architecture that scholars associate with "Indianization" in Southeast Asia (Manguin 2004:292).

In this period, large walled settlements containing ritual brick architecture appear farther north in the middle Mekong region of central Cambodia, but archaeological research has yet to date the construction and occupational histories of these sites. The subsequent kingdom of Chenla probably covered most of modern-day Cambodia (Vickery 1998:43). Approximately 150 inscriptions from the sixth through eighth centuries have been translated; of these, 76 were written in Khmer, 46 contain both Khmer and Sanskrit sections, 27 were written exclusively in Sanskrit, and 1 was written in the Pali language (Vickery 1998:91–92). Since Angkorian descendants of the Funan population spoke Khmer, some scholars (notably Vickery 1994) argue that the Funan population also spoke Khmer. In this scenario, Sanskrit served primarily as a liturgical language.

Figure 10.3 illustrates the distribution of archaeological sites and inscriptions dated to the sixth through the eighth century throughout modern-day Cambodia; the area traditionally recognized as Chenla is hatched. This pre-Angkorian period is poorly known from all viewpoints: archaeological, art historical, and historical. Almost no systematic archaeological research has been undertaken on pre-Angkorian sites, the period is not ushered in by distinctive art styles, and few indigenous inscriptions inform directly on political developments during this period (Vickery 1994:202–4). To reconstruct the Chenla period, previous historians (Briggs 1951; Coedès 1968:65–66) relied on Chinese annals, particularly the History of the Sui, or *Suishu*, which covered the years AD 581–617 and was compiled from AD 629 to 636 (Wilkinson 2000). They placed the Chenla capital to the north, in southern Laos at the site of Wat Phu (Coedès 1968:66).

The political organization of this period was probably less centralized yet more complex than French colonial scholars have portrayed it (Vickery 1994). At the least, Chenla was an "overgrown tribal confederacy" (Sedov 1978:113) of a militaristic character; at the most, seventh-century Chenla comprised a series of competing power centers rather than a single unified state. For example, Tang dynastic annals describe missions from "little countries of the Southern tribes" (Wolters 1974:357) that may have included as many as five pre-Angkorian polities in northwestern Cambodia alone. Leaders of these northwestern principalities vied with each other for power and were subjugated by Jayavarman I (son of Bhavavarman) after circa AD 655 (Vickery 1998:343–46; Wolters 1973, 1974). Nearly three decades after his death, his daughter Jayadevi ascended the throne. The political stability that followed remains anomalous in ancient Cambodia's rather turbulent political history.

Distributional patterning from the limited extant archaeological database provides evidence for ideological continuity from Funan to Chenla. Khmer and Sanskrit inscriptions suggest that local elites built and consecrated shrines

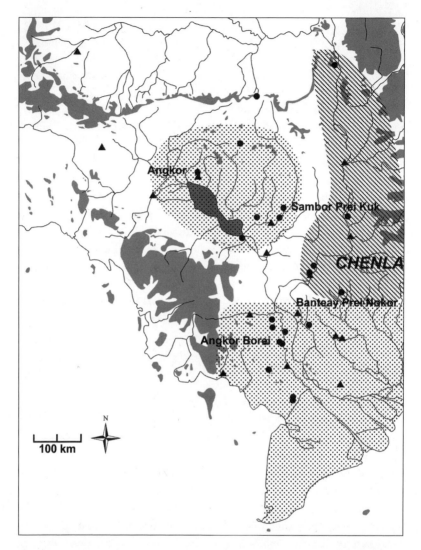

Figure 10.3 Proposed minimal geographic extent, based on extant distributional information on archaeological sites and inscriptions, of the Chenla polity (marked with hatching) and a possible Tonle Sap polity (marked with dot pattern in the area of Angkor), pre-Angkorian period. Gray areas indicate mountain ranges or islands, except for the area southwest of Angkor, which demarcates the Tonle Sap lake. Circles mark sites; triangles mark inscriptions.

and sanctuaries, inscribing their acts of generosity for posterity. Cambodians embraced both Hinduism and Buddhism after the fifth century AD, but the Vaishnavite and Saivite Hindu cults left a deeper material imprint than did Buddhism. The recovery of mitred Vishnu sculptures from sites in the Mekong delta and throughout the coastal peninsular region (Manguin 2004:303) suggests that Vaishnavism predominated to the south, while Saivism was embraced by populations north of the delta and around the Tonle Sap. The appearance of a fused Vishnu/Shiva deity called Harihara in the seventh century AD may signal ideological and political unification of these regions into ancient Cambodia for the first time (Lavy 2003).

Cambodia's rulers in these inscriptions bore Hindu or Vedic names, reflecting an early and intense assimilation of Brahmanical-Hindu ideology into the local ruling ideology. In their adoption of Hindu deities, pre-Angkorian rulers and elite individuals institutionalized some deeply held indigenous practices of ancestor worship (see review in Lavy 2003). That worship of these Indic deities was more important to the elite than to the commoners is likely, in part because of the elites' desire to participate in the Hindu cosmological world that visiting Vaishnavite teachers (*bhakti*) lyrically described (Wolters 1999:109–11). Sites for the construction of local temples and shrines to house Indic images were selected in part based on the location of ancestral spirits that commoners already worshipped. Vishnu and other Brahmanical deities, then, were superimposed on extant spirits (Aeusrivongse 1976:114–15) to produce sites of spiritual and political potency.

The distribution of dated archaeological sites and inscriptions indicates a shift in the center of settlement gravity northward by the mid seventh century AD. The first king of Chenla, Isanavarman, consecrated Indic images and established his first capital at the walled four-hundred-hectare settlement of Sambor Prei Kuk. Approximately two decades after the death of Isanavarman, his descendant Jayavarman II established his capital to the south at Banteay Prei Nokor (Coedès 1968:98; Vickery 1998:346).

The Rise of Angkor

Within a few decades, Jayavarman II moved northwest to the banks of the Tonle Sap. From the end of the eighth to the late ninth century (AD 791–877), almost no Khmer-language inscriptions were produced; vocabulary shifts also characterize this period (Vickery 1998:84–85). Philological evidence, then, suggests a kind of rupture that is poorly understood as yet.

Interestingly, the material record offers evidence for a reconfiguration of pre-existing social and ideological institutions. Notable among these is a shift in political leadership that involved the adoption of the *devaraja* rite and the establishment of a state religion in the form of the Saivite cult of the royal *lingas* on the temple pyramids of Angkor (see Kulke 1978). The direct relationship to the gods, especially Shiva, that this form of statecraft offered to Angkorian rulers gave them substantially more power and legitimacy than their predecessors had.

In declaring himself the Khmer people's *cakravartin,* or universal monarch, in AD 802, Jayavarman II became the first king of the Angkorian period. The dynastic history of the Angkorian state from the tenth century onward is well known and examined elsewhere in great detail (Boisselier 1966; Briggs 1951). Figure 10.4, based on a sample of dated archaeological sites and dated inscriptions, circumscribes the approximate geographic extent of the early Angkorian period (hatched area).

The archaeological record of the early and mature Angkorian periods within Cambodia beyond the capital region in the northwest remains poorly known. Epigraphic research and archaeological surveys in adjacent northeastern Thailand (e.g., Welch 1998) and in the Tonle Sap region (e.g., Pottier 1999; Wolters 1974), however, suggest significant overlap in the dating of sites in northeastern Thailand, in southern Laos, in southern Cambodia, and in northwestern Cambodia. Thus, complex polities may have emerged concurrently in three discrete geographic regions of Cambodia: the Mekong delta, the middle Mekong, and the Tonle Sap region.

Analysis of inscriptions indicates that between the eleventh and thirteenth centuries, the Khmer economy increasingly relied on tribute and corvée labor to support the state (Sedov 1978:123). Subjects were expected to render tribute in both agricultural and manufactured goods and to serve as labor for construction projects and in the military. In concert with military conquests to the west, regional and international trade became important by the eleventh century under the reign of Suryavarman I (Hall 1975, 1979). During this time, the Khmer empire reached its greatest areal extent (fig. 10.5). That much of modern-day Thailand and some of Vietnam lay within its realm is clear from this distributional map of eleventh- to mid-thirteenth-century archaeological sites and inscriptions.

Despite the importance of this period for its economic and military expansions, little documentary or archaeological information exists concerning the domestic and international economy (but see Ricklefs 1966). Local provincial elites appointed by the Khmer rulers controlled a series of local

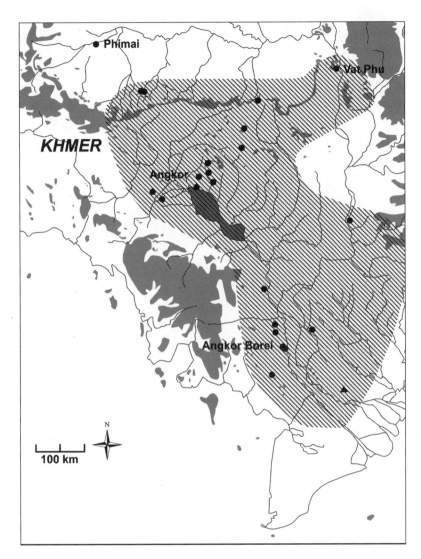

Figure 10.4 Proposed minimal geographic extent, based on extant distributional information on archaeological sites and inscriptions, of the early Angkorian polity (marked with hatching). Gray areas indicate mountain ranges or islands, except for the area southwest of Angkor, which demarcates the Tonle Sap lake. Circles mark sites; triangles mark inscriptions.

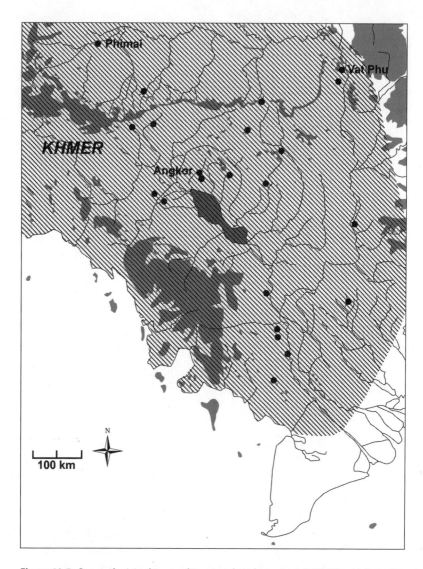

Figure 10.5 Proposed minimal geographic extent, based on extant distributional information on archaeological sites and inscriptions, of the mature Angkorian empire (marked with hatching). Gray areas indicate mountain ranges or islands, except for the area southwest of Angkor, which demarcates the Tonle Sap lake. Circles mark sites.

systems across the Khmer region. The tax and/or tribute that government officials collected from these provincial areas would have been funneled back into the center to support public works such as temple construction. Provincial markets were focal points for local systems, and temples located near these markets linked the Khmer center to its periphery through a series of mutual dependencies. Angkor's participation in international trade with China and South Asia was limited after the eleventh century AD (Hall 1975).

Jayavarman VII was the last great king of Angkor, and successive leaders could not return their country to the prominence the Khmer empire had once held. Warfare became more common in the fourteenth century. After a sustained siege by the Siamese in AD 1430–1431, the Thais sacked the city of Angkor. Multiple factors contributed to the collapse of the Khmer state: structurally unstable relations between the rulers and their elite, economic challenges that an ever-expanding and largely autonomous periphery posed to the center, periodic civil war, and the intrusion of Buddhist ideas into the predominantly Hindu world of Khmer statecraft all contributed (see also Hagesteijn 1987). Cambodia's political center moved south again to the banks of the Mekong River, and the former Khmer capital was left to villagers and monks.

Collapse and Regeneration from Funan to Angkor

The history of the Khmer civilization is characterized by cycles of fragmentation, collapse, and reorganization. Seats of power shifted across space, rulers alternated in their preference of Indic religious denomination, breaks occurred in royal dynastic succession, and the polity grew progressively more inward focused through time. Embedded within this turbulent political and social history are threads of continuity that Oliver Wolters (1999) describes as a cultural matrix of social and ideological institutions; some threads persist from the late first millennium BC until the fall of Angkor circa AD 1432.

Economic and ideological foundations of the Khmer civilization exhibit substantial continuity through time and counterbalance political discontinuities in the kingly reigns that historians generally study. This pattern might well be called "template regeneration" (Bronson, chapter 9). What accounts for this longevity in the Khmer civilization? Bennet Bronson (1988:212) maintains that one reason for the longevity of the Southeast Asian classical states, including Angkor, lay in the absence of "barbarians" at their peripheries, in contrast to the case of northern India. But internal factors were equally if not more important—namely, the domestic economic organization of these polities and the ways in which elites embraced Indic ideologies to garner wealth and legitimize their power. The following discussion concentrates on economic, political, and ideological aspects of the Khmer civilization.

Economic Patterns

Khmer economic organization from the early historic to the mature Angkorian period involved a stable domestic economy of subsistence agriculture and a fluctuating international economy based on trade. Continuity characterizes the agrarian Khmer economy, which perennially relied on locally managed irrigation agriculture, involving flood-recession techniques where possible even during the height of Khmer power from the ninth to the fourteenth century AD (van Liere 1980).

By the Angkorian period, this subsistence economy depended on tribute extracted from the rural provincial population to support the state's administrative and political activities in the core region. In most respects, however, agrarian production remained fixed at the local level. Little evidence exists for a centralized economic system in provincial areas that might have consistently channeled surplus to the center (Welch 1989, 1998).

The only exceptions to this local and regional economic autonomy lay in the support of temples (or "foundations," following Vickery 1998) that formed the core of local communities. These temple estates formed major economic units, controlling farmlands that elites had donated; the produce grown on the estates supported the vast number of attached specialists for the temple. Khmer temple estates absorbed substantial amounts of land, goods, livestock, and labor (field hands, temple assistants, dancers) from local elites and involved local populations.

These local cults (Vickery 1998) or "kin temples" (Hagesteijn 1987) formed an economic and ideological basis of Khmer society by the seventh century AD. Indic notions of karma may partly explain the proliferation of first-millennium religious architecture. Individuals increased their karma for the next life by establishing temples or making donations to extant temples (see also Hagesteijn 1996:189, passim). Entrenched and aspiring elite members recorded their temple offerings in stone. Such activity is clear in the earliest dated Khmer inscription (K. 600) from Angkor Borei in southern Cambodia. This inscription lists donations to the temple/foundation by two elite individuals: nine males, nine females, two children, eighty head of cattle, two buffalo, ten goats, forty coconut trees, and two rice fields (Vickery 1998:277). How much earlier this temple economy might extend back in time awaits chronometric dating of the brick monuments across southern Cambodia and southern Vietnam.

Whereas continuity characterizes ancient Khmer domestic economic organization, discontinuity exists in its international trade orientation. The Funan polities of the early to mid first millennium AD were extensively involved in trade (Hall 1982, 1985; Malleret 1959, 1962), and the most active economic and diplomatic relationships with China occurred before the seventh century AD, during the gradual collapse of the Chinese Tang state (Hall 1979:421–22). Insufficient evidence exists pertaining to Chenla economic organization for scholars to identify points of continuity or discontinuity from its predecessor.

Angkorian period successors to Funan, however, grew increasingly insular. In China's Song dynasty (AD 960–1279), contemporaneous with the period most closely associated with the height of the Khmer empire, records of Khmer tributary missions are scarce compared to missions reported for neighboring polities including Champa (central Vietnam) and southern Sumatra (Wong 1979). During this era, polities in Java and Sumatra developed multiple shipping ports, hosted foreign merchants, and established coinage (Christie 1999). The Khmer empire never developed a standardized currency, instead using exchange equivalents in gold, silver, rice, cloth, cattle, butter, and slaves (Sedov 1978:125), and remained a marginal player in the China–Southeast Asia trade network.

Archaeological research indicates that most successive polities focused instead on the circulation of goods within regions under their direct control (Stark 2004; Welch 1989). The geographic extent of the Khmer empire expanded and contracted according to ruler: selected Angkorian rulers in the tenth, eleventh, and thirteenth centuries had expansionist aims and acquired more land through successful military campaigns. Under these rulers, the Khmer empire controlled more area than did any of its contemporaries in mainland Southeast Asia.

Political Patterns

The documentary record of ancient Cambodia provides an excellent case study in collapse and regeneration. Documentary accounts record the collapse of Funan, internecine struggles within Chenla, the twelfth-century sacking of Angkor by the Chams in the chaos that followed the death of Suryavarman II, and the rapid regeneration of the Khmer empire by its last great ruler, Jayavarman VII. For more than five hundred years before the establishment of Angkor, multiple, interacting polities competed with each other for power and access to material and ideological resources (Jacques 1990:257; Welch 1998:218). The establishment of the Angkorian polity in the ninth century AD did not end this competition, since rival successors and usurpers often fought each other to control the throne (e.g., Briggs 1951; Vickery 1985). Between the ninth and the eleventh century AD, Angkorian rulers established new capitals at least six times.

One reason that Angkorian rulership was not stable lay in the bilateral descent rules that structured Khmer social organization (Kirsch 1976). This descent system, coupled with royal polygamy as kings built alliances through multiple marriages, created multiple competitors for the throne. Of the twenty-seven Angkorian rulers from circa AD 802 to 1432, four were recognized usurpers and seven were "second grade relatives" (following Hagesteijn 1987:163) of the king and lacked legitimate claim to the throne. In fact, the Angkorian military devoted substantial effort to suppressing internal revolts and mutinies at various points in history (Sedov 1978:127).

Perhaps another reason for collapse and regeneration in the Angkorian state lay in its lack of professional generals or a hereditary military. Instead, the state relied primarily on labor from its citizens (Chou Ta-Kuan 1993; Sedov 1978:127) and on alliance networks based on patron-client relationships between the center's ruler and provincial elites (see review in Stark 2004:107–11). One clear example of collapse is depicted in a bas relief on the Bayon that commemorates the state's disintegration in AD 1177 under Cham attack; the new king Jayavarman VII reunified Cambodia for its last great florescence. During most of its existence, then, ancient Khmer civilization was both fragile and loosely integrated. Cycles of consolidation alternated with political fragmentation, and only a few rulers were able to wrest control from the provincial level to effectively centralize the state during their reigns.

Chinese annals and indigenous inscriptions record "men of prowess" (Wolters 1999) in the early historic period who emerged as overlords and established their power over principalities throughout the Khmer lands. Throughout the sequence, these leaders attracted followers and commanded political power and respect, becoming essential components of the Angkorian political system (Mabbett 1977). Such elite individuals were also the leading worshippers of the Indic deities (Wolters 1979:433), appropriating order through practice of Indic rituals, shrine construction, and dedications of these monuments to the Indian deities. Such ritualization and aestheticization of the elite is integral to the process of state formation (Baines and Yoffee 1998:233–36). Pre-Angkorian brick monuments found across Cambodia and southern Vietnam housed Indic images or served as mortuary monuments and materialized elite power through ideology. Such foundations may have been constructed as early as the mid first millennium AD (Vo Si Khai 1998).

Recent analysis of indigenous Khmer inscriptions (Vickery 1986, 1998) suggests that significant breaks occurred in the nature of political leadership from the sixth through eighth centuries AD. Before the eighth century AD, political authority rested in the hands of local hereditary and perhaps matrilineal *poñ,* who were directly responsible for smaller territories. Political transformations during the eighth century AD, however, replaced this leadership structure with a patrilineal descent system of rulers (using the suffix *-varman*).

By the Angkorian era, larger-scale administrative units (including temples) had developed to support their universal monarch/king (*devaraja* or *cakravartin*), and the ruler became responsible for larger and more topographically variable regions. The rules of royal succession may not have changed substantially, however. Elites reckoned descent bilaterally in the pre-Angkorian era (Vickery 1998), and some of the greatest Angkorian kings gained legitimation through the female line (see review in Kirsch 1976).

Ideology and Identity

Some aspects of the religious ideological system remained constant from the early historic to the Angkorian period (e.g., the local adoption of Indic religious ideology, writing systems, and iconography), while others changed within, rather than between, Cambodia's political epochs. Indic statuary appeared in the Mekong basin before the end of the sixth century AD (Dalsheimer and Manguin 1998:96, passim). These representations of the gods Shiva and Vishnu reflect the establishment of local Indic cults in the region (Coedès 1968; Wolters 1979). Recent revisionist writing on Khmer religion and statecraft have modified earlier assumptions that the region was colonized by Brahmins from South Asia, while still underscoring the Southeast Asian adoption of South Asian traditions (Kulke 1990; Mabbett 1997).

Indigenous Southeast Asians selectively adopted elements of Indic religions that fit their needs, alternating between an emphasis on Saivism and one on Vaisnavism (Brown 1996). This ideological orientation toward Hindu cults began in the early historic period and persisted into the Angkorian period. The scope of Khmer religious practice transformed from community-based cults in the early historic period to state-based and state-financed religion by the inception of the Angkorian period in the ninth century AD. So, too, did the content, as Angkorian populations turned increasingly toward Buddhism after Suryavarman I, generally acknowledged to be Buddhist, came to power in the eleventh century (Kulke 1978:33). As increased numbers of Khmers turned away from Hinduism and embraced Buddhism, they directed their donations to Buddhist monasteries instead of (Hindu) state coffers and may have substantially undermined the Angkorian economic base (Hagesteijn 1987).

Elites supported early historic and pre-Angkorian local cults by conducting the requisite Indic practices, by obtaining knowledge of sacred Indian literature, and by making vast outlays of capital to finance the creation of stone sculptures of deities and the brick monuments that housed these creations. Through undertaking such responsibilities, the pre-Angkorian elites regulated power and articulated models of cultural and social order (following Eisenstadt 1988:241). They attracted and maintained entourages and allocated bureaucratic titles such as special counselor, president of the royal council, and town governor (Wolters 1979:433).

While other aspects of the Khmer civilization either changed abruptly or cycled in and out of popularity, this thousand-year period was marked by a growing sense of social identity that was embodied in the celebration of an origin tradition, the widespread use of a single (Khmer) language, and the materialization of this language in the Khmer script. The earliest Khmer-language inscriptions date to the early seventh century AD, but some scholars maintain that populations in central and southern Cambodia had spoken Khmer for centuries before then (e.g., Vickery 1994:205). This development and growth of a Khmer ethnic ideology progressively strengthened as populations in the region alternated between repelling invaders from the east and west and expanding their geopolitical boundaries.

By the ninth century AD, a clearly Khmer identity emerged in the Tonle Sap region that was expressed through both militarism and art. When the Thai army sacked the capital of Angkor in AD 1432, they conquered a distinctly Khmer kingdom. In taking the royal Khmer court back to the Chao Phraya region, the Thais appropriated distinctly Khmer traditions of statecraft, music, and art that reflected a well-developed ethnic and historic identity.

Collapse and Regeneration in Ancient Cambodian Polities

A plethora of publications on Cambodia's ancient history, particularly on Angkor, appears each year, yet the amount of archaeological and paleoenvironmental research undertaken in this region remains modest. Such work is critical to understanding the political ecology of the Khmer empire and of its antecedent political formations and will probably require modifications to our historical reconstructions. However, the outlines of ancient Cambodia's historical trajectory seem reasonably clear. The region witnessed an initial and protracted period of cyclical and contingent power centers throughout the lower Mekong basin. In less than a millennium, political, economic, and ideological power concentrated around the Tonle Sap lake.

Linking multiple Khmer polities into a single, thousand-year-long tradition provides new perspectives on the collapse and regeneration of complex societies in Southeast Asia. Little evidence has thus far been produced for the systematic and sustained deployment of force that characterized some ancient Chinese, Mesoamerican, and Andean empires and that Alan Kolata (chapter 13) describes as "hegemony with sovereignty." Partly for this reason, Cambodia's cycles of collapse and regeneration can be fit within a long-term pattern of resilience and stability (see Adams 1978).

Cambodia's recent geopolitical instability and its deeply entrenched colonialist intellectual traditions have limited the extent to which archaeological research has informed on these long-term patterns of change and resiliency. Both documentary and archaeological data on the Khmer tradition, however, offer intriguing clues to some questions concerning the nature of collapse and regeneration.

Discontinuities are most evident in the succession of political rulership and in geographic shifts in the center of power through time. Yet many aspects of ancient Khmer society remained relatively constant through the centuries and form the Khmer "template" for complex societies. One source of continuity involves the persistence of a rural agrarian economic base, which remained largely unchanged from the early first millennium to the twentieth century. Farming populations provided surplus to coastal communities in the early first millennium AD to support trading ports, and they later channeled surplus to the Angkorian capitals to finance public works constructions. A second continuity lies in the commitment to the local political level; the persistent importance of local (or clan) temples from the Funan to the Angkorian period (see also Sedov 1978) is one expression of this trend. Extant evidence suggests that lower-level administrative apparatuses weathered fluctuations in dynastic rule and shifts in power centers. Throughout the sequence, populations supplemented their indigenous animistic religion with an Indic-derived religious ideology and notions of statecraft. Finally, we see persistence in Khmer sociopolitical organization, which specified social relations and emphasized bilateral descent.

Still other aspects of Khmer society, such as its particular form of religious ideology and its international economic orientation, changed in cycles. While changes in religious ideology remain difficult to understand, shifts in international economic orientation reflect pan–Southeast Asian dynamics. The earliest Khmer civilization was integrally involved in an international maritime trade network because trade routes included the Mekong delta. The seventh-century shift in regional trade patterns south to Sumatra and thus away from the Khmer region occurred with the rise of the trade empire of Srivijaya (Hall 1985).

Viewing the Khmer civilization in its regional and historical context helps explain some of the reasons behind the cyclical patterns discussed here. But explaining why particular continuities and discontinuities characterize ancient Cambodia remains impossible without a more finely textured understanding of the archaeological record, which yields insights on local demographic, technological, and agricultural shifts through time. Future work that combines systematic archaeological research and critical documentary analysis can and should illuminate aspects of resilience and change in the ancient Khmer civilization.

Acknowledgments

I am grateful to Glenn Schwartz for inviting me to participate in the SAA symposium and to Norman Yoffee for his guidance and encouragement. Thanks are also extended to Michael Vickery for conversations and clarification about ancient Khmer history, and to Glenn Schwartz for helpful comments on an earlier draft of this chapter. Amy Commendador prepared graphics used in this chapter. I take full responsibility for any weaknesses in this chapter.

Notes

1. Debates over the nature and impact of South Asian ideology on Southeast Asian state formation continue to rage (e.g., Bellina 1998, 2003; Brown 1996; Christie 1995; Glover 1996; Kulke 1990; Mabbett 1997; Smith 1999).

2. Figures use published information on inscriptions with calendrical dates employing the Indic *çaka* system compiled in Jenner 1980 and Vickery 1998. George Coedès (1937–1966) recorded a larger corpus of inscriptions that have been dated through pa-

leography (de Casparis 1979); these are excluded from the sample. Archaeological site distributions were taken from summary maps in Jessup and Zéphir 1997:2, 12.

3. Twenty-five officially approved dynastic histories cover China's imperial period (e.g., Wilkinson 2000), and a variety of Western-language translations are available (Frankel 1957). Three of these histories specifically describe "Funan": (1) volume 79 of the History of the Jin Dynasty, or *Jinshu*, covers the years AD 265–419 (compiled in AD 644); (2) volume 58 of the History of the Southern Qi, or *Nan Qishu*, covers the years AD 479–502 (compiled from AD 489 through 537); and (3) volume 54 of the History of the Liang Dynasty, or *Liangshu*, covers the years AD 502–556 (compiled from AD 628 through 635). Additional material is located in the following publications: volume 78 of *Nanshi*; volume 222 (part 2) of *Xintangshu*; related articles and material dispersed throughout volume 36 of the *Shujingzhu*; and volume 347 in *Taipingyulan* (also see Ishizawa 1995:13; Pelliot 1903:275–77; and Wheatley 1961:114–15).

4. Some of the tribute items offered to the Chinese court include gold, silver, copper, tin, gharuwood, ivory, peafowl, kingfishers, fruits, and areca nuts. The "Funan" emissaries also offered tame elephants to the Chinese court in AD 357 and a live rhinoceros in AD 539 (Wheatley 1983:111n147).

11 Framing the Maya Collapse
Continuity, Discontinuity, Method, and Practice in the Classic to Postclassic Southern Maya Lowlands
Diane Z. Chase and Arlen F. Chase

Despite substantial new research on both the Classic (AD 250–900) and the Postclassic (AD 900–1542 [1697]) period Maya, views of the Classic Maya collapse and of the changes that took place in the subsequent Postclassic period are very little changed from paradigms established more than thirty years ago. While the Postclassic Maya are no longer viewed as a decadent and declining population, explanations for a regenerated Maya society continue a traditional focus on causal factors such as environmental change or destruction, internal or external warfare, and the rise of mercantilism. We suggest that viewing the Maya from the perspective of "frames"—a methodological approach that is used in other disciplines (see Goffman 1974)—provides a different and potentially more holistic view of the transformation and restructuring of Maya society. Our archaeological research at the sites of Caracol (Belize), Nohmul (Belize), Santa Rita Corozal (Belize), and Tayasal (Guatemala) provides the data for a multiframe analysis. We believe that this perspective not only is more dynamic, but also more clearly indicates the disjunctions of the Terminal Classic (AD 790–900) with bordering time periods and highlights the aspects of Classic period society that are incorporated into the regenerated Postclassic period.

The Classic Maya collapse, defined by the cessation of erecting carved and inscribed stone stelae and altars and by the depopulation of Classic Maya cities in the southern lowlands during the ninth century AD, has been viewed as resulting from a variety of factors. Possible causal explanations include peasant revolts and warfare, ideological predilections, environmental degradation, drought, epidemic disease, and natural disasters such as earthquakes and hurricanes (see Culbert 1973a, 1988). The subsequent reconstituted Postclassic society has been portrayed as more focused on warfare, water, and trade (Chase and Rice 1985). Some have suggested that the Postclassic Maya can be characterized by decentralized and privatized worship (Freidel and Sabloff 1984). Other archaeologists, following Jeremy Sabloff and William Rathje (1975), consider a defining characteristic of the Postclassic Maya to have been mercantilism (e.g., Masson 2002). While there is a long history of publication on the collapse and on the transition between the Classic and the Postclassic period, no single viewpoint is overwhelmingly supported by hard archaeological data, leaving most archaeologists to avoid the question and to note the probability that complex multiple causes were responsible for the collapse (e.g., Sharer 1994; Webster 2002).

There have been critical advances in our knowledge base relative to the Classic Maya collapse. Investigations have revealed key facts that we were unaware of thirty years ago. Importantly, it is now apparent that the collapse was not a single uniform event but rather took place at different times throughout the sites of the southern Maya lowlands (fig. 11.1). Hieroglyphic inscriptions ceased at Dos Pilas at AD 760, when the site was under siege (Demarest 1997), and at Tikal at AD 889, when that site's palaces were being infilled with trash (Harrison 1999). Complicating this picture, however, are the many Maya sites that were occupied past their last monument dates (such as Caracol [A. Chase and D. Chase 2004a:345]). Other sites, which were not overt participants in the Late Classic Maya stela-altar cult, had substantial populations that continued into the Postclassic era (e.g., Lamanai [Pendergast 1986] and Tayasal [A. Chase 1990]). Thus, population decline is not necessarily correlated with a cessation of monument erection or a lack of monuments (see also Webster 2002:187 for Copán and A. Chase and D. Chase 2006 for Caracol). A focus on monument erection alone likely provides a skewed picture of the Maya collapse (e.g., Lowe 1985), but without the monuments as a guide, dating of the latest archaeological occupation at any site can prove difficult. Even advances in radiocarbon dating and in obsidian hydration dating have not resolved the timing of the collapse; instead, these absolute dating methods have been used to argue (somewhat controversially, e.g., Braswell 1992) for lingering populations that lasted for two centuries beyond the dates on the latest stone monuments at sites such as Copán, Honduras (Webster 2002; Webster et al. 1993).

However, our knowledge of the latest Classic period (or "Terminal Classic") Maya has been expanded. It is now apparent that the final monuments in the southern Maya lowlands are often distinct stylistically and iconographically (A. Chase 1985; Laporte and Mejia 2002; Proskouriakoff 1950), although the iconographic themes are not always expressed in the same way at every site. At Seibal and Machaquila, for example, there are changes in

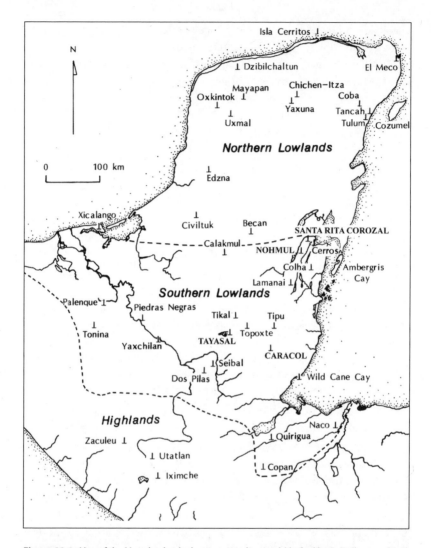

Figure 11.1 Map of the Maya lowlands showing sites discussed (drafted by D. Z. Chase and A. F. Chase).

the dress of rulers (I. Graham 1967; J. Graham 1990), and at Caracol, dual figures engaged in a common action are depicted on the monuments (Beetz and Satterthwaite 1981; A. Chase et al. 1991). Terminal Classic ceramics share some similar iconography with these latest monuments (e.g., Adams 1973), and other artifacts, such as spindle whorls and lithic points, provide additional information. They indicate pan-Maya ties and local variation along with tremendous ranges in access to goods, implying substantial status differentiation. Excavations at many sites have also yielded unfinished building efforts, on-floor debris, and burning—suggesting that site abandonment, when it did occur, may have been rapid (D. Chase and A. Chase 2000; Webster 2002).

We also know more about the Postclassic Maya than we did thirty years ago. Postclassic period Maya settlements are found in substantial numbers but often in strikingly different places than their Classic period counterparts. Postclassic occupation has a focus on low-lying constructions. The barely elevated nature of many of these late buildings and their easy obfuscation in a tropical environment (often being found in "vacant terrain") has not only made the discovery of Postclassic occupation more difficult archaeologically, but has also led to the incorrect characterization of these later sites as being less complex or less stratified than their Classic-era counterparts. However, there are Postclassic interments with substantial indications of status differentiation—even though these, again, are distinct from earlier counterparts. Yet we continue to be hampered in our interpretation of the Postclassic Maya, for despite an increased interest, there has not yet been the same quantity of excavation of Postclassic sites as exists for the earlier Classic period.

Excavation and analytic methodologies may also pose barriers to the study of the regeneration of Maya society. Many Postclassic constructions were not built on elevated platforms; because these buildings employed only line-of-stone base walls, they are almost invisible to archaeological survey in tropical environments. Even late monumental architecture often employed impermanent building materials that had once been covered in thick coats of stucco—stucco that erodes and building materials that decompose under harsh tropical conditions. These same late buildings are frequently also not abundant at the mounded Classic Maya sites that continue to be the prime focus of research for most archaeological projects in the Maya area. Thus, identifying Postclassic occupation using Classic period perspectives usually proves difficult. Excavations undertaken at Tayasal, Guatemala, in 1971 illustrate this point. The excavation strategy adopted at Tayasal initially concentrated on mounded remains and thus resulted in the recovery of largely Classic period artifacts and architecture. Only after the excavation strategy was shifted to vacant-terrain lakeside locales were the sought-after Postclassic buildings and artifacts recovered (A. Chase 1990). Initially, Tayasal excavators also were perplexed by crude lines-of-stone that appeared in the humus levels of several narrow trenches into mounded buildings;

only later in the season—after areal clearing excavations had been undertaken in what had appeared to be vacant-terrain locales—were these crude lines recognized as base walls of buildings.

A focus on ceramic markers or preconceived ideas of style sometimes also can lead to problems in identifying Postclassic and Terminal Classic occupation. At Barton Ramie, Belize, Gordon Willey and his colleagues (1955) initially thought that no Postclassic remains had been found at that site; however, subsequent ceramic analysis showed that Postclassic pottery had been recovered in more than 95 percent of the excavations (Willey et al. 1965:384). Postclassic pottery was not identified in the field; it was only recognized later in laboratory analysis. Similarly, our identification of Terminal Classic occupation may also be clouded, especially as it is primarily based on known ceramic markers. Much Late Classic pottery now appears to have continued in use through the Terminal Classic period without significant modification; only the elite ceramic markers changed from the preceding Late Classic period, and their use was largely restricted to very specific contexts (A. Chase and D. Chase 2004a, 2006). Yet these markers are the ones that traditionally have been used to identify the existence of the Terminal Classic (e.g., Culbert 1973b for Tikal; Adams 1973 for Altar de Sacrificios; Sabloff 1973 for Seibal), potentially resulting in the misdating of non-elite Terminal Classic contexts. Estimates of population levels based solely on the presence or absence of these known Terminal Classic markers likely do not accurately reflect ancient reality. Thus, our current view of the Classic Maya collapse is impeded by methodological shortcomings.

Significantly, high-status Terminal Classic ceramic markers appear in the Maya archaeological record at the same time as substantial changes in burial practices. These changes do not appear to have occurred uniformly throughout the southern Maya lowlands. For example, while the lack of Terminal Classic period burials in traditional eastern mortuary buildings has been confirmed at many sites (Ciudad Ruiz et al. 2003; see also Becker 1999 for Tikal and D. Chase and A. Chase 2004b for Caracol), a new burial locus is not always apparent. Juan Pedro Laporte (1996) has demonstrated a Terminal Classic predilection for interring the dead in western structures—at least in the southeastern Petén region of Guatemala. Thus, major differences also exist between Late Classic and Terminal Classic burial patterns—differences that may not always be identifiable by research using preconceived Late Classic period excavation perspectives.

Approaches to the transformation of Maya society have tended to focus on simple comparisons of Classic and Postclassic material remains (see A. Chase and P. Rice 1985; D. Chase 1981; D. Chase and A. Chase 1992b,

2001, 2004a). As has been pointed out previously by many researchers, the Postclassic Maya generally are described in negative terms relative to their Classic counterparts: no stela and altar erection, no long-count dates, no slipped polychrome pottery, and no monumental architecture. This focus on contrasts is not surprising given that descriptions and modeling of the Maya have tended to emphasize heuristically useful extremes. In-built black-and-white contrasts include whether Maya political organization can be described as a chiefdom or a state and, if a state existed, whether it was centralized or segmentary (Fox et al. 1996; Iannone 2002). Maya cities are described alternatively as urban or as regal-ritual centers (A. Chase et al. 2001; D. Chase et al. 1990; Sanders and Webster 1988; Webster 2002). Classic polities are viewed as balkanized (Dunham 1988; Mathews 1991) or as integrated into "super-states" (Martin and Grube 1995, 2000). In general, the focus of Maya research on the collapse also has been on identifying heuristic polar opposites rather than on exploring continuities or regeneration. These contrastive approaches tend to rigidify theoretical positions and make perceptions of the Maya more static than dynamic.

We suggest that using a different approach—one borrowed from organizational studies—permits a more holistic and dynamic view of the ancient Maya and of the transformation of Maya society.

Organizational Frames

In *Reframing Organizations: Artistry, Choice, and Leadership,* Lee Bolman and Terrence Deal (1997) proposed the use of a four-frame model to provide a more effective overview of organizations. While this four-frame approach was not created for analyzing archaeological cultures, we believe that it can be modified for archaeological purposes and that the combined multiple-frame perspectives can provide useful insight into both the Classic Maya collapse and the Postclassic period regeneration of Maya society (fig. 11.2). The four frames defined by Bolman and Deal (1997) are structural, human resource, political, and symbolic. Each frame is a tool based on distinct assumptions, and each provides a somewhat different perspective from which to view an organization. No frame is "the" frame; rather, each constitutes one "image of reality" (Bolman and Deal 1997:15). "Frames are both windows on the world and lenses that bring the world into focus. Frames filter out some things while allowing others to pass through easily" (Bolman and Deal 1997:12). The hope is that the combined frame perspectives can provide a more holistic view of an organization.

The structural frame defines "social architecture" (Bolman and Deal

Figure 11.2 Organizational frames for consideration of changes in Classic to Postclassic Maya society. *Upper left:* Caracol Archaeological Project (painting by Michael Rothman [copyright held by A. F. and D. Z. Chase]); *upper right:* National Geographic Image Collection (painting by H. M. Herget [1935:559, Plate VII]); *lower left:* Caracol Archaeological Project (painting by Barbara Stahl [copyright held by A. F. and D. Z. Chase]); *lower right:* after Gann 1900:Plate 36.

1997:50)—the different units of the organization. Key to the structural frame are specializations and relationships—the division of labor as well as vertical and lateral units and coordination. Thus, the structural frame focus would be concerned with heterarchy and hierarchy as well as rules, policies, and procedures.

The human resource frame perspective is that "organizations serve human needs," that "people and organizations need each other," and that "when the fit between individual and system is poor, one or both suffer" (Bolman and Deal 1997:102). Human resource–focused organizations are democratic in that individuals have greater control over their activities or work; there also may be some rotation in leadership (Bolman and Deal 1997:132–33). An emphasis on human resources would involve "investing in people," allowing for autonomy and empowerment, providing rewards for efforts, and sharing in success (Bolman and Deal 1997:123, 126–29). Thus, the human resource frame focuses on viewing the organization much like an extended family and is concerned with the degree to which an organization is tailored to people, making individuals feel good about their individual roles.

The political frame considers organizations as composed of coalitions of people (Bolman and Deal 1997:163). Following this perspective, organizational goals are established in ongoing negotiation among stakeholders, and power can derive from various sources—authority, expertise, knowledge, or ability to provide rewards. These multiple sources of power can lessen any single base of authority. Likewise, conflict can come from many directions and sources (cultural, horizontal, or vertical; Bolman and Deal 1997:173). Thus, the political frame focuses on the different interest groups that compete for power and resources, as well as on conflicts and coalitions.

The symbolic frame is concerned with symbols, beliefs, myths, rituals, ceremonies, and metaphor (Bolman and Deal 1997:215–17). Symbols are seen as embodying the culture of the organization and are repeatedly created, re-created, and passed on. Thus, the symbolic frame focuses on organizations as cultures characterized and unified by traditions, rituals, symbols, and ceremonies.

By conscientiously applying these frames to existing archaeological data for the Classic, Terminal Classic, and Postclassic Maya, we can make inroads into understanding what was (and what was not) regenerated in later Maya society.

The Structural Frame

The Late Classic Maya are easily viewed from the structural frame. There are clear units that can be identified, as well as functional groups, such as the specialists that produced distinct artifact classes. There are also status divisions and spatially distinct occupation locations for different status groups. At Caracol, a group of low-status individuals lived immediately outside, but adjacent to, the monumental epicentral architecture. An epicentral royal palace is larger than all the other known palaces at the site (A. Chase and D. Chase 2001a). However, because some of the elite (although not royal) palaces were located in the outlying residential core of Caracol, we can infer that high-status individuals were embedded at widely separated points in the site's urban landscape. At some sites, the structural organization of the city is also evident in public works—causeways that connect parts of the site together or terraces for agricultural production (A. Chase and D. Chase 2001b). Population numbers approached a hundred thousand or more at several sites; however, most sites were substantially smaller. Sites were connected to each other in hierarchical and heterarchical ways. A site hierarchy focused on regional capitals is evident in settlement patterns and hieroglyphic texts. Each of the Classic-era regional capitals in the southern lowlands had its own emblem glyph; however, emblem glyph sites could be subordinate to other emblem glyph sites. We believe that polity size could approximate seven thousand square kilometers (or more; A. Chase and D. Chase 1998).

There is also structure to the economic system. Production was localized in households within sites as well as in specialized sites (such as the chert production at Colha; Shafer and Hester 1983). The economic system incorporated both long-distance trade and household distribution so that at some sites (e.g., Caracol), virtually all households had access to imports such as obsidian, regardless of the status of the household members. At other sites, such as Calakmul, obsidian was not as available or as well distributed (Braswell et al. 1997; Folan et al. 1995). The argument can be made that there was little control exercised on most production but that there was greater control over distribution (A. Chase 1998); however, standardization in production is evident in items, such as ceramics, that have strikingly consistent rim diameters and heights. Functional variation within and standardization among Classic period household groups is also apparent; within residential plaza groups, eastern buildings functioned as the locus of ritual and mortuary activity for most households in the eastern part of the southern lowlands.

Terminal Classic Maya society also contains clear structural elements;

however, the smaller database of household information derived from excavations provides less detail than exists for the preceding Classic period. Nevertheless, certain differences are apparent. Most evident are status distinctions, which are less graded than in the Classic era and more polarized: there are clear "haves" and "have-nots." This is apparent in all material culture but is perhaps most evident in ceramic distributions. Trade items, such as modeled-carved pottery, which often have been used as temporal markers, appear instead to be status-linked items that are only infrequently found in other than elite contexts (A. Chase and D. Chase 2004a, 2006). Standardization in household functional units is also not as evident as in the preceding Classic period; no longer are the eastern structures reserved for ritual purposes and the interment of the dead. Although continuity is evident with the earlier Late Classic occupation at many sites, the Terminal Classic Maya often used existing architecture and spaces in different ways. This can be seen in buildings that close off access to existing structures (e.g., Nohmul Str. 20 [D. Chase and A. Chase 1982]) or in the accumulation of household trash inside buildings that once had ritual, residential, or administrative functions (e.g., Tikal Central Acropolis [Harrison 1999] or Caracol Str. A6 [D. Chase and A. Chase 2000]).

The Postclassic Maya maintained dense populations, but generally in different locations than those occupied by the preceding Late Classic or Terminal Classic period Maya—sometimes in distinct areas within the same locality and other times at a distance. There also were new seats of power; significantly, these did not overlap with the emblem glyph sites of the Classic period. Historic descriptions indicate that movements of people within the southern lowlands also occurred. Specializations continued, as did short- and long-distance trade in chert, obsidian, and other exotic items (such as copper, gold, and *Spondylus* shell). Some unification of art styles may have resulted from population movement, enhanced communication, and trade. Standardization is evident in some pottery. Certain cache figures from Mayapán, Lamanai, and Santa Rita Corozal are nearly identical; significantly, these sites are beyond the area of a single region or state. However, there also was substantial variety in the decorative elaboration of ceramics. Even items as mundane as red-slipped tripod plates are less standardized than in the preceding Classic and Terminal Classic periods (which contradicts one of the arguments for Postclassic mercantile trade and stackable vessels—e.g., Sabloff and Rathje 1975). There are status differences; multiple-room palaces, upright flexed burials covered by small shrines, and elaborate jewelry all can be used as indicators of high status. The elites, however, were not located solely or even predominantly in the center of the site. This is seen in the distribution of multiple-room structures at Santa Rita Corozal and of colonnaded halls at Mayapán. Generally, no one palace was grander or more important than the others. The size of Late Postclassic political units, however, is in question. If Ralph Roys (1957) is correct (but see also Restall 1997), the size of a Postclassic polity was approximately the same as a Classic period regional state, averaging twelve thousand square kilometers (A. Chase and D. Chase 1998:14). Regional capitals are distinguishable at Mayapán, Santa Rita Corozal, and Lamanai and have a distinctive archaeological signature—they are characterized by a greater number of multiple-room constructions and ritual caches. There was standardization in the deposition of ritual items (but not replication, as in Late Classic Caracol), and there were caches located in residential *plazuela* groups. However, the deposition location within Postclassic households was not the same as in the Late Classic; ritual activities generally were not centered on an eastern mortuary construction.

The Human Resource Frame

Elements of the human resource frame have been incorporated in some of the explanations for the Maya collapse, such as in the postulation that there was a peasant revolt. However, this frame is not always easy to identify in the archaeological record, even though the possibility exists for assessing the distribution of resources and/or the degree to which there appears to be democracy or symbolic egalitarianism (e.g., Bolman and Deal 1997:134; see also Blanton 1998).

The Late Classic Maya, at least at Caracol, appear to have maintained a human resource perspective. The site is characterized by symbolic egalitarianism. Virtually all households had eastern shrines that contained interments and caches; ancestor veneration was not solely a prerogative of the royalty (D. Chase and A. Chase 2004b). All households had access to obsidian, shell, chert, and polychrome ceramics (A. Chase and D. Chase 2004b; D. Chase 1998). The prosperity of the site appears to have been shared by all, at least symbolically. Furthermore, during the height of the Late Classic era, neither were iconographic representations of rulers in great evidence on stone monuments nor were their exploits recounted in any detail in hieroglyphic texts. That this egalitarianism was symbolic rather than actual is suggested by stable isotope analysis that shows the presence of distinctive status-linked diets (A. Chase et al. 2001).

The Terminal Classic Maya, in contrast, could not be characterized as human resource oriented. Status distinctions are marked. For known Terminal Classic sites such as Seibal, Ucanal, and Caracol, there appears to have been a purposeful refocus on dynasty in the monuments. In terms of the artifactual record, there is nothing approaching symbolic egalitarianism. Burials and de facto refuse all point to distinctions in access to nonlocal items.

The Postclassic period Maya reestablished symbolic egalitarianism. Household plazuela groups are similarly set up regardless of status. Caches and burials are associated with household groups and are not restricted to elite contexts. There are the same kinds of artifacts in most locations. Contrary to popular opinion (Webster 2002), some Postclassic sumptuous elite burials were made (D. Chase and A. Chase 1988:54–56 for Santa Rita Corozal; Pendergast 1984, 1992:75 for Lamanai), but these tended to be placed within elaborate line-of-stone residential groups and "palaces" rather than in civic architecture. Status differentiation is present; however, as in the Late Classic, the basic contexts of interments are similar among residential groups. Multiple, equivalent-sized palaces also occur at many Postclassic sites, but these structures are somewhat dispersed in the settlement layout rather than being concentrated solely in a site's epicenter (e.g., D. Chase 1986). Ethnohistory suggests that "democracy" might have been realized with joint leadership through something called *multepal*.

The Political Frame

All organizations are composed of coalitions of people that vie for resources with other groups. Conflict and politics become emphasized in difficult times but can follow different trajectories depending on a given political system (Bolman and Deal 1997:164). Following Clayton Alderfer (1980) and L. David Brown (1983), Bolman and Deal (1997:171) note that there are "overbounded systems" with concentrated power and regulations and "underbounded systems" that are loosely controlled; conflict is differentially expressed in these two systems. Alternatively, authority's power in some circumstances may be limited to "zones of indifference" or to "areas that few people care about."

Late Classic society appears to have been overbounded and tightly controlled. However, for Caracol there is a monument gap during the eighth century when no rulers are portrayed (at a time during which other sites experience their greatest monument erection; Webster 2002:209). The archaeological record for Caracol indicates that precisely during this time, when dynastic rulers are less evident, the site experienced its greatest prosperity (as indicated in both the extensive construction of monumental architecture and the presence of artifactual materials that occur in household groups for this time; e.g., D. Chase and A. Chase 2002). Following this Late Classic monument lull—and leading into the Terminal Classic—there are increased depictions of warfare and captives (A. Chase et al. 1991). The monument texts suggest that the conflicting coalitions were mostly external to the site but within the polity, at a twenty-five-kilometer radius from Caracol. Earlier conflict, in contrast, was at a greater distance (A. Chase and D. Chase 1998).

Terminal Classic Maya politics can be gleaned from the stone monuments. While initial Terminal Classic monuments show captives and a continuation of local warfare (A. Chase et al. 1991; Dillon 1982), this quickly changed to an iconography signaling alliances (rather than warfare) with neighboring sites. For the first time at Caracol, more than one person of seemingly equivalent status could be portrayed on a monument. Modeled-carved pottery similarly depicts scenes of alliance. Thus, in the Terminal Classic, external coalitions appear to have been prominent.

Politics and coalitions are also apparent among the Postclassic Maya. No single dynasty appears to have emerged at any site or region (e.g., Roys 1957), in spite of colonial documents created to claim land, titles, and status (such as those of the Xiu; Roys 1943). Ethnohistory suggests that joint rule occurred and that knowledge was power. Archaeology also suggests the existence of multiple elite families and politically shared or rotated leadership. There is no indication of a single grand palace; rather, there are multiple dispersed "palace" residences with elite burials. Unfortunately, however, there are no stone monuments with coeval political history.

The Symbolic Frame

All of Maya culture can be viewed from a symbolic frame. Late Classic Maya society is characterized by monumental architecture—palaces, temples, and large plazas lined with carved stelae and altars. The architecture speaks to the grandeur of each city and the power of its rulers, positioning each dynasty within a cosmological metaphor (e.g., Schele and Mathews 1998). The stone monuments and iconography record the great feats (primarily conquests and captives) of rulers. At the same time, however, Late Classic society, at least at Caracol, is characterized by symbolic egalitarianism. Virtually all household plazuela groups had eastern mortuary shrines and associated caching. Thus, all households had a symbolic location for the interment of ancestors who could be venerated; ancestor veneration was not restricted to the ruling dynasty. Monumental architecture was a relatively constant symbol from site to site in the southern Maya lowlands—with some allowance for stylistic variation. Household ritual appears to have been more locally distinctive within communities and regions. At Caracol, face caches (lidded ceramic urns with an exteriorly modeled human face) and finger bowls (small lip-to-lip bowls containing extracted human fingers) were the norm (D. Chase and A. Chase 1998), as were collective burial locations for select members of the family (D. Chase and A. Chase 1996; a pattern also noted for Tikal [Haviland 1988]).

The Terminal Classic Maya, as mentioned, did not practice symbolic egalitarianism, and the east-structure ritual focus of households (as evidenced by burials and caching) disappeared. Efforts were initially expended, however, at rebuilding and remodeling monumental architecture. At many sites, though, these efforts stopped midstream with site abandonment. At Caracol, rebuilding continued minimally for forty years past the cessation of monument erection and is evident throughout the site epicenter. Initially, rulers were depicted and written about prominently on monuments; they also portrayed themselves with mythical symbols (snakes, sky figures) to bolster their importance. Stucco masks on epicentral pyramids can be related to warfare and central Mexican deities. Thus, the iconography found carved on the stone monuments, modeled in stucco on late architecture, and molded on some ceramics suggests broadened Mesoamerican contacts. These symbols boasted of the grandeur of dynastic rulership but simultaneously placed this rulership within the context of wider coalitions. In fact, there may have been attempts at establishing one or more Terminal Classic empires that were eventually foiled by local squabbles.

The Postclassic period symbolic frame contrasted with the symbolic frames employed during the Late and Terminal Classic periods in that it was characterized by a lessened emphasis on monumental architecture. The symbolic egalitarianism of the Late Classic, however, reappeared. Household rituals, as indicated by caching and incense-burner deposition, were similar throughout a given site. These rituals, in fact, have been interpreted as community-integrating devices for Santa Rita Corozal (D. Chase 1985a, 1985b, 1986; D. Chase and A. Chase 1998). Symbolism was overt in these caches; images and offerings were clearly depicted—dogs, jaguars, people, and gods. Cache contents and deities were personified, and cache contents varied depending upon the calendrical ritual being undertaken. Rather than being replicated in each residential group, cache locations rotated among these groups within the site, thus effectively integrating the community (and not simply extended families) in shared symbolic activity. However, there was not an east-structure focus to ritual. Instead, shrines were located in northern, western, and southern buildings. Shrines were used to mark individual graves as opposed to collective burial locations. Significantly, nearly identical cache figures and incense burners were found at sites a great distance apart, beyond the boundaries of a single state or region. The shared symbolism, when combined with ethnohistoric descriptions of migration, suggests a substantial overlap of culture and population. The widespread presence of a pan-Mesoamerican art style also supports this conclusion, visually emphasizing the broader integrative networks and cultural ties that once existed (Nicholson 1982; Robertson 1970).

Multiframe Interpretations of the Regeneration of Ancient Maya Society

When one views the Postclassic regeneration of Maya society, direct continuity, broken traditions, and resynthesis are all visible. The Late Classic everywhere has clearly identifiable horizontal and vertical structural elements. However, in the archaeological data at Caracol, all frames are evident. In the structural frame, there is a Classic period emphasis on one palace complex (probably related to the ruling dynasty) above all others that is not found in the Postclassic (at least at Santa Rita Corozal). However, a Late Classic Caracol identity and symbolic egalitarianism is also evident in household layout, artifacts, burials, and caches, and this is reflective of both the human resource and the symbolic frame. This combined-frame focus may have been the reason for Caracol's successes and Late Classic prosperity.

During the Terminal Classic, changes in all frames can be identified. Perhaps most evident are variations in the political frame. Initial Terminal Classic monuments focus on veneration of rulers and the re-creation of dynasty. There is increased iconographic evidence for, first, warfare and, then, symbolic ritual alliance with the same nearest neighbors in the Terminal Classic. At the same time, Caracol's Late Classic shared identity and symbolic egalitarianism disappeared in the Terminal Classic, indicating substantial changes in the symbolic and human resource frame. Excavations in Terminal Classic contexts show clear status variation and the polarization of the elite from the rest of society. At Nohmul, a nonlocal elite residence was inserted into a central public plaza (D. Chase and A. Chase 1982). At Caracol, on-floor trash indicates that the site's epicentral palaces continued to be occupied by an elite using a specialized ceramic subcomplex for some forty years after the erection of the site's final stone monument (D. Chase and A. Chase 2000). Eastern-structure mortuary and ritual focus also vanished.

Postclassic Maya organization may be seen as a rejection of the Terminal Classic Maya and as a regeneration of certain aspects of the Classic period organization. The Postclassic is characterized by symbolic egalitarianism and shared rule as opposed to dynasty. This is indicative of a human resource frame focus and is similar to the emphasis found in Late Classic Caracol, but it contrasts with the extreme status distinctions evident among the Terminal Classic Maya. The Postclassic Maya shifted their most populated centers to different locations than their Classic counterparts. There was also great movement of people and blending of traditions—as seen in the "international style" of the Late Postclassic and in historic documents relating to migrations. Importantly, however, no identified Late Postclassic regional capital was placed on top of a Classic period emblem glyph site; this is politically and symbolically significant. The rejection of Classic period dynastic seats of power and monumentality is seen further in the absence of the eastern focus found in Classic-era households. Evidence from Santa Rita Corozal suggests that the idea of a collective ancestral shrine also disappeared—in favor of a Postclassic emphasis on either the individual or the wider community.

Applying frame analysis to the transition from the Classic to the Postclassic period Maya permits us to see that Maya society was continuously regenerating itself through the varied emphasis of different frames in changing situational contexts. Maya society regenerated structurally following the Late Classic period pattern, with the notable loss of the dynastic overlay. Postclassic society existed with more crosscutting mechanisms in place, which have caused it sometimes to be characterized as "heterarchical" or "community oriented." This emphasis on the human resource frame also has been referred to by others, such as Richard Blanton (1998:149–54), as a "corporate strategy." The human resource frame is emphasized in both Late Classic and Postclassic society but not in the Terminal Classic, within which status distinctions are emphasized while local community identities are minimized.

The political frame shows changes on a temporal level, although polity size appears to be roughly similar between the Classic and Postclassic eras. Coalitions always existed. In the Terminal Classic, coalitions appear to have been most prominent not within a site proper but rather within the broader political unit. The emergence of Terminal Classic coalitions may have resulted from imbalances in the overbounded Classic system and likely represent other political changes, perhaps related to postmonument attempts at empire building. The Postclassic period political frame is characterized by intracommunity coalitions without evidence of dynasty. The concept of dynasty, while present, was deemphasized in some Late Classic polities, such as Caracol, although even there attempts were made to reestablish the importance of dynasty in the subsequent Terminal Classic period. Mercantilism was present in Maya society from at least the Late Preclassic period and cannot be credited in and of itself as a causal factor for Postclassic change (with the possible exception of introduced worldviews via trade contacts). Thus, although we have tended to think of Maya society as having devolved, a frame analysis suggests that this was not the case—at least in political and economic terms.

The symbolic frame also witnesses major changes between the Classic and the Postclassic period, particularly in the absence of overt dynastic representations (monumentality, east-structure focus, and stone texts). However, burials and caches were placed in households in both time frames. While Classic period burials in households emphasize the idea of collective ancestral membership within a single family line (D. Chase and A. Chase 2003, 2004b), Postclassic burials in households normally focus on the individual rather than the collective (D. Chase and A. Chase 1988:75–76); during the Classic period, interment in a residential group was ritually timed and highly selective (D. Chase and A. Chase 2004c), often combining the remains of multiple individuals in a single chamber or grave; during the Postclassic, in contrast, family cemeteries of individual graves can be located. Household caching in both the Classic and the Postclassic fostered a sense of unified community; for Late Classic Caracol, similar containers were placed within the same residential venues throughout the urban landscape (D. Chase and A. Chase 2004b), indicating participation by individual descent groups in community-wide rituals; for Late Postclassic Santa Rita Corozal, figurine caches placed within residential groups replicate community-wide rituals that have been recorded ethnohistorically (D. Chase 1985b), thus linking descent groups to community ceremonies. However, the overt symbolism and rarity of the Postclassic figurine assemblages indicates that multiple descent groups participated in the residential ceremonies, thus suggesting that aspects of household caching were regenerated into an even greater integrating mechanism during the Late Postclassic period (D. Chase and A. Chase 1998). While Late Classic Caracol households were unified in their adoption of similar caching practices regardless of status or location, these practices were directly related to honoring ancestors of members of individual household groups. Postclassic period caching, in contrast, seems to have been part of a more public community-related ritual activity; it was conducted not in conjunction with ancestor veneration but rather in concert with calendrical ritual. Thus, major shifts occur in the symbolic frame in the realms of public symbolism and ancestor veneration.

There are lessons to be learned from utilizing organizational frame analysis. As is readily evident, some material indicators may have varied meanings that can be missed without a multiple-frame perspective. Symbolic egalitarianism and the human resource strategy of sharing wealth and successes may be mistaken for a lack of hierarchy or centralization, if care is not exercised in archaeological interpretation (see also Blanton 1998:149–54). Carol Smith (1976) noted similar interpretational problems related to the identification of complex economic and market systems that mimic simple systems in their more evolved form (D. Chase and A. Chase 1992a:313). At Caracol, diet is perhaps the clearest marker of status (A. Chase et al. 2001), which is not surprising if stratification implies differential access to basic resources (as suggested by Morton Fried [1967]). Overemphasizing one frame in an analysis and mixing frames interpretationally are also possible. For instance, ancient Maya monumental architecture is predominantly a symbolic (not a political) indicator. Thus, the lack of monumental temples in the Late Postclassic should be viewed through the symbolic frame and cannot be taken to be directly indicative of political decentralization.

Organizational Change and Regeneration of Postclassic Maya Society

The regeneration of Maya society in the Postclassic period can be seen as a return to certain elements of Classic period society and organization and a rejection of other aspects. It is not just a recombination of existing features; it is also a transformation of the old order. The Terminal Classic period Maya were a major catalyst for this transformation, and many aspects of the Maya Terminal Classic period were distinctive from both the earlier and the later period.

A frame analysis evinces that the Postclassic Maya, rather than being characterized by the presence or absence of physical things such as monumental architecture or stelae, can be better distinguished by delineating organizational changes. The Postclassic period Maya rejected the hereditary ruling dynasty of the Classic period in favor of a system of shared governance. The shared identity of the Late Classic period was replaced by broad-based participation within a single Postclassic period community. The rejection of dynasty and the corresponding focus on shared government and community was likely an outgrowth of the Terminal Classic period attempts at reasserting dynastic leaderships and the deemphasis of symbolic egalitarianism (at least at sites such as Caracol).

Archaeological data suggest that the Terminal Classic Maya focused on structural changes in the organization of Maya sociopolitical organization without sufficient concern for the impact of the human resource perspective. The structural shift witnessed in Postclassic Maya society—with the lack of dynastically oriented monumental architecture and stelae and with the movement of population away from major Classic centers—may be viewed as a negative reaction to the Terminal Classic structure. The depopulation of major centers began at the onset of the Terminal Classic period (Culbert and Rice 1990; Demarest 1997) and is not a purely Postclassic period phenomenon. No known emblem glyph sites were continuously occupied through this transition into the Postclassic era. With the lack of an overarching dynasty came changes in patterns of ancestor veneration. The Postclassic period Maya may have venerated individual ancestors as opposed to the collective group. No longer was there a focal eastern mortuary structure in residential plazuela groups; in fact, the dead were frequently interred individually (as opposed to within family mausoleums). Other evidence of ritual activity confirms a change in focus. Caching returned to prominence during the Postclassic period, and—as was the case during the Late Classic period (at least at Caracol)—caches were found in residential plazuela groups. However, unlike their Classic period counterparts, Postclassic period caches were neither redundant in content nor located in conjunction with eastern mortuary shrines. Community building was strengthened by the overt symbolism of these caches: objects inside them are clearly identifiable, and their placement demonstrates a community-wide focus on directional symbolism and calendric ritual. The caches were not merely replicated, they were functionally interdependent.

In summary, the Postclassic period regeneration of Maya society is both more complex and more continuous than has often been suggested. The Terminal Classic Maya, in contrast, provide evidence of substantial disjunction between the earlier and later periods. We believe that the transformation of Maya society was an intentional move from the more autocratic Terminal Classic organization to a more democratic Postclassic structure—with a concomitant focus on human resources (as exhibited by symbolic egalitarianism) and a symbolic frame that confirmed the focus on community integration. Only by viewing the Maya diachronically and contextually through multiple perspectives or frames can we gain a more holistic and complex view of the collapse and regeneration of Maya society.

Acknowledgments

The research reported on here has been funded by a wide variety of sources. The research at Santa Rita Corozal, Belize, was funded by the Explorer's Club, the National Science Foundation (BNS-8318531 and BNS-8509304), Sigma Xi, and private sources. The work at Caracol, Belize, has been funded by the Ahau Foundation, the Dart Foundation, the Government of Belize, the Foundation for the Advancement of Mesoamerican Studies, Inc., the Harry Frank Guggenheim Foundation, the Institute of Maya Studies, the J. I. Kislak Foundation, the National Science Foundation (BNS-8619996, SBR-9311773, SBR-9708637, and DBI-0115837), the Stans Foundation, the United States Agency for International Development, and the University of Central Florida Trevor Colbourn Endowment. The authors would like to thank two anonymous reviewers for their comments; Glenn Schwartz also provided an extremely conscientious edit of an earlier version of this chapter. The authors, however, assume full responsibility for any errors that may still exist. Many articles published on Caracol may be found as pdf files at http://www.caracol.org.

12 Postclassic Maya Society Regenerated at Mayapán

Marilyn A. Masson, Timothy S. Hare, and
Carlos Peraza Lope

Most prior studies of collapse in the Maya area focus on the abandonment, decline, and transformation of Late or Terminal Classic period polities, which suffered far more permanent and damaging regional-scale demographic consequences than earlier cyclic fluctuation in polity fortunes (e.g., Culbert 1988; Demarest et al. 2004; Marcus 1993; Robles and Andrews 1986; Sabloff and Henderson 1993). The Postclassic period at Mayapán, a successor capital in northern Yucatán (fig. 12.1) that was unrivaled in size and power, presents an opportunity to examine how Maya society was transformed after collapse. At Mayapán, we can examine which institutions were changed, discarded, recycled, or retained from the past during regenerative processes occurring over the two centuries preceding the city's formation (AD 900–1100). This chapter builds on previous approaches to the study of social change at Postclassic Maya sites (A. Chase and Rice 1985; D. Chase and A. Chase 1988; Graham 1987; Masson 1997, 2000; Pendergast 1986; Rice and Rice 2004). We focus here on comparisons of political, religious, and economic institutions at Mayapán with those of the Classic period in our assessment of Postclassic regeneration.

An improved understanding of Postclassic regenerated society will emerge when we can more accurately pinpoint when Terminal Classic occupation ended and Late Postclassic sites were founded. The interval between around AD 1000–1150, poorly understood in this region, may represent a transition during which Chichén Itzá and its contemporaries waned until the coalescence of Mayapán (Andrews et al. 2003:152–53). This temporal intersection marks the metamorphosis of structures of Classic northern Maya society.

At Mayapán, a new regional capital was founded out of the collapse of

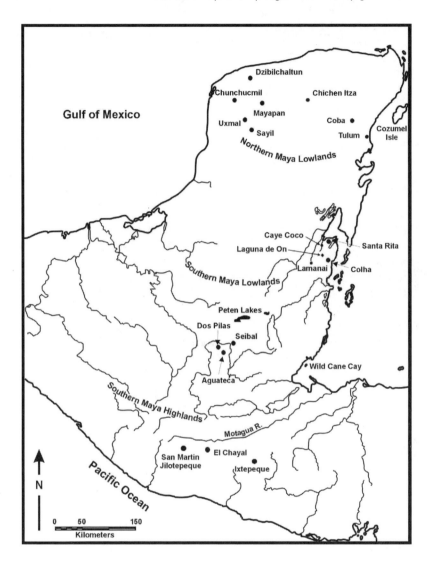

Figure 12.1 Location of Mayapán and other sites mentioned in text. (Map drafted by Pamela Headrick.)

the megacenter of Chichén Itzá and its affiliates in a process that exhibits aspects of both the template and the stimulus diffusion form of regeneration outlined by Bennet Bronson (chapter 9). Mayapán replicated major political institutions and monumental features (figs. 12.2, 12.3) derived from the Chichén Itzá template (Pollock et al. 1962), such as quadripartite and

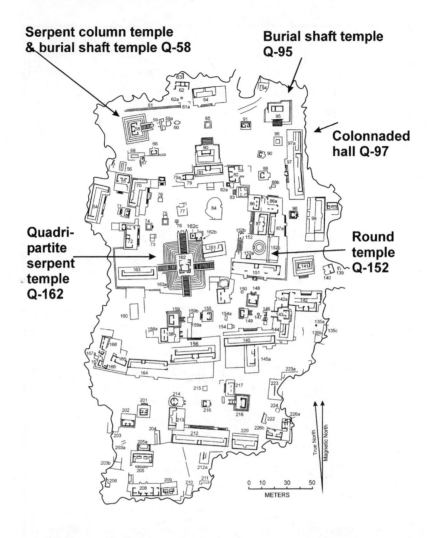

Serpent column temple & burial shaft temple Q-58

Burial shaft temple Q-95

Colonnaded hall Q-97

Quadri-partite serpent temple Q-162

Round temple Q-152

Figure 12.2 Mayapán feature types that resemble earlier versions at Chichén Itzá.

single-staircase serpent temples, round temples, colonnaded halls, and art programs suggesting paired offices and multiple assemblies. However, Mayapán rejected and excluded other architectural conventions of Chichén, such as recording long-count dates, names, and actions in carved stone; the use of cenotes for massive offerings; ballcourts; gallery patio features; and certain housing styles (Freidel 1981a:317, 321–23). As a further distinc-

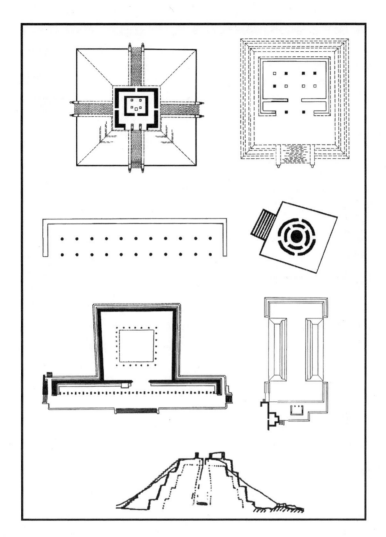

Figure 12.3 Chichén Itzá features that precede later versions at Mayapán: (*top row, left*) quadripartite serpent temple; (*top row, right*) serpent temple; (*second row, left*) colonnaded hall; (*second row, right*) round temple. Feature types at Chichén Itzá not found at Mayapán: (*third row, left*) gallery patio structure; (*third row, right*) ballcourt. Burial shaft temple Q-95 at Mayapán, cross section (*bottom, center*), resembling burial shaft in High Priest's Grave temple at Chichen Itzá (*see top left*). (Illustrations are modified from, starting at top left, Pollock et al. 1962:back-pocket map of main group; Thompson 1938:fig. 1; Ruppert 1952:figs. 42 and 74; http://www.mesoweb .com/chichen/resources/map/EntireMap.html; Ruppert 1950:fig. 4, 1952:fig. 49; Shook 1954:fig. 1. Prepared by Bradley Russell.)

tion from Chichén Itzá, Mayapán's lords rekindled traditions of the more distant Classic period, such as carved stelae, perhaps as part of a strategic revitalization (Masson 2000:250). This additional strategy more closely fits Bronson's "stimulus diffusion."

Models for cultural reproduction and transformation described by Marshall Sahlins for historic Pacific societies at the time of European contact outline aspects of Bronson's template regeneration. Sahlins (1981, 1995) demonstrates ways in which society's structural institutions are reproduced from the historical memories and varying agendas of actors. A theoretical threshold exists whereby the reproduction of a structure alters it to such a degree that transformation takes place. Transformation occurs because of internal or external circumstances that drive change, but emergent institutions are nonetheless created from historical elements that are recombined, sometimes with new material, to meet the needs of new cultural realities. The theoretical foundations of Sahlins's approach to structural change and his challenge to explain this change in local historical contexts are pertinent to the archaeological study of collapse and regeneration, postmodern critique notwithstanding (Obeyesekere 1992; Sahlins 1995). The evidence reviewed in this chapter is used to argue that many institutions at Mayapán were reproduced, selectively, from Chichén Itzá and its Classic period predecessors, but we also highlight important differences in the development of priestly and mercantile sectors at Mayapán. International influences were also incorporated by the city's ruling regimes, an issue treated in detail elsewhere (Milbrath and Peraza 2003).

Background

Recent interpretations of Chichén Itzá's chronology argue that the city's supreme hold over the northwestern Yucatán ended before AD 1100 (Andrews et al. 2003:152) and that Mayapán rose soon afterward (Milbrath and Peraza 2003; Peraza and Masson n.d.). The northern capital, Chichén Itzá, rose to power during the same Terminal Classic centuries when other northern and southern kingdoms met their demise (Andrews et al. 2003). The formation of the Chichén Itzá conquest state (Kepecs et al. 1994; Ringle et al. 1998) and its expanded international economy probably knocked the economic wind out of older, inland southern states that were already suffering from political conflict and other problems. Some Terminal Classic settlements of northeastern Belize and coastal Quintana Roo, located near the newly recharged Caribbean trading routes, show signs of orienting their production economies toward northern networks and adopting politico-religious symbols shared with Chichén Itzá (Freidel and Sabloff 1984; Masson and Mock 2004; Pendergast 1986).

By the time the Mayapán state formed during the twelfth–thirteenth centuries AD, the collapse most pertinent to this site and its hinterlands was that of the Chichén Itzá hegemony. The rise of Mayapán is historically attributed to its usurpation of Chichén Itzá's dominant position, and Mayapán's new lords claimed to restore local traditions and expel the foreign elements (for a summary, see Masson 2000:250).

Mayapán's architecture and areal extent are far larger than those of any of its contemporaries—the city covers an expanse of 4.5 square kilometers in the walled portion alone (fig. 12.4), and survey outside the wall suggests that many more dwellings exist beyond this boundary (Russell and Ormsby 2003). Put succinctly, Mayapán is "primate" in its size compared to other contemporary settlements of the Maya area (Smith 2005). Colonial sources reveal the city's centralizing tendencies in descriptions of the ranked confederacy of town leaders who founded the city and formed its ruling bureaucracy. Mayapán was a centralized nucleus, in contrast to a decentralized realm of weaker polities across the peninsula and into the southern lowlands.

Although past views of Late Postclassic Maya society at Mayapán and elsewhere were laden with assumptions of decadence, decay, and ruin (e.g., Pollock 1962:17; Proskouriakoff 1962:136; Thompson 1957:624), new studies over the past twenty years have cultivated a more objective, cross-cultural assessment (e.g., A. Chase and Rice 1985; D. Chase and A. Chase 1988; Graham 1987; Pendergast 1986). Sites such as Mayapán, Tulum, and Santa Rita Corozal continued the Chichén Itzá tradition of cosmopolitanism that incorporates international art and architectural styles shared with highland Mexico and elsewhere in Postclassic Mesoamerica (Milbrath and Peraza 2003; Miller 1982; Proskouriakoff 1962; Smith and Berdan 2003a). The effigy censers of Mayapán represent a hallmark Postclassic tradition in which deities and possible ancestors were portrayed in resplendent composite molded, modeled, stuccoed, and painted ceramic statues. These censers were key elements in calendrical rituals (D. Chase 1985a) practiced at Mayapán and virtually all other Postclassic Maya sites reported throughout the Yucatán peninsula, Belize, Guatemala, and the Maya highlands. Much other artistic and literary information has unfortunately been eroded, destroyed, or made invisible because of the popularity of stucco plaster and paint for murals and stelae and the widespread use of bark chapter codex books.

What new information has emerged from recent research that can refine our understanding of Late Postclassic Maya developments? Here we compare

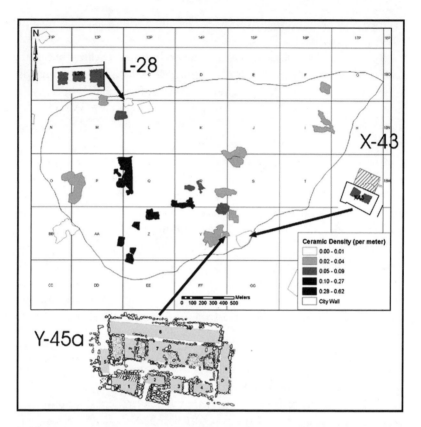

Figure 12.4 Map of Mayapán showing parameters of city wall; mapped fields; structures L-28, Y-45a, and X-43; and ceramic densities by field from surface collections (drafted by Timothy Hare and Bradley Russell).

Mayapán's leadership and economic institutions to those of the Classic period to assess the reproduction and transformation of key components of Maya society over time.

Political, Religious, and Mercantile Institutions at Mayapán

Lords and Priests

Recent multiactor art programs found in the two colonnades flanking the Castillo (Milbrath and Peraza 2003; Peraza 1998) reflect the multiple patron gods or ancestors of members of Mayapán's ruling council (*multepal*), which was dominated by members of one paramount family at a time

(Ringle and Bey 2001). Internally ranked councils such as those of Mayapán have precedents in the Classic period at a variety of northern sites including Chichén Itzá (Andrews et al. 2003:153; Grube 1994; Ringle and Bey 2001). More inclusive, shared leadership emerged at the end of the Classic period in response to the rising power of local elite families as reflected in art, architecture, and hieroglyphic programs of southern sites (Schele and Freidel 1990:274–305, 320–45). This late southern power-sharing accompanied the decline of the institution of divine kingship and paved the way for a transformation of rulership at Chichén Itzá, as well as some of its Puuc hills contemporaries (Carmean et al. 2004:427, 437) and ultimately Mayapán (Freidel 1981a:331).

The presence of a large number of influential merchants and priests would have limited the political power of Postclassic Maya lords. Cross-culturally, the increasing power of merchants or religious officials contributes to the decentralization of political nuclei (Eisenstadt 1980, 1981). Mayapán, like Chichén Itzá, endeavored to centralize Shmuel Eisenstadt's three categories of elite power (economic, religious, political). Members of the city's noble families held the highest political seats, engaged in the most influential long-distance mercantile activity, and held priestly offices (Landa 1941:90; Tozzer 1941:27n147).

The relationship between the priesthood and political offices at Mayapán and other contemporaneous sites could have been either an unbeatable partnership or the basis for fatal divisions. To what extent were political power institutions distinct from religious ones during the Postclassic period? The separation of such offices, or what Eisenstadt terms the "transcendental and mundane orders," is an important process that results in alternative elite sectors of society capable of exerting power somewhat autonomously from political rulers. The rise of formal religious sects also contributes to the development of ideological political codes by which rulers are held accountable, as they are judged by elites holding code-enforcing offices (Eisenstadt 1981).

In the Classic period, attendants are sometimes present in texts and images, but they are members of noble families or they are subordinate lords attending to or assisting kings. We know little of the existence of Classic period priests, whose specific titles ("Ah Kin") are scarcely mentioned in the texts, although some "political" titles could have carried ritual responsibilities (Houston and Stuart 2001:60). The paucity of priestly titles stands in contrast to political, military, and scribal glyphs present in Classic period texts. This implies that a powerful, separate class of hierarchically ranked priests may not have been well developed at Classic period cities. Rather, religious and mundane political duties may have been bound together in political offices. If true, this is a major difference from the Postclassic period.

Diego de Landa (1941:40) describes twelve high priests in residence at Mayapán. High priests possessed the title "Ah Kin Mai" (or "Ahau Can Mai"), and other lower-ranked religious offices also existed (Landa 1941:27). Chilam Balam priestly officials operated out of towns that were contemporary with Mayapán and postdated the city's fall. These individuals were not easily controlled by political authorities; their commentary, couched in prophetic histories, includes a critique of the Mayapán regime (e.g., Masson 2000).

The degree to which religious offices and institutions operated independently of political power is difficult to assess for the Postclassic. Some degree of complementarity is implied by the co-rulership of Petén Lakes polities by a political leader and a high priest (Jones 1998:94). One Mayapán account describes a priest, Ah K'in Kob'a, and another official named Kawich who "presided at the center" (Edmonson 1986:81; Pugh 2001:250; Roys 1962:79), a phrase that suggests power sharing. While Petén Lakes co-leadership roles may have formally reconciled potentially competitive sources of power, the existence of separate priestly offices represented a potential threat to political regimes by providing an organized faction capable of making rulers accountable or encouraging dissent. Although one informant's account relays that elites sponsored ceremonies in religious facilities at Mayapán (Tozzer 1941:27n147), the existence of separate priestly titles ("Ah Kin," "Chilam," etc.) indicates the conceptual distinctiveness of lords and priests.

Sources on Mayapán illustrate this divide along which Late Postclassic power structures could have easily fissioned. Landa (1941:27) claimed that priests were recruited from sons of noble families or moved into hereditary positions occupied by their fathers. In a famous case described by Landa, a high-ranking Xiu faction priest (Ah Xupan) from Mayapán became the founder of the post-Mayapán Xiu dynasty at the center of Mani (Landa 1941:40; Tozzer 1941:36). He married his daughter to a nobleman named Ah Chel, who founded the center and province of Ah Kin Chel, aided by political and religious knowledge obtained from his father-in-law (Landa 1941:40). Another case of a former priest who became a political ruler is described by Alfred M. Tozzer (1941:35n173) regarding an individual named Uxmal Chac of Uxmal. These accounts suggest that Late Postclassic priests (and merchants) may have increased in number or may have had increased political influence compared to their barely referenced counterparts of the Classic period.

In discussing Chichén Itzá, William M. Ringle (2004:213) suggests that the art of the city indicates the existence of dual offices of priests and lords and their accompanying councils. To a great extent, Mayapán appears to have reproduced the institution of the priesthood from Chichén Itzá, and Mayapán's Hall of the Sun Disk murals show sun disk figures descending at the behest of paired practitioners wielding serpent staffs. These may be sun-framed portraits of the city's major dynasts and their attendant conjuring or anointing priests. Many halls at Mayapán have art that portrays multiple individuals rather than single or hierarchically ranked actors.

In sum, southern Classic period sites show no evidence of a separate priestly class, but the office of the divine king and affiliated subordinate hierarchies had fissioned into separate institutions of lordship and priesthood by the time Chichén Itzá rose to power. While Postclassic lords may still have claimed some divine or supernatural origins or privileges, they did not exclusively perform ritual and relied upon priestly specialists for many such tasks. However, members of ruling families probably filled the ranks of the priesthood and had close ties to noble houses of governing lords.

Merchants

Merchants are known from the Classic period, but as with the priesthood, the evidence concerning them is relatively sparse. While portrayals of merchant figures occasionally occur on Classic period polychrome vessels (Taube 1992:90), they are much more common in Postclassic effigy censers. These individuals, perhaps historical individuals or representatives of the merchant deity Ek Chuah (God M), are seen in the context of royal courts and were probably linked to tribute offerings or the exchange of prestige items destined for royal circulation. Tiers of merchant activity are recorded for the contact period, ranging from long-distance traders to petty vendors operating solely within the confines of a single settlement (Feldman 1978).

At Postclassic Mayapán, noble family members were engaged in long-distance trade (Roys 1962), and our investigations suggest that affluent families apart from those of the governing council probably also engaged in distant mercantile activity. A recently excavated large house (Y-45a), located 900 meters southeast of the monumental zone and 150 meters from the southern portion of the city wall (fig. 12.4), probably was associated with an affluent family from the nongoverning lesser elites. This eight-room structure was rapidly abandoned, with belongings on the surface broken and then buried with stones and dirt, probably at the time of the city's violent demise circa AD 1441 (Masson and Peraza 2004). The vessel assemblage from this house included abundant examples of pots that may have originated from the Petén Lakes (Prudence Rice, personal communication to Carlos Peraza, July 2004) and Gulf Coast. Among the ritual censers present were smashed ceramic cacao pod effigies; cacao beans were widely used as money at Mayapán, and cacao effigies that were held by deity censers are ubiquitous in collections from the site. The presence of two storerooms at the house as well as numerous exotic vessels and cacao effigies strongly implies the occupants' involvement in mercantile activities.

Postclassic Economic Institutions and Classic Precedents

Economic change has been commonly invoked to explain Classic to Postclassic changes in the context of world-systems approaches (Blanton and Feinman 1984; Kepecs and Kohl 2003). Higher levels of commercialization of the Postclassic economy in the Maya area and elsewhere are inferred from documentary evidence about levels of market exchange at Spanish contact (Freidel 1981b; Smith and Berdan 2003b:7). Postclassic interregional market development and international world-system-type interaction are thought to have been greater than during the Classic period (Blanton et al. 1993; Smith and Berdan 2003b).

Some maintain that marketplaces probably existed at certain Classic sites (Folan et al. 2001:234; Jones 1996; Ruppert 1952:fig. 45; Tourtellot and Sabloff 1994:88–90). Richard E. Blanton and colleagues (1993:219–24) propose that the markets of Classic Maya society were primarily regional, confined to small, spatially bound territories (e.g., "solar" market systems [A. Chase 1998; West 2002]), and that greater market exchange of interregional goods was a Postclassic development. This proposal has found some support in distributional studies (Kepecs 2003; Masson 2001; Sabloff and Rathje 1975; West 2002). Comparing household production and consumption patterns is a useful approach to this problem (Hirth 1998; Smith and Heath-Smith 1994).

At some Classic period sites such as Caracol (A. Chase 1998) and Chunchucmil (Dahlin and Ardren 2002), market development is thought to have been considerable, perhaps qualitatively or quantitatively no different from the Postclassic (Chase and Chase, chapter 11). This assertion challenges previous work (Masson 2000; Sabloff and Rathje 1975) that attributes a major role to mercantile/commercial development in explaining changes in Late Postclassic social and political organization. Most scholars would generally agree that aspects of Late Postclassic international commerce were preceded and perhaps exceeded in some respects by the Terminal Classic developments witnessed for the primate city of Chichén Itzá (Ringle et al. 1998), although few have applied economic data to this supposition (for some exceptions, see Connor 1983; Kepecs 1998; Rice 1984; West 2002). Fully quantified assemblages rather than presence/absence studies are needed for comparison. We assert that the importance of distant goods (such as obsidian) to the daily economy of all members of society was far greater during the Postclassic than the Classic period at most sites prior to Chichén Itzá (Masson 1997, 2000; Sabloff and Rathje 1975).

Gifting and Tribute

Elite association with luxury manufacture and a gifting economy is observed in the Classic period (Ball 1993; Freidel et al. 2002; Inomata and Stiver 1998; Reents-Budet 1994), and a clear continuity with the Postclassic is observed. For the contact period, Landa (1941:92, 106, 141, 158) reports numerous feasts and ceremonies at which textiles, food, and other offerings were lavished on attendees, and a production economy of luxury items at Mayapán was probably linked to gifting. Ornament and fine craft production and consumption contexts are concentrated at upper-status houses or at small dwellings nearby, indicated by artistic debris such as pigments, worked stalactites, figurine molds, palettes, and marine shell. Luxury trade items such as copper bells and greenstone axes are also more common in upper-status contexts.

Of a list of tribute items requested by Mayapán (Landa 1941:26)—including birds, maize, honey, salt, fish, game, cloth, and "other things"—only game, fowl, and fish can be expected to show up archaeologically on a systematic basis. In one of Tozzer's notes (1941:30n159), birds, cotton mantles, exotic stones, and "everything produced in the country" are listed as tribute. If everything was a potential tribute item, there is great difficulty in isolating tribute goods production or consumption archaeologically. Greater consumption of young mammals (deer, dog, peccary) within the monumental zone is documented relative to outlying house lots by our recent faunal analysis. This age distribution pattern may indicate the value of young animals as tribute offerings to central elites.

It is noteworthy that Landa was unimpressed by Mayapán's tribute demands on subject polities and inferred that Mayapán was a relatively weak political center. From our point of view, the evidence for weak tribute obligations implies a greater importance of other mechanisms of exchange, that is, markets. Landa neglected to note, as other sources do (Roys 1962:50), that Mayapán requested military service from its subordinates instead of more hens. Historic sources also claim that Mayapán's representatives oversaw cacao production in distant southern lands (Honduras or Belize), probably owing to the importance of cacao as a market currency (Tozzer 1941:37n179, 94n417). Mayapán may have extracted cacao from distant plantations as tribute, but the documents are not specific on this point. Classic period hieroglyphic, iconographic, and residue studies also highlight this crop's long-term significance prior to Mayapán (Powis et al. 2002; Stuart 1988), including its use as tribute payment (e.g., Miller 2000:fig. 374).

External Resources for Currencies

Three crucial resources were more plentiful outside of the Mayapán environs yet formed the basis of marketplace currency used at the site. These include cacao, cotton mantles (Feldman 1985:21–23; Tozzer 1941:94), and marine shell ornaments (Landa 1941:96). The site was dependent on distant regions for supplemental quantities of cacao beans and textiles beyond what it could produce locally, and raw marine shells came from coastal sites. At the Belize sites of Laguna de On and Caye Coco, spindle whorl/ceramic sherd ratios were .002 (32/12,382) and .0001 (34/32,000) respectively. In contrast, only 3 spindle whorls were recovered at Mayapán among over 100,000 sherds outside of the monumental zone (2001, 2002 seasons), yielding a ratio of less than .00003. While a few weavers were present at Mayapán, clearly the intensity of mantle production was much higher in the Chetumal polity area (northeastern Belize/southeastern Quintana Roo), and traders from the city probably obtained cloth from there as well as from other polities (Piña Chan 1978; Tozzer 1941:30n159). A similar paucity of weaving is indicated by the numbers of whorls reported for Dzibilchaltun, Yucatan (n=25 [complete examples]), according to Jennifer T. Taschek (1994:215, 219). Although Taschek quantifies only complete artifacts, this low number may reflect the relative rarity of weaving industries in Yucatán in general. In contrast, 76 spindle whorls were reported from Cozumel Island, Quintana Roo (Phillips 1979). These data may highlight an important long-term dependency on east coast cotton textiles from the Quintana Roo and Belize areas.

Elites are linked to shell ornament production at Mayapán and the Belize sites of Laguna de On and Caye Coco (Masson 2003). Milpa 1, an area immediately to the west of the monumental zone, has 33–77 percent more shell-working debris than elsewhere at Mayapán. Tozzer (1941:95–96n418) mentions the use of "red" stone or shell beads in exchange, but the archaeo-logical record reveals a large suite of stone and shell beads and other orna-ments of varied form. In addition to their use as an exchange equivalency, shell ornaments probably also decorated prestigious costumes and were used for special purposes such as chastity objects (Tozzer 1941:106n488). David Freidel and colleagues (2002) highlight the close link between the value of precious items for status display and the consequent economic relative value of these items in exchange.

The importance of shell ornaments was reproduced closely from the past. For example, shell disk beads, cut *Olivella* beads, and *Spondylus* pecto-rals occur in Classic (Taschek 1994:figs. 6–9, 12) and Postclassic contexts at Mayapán and northern Belize sites. Tinklers and disk beads were also made as ornaments in the Preclassic (Buttles 1992:figs. 16, 20). As similarities in ornament forms are observed over time, their use as a currency for market-place or other forms of exchange could have earlier precedents.

Obsidian Distribution

Obsidian is the one durable material that reached Mayapán from distant locations, along with less-durable items such as cacao, cotton, salt, and perhaps honey, wood, fish, dyes, copal, and other forest products (Jones 1989; Piña Chan 1978). More-equitable proportions of obsidian were re-covered from different contexts at the Belize sites compared to Mayapán, where some contexts had more than 90 percent obsidian and others had none (table 12.1). In contrast, nearly 84 percent of the Belize site contexts had 40–89 percent obsidian in their household stone tool assemblage (Mas-son and Chaya 2000). The contexts with the greatest amount of obsidian at Mayapán are those located in the upper-status district of Milpa 1, next to the monumental center. Mayapán's distribution shows greater social in-equality in terms of access to this distant product, as might be expected for a more highly stratified center. Also noteworthy is the fact that the Belize sites possessed a larger overall proportion of obsidian than is found at May-apán: 66–75 percent of all stone tools, including utilized flakes, as opposed to 37 percent at Mayapán. This suggests that the Belize sites' position closer to the southern source created opportunities to obtain more obsidian from coastal traders. Mayapán obtained less obsidian, of which the elites had a disproportionately large share.

This sort of daily dependency on utility items from far away highlights the interregional nature of exchange. However, data from Classic period

Table 12.1 Obsidian at Belize sites and Mayapán

Interval category[a] (% obsidian)	Mayapán[b]	Caye Coco/Laguna de On[b]
0	25.0%	0%
20–39	9.6%	16.1%
40–69	26.9%	61.3%
70–89	21.2%	22.6%
90 or more	17.3%	0%

a. Interval categories quantify obsidian as a percentage of all stone tools recovered (obsidian and nonobsidian, formal tools and utilized flakes).
b. Percentage of Postclassic archaeological contexts with proportions falling in each interval.

Tikal illustrate the complex nature of obsidian consumption in the low-lands over time. Prudence Rice (1984:table 3) previously noted an increase in obsidian-to-chert ratios in Postclassic contexts of the Petén Lakes relative to the Classic period. Although problems with data collection thwart some efforts to quantify lithic debris at Tikal, Hattula Moholy-Nagy has recently made admirable attempts to overcome this (1997, 1999). There is much obsidian at Classic period Tikal; in one case, a ratio of obsidian (all pieces [including artifacts and debitage], $n=65,920$) to chert tools ($n=6,642$) can be calculated (Moholy-Nagy 1997:table 2) at 9.9 obsidian pieces per chert tool, higher than our ratios for either the Belize sites or Mayapán. One major difference is that obsidian pieces are generally concentrated in special-purpose contexts at Tikal, such as chamber burials (Moholy-Nagy 1999; Spence 1996), as opposed to the domestic midden contexts at Mayapán and the Belize sites. Moholy-Nagy's distributional analysis of green obsidian illustrates this pattern, although it also shows that upper-status-range structures and intermediate-sized structures have about three times more green obsidian than do small structures. This pattern resembles that of Mayapán, since Milpa 1 contexts have about three times more obsidian than do areas more distant from the main plaza.

What can be inferred from these comparisons? Elites at primary centers such as Postclassic Mayapán and Classic Tikal were able to acquire larger quantities of obsidian, and this material was distributed in similar ratios among upper- (and middle- for Tikal) status groups compared to lower-status groups. However, obsidian was utilized by upper-status groups in different ways, often cached in particular contexts at Tikal and used alongside local lithic tools at Mayapán. The effect of a well-developed hierarchy is visible in the top-down control of obsidian distribution at both sites, but the use context of this material suggests that it was used less as a prestige item at Mayapán. Obsidian was but one item brought in by long-distance trading activities at Mayapán, and its use as a daily utilitarian object may signal its changing role as a bulk utilitarian item (Masson and Chaya 2000; Rice 1984, 1987). Archaeologists have long noted that there are more obsidian artifacts at Postclassic sites than at Classic ones, apart from sites near obsidian sources. Through these patterns we see a transformation in the consumer use of at least one distant-exchange commodity.

Local Subsistence Production

Mayapán's local economy depended on nearby communities to acquire needed raw materials for basic production. Chert and chalcedony debris and tools are common at Mayapán, and most are from a white patinated chalcedony source not located at the site. The paucity of primary flakes and cores suggests that prepared preforms were brought to the site for the manufacture of bifacial tools, including knives and axes.

Tools produced from these raw materials were used throughout the city, and a good deal of manufacturing was probably devoted to meeting local needs. Workshops of varying intensity are dispersed throughout the site in association with non-elite house lot compounds. At Classic period Tikal, similar patterns of chert production have been reported (Becker 1973:398; Moholy-Nagy 1997). Scott L. Fedick (1991:111) observes that more primary production took place in sites beyond Tikal's boundaries and that debitage within the city was related to later stages of biface production.

Open spaces within and between house lots inside of the city wall at Mayapán would have been suitable for gardens or orchards as well as human-made moisture-trap depressions (*sascaberas*) located next to many houses. Land was also available outside the city wall, where small field houses, agricultural storage features, and dispersed residences have been recorded (Russell and Ormsby 2003). Small wedge-shaped axes found at Mayapán were probably used for clearing slash-and-burn agricultural plots.

In contrast, residents of the Belize political centers of Santa Rita Corozal (Dockall and Shafer 1993) and Caye Coco, as well as small settlements such as Laguna de On, produced few of their own formal stone tools. Instead, they obtained formal tools through exchange with the site of Colha, and local manufacture was restricted to idiosyncratic expedient tools or opportunistic recycling.

Classic period economic patterns vary according to the availability of local resources and the size and location of particular sites (Graham 2002). Community specialization has been documented, although never exclusively, as if settlements were loath to forfeit their subsistence autonomy. Settlements could specialize in agriculture (McAnany 1994) or supplement cultivation with lithic (King 1994, 2000:151) or ceramic (Fry 2001) production.

In summary, local subsistence production shows much variation across Classic and Postclassic landscapes. Mayapán, like Classic period Tikal, imported raw materials and engaged in late-stage stone toolmaking. As at some Classic cities, agricultural production also occurred at Mayapán. Although dependent on supporting communities for raw materials, these major cities attained a greater degree of independence by encouraging some local production of basic goods essential for daily life. Unlike Tikal (Fry 1980), Mayapán may have had utilitarian production of pottery, as implied by Clifford Brown (1999:574, 584), perhaps indicating an even greater concern with self-sufficiency in the utilitarian economy. While the earlier northern city of Chunchucmil (Dahlin and Ardren 2002) is an important exception, Puuc settlements also tended to some of their own basic needs, leading to their description as "garden cities" (Tourtellot and Sabloff 1994).

Settlement Patterns and Socioeconomic Status

House-lot boundary walls (*albarradas*) are present at Mayapán and earlier Classic period sites such as Dzibilchaltun, Chunchucmil (Dahlin and Ardren 2002; Garza and Kurjack 1984), and Coba (Folan et al. 1983). Albarradas surround domestic feature clusters, defining both elite and commoner compounds (Brown 1999:76–79; Bullard 1952, 1954), and their replication at Mayapán reveals the reproduction of a specific practice critical for identifying social units at particular sites. Despite these similarities between Mayapán and Dzibilchaltun, along with those discussed below, it is notable that domestic plans exhibit far less variation at Mayapán. This observation led Freidel (1981a:319–20) to suggest greater unity in social norms that affected house construction at Mayapán compared to the earlier site.

In a thoughtful comparison of domestic settlement patterns at Seibal and other sites, Gair Tourtellot (1988:table 45, 339–41) observed that more houses occur in isolation or in groups of two structures at Mayapán relative to Late/Terminal Classic Seibal, where more multihouse groups of three or more structures are present. He noted that Classic period Dzibilchaltun displays a similar pattern to that of Mayapán, with even more single structures observed. Tourtellot proposed that Mayapán and Dzibilchaltun had labor institutions—such as military corvée service at the former or temporary salt-bed working at the latter—that would have encouraged the part-time occupation of small houses by nuclear families resettled from their more permanent homes.

The pattern of more-abundant nuclear family dwellings at Mayapán is a potential reproduction of Classic period patterns at nearby Dzibilchaltun. While craft manufacturing house groups occur more often as isolated structures, compared to larger groups engaged in agrarian production (King 1994, 2000; McAnany 1994, 1995; Tourtellot 1988), many outlying isolated dwellings do not yield evidence of craft production at Mayapán.

Investigations of two small houses near the city wall, L-28 and X-43 (fig. 12.4), lend support for Tourtellot's model and provide no indication that the occupants of either house worked in agriculture or crafts. Neither house was occupied for long, indicating a limited stay at the city. Similar-sized houses closer to (within 500 meters of) the monumental center had twenty-nine times more lithic flakes and ten times more pottery than X-43, and L-28 has densities comparable to those found at X-43. Proportions of projectile points are above the site average for these structures' lithic assemblages, which could imply military service (Masson and Peraza 2004).

Tourtellot's suggestion that supporting classes were brought to Mayapán finds support in Landa´s account, which describes the initial establishment of the site as a seat of noble families of the confederation, followed by the recruitment of supporting residents "to provide services" (Landa 1941:26). Our settlement data support Landa's account, as structure density, structure size, and artifact density decrease with distance from the monumental center in the thirty-six sample areas studied (e.g., ceramic distributions; fig. 12.4).

In the regeneration of complex society at Mayapán, settlement patterns suggest a purposeful directive that drew lower-ranked families to the city. These residents were probably recruited from allied or subordinate polities, including those whose elites had resettled at the city's center. Comparisons with some Classic period sites suggest that this strategy was not new. Developmental surges in population growth and rapid construction of temples and palaces are associated with the coalescence of power at Petexbatun polities, including Dos Pilas (Demarest 1997:218–19) and nearby sites (Escobedo

1997:317; Inomata 1997:341, 347; Valdés 1997:324, 329). The parallels between Mayapán and Dzibilchaltun indicate that urban centers of western Yucatán persisted in luring laborers and small family units to provide services, a compelling case of structural reproduction.

Selective Transformation in the Regeneration of Mayapán

The evidence presented above indicates that Mayapán selectively regenerated political, religious, and economic institutions from the predecessor capitals of Chichén Itzá and prior Classic period sites. The creation of the city was not simply a template regeneration (Bronson, chapter 9) but involved calculated acts informed by historical memory that were selective in nature. Founding regimes of Mayapán claimed to reject Chichén Itzá's foreign ways, while at the same time they emulated key political, religious, and architectural features of this polity. Some institutions and structures were new or markedly amplified; others harked back to Classic models.

Like Chichén Itzá, Mayapán incorporated an outward-looking cosmopolitan style of art and architecture that fused earlier traditions and links with Gulf Coast Mexican groups and beyond (Milbrath and Peraza 2003). But Mayapán distinguished itself from Chichén Itzá in multiple aspects, including major ceramic changes; rejection of selected architectural features (gallery-patio, ballcourt, house style as noted by Freidel [1981a:317], etc.); reinstating the Classic institution of stela erection; creating an elaborate effigy censer tradition; inventing a sacrificial burial shaft temple tradition unique to Mesoamerica; altering obsidian exchange supply networks (Andrews et al. 1989); and establishing a highly nucleated city that contrasts with Chichén's vast sprawl.

Like Classic period Dzibilchaltun, Mayapán manifests a settlement pattern that reflects unusually large numbers of nuclear families (Tourtellot 1988:339), perhaps indicative of city-oriented work patterns. Military service was probably one important occupation for residents of small, isolated Mayapán houses.

New political developments in Postclassic Mayapán include powerful families competing for control of Mayapán's government. The institution of the priesthood seems more developed at Mayapán and Chichén Itzá compared to earlier sites; religious and secular duties fissioned into specialized, dual, complementary offices occupied by members of noble houses. Long-distance merchants included members of governing houses as well as other affluent families.

Various economic institutions were reproduced from the past, including a prestige economy, gifting and tribute, and local, regional, and distant exchange in goods essential to daily life. The local economy relied on a regional supply system, importing raw materials for elite-based shell working and commoner-based stone toolmaking, a strategy paralleling earlier patterns of dependency reported for Classic period sites. The use of cacao as currency or payment was a practice shared by both the Classic period and the Postclassic period, and similarities in shell ornaments over time imply their long-term use as an exchange medium as well.

However, the political economy of Mayapán consumed far more products from afar than it produced for interregional networks. Mayapán traders imported southern cacao, cotton mantles, honey, and other riches in exchange for slaves (Landa 1941:35–36; Tozzer 1941:35), salt obtained en route, or shell or cacao bean currencies.

This amplification of long-distance trade was a critical factor that has been linked to the growth of the merchant sector (Sabloff and Rathje 1975), which—along with the rise of the priesthood—formed major competitive pools of social power and checked the inflation of political hierarchy. This triadic, magnified confrontation of merchants, priests, and lords or military captains is perhaps the most conspicuous institutional change from earlier times, although Late Classic power struggles forecast the transformation to more inclusive modes of government toward the end of some southern dynasties (Schele and Freidel 1990:274–305, 320–45). The completion of this political metamorphosis is evident at Mayapán, where the art and architecture successfully obscure the identities of any single, dominant rulers, including those known to us from colonial ethnohistory.

As Eisenstadt (1980:842) notes, "In different civilizations and historical settings a variety of combinations of continuity and change in different spheres of institutional life took place." When we consider broader patterns of regeneration for the Postclassic Maya case, a model of selective transformation of particular institutions, with variation according to factors of political geography, is evident.

Acknowledgments

We are grateful to Jeremy Sabloff, Glenn Schwartz, and two anonymous reviewers for their valuable suggestions regarding this chapter, although all errors and interpretations are the sole responsibility of the authors. Research at Mayapán is supported by the Foundation for the Advancement of Mesoamerican Studies and the National Science Foundation (grant number 1018919).

13 Before and After Collapse
Reflections on the Regeneration of Social Complexity
Alan L. Kolata

This book addresses an extraordinarily complicated sociohistorical phenomenon: the regeneration of cultural complexity in the aftermath of state collapse. The case studies presented here graphically demonstrate the highly variable nature of this process. One might be tempted to say that each case of societal regeneration is unpredictable, historically contingent, unique, and therefore analyzable only in its own terms. Most of the authors in this book do, in fact, present empirically rich instances of regeneration processes that pertain to highly specific historical, cultural, and environmental circumstances. Generally eschewing the comparative impulse, these authors emphasize the contingent and locally embedded quality of the social regeneration of complexity. One can readily understand this perspective given the exceptionally variable social and historical trajectories through which complex societies developed globally. Some contributors (most notably Bronson and Schwartz), however, explicitly grapple with more general theoretical frameworks that may enable intriguing comparisons across time, space, and cultural traditions.

As Glenn Schwartz perceptively notes in his introductory chapter, the regeneration of social complexity in the wake of the collapse of urbanized, state-level societies and empires has rarely been a topic of sustained scholarly analysis, despite its inherent value for comparative historical and social science research. This may be because the aftermath of empire is often imagined as a period of cultural degradation, a backsliding into "dark ages" shorn of the rich material trappings of imperial splendor. The initial decline of social complexity after state collapse apparently renders this period of transformation less compelling as an object of analysis for many historians, art historians, and archaeologists. The study of "high civilization" still remains the holy grail of historical scholarship. But this is at once a parochial and an elitist conception, one that fails to acknowledge that the regeneration of cultural complexity, in whatever forms it takes, is a complex process of social change fascinating in its own right. Principled theoretical and empirical analyses of regeneration in the aftermath of collapse have enormous potential for informing us about the structural nature of complex society and the processes through which states and empires are formed and sustained in the first instance. The various chapters of this book represent richly varied attempts to explore this potential both through empirical analysis of individual case studies and through more general, comparative perspectives.

To understand the regeneration of social complexity after some form of state disintegration or collapse, one must recognize and account for the historical specificities of prior structures of rule, authority, and governmentality. By "governmentality" here I mean the socially and historically contingent crucible of coercion and consent that composes the underlying lineaments of state power. Regeneration of social complexity, if such occurred after collapse of a state formation, can follow any number of structural pathways, depending on the nature of various externalities present during the reconstitution of complex society. Such externalities might include the social, political, economic, and environmental processes by which state collapse was engendered in the first instance, or the nature of historical, political, and economic relationships with neighboring states. In short, the conditions of possibility for the social regeneration of complexly structured societies, as well as the specific character of that regeneration, are directly dependent upon the principles and structures of government prior to collapse.

Any convincing analysis of the regeneration of social complexity after state collapse must account for the "time-binding" material and social effects of prior governmental actions—the specific political ecology of the state prior to its disintegration. The analysis of political disruption must take account of the historical continuities between pre- and postcollapse social formations as much as the nature of the disjunctions produced in the aftermath of state disintegration. One can readily imagine, for instance, that it matters considerably for such an analysis whether the historical trajectory of state formation and governance entailed the forceful imposition of direct control over territories, resources, and populations by some form of dominant political, economic, and military power, or whether state structure and governance was sustained through indirect networks of political alliance, social exchange, and commodity circulation via trade and mutually accepted tributary or clientage relationships.

The former circumstance involves the imposition of hegemony and sovereignty over subjugated peoples by authorities that govern with the full panoply of the instruments of daily administration, surveillance, persuasion, co-optation, and coercion. Here territorial annexation, imposition of externally derived laws and regulations, cultural absorption of subject populations, and often a powerful, colonial ideology of a "civilizing mission" are central to the dynamics of state formation and expansion. A necessary institutional correlate of the colonizing state is the forceful deployment of military and police power. The physical embodiment of this power often includes chains of strategically placed fortresses, garrisons, and fortified walls, but also new colonial towns imposed in the countryside, often with streets laid out in visually transparent grid or radial forms to enhance, in theory at least, the capacity for surveillance, tracking, and ultimately taxing of populations of the subject cities and their near hinterlands. The strategy of hegemony and sovereignty, in other words, reflects the logic and the logistics of empire.

The latter circumstance, in contrast, represents a case in which a state dominates populations without actually administering them directly—a form of governance that can be termed hegemony without sovereignty. In this instance, power and influence are exercised not by unilateral imposition of administrative regulations or centrally controlled bureaucracy but rather by the strategic application of force—tactical force, not generalized military oppression—and the demonstration effects of cultural superiority, awesome displays of material wealth, sumptuousness, conspicuous consumption, and superior military capability (Sahlins 2004).[1] The intrusive, material presence of the state in local communities is much reduced, often absent altogether, in favor of the co-optation of local institutions and facilities, while the displays of superiority (the demonstration effects) are frequently limited to capitals, where they may impress and overawe local elites. The mere potential for direct military intervention, territorial subjugation, and social incorporation is sufficient to ensure the political and economic subordination of these subject populations. The dominant state exercises hegemony without the need for or logistical difficulties of maintaining sovereignty. Here the shared perception of overwhelming power obviates the need for its systematic exercise. The social and economic costs of this principle of power are correspondingly lower than that of the colonizing state, which must bear the extraordinary burden of subduing and directly governing an often truculent and resistant population.

But why do I claim that it matters significantly to the analysis of the regeneration of complex society whether the political ecology of states prior to collapse varied along these lines—that is, along the continuum from what we can gloss schematically as direct-to-indirect rule? First, I would argue that these distinct modes of political control (and, as discussed below, the depth of their temporal persistence) generate differing degrees of transformation in everyday practices, habitual social relations, and, ultimately, the historical consciousness of subject populations, and further that the intensity of this transformation of historical consciousness shapes the character and trajectory of social regeneration in the wake of state disintegration. From this perspective, ordinary peoples' prevailing attitudes, perceptions, and practices played out in the course of their everyday lives, not simply political and economic institutions, become analytically critical variables.

In the case of the colonizing state (hegemony with sovereignty), the ubiquity of instruments of social control—foreign governors wielding authority through military force; imposed systems of revenue collection, taxation, tariffs, and tribute; subordination of once-autonomous local authorities; expropriation of local land, water, and other natural resources; graphic displays of extreme violence against local resistance; erection of highly visible public monuments such as palaces, temples, shrines, government schools, offices, warehouses, forts, prisons, and the foundation of entirely new colonial cities commemorating and glorifying the power of the state—serve, over time, to alter and even suborn autochthonous social identities and senses of cultural independence. In a kind of society-wide "Stockholm syndrome," subject populations often move their perception of newly dominant authorities from fear and loathing to identification, collaboration, and emulation. They often become complicit in their own domination. In short, historical consciousness may be so thoroughly transformed that the dominated and the dominators come to broadly share the new ideology of social relations and governance. The political subjugation of local populations becomes naturalized. Foreign authorities and, even more important, foreign "ways of being" become embedded in the total social fabric, radically transforming if not erasing locally specific identities and social relationships. This is not to say, however, that resistance to the colonizing state necessarily disappears. Vigorous local opposition may continue, particularly in covert fashion. But accommodation to the state in its various degrees and intensities of political presence defines the terms of engagement of that resistance.

In the case of a state formation structured according to a political strategy of hegemony without sovereignty, the effects on historical consciousness of the subjugated populations may be rather less transformative, more fluid, and potentially evanescent. Daily social interactions follow familiar rhythms without the continual presence of foreign authorities. The material presence and sheer physical artifacts of the superordinate state rarely dominate local cityscapes. Foreign-occupied military garrisons and foreign-conceived and -imposed colonial new towns are few and far between, or entirely absent. Social intercourse between state authorities and subject populations is highly constrained both spatially (to capitals or trading entrepôts, for instance) and often temporally as well, occurring only during a few prescribed moments (such as periods of tribute collection). Local patterns of work, worship, and leisure continue fundamentally unaltered. Foreign ways of being are less apparent, less palpable, consigned most often to occasional encounters in highly conventionalized, scripted social contexts. Multiple or unanticipated juxtapositions of the foreign and the local are rare and do not constitute the fundamental texture of social life.

Of course, this does not mean that in a complex state formation structured through the exercise of hegemony without sovereignty, social impacts on subject populations are negligible. As a major instance of such impact, all states extract surplus from subject populations whether in labor or in kind, or both. Taxation of labor, product, or species will often be considerably onerous, even though the institutional forms of extraction remain local. Surplus inevitably flows away from the local communities into the coffers of both the local authorities (as was likely the case prior to foreign domination) and that of the distant, foreign elites. Although social and, especially, economic impacts on subject populations are considerable, they are periodic, not chronic, and framed in terms of very specific social domains; they do not seep into daily social practice or necessarily transform people's understanding of themselves or their place in the world.

This distinction between state-deployed strategies of hegemony and sovereignty versus hegemony without sovereignty can be further explored by conceiving the difference in impact on subject populations in terms of another analytical distinction—that between orthodoxy and orthopraxy. This distinction will be particularly important later when I explore the various pathways, trajectories, and outcomes of the regeneration of complex societies after an event or process of state collapse. Orthodoxy and orthopraxy are subtly different forms of the relationship between belief and behavior.

By orthodoxy here I mean circumstances under which subject populations adopt and practice state ideology that serves to bind them closely to dominant patterns of behavior prescribed and sanctioned by state authorities. In the case studies of the preindustrial states examined in this book, orthodoxy is framed most often in terms of state religions and related cult practices. Such state religions inculcate concepts of the proper social relationships between rulers and the ruled, create a sense of shared meaning between state authorities and their subjects, legitimize the actions of central authorities, and, in some sense, define the terms of social belonging and citizenship in society.

Often such religious practice is tied spatially and materially to visually salient state temples, shrines, and pilgrimage centers. These state-authorized and -constructed spaces become touchstones for public gatherings and therefore for the expression of popular culture and publicly shared attitudes. Significantly, one finds that such temples (within major cities at least) are contiguous with other state-constructed spaces and structures, such as central plazas, palaces, elite residences, and perhaps most important of all, state-regulated marketplaces. This physical contiguity of state-identified places and the institutions they materialize shapes the daily spatial practice of state subjects. They become critical nodes in the social networks that people inhabit on a daily basis. Because access to and social relationships within these spaces are shaped by the needs and priorities of the state, these physical spaces are important vehicles for inculcating socioreligious orthodoxy.

State religions can also change the definition and experience of time and therefore the collective daily activities organized in temporal cycles that are critical to social reproduction. Frequently, state religions introduce new calendars, calendrical systems, and related forms of time reckoning that serve to inscribe new senses of temporal value. In the preindustrial world, such calendars are normally linked to specific rhythms of production, particularly in agricultural practice. By temporally coordinating agriculture and labor through new systems of time reckoning, the state achieves a measure of control over the social forces of production. Surplus production, in particular, is extracted through the spatial and temporal frames of reference of the dominant state authorities. That is, state religion and state business merge or interpenetrate as a bundle of related, daily practices and activities. Religion and economics become part of a socially and conceptually seamless set of practices.

Subjects come to live and experience their social worlds in terms of the spatial and temporal frames of reference constructed and authorized by the state. By significantly altering or introducing new spatial and temporal frames of reference, the state in essence achieves a measure of discipline over its subjects' social, political, and economic behavior, challenging and often changing local practices. Over a period of time, perhaps a generation or two, this habituated social action engraves a kind of mental template of what is defined as acceptable actions and proper thought. In Orwellian terms, the state achieves, particularly in its leading subjects, a measure of "mind control" through its involvement in the production and consumption of spatial, temporal, and material value. State orthodoxy defines what, where, when, how, and why certain social actions are valued, as well as who may have access to the material and social benefits generated by the state. Just as importantly, a state-imposed doxology defines who can be excluded from these benefits. That is, state authorities define and implement the system of incentives and punishments that motivate or inhibit culturally prescribed and culturally proscribed behaviors among its subjects.

Orthodoxy, in other words, is intimately associated with the process of the transformation of historical consciousness. Habitual social, economic, religious, and ideological practice is intimately bound to belief. Believers become citizens; citizens become believers. Subjects aspire to the values promoted by state authorities, often through religious practice. New communities of worship and social belonging are among the most effective vehicles for the transformation of historical consciousness that, in political terms, can be glossed as the transformation of subjects into citizens. In the world of orthodoxy, behavior and belief become isomorphic: subjects of the state do what they believe, and they believe what they do. Subjects become stakeholders and, in the process, willing agents of the state's social, economic, political, and cultural agendas and its status quo. In the calculus of cost versus value, orthodox citizens benefit from conforming their behavior to the dominant beliefs and practices of the state.

I suggest that the adoption of orthodoxy is more likely to occur in the context of a state structured through a strategy of hegemony and sovereignty—a context in which daily behaviors are suffused within, defined, controlled, or heavily influenced by state instruments of social control. The very social and physical ubiquity of the state, its institutions, material practices, strategies of governance, beliefs, and value systems, condition the manner in which individuals experience their world. The relevant social memories, religious practices, and institutions become those of the dominant state and its elite authorities, not those of the incorporated subjects. Local identity is not necessarily entirely subsumed in or erased by the foreign value system, but it is certainly transformed and, in complex ways, hybridized by interaction with the dominant value system. Of course, hybridization may flow in either direction or both simultaneously—from dominant elites to local subjects, and from local subjects to dominant elites—but the relevant point is that value shifts inevitably occur, and the resulting system can become the taken-for-granted institutional, social, and behavioral framework for society. In short, orthodoxy becomes naturalized, the normative state of affairs.

By orthopraxy, I mean social forms of practice that come close to dominant patterns of behavior without adopting the underlying meaning or worldview inscribed in such practices. Subjects behave (publicly at least) in a fashion consistent with the expectations of state authorities. They may do so to avoid punishment or, perhaps just as likely, to extract social, political, or economic benefits from the dominant state and its institutions. The behavior of local subjects is strategically mimetic and does not constitute thoroughgoing assimilation or conversion, as is the case with orthodox beliefs. Local elites expand their own influence and authority by establishing mutualistic or symbiotic social relationships with state authorities without adopting the underlying value system of the dominant state. Emulation and deference are effective tools for creating and sustaining these important social networks.

Orthopraxy, however, is not a dilute or incomplete form of orthodoxy in which state doxology and values are misunderstood or inadequately inculcated in subjects. Rather, orthopraxy generates a unique synthesis of foreign (dominant) and local (subordinate) beliefs; expresses its own value system that may partially incorporate, transform, or even reject foreign elements; and, importantly, constitutes its own political strategy. In contrast to the power of orthodox beliefs, when thoroughly assimilated by subject populations, to effect a transformation of historical consciousness, orthopraxic behaviors do not readily result in such substantive changes in local beliefs and practices, core value systems, or metaphysical understandings of space, time, and history. Local beliefs, values, and social memories are not subsumed or erased in the dominant system. Rather, they retain their integrity and local meaning, even if they are partially transformed by foreign concepts and institutional practices as they interpenetrate them. Local elites and their subjects pattern their behavior on the model of the dominant social actors, but they do not become like those actors except as they consciously choose to do so. In effect, unlike orthodoxy, orthopraxy produces strategic subjects, not committed citizens.

Parallel to my thoughts on the proposed close relationship of orthodoxy to states organized according to principles of hegemony and sovereignty, I would argue that orthopraxy is more likely to occur under conditions of dominance structured by a strategy of hegemony without sovereignty. The rationale for this hypothesis is straightforward, and I will not belabor the point. Simply framed, the relative material, social, and political absence of a state that elects to exercise hegemony through indirect instruments of power inhibits the consolidation and convergence of belief, value, and behavior that induces committed forms of orthodoxy. The relationship of state to subject under a regime of hegemony without sovereignty is framed most often as a periodic, extractive proposition, rather than as a fully realized incorporation of local subjects into the political sphere. State authorities skim the economic surplus of subjects through episodic tribute and taxation, but they rarely engage in the social control of daily life. Political relations focus on interactions between state and local elites; that is, the bulk of the subject population constitute economic subjects, not political subjects. As a result, substantive value shifts and the hybridization of beliefs and social practices among all but a few local elites rarely occur. Absent a "civilizing mission," the mass conversion experience characteristic of orthodoxy never takes root. Habituated social practices remain deeply embedded in local ways of belief and being. Orthopraxy does not entail the rejection or transformation of local identities, values, institutions, and social practices, but rather constitutes a strategic positioning of these local cultural expressions in terms of the value system of the state. Instead of a transformation of historical consciousness among subjects as occurs with orthodoxy, we see multiple local accommodations to the political and economic realities of a dominant power. Such accommodations, however, do not entail acceptance of the implicit social and moral order on which that dominant power is based. In short, orthopraxy is a form of situational, pragmatic social practice formed in the crucible of unequal power relations.

How, then, do we apply these various theoretical concepts of hegemony, sovereignty, orthodoxy, and orthopraxy to the analysis of the regeneration of complex society in the aftermath of state collapse? First, I would argue that what is regenerated after collapse may be dependent on the extent to which the historical consciousness (and therefore the daily social, political, ideological, and cultural practices of subject populations) has been transformed. An initial hypothesis might propose that the regeneration of complex society after state collapse is more likely to occur in contexts in which the predecessor state held both hegemony and sovereignty over subject populations for a considerable period of time (several generations) and therefore succeeded in significantly transforming the historical consciousness of these populations. In such a historical context, the ubiquitous physical and social presence of the state serves, over time, to ingrain social habits, political structures, patterns of production and consumption, and, not least, familiarity with and acceptance of hierarchical institutions and specific forms of class relations. The status quo ante becomes the natural, familiar model for regenerating and reproducing state formations. Here the intriguing concept of "template regeneration" proposed by Bennet Bronson (chapter 9) is particularly apropos.

By "template regeneration," Bronson means that the regeneration of complex society follows a culturally well-understood and historically in-grained model of social and political organization, such that states and empires reappear periodically after periods of disintegration with essentially the same structure. According to Bronson, such regenerated states are "faithful copies of their predecessors" that adhere to replicated social practices, "government organization, institutions, language, cultural manifestations, and style." Bronson attributes the virtual isomorphic character of such regenerated states to the power of literacy and to bureaucratic structures obsessed with detailed record keeping. He believes that such practices of reading, writing, and record keeping permitted the reemergent state to copy the institutions and cultural styles of their predecessors with high fidelity and essentially re-create the past. Not surprisingly, Bronson points to the ancient Chinese empire(s) as his principal exemplar of template regeneration, given the high cultural value placed by the Chinese on literacy, bureaucracy, mensuration/standardization, and hierarchical institutions.

This assumes, of course, that the Chinese (or other template regenerating states) held a norm or ideal of history as the "unadorned reporting of things that had happened, free of distortion, addition or omission, as though it were possible to record human actions in words as faithfully as a musical performance might be recorded by an infallible phonograph" (Nelson 1973:40) and further that the means of transmitting historical tradition across generations was principally via the written word. Both of these assumptions can be questioned—if not, perhaps, in the Chinese case, most certainly in other cultural and historical contexts (such as the Andes, Mesoamerica, sub-Saharan Africa) where plastic and textile art, storytelling, folk tales, music, dance, and other forms of performative acts serve as a principal vehicle for the transmission of historical knowledge.

In other words, I would extend Bronson's notions of how and why template regeneration occurs by noting that this was not simply a matter of technography, that is, occurring merely through the quality and fidelity of written records. Rather, cases of template regeneration may equally be a product of perduring ideologies, worldviews, and daily social practices, however these were transmitted across generations (orally, the written word, plastic arts, performative scripts). Miriam Stark's (chapter 10) discussion of the sequential, recursive emergence of structurally isomorphic state formations in Southeast Asia is a particularly interesting instance of template regeneration that does not depend exclusively on literacy and the transmission of detailed historical records. Although the pre-Angkor and Angkor period Khmer states employed scripts written in Sanskrit and Old

Khmer, these texts (particularly those written in Sanskrit) generally concern details of dynastic succession, dedications recounting the establishment of religious foundations, and imprecations to various Indic deities. Michael Vickery's (1998) tour de force of historical scholarship demonstrated that the Old Khmer texts do provide a richer description of local sociological, political, and economic structures than had been previously appreciated. Still, these inscriptions do not constitute the kind of highly detailed histori- cal archive that Bronson suggests was essential for template regeneration. As Stark proposes, the "Khmer template" derived from long-term conti- nuities in local-level political structures ("local" here meaning down to the sociological scale of villages and their surrounding hinterlands) and in tra- ditional modes of production, principally wet-rice agriculture and fishing.

A very similar argument can be seen in Gordon McEwan's (chapter 6) treat- ment of the emergence of the Inca empire. He effectively argues that the Inca were consciously drawing on historical models of ecological adaptations, ad- ministrative structures, political organizations, and, most importantly, ideo- logical concepts of political legitimacy prevalent in the predecessor empires of Tiwanaku and Wari. Here, though, one might suggest along with McEwan that the structural template regenerated by the Inca was not completely isomorphic with the past; it was not a "faithful copy" of its predecessors, in Bronson's terms. Rather, the "Inca template" combined elements of structural continuity, partic- ularly at the level of local political administration (as in the case of the Khmer), with political innovations that built upon but nevertheless transformed the Wari and Tiwanaku templates.

These cases bear some similarity to Bronson's "stimulus regeneration" (the mobilization of social memory, real or imagined, to legitimate structures of hierarchy) but still retain elements of the process of template regeneration. So perhaps we might seek to extend Bronson's typology by proposing a conceptual hybrid of some sort between stimulus and template regeneration to account for these cases. In these sociohistorical contexts, the transmission of a structural template for state formations across generations was not the product of didactic readings of preserved historical archives by mandarins but rather resulted from daily sociocultural practice and long-term persistence in ideology and worldview. In short, the mode and technology of structural template transmission is not re- ally the principal issue here. More importantly, template regeneration can be con- ceptualized as another term for a process of social regeneration stemming from shared historical consciousness of proper social, moral, and governmental order: the practice of orthodoxy rather than orthopraxy.

As is made clear by several chapters in this volume, that which is regenerated after collapse is not always a duplicate or "structural template" of the prior state. Often the very ruptures of collapse generate new institutions, new social practices, and (most interesting from my perspective) new forms of historical consciousness. The fascinating case studies described by Ellen Morris for the First Intermediate Period in Egypt (chapter 4), by Diane and Arlen Chase for the Classic–Terminal Classic–Postclassic Maya transitions (chapter 11), and by Christina Conlee for the post-Wari setting in the Nasca region of Peru (chapter 7) emphasize that social inversions, new forms of class relations, emergent wealth, and shared power regimes complicate presumptive models of divine kings, centralized bureaucratic administration, and the bifurcated class relations of nobles versus commoners. In these historically and culturally distinctive situations, state collapse appears to generate not a rejuvenated template of prior governmentality but in some sense a polar opposite.

In each of these cases, we see the emergence of pluralizing ideologies, new regimes of collective, decentralized authority, enhanced social mobility, and even a socially sanctioned aversion to prior authoritarian regimes. So, rather than the regeneration of similar institutions of power, governance, and sociocultural practices, we may in postcollapse scenarios see the emergence of new forms of socially complex institutions—new class relations, new patterns of production, new forms of the circulation of wealth, and a pluralizing of ideology (even if these innovative forms are imagined by their creators to represent a legitimate continuity from the past). In these instances, some institutions, class relations, and patterns of production may be retained from the precollapse polity. Often, however, these social-structural forms will reflect the historical circumstances of the collapse process (which in most instances was likely to have been socially traumatic to a significant part of the society's population), and the process of collapse and reconstitution will result in new forms of complexity.

Often such new forms of social complexity derive from a foreign source and from external models of organizing social and economic relationships. As Schwartz (chapter 1) perceptively remarks, any analysis of the regeneration of social complexity must pay keen attention to the "teleconnections" of societies across extensive geographic space. In this vein, the contributions of Stark (chapter 10) and Marilyn Masson, Timothy Hare, and Carlos Peraza Lope (chapter 12) demonstrate that "internationalism" in the form of sea-borne, long-distance trade and mercantile activities drove significant social change and heavily influenced (in the case of the Khmer states) or even broke (in the case of the Postclassic Maya) preexisting structural templates of social complexity. In these cases, connectedness and interdependency rather than autonomy and autarky provide the social conditions for the regeneration of complexity. Emerging from this complex interplay of societies and economies is the development of a political landscape of multiple self-organized, competing polities rather than a monolithic imperial presence.

Of course, as Kenny Sims (chapter 8) trenchantly observes, in some cases the regeneration of centralized authority fails to occur after the collapse of empire. Local political formations retain a postcollapse preference for noncomplex, independent, and stubbornly autonomous structures. In these instances, as Sims suggests, local populations were probably little invested in imperial institutions and value systems that, from the local perspective, were perceived as alien and economically burdensome impositions. In other words, when regeneration of social complexity does not occur, the previous state or empire probably governed by a strategy of hegemony without sovereignty and effected no significant transformation of the historical consciousness of its subject populations. The state in these instances produced not citizens but strategic subjects who did not ideologically hew to state orthodoxy. Rather, they adopted a strategy of orthopraxy to negotiate daily life under the dominion of empire, adopting the external appearances of dominant values and practices without fundamentally changing their underlying local value systems and worldviews. When the empire collapsed, their strategic mimesis of state institutions, values, and social practices disappeared with it.

Empires generate significant social, cultural, and economic opportunities for some subjects while simultaneously imposing great burdens on others, creating significant tension through the attempted transformation (successful or not) of local social structures. Imperial regimes and other similarly centralized state hierarchies often seek to radically restructure modes of production and consumption among newly subject populations to accelerate economic revenues. Often these schemes take the form of highly specialized, labor-intensive systems of production that are high risk–high return propositions. Overinvestment in capital- and labor-intensive modes of production, such as massive irrigation systems tied to variable hydrological regimes, frequently results in high short-term economic gains but social and ecological disaster in the long run.

In some instances, such high risk–high return systems can persist for several generations, as in the case of the Tiwanaku state in the Andean high plateau (Kolata 1996; Kolata [ed.] 2003). In the specific case of Tiwanaku, centuries of considerable demographic expansion and increasing social complexity were underwritten by the productive capacity of a highly specialized agricultural system. However, the complex and technically specialized character of Tiwanaku's production system rendered it vulnerable to an extreme environmental impact. The ability of the Tiwanaku state to adapt to deteriorating climatic conditions that ensued in the mid twelfth century and persisted for nearly three hundred years was compromised by its overreliance on a single, highly specialized production system. After Tiwanaku's mid-twelfth-century collapse, social complexity as indexed by urban formations and multilayered political hierarchies did not reemerge in the Tiwanaku heartland for nearly three centuries. As Garrett Hardin (1993:101) observed, "Technology is a blessing, to be sure, but every blessing has its price. The price of increased complexity is increased vulnerability."

Similarly, John Nichols and Jill Weber (chapter 3) and Lisa Cooper (chapter 2) imply that the conditions for the regeneration of social complexity are frequently tied to the relative flexibility of indigenous production systems and their ability to respond to changing social and ecological circumstances. Such strategies may include diversifying subsistence portfolios or decoupling urban settlements from overarching political formations to promote, in Nichols and Weber's felicitous phrase, "integrated strategies of resilience." The ecological and social tensions of empire rarely permit or foster strategies of economic resilience and in fact are more often associated with the imposition of structural rigidities, as was the case with Tiwanaku. Such structural rigidities render the regeneration of social complexity under changed ecological and social circumstances extremely problematic.

As is abundantly clear from the contributions to this volume, the social regeneration of complexity after state collapse can follow multiple historical pathways, each with its own contour of specificity. But these pathways are not infinite in variety; many share significant structural features and sociohistorical commonalities. What we need now, of course, is more nuanced comparative archaeological and historical research that will give us the empirical warrants to categorize and understand differentiated forms of state collapse and social regeneration. Useful discussion of the regeneration of social complexity requires us to negotiate the analytically fraught passage between the Scylla of historical contingency (the history of event) and the Charybdis of comparative societal structure (the history of structure). The contributors to this volume challenge us all to explore more deeply how structure and event under circumstances of state collapse and regeneration interrelate in complicated ways.

Note

1. I thank Marshall Sahlins for bringing the concept of hegemony without sovereignty to my attention. See Sahlins 2004 for an extended discussion of this concept in the context of ancient Greece.

14 Notes on Regeneration
Norman Yoffee

It's been eighteen years since the *anno mirabile* of 1988, when Joseph Tainter's *Collapse of Complex Societies* and George Cowgill's and my edited volume, *The Collapse of Ancient States and Civilizations,* appeared. These studies have resonated in archaeological theory, since they emphasized that social change was not simply a process of mutually supportive interactions that produced an irreversible succession of levels of holistic integration. They challenged views that human social systems inherently tend to persist or expand and required that levels be broken down into social groupings of partly overlapping and partly opposing fields of action that lend the possibility of instability as well as stability to overarching social institutions. Collapse studies also call attention to what happens after collapse, since collapse seldom connotes the death of a civilization as opposed to the end of a particular form of government. The studies of "regeneration" in this volume explicitly explore issues of what happens beyond collapse.

Of course, what happens beyond collapse depends on what it was that underwent the collapsing, why collapse occurred, and what institutions were left in place after collapse. Although the term *collapse* usually implies a downward change from something more complex and larger to something else that is less complex and smaller, one might also consider collapse as a movement from a relatively more stable condition to one that is less stable. For example, Steven Falconer and Stephen Savage (1995) have argued that Syria/Palestine in the Middle Bronze Age was a "heartland of villages," and Lisa Cooper in this volume (chapter 2) presents the variations on this theme. Thus, if stability connotes village life, then the appearance of urban sites in the region—which were based, in part, on connections with outsiders and were unstable—could be called a collapse! Of course, such unstable urbanism itself collapsed into the village life from which it sprang. Archaeologists (and others) are not used to talking about the rise of more complex social systems as a collapse, and I'm not saying that they should begin to do so. I do wish to point out, however, that trends toward less-complex social organizations need not be thought of as failures of those more-complex organizations, and there is an important example of this principle in one of the chapters in this volume (by Kenny Sims). I also must note that if collapse can be multidirectional, resulting in both more- and less-complex societies, it is simply a species of social change that must be investigated in its appropriate larger temporal and spatial sequences. Logically, then, regeneration—meaning the return to a condition (albeit with significant adjustments) after a collapse—is not necessarily a new category of research or theory, but a more focused attention on a kind of social change.

Comparative studies of social phenomena need to ensure that the comparisons, especially the scale of the social units being compared, are useful. There is no point in comparing the rise, abandonment or partial abandonment, and rise again of particular sites with whole regions or states or civilizations. That having been said, I turn to brief notes on the chapters in this volume.

One of the most interesting points about regeneration that was stressed in many chapters is that new opportunities were presented to peripheral regions and secondary elites in the aftermath of the collapse of ancient states. Ellen Morris (chapter 4) shows that the collapse of Old Kingdom Egypt—accompanied by diminished flood levels of the Nile, famine, and political chaos—led to trends toward increased social mobility in the succeeding First Intermediate Period. Although there were always local power structures, craftspeople, and avenues of resistance to the central state in Egypt, these were effectively suppressed in the heyday of the Old Kingdom. In the decentralized environment of the First Intermediate Period, however, and into the Middle Kingdom, rich tombs of nonofficials were erected, and social competition became a topic in literature. Eventually, the ideology of statecraft in Egypt provided the model for the regeneration of the centralized state, but changes in that ideology took into account the experience of the First Intermediate Period.

In the chapters by Diane and Arlen Chase (chapter 11) and by Marilyn Masson, Timothy Hare, and Carlos Peraza Lope (chapter 12), the regeneration of Maya cities and states depended on more than the reassertion of the ideology of Classic Maya statecraft. Although the major sites of the Classic Maya in the Petén had been progressively abandoned in the ninth and tenth centuries and reoccupied only by "squatters" (Webster 2002), other Maya sites, especially to the north in Yucatán, were founded or grew in size and complexity. Although these sites were constructed not according to Classic

Maya models, not everything changed. This was not simply an economizing movement from "monstrous visual symbols" to more demotic architecture and a vigorous market economy (according to Masson and her coauthors) and away from an economy and political system that was based in state-sponsored ritual (as in the Classic period). Rather, in Postclassic cities, the Maya created a new amalgam of Classic symbols and those from a "Mexican" belief system. New political formations, regional alliances, and regional economic interactions ensued in the Postclassic. What had collapsed were not only the Classic Maya city-states, but also the ideology supporting them. Regeneration could take place only in the drastic rearrangement of social and ideological systems. The establishment of new landscapes and the creation of new social memories (and the forgetting of others) were, perhaps, not so much evidence of failures of the past as new opportunities for those people who lived on the margins of the Classic Maya core.

The chapters on Andean archaeology by Christina Conlee (chapter 7), Gordon McEwan (chapter 6), and Kenny Sims (chapter 8) all concern the opportunities presented by the collapse of the Wari and Tiwanaku expansionist states. The opportunities, however, resulted in different kinds of regenerations. Conlee's chapter, like Ellen Morris's on Egypt, emphasizes that the collapse of the Wari state presented the chance for local elites to increase their status. In her study of the site of La Tiza, the evidence is for local aggregation and local ritual behavior at a central pilgrimage site in which ritual elites held much power. McEwan argues that the collapse of Wari presented a "fortuitous set of circumstances" that allowed the Inca, first competing with rivals such as the Chanca confederation, to meld old ways of statecraft with invented traditions that legitimized their expansion. Sims discusses the situation in Moquegua, in which Tiwanaku and Wari colonial regimes competed for resources and labor. He envisions that the local elites, traditional nobility in Moquegua, increased their status and power by serving as middle officials for the states and were able through their access to labor to serve the invading states. With the collapse of those states, however, these elites were faced with resistance to centralization. Commoners and secondary elites rejected the old symbols and markers of prestige and power. This lack of regeneration was far from a failure, however. It was a positive assertion of local ways and resistance to central authority.

Bennet Bronson (chapter 9) calls our attention to kinds of false regeneration, stimulus regeneration, and template regeneration. The chapters by John Nichols and Jill Weber (chapter 3) and Miriam Stark (chapter 10) might all fall under template regeneration. They differ, however, in that

Stark's case is one of formulation of the template, and this would also hold for the rise of states in northern China (discussed by Liu Li at the SAA symposium in Milwaukee but not included in this volume; see Liu and Chen 2003). The Chinese case is so new and important for the concept of "template regeneration" that it deserves at least brief discussion here.

The earliest state in north China was probably centered on the city of Erlitou (ca. 1900–1500 BC). This collapsed in favor of the state centered at Zhengzhou (ca. 1600–1400 BC), whose collapse was followed by other competing cities, the most famous of which is the late Shang dynasty capital of Anyang (ca. 1250–1046 BC). Later Han (206 BC–AD 220) historians invented the Chinese dynastic cycle to imply that China was always ruled by dynasties, and the collapse of one was followed by the regeneration of another one. Such regeneration was molded by the model of statecraft that was carried by Confucian literati, semiautonomous elites who were also the bureaucrats of the state (Hsu 1988). Governments fell in China for the reasons that governments fall, but the literati were able to regenerate the state more or less on the timeless model they maintained, preserved, and reproduced. The earliest states in China, however, which were really competing cities that brought into their orbits outlying towns and regions with their needed resources (in the opinion of Yoffee 2005), had no such model of statecraft. That ideology and the literati who safeguarded it did not emerge until the late first millennium BC. The earliest states were not part of any dynasty, and the template of Chinese statecraft was only in a formative stage (if one takes a teleological position on the development of the Han state). Important features of the earliest states were the bronzes that were controlled by kings and enabled their claims to rule nonkinsmen (Chang 1983) and the use of oracle bones that also connected the ruler with the world of the ancestors in new ways. Those who inscribed the oracle bones formed a kind of protobureaucracy that set the stage for the transformation of later Confucian principles into a "template-making" institution with its organization of literati. Collapse of the earliest cities and states followed by the rise of other early states is not, in my view, an example of regeneration, at least not one of the kind that is stipulated in the Chinese dynastic cycle. Regeneration doesn't just happen; it has to be engineered.

Stark's chapter seems to illustrate the birth of a template of the Khmer state in mainland Southeast Asia (chapter 10). She shows that many interacting small polities from the mid first millennium AD through the mid second millennium were fragile and only loosely integrated. Stimulated by economic ties with China and with significant influence from India—both in economic and in ideological terms (Wheatley 1975)—the Khmer elites forged new systems of power and governance. The collapse of old polities and the rise of new ones in Southeast Asia seems less an example of regeneration than one of state formation.

John Nichols and Jill Weber's chapter details the collapse and regeneration of Tell Umm el-Marra within a larger region of Syrian states and statelets, all influenced in one way or other by contacts with earlier Mesopotamian states (chapter 3). In early Mesopotamian history, there were many collapses of states and empires, but these were all followed by the regeneration of new states and empires. There are a few instances of sites being abandoned and then reoccupied (e.g., Uruk and Nippur in the late Old Babylonian period [Stone 1977; van Ess 1991]), but most urban places, with variations in the density of occupation and political leadership, flourished uninterruptedly for roughly three thousand years.

In the second half of the second millennium BC, new regional states of (Kassite) Babylonia and Assyria arose. In the first millennium BC, Assyria was the greatest empire in the world. It fell in the late 600s but did not regenerate. Babylonia, which replaced it as the dominant state in western Asia, was conquered by Cyrus the Great of Persia in 539 BC. Thereafter, there was no Mesopotamian state, the rulers of Mesopotamia did not think of themselves as Mesopotamians, and the gods and languages of Mesopotamia were only options to the people living in Mesopotamia, who could also choose among many other belief systems. Exploring the differences in the collapse, regeneration, and nonregeneration of these two states is an interesting exercise in assessing change and continuity (Yoffee 2005).

The collapse of Assyria was not followed by the regeneration of an Assyrian state, and for good reasons. In the fourteenth century BC, the Assyrian state effected its independence of rivals by investing strong kings with an increasingly large and influential military establishment. Kings progressively disenfranchised local elites and their councils, increased the effectiveness of the military, conquered new territory, and frequently deported defeated peoples to various parts of its growing empire. Although these policies led to an increasingly centralized Assyrian state and an unprecedented military supremacy, there was a price. When the Assyrian army became bogged down in a civil war with Babylonia from 652 to 648 BC, conquered provinces took the opportunity to rebel. Foreign enemies in the north and the east consolidated their opposition to Assyria. From 616 to 610 BC, the enemies of Assyria conquered and sacked the major cities of Assyria. By this time, the population in Assyria was a mixture of peoples, Assyrians and others, both in the cities and in the countryside, and the traditional Assyrian nobility had been replaced by military leaders and bureaucrats who owned agricultural land and villages. With the defeat of the king and the army there was not only the end of the Assyrian government. The removal of natural ties between the local, rural people—who were largely non-Assyrian—and their traditional leaders had been effected by the Assyrian kings themselves. Such non-Assyrian elites as existed had little reason to follow Assyrian models and to rebuild the Assyrian state.

In Babylonia, Cyrus and succeeding Persian rulers who ruled the land honored Babylonian traditions, refurbished temples, and were regarded by Babylonians as rightful rulers of the land. They had no choice in this matter. Famous for their policies of toleration of all local belief systems as long as these did not challenge the legitimacy of their rule, Persian kings claimed in effect that regeneration of the Mesopotamian state was irrelevant. The Persian state *was* the Mesopotamian state. But was it? Over time, being Mesopotamian was only one of the available orientations for the citizens of the land, and they chose progressively to abandon their Mesopotamianness under Achaemenid Persian, Hellenistic, and then other Persian dynasties (see more fully in Rempel and Yoffee 1999; Yoffee 2005).

The chapters in this volume show that "regeneration" requires research into ideology: Why is the past recalled or one part of the past emphasized and other parts forgotten? Who is vested with preserving the past, and what are the opportunities for rebuilding it or resisting such rebuilding? Studies of regeneration, like those of collapse, require that archaeologists reckon on the active participation of individuals who make choices among the multiple and overlapping identities available to them. We must ask who profits from which choices and who does not. These questions are quite different from many of the old preoccupations of archaeologists who sought to identify types of societies, focused on political institutions, and tended to ignore the different classes of people within a society and their various interests and identities. The archaeology of the new millennium is witnessing the collapse of many old and tired questions, and the field is consequently being (happily) regenerated as a result.

References

Abercrombie, T. A.

1998   *Pathways of Memory and Power: Ethnography and History among an Andean People.* Madison: University of Wisconsin Press.

Abrams, E., and D. Rue

1988   The Causes and Consequences of Deforestation among the Prehistoric Maya. *Human Ecology* 16:377–95.

Adams, R. E. W.

1973   Maya Collapse: Transformation and Termination in the Ceramic Sequence at Altar de Sacrificios. Pp. 133–63 in T. P. Culbert, ed., *The Classic Maya Collapse.* Albuquerque: University of New Mexico Press.

Adams, R. McC.

1978   Strategies of Maximization, Stability, and Resilience in Mesopotamian Society, Settlement, and Agriculture. *Proceedings of the American Philosophical Society* 122:329–35.

1988   Contexts of Civilizational Collapse. Pp. 20–43 in N. Yoffee and G. L. Cowgill, eds., *The Collapse of Ancient States and Civilizations.* Tucson: University of Arizona Press.

2001   Complexity in Archaic Societies. *Journal of Anthropological Archaeology* 20(3): 345–60.

Aeusrivongse, N.

1976   The Devaraja Cult and Khmer Kingship at Angkor. Pp. 107–48 in K. R. Hall and J. K. Whitmore, eds., *Explorations in Early Southeast Asian History: The Origins of Southeast Asian Statecraft.* Michigan Papers on South and Southeast Asian Studies. Ann Arbor: University of Michigan Press.

Akkermans, P.M.M.G., and G. M. Schwartz

2003   *The Archaeology of Syria: From Complex Hunter-Gatherers to Early Urban Societies (ca. 16,000–300 BC).* Cambridge: Cambridge University Press.

Albarracin-Jordan, J.

1996   *Tiwanaku: arqueología regional y dinámica segmentaría.* La Paz: Plural Editores.

Aldenderfer, M. S., ed.

1993   *Domestic Architecture, Ethnicity, and Complementarity in the South-Central Andes.* Iowa City: University of Iowa Press.

Alderfer, C. P.

1980 Consulting to Underbounded Systems. Pp. 267–95 in C. P. Alderfer and C. Cooper, eds., *Advances in Experiential Social Processes,* vol. 2. New York: Wiley.

Alfaro de Lanzone, L. C.

1978 Informe final del proyecto Huayurí. Report submitted to the Insituto Nacional de Cultura, Lima, Peru.

Algaze, G.

2001 The Prehistory of Imperialism: The Case of Uruk Period Mesopotamia. Pp. 27–84 in M. Rothman, ed., *Uruk Mesopotamia and Its Neighbors: Cross-Cultural Interactions in the Era of State Formation.* Santa Fe: School of American Research.

al-Jadir, W.

1967 Le Travail du Cuir. *Sumer* 23:193–201.

al-Maqdissi, M., M. Luciani, D. Morandi Bonacossi, M. Novák, P. Pfälzner, eds.

2002 *Excavating Qatna,* vol. 1. Documents d'Archéologie Syrienne IV. Damascus: Salhani.

Andreades, A.

1933 *A History of Greek Public Finance,* vol. 1. Cambridge: Harvard University Press.

Andrews, A. P., E. Wyllys Andrews, and F. Robles Castellanos

2003 The Northern Maya Collapse and Its Aftermath. *Ancient Mesoamerica* 14:1–6.

Andrews, A. P., F. Asaro, H. V. Michel, F. H. Stross, and P. Cervera Rivero

1989 The Obsidian Trade at Isla Cerritos, Yucatán, Mexico. *Journal of Field Archaeology* 16:355–63.

Archi, A.

1998 The Regional State of Nagar according to the Texts of Ebla. Pp. 1–15 in M. Lebeau, ed., *About Subartu: Studies Devoted to Upper Mesopotamia.* Turnhout: Brepols.

1999 Aleppo in the Ebla Age. *Annales Archéologiques Arabes Syriennes* 43:131–36.

Archi, A., and M. G. Biga

2003 A Victory over Mari and the Fall of Ebla. *Journal of Cuneiform Studies* 55:1–42.

Astour, M. C.

1992 An Outline of the History of Ebla, Part 1. Pp. 3–82 in C. H. Gordon and G. A. Rendsburg, eds., *Eblaitica: Essays on the Ebla Archives and Eblaite Language,* vol. 3. Winona Lake, Ind.: Eisenbrauns.

Aubet, M. E.

1993 *The Phoenicians in the West.* Cambridge: Cambridge University Press.

Baines, J., and N. Yoffee

1998 Order, Legitimacy, and Wealth in Ancient Egypt and Mesopotamia. Pp. 199–260 in G. Feinman and J. Marcus, eds., *Archaic States.* Santa Fe: School of American Research.

Ball, J. W.

1993 Pottery, Potters, Palaces, and Polities: Some Socioeconomic and Political Implications of Late Classic Maya Ceramic Industries. Pp. 243–72 in J. A. Sabloff and J. Henderson, eds., *Lowland Maya Civilization in the Eighth Century AD.* Washington, D.C.: Dumbarton Oaks.

Bandy, M., A. Cohen, P. Goldstein, A. Cardona, and A. Oquiche

1996   The Tiwanaku Occupation of Chen Chen (M1): Preliminary Report of the 1995
          Salvage Excavations. 61st Annual Meeting of the Society for American Archaeol-
          ogy, New Orleans, 1996.

Bard, K.

1989   The Evolution of Social Complexity in Predynastic Egypt. *Journal of Mediter-
          ranean Archaeology* 2:223–48.

Bauer, B. S.

1990   *State Development in the Cusco Region: Archaeological Research on the Incas in
          the Province of Paruro.* Ph.D. dissertation, University of Chicago.

1992   *The Development of the Inca State.* Austin: University of Texas Press.

Bauer, B. S., and A. Covey

2002   Processes of State Formation in the Inca Heartland (Cuzco, Peru). *American
          Anthropologist* 104(3):846–64.

Bawden, Garth

1993   An Archaeological Study of Social Structure and Ethnic Replacement in Resi-
          dential Architecture of the Tumilaca Valley. Pp. 42–54 in M. S. Aldenderfer, ed.,
          *Domestic Architecture, Ethnicity, and Complementarity in the South-Central An-
          des.* Iowa City: University of Iowa Press.

Becker, M. J.

1973   Archaeological Evidence for Occupational Specialization among the Classic Pe-
          riod Maya at Tikal, Guatemala. *American Antiquity* 38:396–406.

Becker, M. J., C. Jones, and J. McGinn

1999   *Excavations in Residential Areas of Tikal: Groups with Shrines.* Tikal Report no.
          21. University Museum Monograph 104. Philadelphia: University Museum.

Beetz, C. P., and L. Satterthwaite

1981   *The Monuments and Inscriptions of Caracol, Belize.* University Museum Mono-
          graph 45. Philadelphia: University Museum.

Bell, B.

1971   The Dark Ages in Ancient History, I: The First Dark Age in Egypt. *American
          Journal of Archaeology* 75:1–26.

Bellina, B.

1998   La formation des réseaux d'échanges reliant l'Asie du Sud et l'Asie du Sud-Est à
          travers le matériel archéologique (VIᵉ siècle av. J.-C.–VIᵉ siècle ap. J.-C.): Le cas
          de la Thaïlande et la Péninsule Malaise. *Journal of the Siam Society* 86(1–2):89–
          105.

2003   Beads, Social Change, and Interaction between India and Southeast Asia. *Anti-
          quity* 77:285–97.

Benavides, M.

1971   Análisis de la cerámica Huarpa. *Revista del Museo Nacional* 37:63–88.

Bennet, J.

1998   The Linear B Archives and the Kingdom of Nestor. Pp. 111–33 in J. Davis, ed.,
          Sandy Pylos. Austin: University of Texas Press.

Bentley, G. C.

1986   Indigenous States of Southeast Asia. *Annual Review of Anthropology* 15:275–305.

Ben-Tor, A.

2000   Hazor and the Chronology of Northern Israel. *Bulletin of the American Schools
          of Oriental Research* 317:9–15.

Berenguer, J., and P. Dauelsberg
1989   El norte grande en la orbita de Tiwanaku (400 a 1200 d.c.). Pp. 129–80 in J. Hidalgo, V. Schiappacasse, H. Niemeyer, C. Alduante, and S. Ivan, eds., *Culturas de Chile: Prehistoria desde sus orígenes hasta los albores de la conquista.* Santiago: Editorial Andres Bello.

Bermann, M., P. Goldstein, C. Stanish, and L. Watanabe
1989   The Collapse of the Tiwanaku State: A View from the Osmore Drainage. Pp. 269–85 in D. S. Rice, C. Stanish, and P. R. Scarr, eds., *Ecology, Settlement, and History in the Osmore Drainage, Peru.* BAR International Series 545(ii). Oxford: BAR.

Bierling, M., ed.
2002   *The Phoenicians in Spain.* Winona Lake, Ind.: Eisenbrauns.

Binford, M. W., A. L. Kolata, M. Brenner, J. W. Janusek, M. T. Seddon, M. Abbott, and J. H. Curtis
1997   Climate Variation and the Rise and Fall of an Andean Civilization. *Quaternary Research* 47:235–48.

Bisel, S. C., and L. Angel
1985   Health and Nutrition in Mycenaean Greece. Pp. 197–210 in N. Wilkie and W. Coulson, eds., *Contributions to Aegean Archaeology.* Dubuque: Kendall/Hunt.

Bishop, P., D. Sanderson, and M. T. Stark
2003   Dating Pre-Angkorian Canals in the Mekong Delta, Southern Cambodia, Using Radiocarbon and OSL. *Journal of Archaeological Science* 31(3):319–36.

Blanton, R. E.
1983   Factors Underlying the Origin and Evolution of Market Systems. Pp. 51–66 in S. Ortiz, ed., *Economic Anthropology: Topics and Theories.* Lanham, Md.: University Press of America.

1998   Beyond Centralization: Steps toward a Theory of Egalitarian Behavior. Pp. 135–72 in G. Feinman and J. Marcus, eds., *Archaic States.* Santa Fe: School of American Research.

Blanton, R. E., and G. M. Feinman
1984   The Mesoamerican World System. *American Anthropologist* 86:673–82.

Blanton, R. E., G. M. Feinman, S. A. Kowalewski, and P. N. Peregrine
1996   A Dual-Processual Theory for the Evolution of Mesoamerican Civilizations. *Current Anthropology* 37:1–14.

Blanton, R. E., S. A. Kowalewski, G. M. Feinman, and L. M. Finsten
1993   *Ancient Mesoamerica: A Comparison of Change in Three Regions.* 2nd ed. Cambridge: Cambridge University Press.

Blom, D. E., B. Hallgrimsson, L. Keng, M. C. Lozada, and J. E. Buikstra
1998   Tiwanaku "Colonization": Bioarchaeological Implications for Migration in the Moquegua Valley, Peru. *World Archaeology* 30(2):238–61.

Boisselier, J.
1966   *Le Cambodge.* Paris: Picard.

Bolman, L. G., and T. E. Deal
1997   *Reframing Organizations: Artistry, Choice, and Leadership.* 2nd ed. San Francisco: Jossey-Bass.

Bourdonneau, E.
2003   The Ancient Canal System of the Mekong Delta. Pp. 257–70 in A. Karlström and

A. Källén, eds., *Fishbones and Glittering Emblems: Southeast Asian Archaeology 2002.* Stockholm: Museum of Far Eastern Antiquities.

Bourriau, J.
1988   *Pharaohs and Mortals: Egyptian Art in the Middle Kingdom.* Cambridge: Cambridge University Press.

Bouzek, J.
1982   Climatic Changes and Central European Prehistory. Pp. 192–211 in A. Harding, ed., *Climate Change in Later Prehistory.* Edinburgh.

Bowersock, G. W.
1988   The Dissolution of the Roman Empire. Pp. 165–75 in N. Yoffee and G. Cowgill, eds., *The Collapse of Ancient States and Civilizations.* Tucson: University of Arizona Press.

Bradley, R.
1999   *Paleoclimatology.* 2nd ed. San Diego: Academic Press.

Branigan, K., ed.
2001   *Urbanism in the Aegean Bronze Age.* Sheffield: Sheffield Academic Press.

Braswell, G. E.
1992   Obsidian Hydration Dating, the Coner Phase, and Revisionist Chronology at Copan, Honduras. *Latin American Antiquity* 3(2):130–47.

Braswell, G. E., J. D. Gunn, M. del Rosario Dominguez C., W. J. Folan, and M. D. Glascock
1997   Late and Terminal Classic Obsidian Procurement and Lithic Production at Calakmul, Campeche, Mexico. Paper presented at the 63rd Annual Meeting of the Society for American Archaeology, Seattle.

Breasted, J. H.
1988   *Ancient Records of Egypt I: The First to the Seventeenth Dynasties.* London: Histories and Mysteries of Man (reprint).

Briggs, L. P.
1951   *The Ancient Khmer Empire.* Philadelphia: American Philosophical Society.

Bronson, B.
1979   The Late Prehistory and Early History of Central Thailand with Special Reference to Chansen. Pp. 315–36 in R. B. Smith and W. Watson, eds., *Early South East Asia.* New York: Oxford University Press.
1988   The Role of Barbarians in the Fall of States. Pp. 196–218 in N. Yoffee and G. Cowgill, eds., *The Collapse of Ancient States and Civilizations.* Tucson: University of Arizona Press.

Brown, C. T.
1999   *Mayapán Society and Ancient Maya Social Organization.* Ph.D. dissertation, Tulane University.

Brown, L. D.
1983   *Managing Conflict at Organizational Interfaces.* Redding: Addison-Wesley.

Brown, R.
1996   *The Dvâravatî Wheels of the Law and the Indianization of South East Asia.* New York: E. J. Brill.

Browne, D. M.
1992   Further Archaeological Reconnaissance in the Province of Palpa, Department

of Ica, Peru. Pp. 17–116 in N. J. Saunders, ed., *Ancient America: Contributions to New World Archaeology.* Oxbow Monograph 24. Oxford: Oxbow Books.

Browne, D. M., and J. P. Baraybar

1988   An Archaeological Reconnaissance in the Province of Palpa, Department of Ica, Peru. Pp. 299–325 in N. J. Saunders and O. de Montmollin, eds., *Recent Studies in Pre-Columbian Archaeology.* BAR International Series 421(ii). Oxford BAR.

Bruins, H., J. van der Plicht, and A. Mazar

2003a   ¹⁴C Dates from Tel Rehov: Iron-Age Chronology, Pharaohs, and Hebrew Kings. *Science* 300:315–18.

2003b   Response to "Comment on ¹⁴C dates from Tel Rehov: Iron-Age Chronology, Pharaohs, and Hebrew Kings." *Science* 302:568c.

Brumfiel, E. M.

1994   Factional Competition and Political Development in the New World: An Introduction. Pp. 3–13 in E. M. Brumfiel and J. W. Fox, eds., *Factional Competition and Political Development in the New World.* Cambridge: Cambridge University Press.

Brumfiel, E. M., and J. W. Fox, eds.

1994   *Factional Competition and Political Development in the New World.* Cambridge: Cambridge University Press.

Brunton, G.

1927   *Qau and Badari I.* London: British School of Archaeology in Egypt.

Buccellati, G.

1997   Amorites. Pp. 107–11 in E. Meyers, ed., *The Oxford Encyclopedia of Archaeology in the Ancient Near East.* Oxford: Oxford University Press.

Bullard, W. R., Jr.

1952   Residential Property Walls at Mayapan. *Current Reports No. 3,* pp. 36–44. Washington, D.C.: Carnegie Institute Department of Archaeology.

1954   Boundary Walls and House Lots at Mayapan. *Current Reports No. 13,* pp. 234–53. Washington, D.C.: Carnegie Institute Department of Archaeology.

Burger, R., K. L. Mohr Chávez, and S. J. Chávez

2000   Through the Glass Darkly: Prehispanic Obsidian Procurement and Exchange in Southern Peru and Northern Bolivia. *Journal of World Prehistory* 14(3):267–362.

Bürgi, P.

1993   *The Inka Empire's Expansion into the Coastal Sierra Region West of Lake Titicaca.* Ph.D. dissertation, University of Chicago.

Burke, M. L.

1964   Lettres de Numušda-Nahrâri et de trois autres correspondants à Idiniatum. *Syria* 41:67–103.

Buttles, P. J.

1992   *Small Finds in Context: The Preclassic Artifacts of Colha, Belize.* M.A. thesis, University of Texas, Austin.

Butzer, K.

1976   *Early Hydraulic Civilization in Egypt: A Study in Cultural Ecology.* Chicago: University of Chicago Press.

Cameron, C. M.

1993   Abandonment and Archaeological Interpretation. Pp. 3–7 in C. M. Cameron and S. A. Tomka, eds., *Abandonment of Settlements and Regions: Ethnoarchaeological and Archaeological Approaches.* Cambridge: Cambridge University Press.

Cannon, A.

1989   The Historical Dimension in Mortuary Expressions of Status and Sentiment. *Current Anthropology* 30:437–58.

Carmean, K., N. Dunning, and J. K. Kowalski

2004   High Times in the Hill Country: A Perspective from the Terminal Classic Puuc Region. Pp. 424–49 in A. A. Demarest, P. M. Rice, and D. S. Rice, eds., *The Terminal Classic in the Maya Lowlands: Collapse, Transition, and Transformation.* Boulder: University of Colorado Press.

Carmichael, P. H.

1988   *Nasca Mortuary Customs: Death and Ancient Society on the South Coast of Peru.* Ph.D. dissertation, University of Calgary.

1998   Nasca Ceramics: Production and Social Context. Pp. 213–31 in I. Shimada, ed., *Andean Ceramics: Technology, Organization, and Approaches.* Philadelphia: University Museum.

Catagnoti, A.

1992   Le royaume de Tuba et ses cultes. Pp. 23–28 in J. Durand, ed., *Florilegium Marianum: Recueil d'études en l'honneur de Michel Fleury.* Paris: Société pour l'Étude du Proche-Orient Ancien.

Chang, K. C.

1983   *Art, Myth, and Ritual: The Path to Political Authority in Ancient China.* Cambridge, Mass.: Harvard University Press.

Charlton, T. H., and D. L. Nichols

1997   Diachronic Studies of City-States: Permutations on a Theme—Central Mexico from 1700 BC to AD 1600. Pp. 169–208 in D. Nichols and T. Charlton, eds., *The Archaeology of City-States: Cross-Cultural Approaches.* Washington, D.C.: Smithsonian Institution Press.

Chase, A. F.

1985   Troubled Times: The Archaeology and Iconography of the Terminal Classic Southern Lowland Maya. Pp. 103–14 in M. G. Robertson and V. M. Fields, eds., *Fifth Palenque Round Table, 1983,* vol. 7. San Francisco: Pre-Columbian Art Research Institute.

1990   Maya Archaeology and Population Estimates in the Tayasal-Paxcaman Zone, Peten, Guatemala. Pp. 149–65 in T. P. Culbert and D. S. Rice, eds., *Prehistoric Population History in the Maya Lowlands.* Albuquerque: University of New Mexico Press.

1998   Planeación civica e integración de sitio en Caracol, Belize: Definiendo una economia administrada del periodo clasico Maya. *Los investigaciones de la cultura Maya* 6(1):26–44. Campeche: University Autonoma de Campeche.

Chase, A. F., and D. Z. Chase

1998   Late Classic Maya Political Structure, Polity Size, and Warfare Arenas. Pp. 11–29 in A. Ciudad Ruiz, et al., eds., *Anatomia de una civilizacion: Aproximaciones interdisciplinarias a la cultura Maya.* Madrid: Sociedad Espanola de Estudios Mayas.

2001a   The Royal Court of Caracol, Belize: Its Palaces and People. Pp. 102–37 in T. Inomata and S. D. Houston, eds., *Royal Courts of the Ancient Maya,* vol. 2: *Data and Case Studies.* Boulder, Colo.: Westview Press.

2001b   Ancient Maya Causeways and Site Organization at Caracol, Belize. *Ancient Meso-america* 12(2):273–81.

2004a   Terminal Classic Status-Linked Ceramics and the Maya "Collapse": De Facto Refuse at Caracol, Belize. Pp. 342–66 in D. Rice, P. Rice, and A. Demarest, eds., *The Terminal Classic in the Maya Lowlands: Collapse, Transition, and Transformation.* Boulder: University of Colorado Press.

2004b   Exploring Ancient Economic Relationships at Caracol, Belize. *Research Reports in Belizean Archaeology* 1:115–27.

2006   Contextualizing the Collapse: Hegemony and Terminal Classic Ceramics from Caracol, Belize. *In* C. Varella and A. Foias, eds., *Geographies of Power: Understanding the Nature of Terminal Classic Pottery in the Maya Lowlands.* Oxford: BAR. (in press)

Chase, A. F., D. Z. Chase, and C. White

2001   El paisaje urbano Maya: La integración de los espacios construidos y la estructura social en Caracol, Belice. Pp. 95–122 in A. Ciudad Ruiz, M. J. Iglesias Ponce de Leon, and M. Del Carmen Martinez, eds, *Reconstruyendo la ciudad Maya: El urbanismo en las sociedades antiguas.* Madrid: Sociedad Espanola de Estudios Mayas.

Chase, A. F., N. Grube, and D. Z. Chase

1991   *Three Terminal Classic Monuments from Caracol, Belize.* Research Reports on Ancient Maya Writing no. 36. Washington, D.C.: Center for Maya Research.

Chase, A. F., and P. M. Rice, eds.

1985   *The Lowland Maya Postclassic.* Austin: University of Texas Press.

Chase, D. Z.

1981   The Maya Postclassic at Santa Rita Corozal. *Archaeology* 34(1):25–33.

1985a   Ganned But Not Forgotten: Late Postclassic Archaeology and Ritual at Santa Rita Corozal, Belize. Pp. 104–25 in A. Chase and P. Rice, eds., *The Lowland Maya Postclassic.* Austin: University of Texas Press.

1985b   Between Earth and Sky: Idols, Images, and Postclassic Cosmology. Pp. 223–33 in M. G. Roberston, ed., *Fifth Mesa Redonda de Palenque,* vol. 6. San Francisco: Pre-Columbian Art Research Institute.

1986   Social and Political Organization in the Land of Cacao and Honey. Pp. 347–77 in J. Sabloff and E. W. Andrews, eds., *Late Lowland Maya Civilization.* Albuquerque: University of New Mexico Press.

1998   Albergando a los muertos en Caracol, Belice. *Los investigadores de la cultura Maya* 6(1):9–25. Universidad Autonoma de Campeche.

Chase, D. Z., and A. F. Chase

1982   Yucatec Influence in Terminal Classic Northern Belize. *American Antiquity* 47:596–614.

1988   *A Postclassic Perspective: Excavations at the Maya Site of Santa Rita Corozal, Belize.* Monograph 4. San Francisco: Pre-Columbian Art Research Institute.

1992a   An Archaeological Assessment of Mesoamerican Elites. Pp. 303–17 in D. Chase and A. Chase, eds., *Mesoamerican Elites: An Archaeological Assessment.* Norman: University of Oklahoma Press.

1992b   Die Maya der Postklassik. Pp. 257–77 in N. Grube, ed., *Die Welt der Maya.* Mainz: Phillipp von Zabern.

1996   Maya Multiples: Individuals, Entries, and Tombs in Structure A34 of Caracol, Belize. *Latin American Antiquity* 7(1):61–79.

1998   The Architectural Context of Caches, Burials, and Other Ritual Activities for the Classic Period Maya (as Reflected at Caracol, Belize). Pp. 299–332 in S. Houston, ed., *Function and Meaning in Classic Maya Architecture.* Washington, D.C.: Dumbarton Oaks.

2000   Inferences about Abandonment: Maya Household Archaeology and Caracol, Belize. *Mayab* 13:67–77.

2001   Underlying Structure in Maya Persistence: An Archaeological Perspective. *Acta Mesoamericana* 12:37–50 (special issue, U. Hostettler and M. Restall, eds.).

2002   Classic Maya Warfare and Settlement Archaeology at Caracol, Belize. *Estudios de cultura Maya* 22:33–51.

2003   Secular, sagrado, y revisitado: La profanacion, alteracion, y reconsagracion de los antigos entierros Mayas. Pp. 255–77 in A. Ciudad Ruiz, M. H. Ruz Sosa, et al., eds., *Antropologia de la eternidad: La muerte en la cultura Maya.* Publication no. 7. Madrid: Sociedad Espanola de los Estudios Mayas.

2004a   Hermeneutics, Transitions, and Transformations in Classic to Postclassic Maya Society. Pp. 342–66 in D. Rice, P. Rice, and A. Demarest, eds., *The Terminal Classic in the Maya Lowlands: Collapse, Transition, and Transformation.* Boulder: University of Colorado Press.

2004b   Archaeological Perspectives on Classic Maya Social Organization from Caracol, Belize. *Ancient Mesoamerica* 15:111–19.

2004c   Patrones de enterramiento y cíclos residenciales en Caracol, Belice. Pp. 203–30 in R. Cobos, ed., *Culto funerario en la sociedad Maya: Memoria de la Cuarta Mesa Redonda de Palenque.* Mexico City: INAH.

Chase, D. Z., A. F. Chase, and W. A. Haviland

1990   The Classic Maya City: Reconsidering "The Mesoamerican Urban Tradition." *American Anthropologist* 92:499–506.

Chatfield, M.

1998   Ceramics from the Site of Chokepukio, Cuzco, Peru. Paper delivered at the 63rd annual meeting of the Society for American Archaeology, Seattle.

Chavez, K. L. M.

1980   The Archaeology of Marcavalle, an Early Horizon Site in the Valley of Cuzco, Peru: Part I. *Baessler Archiv, neue Folge* 28(2):203–329.

1986   Early Tiahuanaco-related Ceremonial Burners from Cuzco, Peru. *Dialogo Andino* 4:137–78.

Childe, V. G.

1950   The Urban Revolution. *Town Planning Review* 21:3–17.

Chou Ta-Kuan

1993   *Mémoires sur les coutumes du Cambodge de Tcheou Ta-kouan (Chen-la feng t'u chi).* Revised ed., Paul Pelliot, trans. Paris: Librairie d'Amérique et d'Orient.

Christie, J. W.

1990   Trade and State Formation in the Malay Peninsula and Sumatra, 300 BC–AD 700. Pp. 39–60 in J. Kathirithamby-Wells and J. Villiers, eds., *The Southeast Asian Port and Polity: Rise and Demise.* Singapore: National University of Singapore.

1995   State Formation in Early Maritime Southeast Asia: A Consideration of the Theories and the Data. *Bijdragen Tot De Taal-, Land -en Volkenkunde* 151(2):235–88.

1999   Asian Sea Trade between the Tenth and Thirteenth Centuries and Its Impact on the States of Java and Bali. Pp. 221–70 in H. P. Ray, ed., *Archaeology of Seafaring*. Cambridge: Cambridge University Press.

Ciudad Ruiz, A., M. Humberto Ruz Sosa, and M. J. Iglesias Ponce de Leon

2003   *Antropologia de la eternidad: La muerte en la cultura Maya.* Publication no. 7. Madrid: Sociedad Espanola de los Estudios Mayas.

Cline, E.

1994   *Sailing the Wine-Dark Sea: International Trade and the Late Bronze Age Aegean.* Oxford: BAR.

Cline, E., and D. Harris-Cline, eds.

1998   *The Aegean and the Orient in the Second Millennium.* Aegaeum 18. Liège: Université de Liège.

Coedès, G.

1937–66 *Inscriptions du Cambodge*, vols. 1–8. Paris: E. de Boccard.

1968   *The Indianized States of Southeast Asia.* W. Vella, ed.; S. B. Cowing, trans. Honolulu: East-West Center Press.

Conlee, C. A.

2000   *Late Prehispanic Occupation of Pajonal Alto, Nasca, Peru: Implications for Imperial Collapse and Societal Reformation.* Ph.D. dissertation, University of California, Santa Barbara.

2003   Local Elites and the Reformation of Late Intermediate Period Sociopolitical and Economic Organization in Nasca, Peru. *Latin American Antiquity* 14(1):47–65.

2005   The Restructuring and Democratization of Power in Late Prehispanic Nasca. Pp. 211–23 in C. A. Conlee, D. Ogburn, and K. Vaughn, eds., *The Foundations of Power in the Prehispanic Andes.* Archaeological Papers of the American Anthropological Association no. 14. Berkeley: University of California Press.

Conlee, C. A., and A. R. Rodríguez

2002   Informe del Proyecto La Tiza 2002. Report submitted to the Instituto Nacional de Cultura, Lima, Peru.

Conlee, C. A., and K. Schreiber

2006   The Role of Local Elites in the Balkanization and Reformation of Post-Wari Society in Nasca, Peru. Chapter 5 in C. Elson and A. Covey, eds., *Intermediate Elite Agency in Precolumbian States and Empires.* Tucson: University of Arizona Press. (in press)

Connor, J. G.

1983   *The Ceramics of Cozumel, Quintana Roo, Mexico.* Ph.D. dissertation, University of Arizona.

Cook, A.

1984–85 The Middle Horizon Ceramic Offerings from Conchopata. *Ñawpa Pacha* 22–23:91–126.

2001   Huari D-shaped Structures, Sacrificial Offerings, and Divine Rulership. Pp. 137–64 in E. P. Benson and A. G. Cook, eds., *Ritual Sacrifice in Ancient Peru: New Discoveries and Interpretations.* Austin: University of Texas Press.

Cooper, E. N.

1997   *The Middle Bronze Age of the Euphrates Valley, Syria: Chronology, Regional Interaction, and Cultural Exchange.* Ph.D. dissertation, University of Toronto.

1998   The EB-MB Transitional Period at Tell Kabir, Syria. Pp. 271–80 in M. Fortin and O. Aurenche, eds., *Espace naturel, espace habité en Syrie du nord (10e–2e millénaires av. J.-C.).* Lyon: Maison de L'Orient Méditerranéen.

1999   The EB-MB Transitional Period at Tell Kabir, Syria. Pp. 321–32 in G. del Olmo Lete and J.-L. Montero Fenollós, eds., *Archaeology of the Upper Syrian Euphrates—The Tishrin Dam Area: Proceedings of the International Symposium Held at Barcelona, Jan. 28th–30th, 1998.* Barcelona: Editorial Ausa.

2001   Archaeological Perspectives on the Political History of the Euphrates Valley, during the Early Second Millennium BC. Pp. 79–86 in M. Fortin, ed., *Canadian Research On Ancient Syria.* Québec: Musée de la Civilisation à Québec.

Costin, C. L.

1998   Introduction: Craft and Social Identity. Pp. 3–16 in C. L. Costin and R. P. Wright, eds., *Craft and Social Identity.* Arlington, Va.: American Anthropological Association.

Costin, C. L., and T. K. Earle

1989   Status Distinction and Legitimation of Power as Reflected in Changing Patterns of Consumption in Late Prehispanic Peru. *American Antiquity* 54(4):691–714.

Courty, M.

2001   Evidence at Tell Brak for the Late ED III/Early Akkadian Air Blast Evident (4 kyr BP). Pp. 367–72 in D. Oates, J. Oates, and H. McDonald, eds., *Excavations at Tell Brak, vol. 2: Nagar in the Third Millennium BC.* Cambridge: British School of Archaeology in Iraq.

Courty, M., and H. Weiss

1997   The Scenario of Environmental Degradation in the Tell Leilan Region, NE Syria, during the Late Third Millennium Abrupt Climate Change. Pp. 107–47 in H. Dalfes, G. Kukla, and H. Weiss, eds., *Third Millennium BC Climate Change and Old World Collapse.* Berlin: Springer-Verlag.

Covey, R. A.

2000   Inka Administration of the Far South Coast of Peru. *American Antiquity* 11(2):119–38.

Cowgill, G. L.

1988   Onward and Upward with Collapse. Pp. 244–76 in N. Yoffee and G. Cowgill, eds., *The Collapse of Ancient States and Civilizations.* Tucson: University of Arizona Press.

Crielaard, J.-P.

1999   Production, Circulation, and Consumption of Early Iron Age Pottery (Eleventh to Seventh Century BC). Pp. 49–81 in J.-P. Crielaard, V. Stissi, and G. van Wijngaarden, eds., *The Complex Past of Pottery.* Amsterdam: J. C. Gieben.

Culbert, T. P.

1988   The Collapse of Classic Maya Civilization. Pp. 69–101 in N. Yoffee and G. Cowgill, eds., *The Collapse of Ancient States and Civilizations.* Tucson: University of Arizona Press.

Culbert, T. P., ed.

1973a   *The Classic Maya Collapse.* Albuquerque: University of New Mexico Press.

1973b   The Maya Downfall at Tikal. Pp. 63–92 in T. P. Culbert, ed., *The Classic Maya Collapse.* Albuquerque: University of New Mexico Press.

Culbert, T. P., and D. S. Rice, eds.

1990   *Prehistoric Population History in the Maya Lowlands.* Albuquerque: University of New Mexico Press.

Curvers, H. H., and G. M. Schwartz

1997   Umm el-Marra: A Bronze Age Urban Center in the Jabbul Plain, Western Syria. *American Journal of Archaeology* 101:201–27.

Dahlin, B. H., and T. Ardren

2002   Modes of Exchange and Regional Patterns: Chunchucmil, Yucatan. Pp. 249–84 in M. A. Masson and D. A. Freidel, eds., *Ancient Maya Political Economies*. Walnut Creek, Calif.: Altamira Press.

Dalfes, H. N., G. Kukla, and H. Weiss, eds.

1997   *Third-millennium BC Climate Change and Old World Collapse*. Berlin: Springer-Verlag.

Dalsheimer, N., and P.-Y. Manguin

1998   Visnu mitrés et réseaux marchands en Asie du Sud-Est: nouvelles données archéologiques sur le Ier millénaire ap. J.-C. *Bulletin de L'École Française d'Extrême-Orient* 85:87–123.

D'Altroy, T., and T. K. Earle

1985   Staple Finance, Wealth Finance, and Storage in the Inca Political Economy. *Current Anthropology* 26:187–206.

Danti, M., and R. Zettler

1998   The Evolution of the Tell es-Sweyhat (Syria) Settlement System in the Third Millennium BC. Pp. 209–28 in M. Fortin and O. Aurenche, eds., *Espace naturel, espace habité en Syrie du nord (10ᵉ–2ᵉ millénaires av. J.-C.)*. Lyon: Maison de l'Orient Méditerranéen.

2002   Excavating an Enigma: The Latest Discoveries from Tell es-Sweyhat. *Expedition* 44:36–45.

Dao Lin Côn

1998   The Oc Eo Burial Group Recently Excavated at Go Thap (Dong Thap Province, Viêt Nam). Pp. 111–17 in P.-Y. Manguin, ed., *Southeast Asian Archaeology 1994*. Hull, U.K.: Centre for Southeast Asian Studies.

De Angelis, F.

2000   Estimating the Agricultural Base of Greek Sicily. *Papers of the British School at Rome* 68:111–48.

2002   Trade and Agriculture at Megara Hyblaia. *Oxford Journal of Archaeology* 21:299–310.

de Casparis, J. G.

1979   Palaeography as an Auxiliary Discipline in Research on Early South East Asia. Pp. 380–95 in R. B. Smith and W. Watson, eds., *Early South East Asia*. New York: Oxford University Press.

Demarest, A. A.

1997   The Vanderbilt Petexbatun Regional Archaeological Project 1989–1994: Overview, History, and Major Results of a Multidisciplinary Study of the Classic Maya Collapse. *Ancient Mesoamerica* 8(2):209–27.

Demarest, A. A., P. M. Rice, and D. S. Rice, eds.

2004   *The Terminal Classic in the Maya Lowlands: Collapse, Transition, and Transformation*. Boulder: University of Colorado Press.

DeMarrais, E.

2002   Comments in "Editorial," by S. Stoddart and C. Malone. *Antiquity* 291:4–6.

DeMarrais, E., L. Jaime Castillo, and T. Earle

1996   Ideology, Materialization, and Power Strategies. *Current Anthropology* 37:15–31.

de Polignac, F.

1995   Repenser "la cité"? Pp. 7–19 in M. Hansen and K. Raaflaub, eds., *Studies in the Ancient Greek Polis*. Historia Einzelschrift 95. Stuttgart: Franz Steiner.

Dever, W.

1989   The Collapse of the Urban Early Bronze Age in Palestine—Toward a Systemic Analysis. Pp. 225–46 in P. de Miroschedji, ed., *L'urbanisation de la Palestine à l'âge du Bronze ancien*. BAR International Series 527(ii). Oxford: BAR.

1995   Social Structure in the Early Bronze IV Period in Palestine. Pp. 282–96 in T. Levy, ed., *The Archaeology of Society in the Holy Land*. New York: Facts on File.

de Vogüé, M.

1865   *Syrie centrale: Architecture civile et réligieuse du 1er au VIIe siècle*, vol. 1. Paris: Noblet et Baudry.

Dillehay, T. D., and A. Lauturo Nuñez

1988   Camelids, Caravans, and Complex Societies in the South-central Andes. Pp. 603–634 in N. Saunders and O. de Montmollin, eds., *Recent Studies in Pre-Columbian Archaeology*. BAR International Series. Oxford: BAR.

Dillon, B. D.

1982   Bound Prisoners in Maya Art. *Journal of New World Archaeology* 5(1):24–45.

Dockall, J. E., and H. J. Shafer

1993   Testing the Producer-Consumer Model for Santa Rita Corozal, Belize. *Latin American Antiquity* 4:158–79.

Donlan, W.

1997   The Homeric Economy. Pp. 649–67 in I. Morris and B. Powell, eds., *A New Companion to Homer*. Leiden: E. J. Brill.

Dornemann, R.

1979   Tell Hadidi: A Millennium of Bronze Age City Occupation. Pp. 113–52 in D. N. Freedman, ed., *Archaeological Reports from the Tabqa Dam Project, Euphrates Valley, Syria*. Cambridge: American Schools of Oriental Research.

1985   Salvage Excavations at Tell Hadidi in the Euphrates River Valley. *Biblical Archaeologist* 48:49–59.

Dossin, G.

1950   *Correspondance de Samsi-Addu*. Paris: Archives Royales de Mari I.

Driessen, J., I. Schoep, and R. Laffineur, eds.

2002   *Monuments of Minos: Rethinking the Minoan Palaces*. Aegaeum 23. Liège: Université de Liege.

Dunham, P.

1988   Maya Balkanization and the Classic Florescence: Golden Age or Incipient Collapse. Paper presented at 87th Annual Meeting of the American Anthropological Association, Phoenix.

Durand, J.-M.

1988   *Archives epistolaires de Mari I*. Archives royales de Mari 26. Paris: Édition Recherches sur les Civilisations.

1989   L'assemblée en Syrie à l'époque pré-amorite. Pp. 27–44 in P. Fronzaroli, ed., *Miscellanea Eblaitica*, vol. 2. Florence: Università di Firenze.

1990   Le cité-état d'Imâr à l'époque des rois de Mari. *Mari, Annales de Recherches Interdisciplinaires* 6:39–92.

Edmonson, M. S.

1986   *Heaven Born Mérida and Its Destiny: Book of the Chilam Balam of Chumayel.* Austin: University of Texas Press.

Eisenstadt, S. N.

1964   Social Change, Differentiation, and Evolution. *American Sociological Review* 29(3):375–86.

1969   *The Political Systems of Empires: The Rise and Fall of the Historical Bureaucratic Societies.* New York: Free Press.

1980   Cultural Orientations, Institutional Entrepreneurs, and Social Change: Comparative Analysis of Traditional Civilizations. *American Journal of Sociology* 85:840–69.

1981   Cultural Traditions and Political Dynamics: The Origins and Modes of Ideological Politics. *British Journal of Sociology* 32:155–81.

1988   Beyond Collapse. Pp. 236–43 in N. Yoffee and G. Cowgill, eds., *The Collapse of Ancient States and Civilizations.* Tucson: University of Arizona Press.

Emberling, G.

1997   Ethnicity in Complex Societies: Archaeological Perspectives. *Journal of Archaeological Research* 5(4):295–344.

Escobedo, H. L.

1997   Arroyo de Piedra: Sociopolitical Dynamics of a Secondary Center in the Petexbatun Region. *Ancient Mesoamerica* 8:307–20.

Fagan, B.

2004   *The Long Summer: How Climate Changed Civilization.* New York: Basic Books.

Falconer, S. E.

1987   *Heartland of Villages: Reconsidering Early Urbanism in the Southern Levant.* Ph.D. dissertation, University of Arizona.

1994   Village Economy and Society in the Jordan Valley: A Study of Bronze Age Rural Complexity. Pp. 121–42 in G. M. Schwartz and S. E. Falconer, eds., *Archaeological Views from the Countryside: Village Communities in Early Complex Societies.* Washington, D.C.: Smithsonian Institution Press.

Falconer, S., and S. Savage

1995   Heartlands and Hinterlands: Alternative Trajectories of Early Urbanism in Mesopotamia and the Southern Levant. *American Antiquity* 60:37–58.

Falsone, G.

1998   Tell Shiyukh Tahtani on the Euphrates: The University of Palermo Salvage Excavations in North Syria (1993–94). *Akkadica* 109–10:22–64.

1999   Tell Shiyukh Tahtani. Pp. 137–42 in G. del Olmo Lete and J.-L. Montero Fenollós, eds., *Archaeology of the Upper Syrian Euphrates—The Tishrin Dam Area: Proceedings of the International Symposium Held at Barcelona, Jan. 28th–30th, 1998.* Barcelona: Editorial Ausa.

Faulkner, R. O.

1962   *A Concise Dictionary of Middle Egyptian.* Oxford: Griffith Institute.

Fedick, S.

1991   Chert Tool Production and Consumption among Classic Period Maya Households. Pp. 103–18 in T. R. Hester and H. J. Shafer, eds., *Maya Stone Tools: Selected Papers from the Second Maya Lithic Conference.* Monographs in World Archaeology no. 1. Madison, Wisc.: Prehistory Press.

Feinman, G.

1998 Scale and Social Organization: Perspectives on the Archaic State. Pp. 95–134 in G. Feinman and J. Marcus, eds., *Archaic States*. Santa Fe: School of American Research Press.

Feldman, L. H.

1978 Moving Merchandise in Protohistoric Central Quauhtemallan. Pp. 7–17 in T. A. Olee Jr. and C. Navarrete, eds., *Mesoamerican Communication Routes and Cultural Contacts*. Paper no. 40. Provo, Utah: New World Archaeological Foundation.

1985 *A Tumpline Economy: Production and Distribution Systems in 16th-century Eastern Guatemala*. Culver City: Labyrinthos.

Finkbeiner, U.

1997 'Abd. *In* H. Weiss, ed., Archaeology in Syria. *American Journal of Archaeology* 101:97–101.

1999–2000 Emar and Balis 1996–1998: Preliminary Report of the Joint Syrian-German Excavations with the Collaboration of Princeton University. *Berytus* 44:5–34.

2001 Emar 2001: Bericht über die 4, Kampagne der syrisch-deutschen Ausgrabungen. *Baghdader Mitteilungen* 33:2–21.

Finkelstein, I.

1996 The Archaeology of the United Monarchy: An Alternative View. *Levant* 28:177–87.

1999 Hazor and the North in the Iron Age: A Low Chronology Perspective. *Bulletin of the American Schools of Oriental Research* 314:55–70.

2004 Tel Rehov and Iron Age Chronology. *Levant* 36:181–88.

Finkelstein, I., and E. Piasetsky

2003 Comment on "^{14}C dates from Tel Rehov: Iron-Age Chronology, Pharaohs, and Hebrew Kings." *Science* 302:568b.

Finkelstein, I., and N. Silberman

2001 *The Bible Unearthed*. New York: Free Press.

Finkelstein, J. J.

1966 The Genealogy of the Hammurapi Dynasty. *Journal of Cuneiform Studies* 20:95–118.

Flannery, K. V.

1999 Process and Agency in Early State Formation. *Cambridge Archaeological Journal* 9:3–21.

Fleming, D. E.

2004 *Democracy's Ancient Ancestors: Mari and Early Collective Governance*. Cambridge: Cambridge University Press.

Fogel, R.

1993 New Sources and New Techniques for the Study of Secular Trends in Nutritional Status, Health, Mortality, and the Process of Aging. *Historical Methods* 26:5–43.

Folan, W. J., J. D. Gunn, and M. del Rosario Domínguez Carrasco

2001 Triadic Temples, Central Plazas, and Dynastic Palaces: A Diachronic Analysis of the Royal Court Complex, Calakmul, Campeche, Mexico. Pp. 223–65 in T. Inomata and S. D. Houston, eds., *Royal Courts of the Maya*, vol. 2: *Data and Case Studies*. Boulder, Colo.: Westview Press.

Folan, W., E. R. Kintz, and L. A. Fletcher

1983 *Coba: A Classic Maya Metropolis*. New York: Academic Press.

Folan, W. J., J. Marcus, S. Pincemin, M. del Rosario Dominguez Carrasco, L. Fletcher, and A. Morlaes Lopez

1995   Calakmul, Campeche: New Data from an Ancient Maya Capital in Campeche, Mexico. *Latin American Antiquity* 6:310–34.

Fox, J. W., G. W. Cook, A. F. Chase, and D. Z. Chase

1996   Questions of Political and Economic Integration: Segmentary versus Centralized States among the Ancient Maya. *Current Anthropology* 37(5):795–801.

Foxhall, L.

1995   Bronze to Iron: Agricultural Systems and Political Structures in Late Bronze Age and Early Iron Age Greece. *Annual of the British School at Athens* 90:239–50.

Frank, A. G.

1993   Bronze Age World System Cycles. *Current Anthropology* 34:383–429.

Frankel, H. H.

1957   *Catalogue of Translations from the Chinese Dynastic Histories for the Period 220–960.* Supplement no. 1. Berkeley: University of California Press.

Frankenstein, S.

1997   *Arqueologia del colonialismo: El impacto fenicio y griego en el sur de la Peninsula Ibérica y el suroeste de Alemania.* Barcelona: Critica.

Franklin, N.

2004   Metrological Investigations at 8th and 9th Century Samaria and Megiddo, Israel. *Mediterranean Archaeology and Archaeometry* 4:83–92.

Freidel, D. A.

1981a   Continuity and Disjunction: Antedecents of the Late Postclassic Settlement Patterns in Northern Yucatan. Pp. 311–32 in Wendy Ashmore, ed., *Lowland Maya Settlement Patterns.* Albuquerque: University of New Mexico/School of American Research.

1981b   The Political Economics of Residential Dispersion among the Lowland Maya. Pp. 371–82 in W. Ashmore, ed., *Lowland Maya Settlement Patterns.* Albuquerque: University of New Mexico Press.

Freidel, D. A., K. Reese-Taylor, and D. Mora-Marin

2002   The Origins of Maya Civilization: The Old Shell Game, Commodity, Treasure, and Kingship. Pp. 41–86 in M. A. Masson and D. A. Freidel, eds., *Ancient Maya Political Economies.* Walnut Creek, Calif.: Altamira Press.

Freidel, D. A., and J. A. Sabloff

1984   *Cozumel: Late Maya Settlement Patterns.* New York: Academic Press.

Freter, A.

1994   The Classic Maya Collapse at Copan, Honduras. Pp. 160–76 in G. Schwartz and S. Falconer, eds., *Archaeological Views from the Countryside: Village Communities in Early Complex Societies.* Washington, D.C.: Smithsonian Institution Press.

Fried, M. H.

1967   *The Evolution of Political Society.* New York: Random House.

Fry, R. E.

1980   Models of Exchange for Major Shape Classes of Lowland Maya Pottery. Pp. 3–18 in R. E. Fry, ed., *Models and Methods in Regional Exchange.* SAA Papers no. 1. Washington, D.C.: Society for American Archaeology.

2001   The Peripheries of Tikal. Pp. 143–70 in J. A. Sabloff, ed., *Tikal: Dynasties, Foreigners, and Affairs of the State*. Santa Fe: School of American Research Press.

Gadd, C. J.

1940   Tablets from Chagar Bazar and Tall Brak, 1937–38. *Iraq* 7:22–66.

Gagarin, M.

1986   *Early Greek Law*. Berkeley: University of California Press.

Galaty, M., and W. Parkinson, eds.

1999   *Rethinking Mycenaean Palaces*. Los Angeles: University of California Press.

Gann, T. W.

1900   Mounds in Northern Honduras. *Nineteenth Annual Report of the Bureau of American Ethnology 1897–1898, Part 2*, pp. 655–92. Washington, D.C.

García M.

1990   *Excavación arqueológica en el cementerio de Chen Chen, Moquegua: Una interacción de contextos funerarios, Tiwanaku/Wari*. Licenciado thesis, Universidad Católica Santa Maria, Arequipa, Peru.

Gardiner, A. H.

1933   The Dakhleh Stela. *Journal of Egyptian Archaeology* 19:19–30.

Garnsey, P.

1988   *Famine and Food Supply in the Graeco-Roman World*. Cambridge: Cambridge University Press.

Garza, S. T., and E. B. Kurjack

1984   Organizacion social y asentamientos Mayas prehispanicos. *Estudios de cultura Maya* 15:19–28.

Gasparini, G., and L. Margolies

1980   *Inca Architecture*. Patricia J. Lyon, trans. Bloomington: University of Indiana Press.

Gilboa, A., and I. Sharon

2001   Early Iron Age Radiometric Dates from Tel Dor. *Radiocarbon* 43:1343–51.

Gill, R. B.

2000   *The Great Maya Droughts: Water, Life, and Death*. Albuquerque: University of New Mexico Press.

Gitin, S.

1997   The Neo-Assyrian Empire and Its Western Periphery. Pp. 77–104 in S. Parpola and R. M. Whiting, eds., *Assyria 1995*. Helsinki: Neo-Assyrian Text Corpus Project.

2001   The Tel Miqne-Ekron Silver Hoards: The Assyrian and Phoenician Connections. Pp. 27–48 in M. Balmuth, ed., *Hacksilber to Coinage: New Insights into the Monetary History of the Near East and Greece*. New York: American Numismatic Society.

Glover, I.

1996   Recent Archaeological Evidence for Early Maritime Contacts between India and Southeast Asia. Pp. 129–58 in H. Ray, ed., *Tradition and Archaeology: Early Maritime Contacts in the Indian Ocean*. New Delhi: Manohar Press.

Glowacki, M.

1996   *The Huari Occupation of the Southern Highlands of Peru: A Ceramic Perspective from the Site of Pikillacta*. Ph.D. dissertation, Brandeis University.

2002   The Huaro Archaeological Site Complex: Rethinking the Wari Occupation of Cuzco. Pp. 267–86 in W. Isbell and H. Silverman, eds., *Andean Archaeology*. New York: Kluwer Academic/Plenum.

Goffman, E.

1974   *Frame Analysis*. Cambridge, Mass.: Harvard University Press.

Goldstein, P.

1985   *Tiwanaku Ceramics of the Moquegua Valley, Peru*. Master's thesis, University of Chicago.

1989a   *Omo, a Tiwanaku Provincial Center in Moquegua*. Ph.D. dissertation, University of Chicago.

1989b   The Tiwanaku Occupation of Moquegua. Pp. 219–54 in R. Don, C. Stanish, and P. R. Scarr, eds., *Ecology, Settlement, and History in the Osmore Drainage, Peru*. BAR International Series 545. Oxford: BAR.

1993a   House, Community, and State in the Earliest Tiwanaku Colony: Domestic Patterns and State Integration at Omo M12, Moquegua. Pp. 25–41 in M. S. Aldenderfer, ed., *Domestic Architecture, Ethnicity, and Complementarity in the South-central Andes*. Iowa City: University of Iowa Press.

1993b   Tiwanaku Temples and State Expansion: A Tiwanaku Sunken-court Temple in Moquegua, Peru. *Latin American Antiquity* 4(1):22–47.

Goldstein, P., and B. Owen

2001   Tiwanaku en Moquegua: las colonias altiplánicas. Pp. 139–68 in P. Kaulicke and W. H. Isbell, eds., *Boletín de arqueología*, vol. 5. Lima: Pontificia Universidad Católica del Perú.

Gordon, S.

1979   Recovery from Adversity in Eighteenth-century India: Re-thinking "Villages," "Peasants," and Politics in Pre-modern Kingdoms. *Peasant Studies* 8(4):61–80.

Graffam, G.

1992   Beyond State Collapse: Rural History, Raised Fields, and Pastoralism in the South Andes. *American Anthropologist* 94:882–904.

Graham, E. A.

1987   Terminal Classic to Early Historic Period Vessel Forms from Belize. Pp. 73–98 in P. Rice and R. Sharer, eds., *Maya Ceramics*. BAR International Series 345. Oxford: BAR.

2002   Perspectives on Economy and Theory. Pp. 398–418 in M. A. Masson and D. A. Freidel, eds., *Ancient Maya Political Economies*. Walnut Creek, Calif.: Altamira Press.

Graham, I.

1967   *Archaeological Explorations in El Peten, Guatemala*. Middle American Research Institute Publication 33. New Orleans: Tulane University Press.

Graham, J. A.

1990   Monumental Sculpture and Hieroglyphic Inscriptions. *Excavations at Seibal, Department of Peten, Guatemala*. Peabody Museum of Archaeology and Ethnology, Memoir 17, no. 1. Cambridge, Mass.: Harvard University Press.

Grube, N.

1994   Hieroglyphic Sources for the History of Northwest Yucatan. Pp. 316–58 in H. J. Prem, ed., *Hidden among the Hills: Maya Archaeology of the Northwest Yucatan Peninsula*. Acta Mesoamericana, vol. 7. Markt Schwaben: Anton Saurwein.

Habachi, L.
1963   King Nebhepetre Mentuhotp: His Monuments, Place in History, Deification, and Unusual Representations in the Form of Gods. *Mitteilungen des deutschen archäologischen Instituts* 19:16–52.

Hagesteijn, R.
1987   The Angkor State: Rise, Fall, and In Between. Pp. 154–69 in H.J.M. Claessen and P. van de Velde, eds., *Early State Dynamics.* Studies in Human Society, vol. 2. New York: E. J. Brill.
1996   Lack of Limits: Cultural Aspects of State Formation in Early Continental Southeast Asia. Pp. 187–204 in H.J.M. Claessen and J. G. Oosten, eds., *Ideology and the Formation of Early States.* New York: E. J. Brill.

Hall, K. R.
1975   Khmer Commercial Developments and Foreign Contacts under Sûryavarman I. *Journal of the Economic and Social History of the Orient* 18(3):318–36.
1979   Eleventh-century Commercial Developments in Angkor and Champa. *Journal of Southeast Asian Studies* 10(2):420–34.
1982   The "Indianization" of Funan: An Economic History of Southeast Asia's First State. *Journal of Southeast Asian Studies* 13:81–106.
1985   *Maritime Trade and State Development in Early Southeast Asia.* Honolulu: University of Hawaii Press.
1992   Economic History of Early Southeast Asia. Pp. 183-275 in Nicholas Tarling, ed., *The Cambridge History of Southeast Asia,* vol. 1: *From Early Times to c. 1800.* Cambridge: Cambridge University Press.

Hallo, W. W.
1964   The Road to Emar. *Journal of Cuneiform Studies* 18:57–88.

Halstead, P.
2001   Mycenaean Wheat, Flax, and Sheep: Palatial Intervention in Farming and Its Implications for Rural Society. Pp. 38–50 in S. Voutski and J. Killen, eds., *Economy and Politics in the Mycenaean Palace States.* Proceedings of the Cambridge Philological Society, supp. vol. 27.

Hardin, G.
1993   *Living within Limits: Ecology, Economics, and Population Taboos.* New York: Oxford University Press.

Harris, W. V.
1989   *Ancient Literacy.* Cambridge, Mass.: Harvard University Press.

Harrison, P. D.
1999   *The Lords of Tikal.* London: Thames and Hudson.

Hastorf, C. A.
1993   *Agriculture and the Onset of Political Inequality before the Inka.* Cambridge: Cambridge University Press.

Ha Van Tan
1986   Oc Eo: Endogenous and Exogenous Elements. *Vietnam Social Sciences* 1–2(7–8):91–101.

Havighurst, A. F., ed.
1976   *The Pirenne Thesis: Analysis, Criticism, and Revision.* Lexington, Mass.: Heath.

Haviland, W. A.
1988   Musical Hammocks at Tikal: Problems with Reconstructing Household Com-

position. Pp. 121–34 in R. Wilk and W. Ashmore, eds., *Household and Community in the Mesoamerican Past.* Albuquerque: University of New Mexico Press.

Hayes, W.

1971   The Middle Kingdom in Egypt: Internal History from the Rise of the Herakleopolitans to the Death of Ammenemes III. Pp. 464–531 in I. E. S. Edwards et al., eds., *The Cambridge Ancient History I, Part 2.* 3rd ed. Cambridge: Cambridge University Press.

Heimpel, W.

2003   *Letters to the King of Mari: A New Translation with Historical Introduction, Notes, and Commentary.* Winona Lake, Ind.: Eisenbrauns.

Heinrich, E., E. Strommenger, D. R. Frank, W. Ludwig, D. Sürenhagen, E. Töpperwein, H. Schmid, J-C. Heusch, K. Kohlmeyer, D. Machule, M. Wäfler, and T. Rhode

1974   Vierter vorläufiger Bericht die von der deutschen Orient-Gesellschaft in Habuba Kabira und in Mumbaqat. *Mitteilungen der deutschen Orient-Gesellschaft* 106:5–52.

Heinrich, E., E. von Schuler, H. Schmid, W. Ludwig, E. Strommenger, and U. Seidl

1969   Bericht über die von der deutschen Orient-Gesellschaft mit Mitteln der Stiftung Volkswagenwerk im Euphrattal bei Aleppo. *Mitteilungen der deutschen Orient-Gesellschaft* 101:28–67.

Herget, H. M.

1935   Portraits of Ancient Mayas. *National Geographic Magazine* 68(5):553–60.

Heusch, J.-C.

1980   Tall Habuba Kabira im 3. und 2. Jahrtausend: Die Entwicklung der Baustruktur. Pp. 159–78 in J.-C. Margueron, ed., *Le Moyen Euphrate: Zone de contacts et d'échanges.* Leiden: E. J. Brill.

Higham, C.F.W.

1989   The Later Prehistory of Mainland Southeast Asia. *Journal of World Prehistory* 3(3):235–82.

2002   *Early Cultures of Mainland Southeast Asia.* Bangkok: River Books.

Hiltunen, J.

1999   *Ancient Kings of Peru: The Reliability of the Chronicle of Fernando de Montesinos.* SHS Bibliotheca Historica 45. Helsinki: SHS.

Hiltunen, J., and G. McEwan

2004   Knowing the Inca Past. Pp. 237–54 in H. Silverman, ed., *Andean Archaeology.* London: Blackwell.

Hirth, K.

1998   The Distributional Approach. *Current Anthropology* 39(4):451–76.

Hodell, D., M. Brenner, J. H. Curtis, and T. Guilderson

2001   Solar Forcing of Drought Frequency in the Maya Lowlands. *Science* 292:1367–70.

Hodges, R., and D. Whitehouse

1983   *Mohammed, Charlemagne, and the Origins of Europe: Archaeology and the Pirenne Thesis.* Ithaca, N.Y.: Cornell University Press.

Holland, T. A.

1976   Preliminary Report on Excavations at Tell Sweyhat, Syria, 1973–4. *Levant* 8:36–70.

1977a   Preliminary Report on Excavations at Tell es-Sweyhat, Syria 1975. *Levant* 9:36–65.

1977b   Incised Pottery from Tell Sweyhat, Syria, and Its Foreign Connections. Pp. 127–57 in J.-C. Margueron, ed., *Le Moyen Euphrate: Zone de contacts et d'échanges.* Strasbourg: E. J. Brill.

Horne, L.
1993   Occupational and Locational Instability in Arid Land Settlement. Pp. 43–53 in C. M. Cameron and S. A. Tomka, eds., *Abandonment of Settlements and Regions.* Cambridge: Cambridge University Press.

Houston, S. D., and D. Stuart
2001   Peopling the Classic Maya Court. Pp. 54–83 in T. Inomata and S. D. Houston, eds., *Royal Courts of the Ancient Maya,* vol. 1: *Theory, Comparison, Synthesis.* Boulder, Colo.: Westview Press.

Hsu, Cho-yun
1988   The Roles of the Literati and of Regionalism in the Fall of the Han Dynasty. Pp. 176–95 in N. Yoffee and G. L. Cowgill, eds., *The Collapse of Ancient States and Civilizations.* Tucson: University of Arizona Press.

Hutterer, K. L.
1982   Early Southeast Asia: Old Wine in New Skins?—A Review Article. *Journal of Asian Studies* 41(3):559–70.

Iannone, G.
2002   Annales History and the Ancient Maya State: Some Observations on the "Dynamic Model." *American Anthropologist* 104(1):68–78.

ibn Khaldun
1969   *The Muqaddimah: An Introduction to History.* F. Rosenthal, trans. Princeton: Princeton University Press.

Ilan, D.
1995   The Dawn of Internationalism—The Middle Bronze Age. Pp. 297–319 in T. Levy, ed., *The Archaeology of Society in the Holy Land.* New York: Facts on File.

Inomata, T.
1997   The Last Day of a Fortified Classic Maya Center: Archaeological Investigations at Aguateca, Guatemala. *Ancient Mesoamerica* 8:337–52.

Inomata, T., and L. R. Stiver
1998   Floor Assemblages from Burned Structures at Aguateca, Guatemala: A Study of Classic Maya Households. *Journal of Field Archaeology* 25:431–52.

Isbell, B. J.
1977   "Those Who Love Me": An Analysis of Andean Kinship and Reciprocity within a Ritual Context. Pp. 81–105 in R. Bolton and E. Mayer, eds., *Andean Kinship and Marriage.* Special Publication of the American Anthropological Association, vol. 7. Washington, D.C.: American Anthropological Association.

Isbell, W. H., C. C. Brewster-Wray, and L. E. Spickard
1991   Architecture and Spatial Organization at Huari. Pp. 19–53 in W. H. Isbell and G. McEwan, eds., *Huari Administrative Structure: Prehistoric Monumental Architecture and State Government.* Washington, D.C.: Dumbarton Oaks.

Isbell, W., and G. F. McEwan
1991   A History of Huari Studies and Introduction to Current Interpretations. Pp. 1–18 in W. H. Isbell and G. McEwan, eds., *Huari Administrative Structure: Prehistoric Monumental Architecture and State Government.* Washington, D.C.: Dumbarton Oaks.

Isbell, W. H., and K. J. Schreiber

1978   Was Huari a State? *American Antiquity* 43(3):372–89.

Ishizawa, Y.

1995   Chinese Chronicles of 1st–5th Century AD Funan, Southern Cambodia. Pp. 11–31 in R. Scott and J. Guy, eds., *South East Asia and China: Art, Interaction, and Commerce.* Colloquies on Art and Archaeology in Asia no. 17. London: Percival David Foundation of Chinese Art, London School of Oriental and African Studies.

Jacques, C.

1979   "Funan," "Zhenla": The Reality Concealed by These Chinese Views of Indochina. Pp. 371–79 in R. B. Smith and W. Watson, eds., *Early South East Asia.* New York: Oxford University Press.

1990   New Data on the VII–VIIIth Centuries in the Khmer Land. Pp. 251–59 in I. Glover and E. Glover, eds., *Southeast Asian Archaeology 1986.* BAR International Series 61. Oxford: BAR.

1995   China and Ancient Khmer History. Pp. 32–40 in R. Scott and J. Guy, eds., *South East Asia and China: Art, Interaction, and Commerce.* Colloquies on Art and Archaeology in Asia no. 17. London: Percival David Foundation of Chinese Art, London School of Oriental and African Studies.

Janusek, J. W.

2002   Out of Many, One: Style and Social Boundaries in Tiwanaku. *Latin American Antiquity* 13(1):35–61.

Jenner, P. N.

1980   *A Chrestomathy of Pre-Angkorian Khmer.* Southeast Asia Paper no. 20. Honolulu: University of Hawaii Asian Studies Program.

Jessup, H. I., and T. Zéphir, eds.

1997   *Sculpture of Angkor and Ancient Cambodia: Millenium of Glory.* Washington, D.C.: National Gallery of Art.

Jones, C.

1996   *Excavations in the East Plaza of Tikal.* Tikal Reports no. 16. Philadelphia: University Museum.

Jones, G. D.

1989   *Maya Resistance to Spanish Rule: Time and History on a Colonial Frontier.* Albuquerque: University of New Mexico Press.

1998   *The Conquest of the Last Maya Kingdom.* Stanford: Stanford University Press.

Joyce, A. A., A. Bustamante, and M. N. Levine

2001   Commoner Power: A Case Study from the Classic Period Collapse on the Oaxaca Coast. *Journal of Archaeological Method and Theory* 8:303–42.

Katz, F.

1972   *The Ancient American Civilizations.* New York: Praeger.

Kaufman, H.

1988   The Collapse of Ancient States and Civilizations as an Organizational Problem. Pp. 219–35 in N. Yoffee and G. Cowgill, eds., *The Collapse of Ancient States and Civilizations.* Tucson: University of Arizona Press.

Kemp, B.

1990   The Cultural Setting. Pp. 10–16 in G. Robins, ed., *Beyond the Pyramids: Egyptian Regional Art from the Museo Egizio, Turin.* Atlanta: Emory University Museum.

Kenoyer, J. M.

2005   Culture Change during the Late Harappan Period at Harappa: New Insights on Vedic Aryan Issues. Pp. 21–49 in L. L. Patton and E. F. Bryant, eds., *Indo-Aryan Controversy*. London: RoutledgeCurzon.

Kepecs, S.

1998   Diachronic Ceramic Evidence and Its Social Implications in the Chikinchel Region, Northeast Yucatan, Mexico. *Ancient Mesoamerica* 9:121–36.

2003   Chikinchel. Pp. 259–68 in M. E. Smith and F. F. Berdan, eds., *The Postclassic Mesoamerican World*. Salt Lake City: University of Utah Press.

Kepecs, S., G. M. Feinman, and S. Boucher

1994   Chichén Itzá and Its Hinterland: A World Systems Perspective. *Ancient Mesoamerica* 5:141–58.

Kepecs, S., and P. Kohl

2003   Conceptualizing Macroregional Interaction: World-Systems Theory and the Archaeological Record. Pp. 14–20 in M. E. Smith and F. F. Berdan, eds., *The Postclassic Mesoamerican World*. Salt Lake City: University of Utah Press.

Killen, J.

1985   The Linear B Tablets and the Mycenaean Economy. Pp. 241–305 in A. Morpurgo Davies and Y. Duhoux, eds., *Linear B: A 1984 Survey*. Louvain-la-Neuve: Cabay.

King, E.

1994   Preliminary Report on the Colha Settlement Survey: The 1983 and 1984 Seasons. Pp. 17–24 in T. R. Hester, H. J. Shafer, and J. D. Eaton, eds., *Continuing Archaeology at Colha, Belize*. Austin: Texas Archeological Research Laboratory.

2000   *The Organization of Late Classic Lithic Production at the Prehistoric Maya Site of Colha, Belize: A Study in Complexity and Hierarchy*. Ph.D. dissertation, University of Pennsylvania.

Kirsch, A. T.

1976   Kinship, Genealogical Claims, and Societal Integration in Ancient Khmer Society: An Interpretation. Pp. 345–62 in D. Cowan and O. W. Wolters, eds., *Southeast Asian History and Historiography*. Ithaca, N.Y.: Cornell University Press.

Kitchen, K.

1986   *The Third Intermediate Period in Egypt (1100–650 BC)*. 2nd ed. Warminster: Aris and Phillips.

Klengel, H.

1983   The Middle Euphrates and International Trade in the Old Babylonian Period. *Annales archéologiques arabes syriennes* 34:25–32.

1992   *Syria, 3000–300 BC*. Berlin: Akademie Verlag.

Knobloch, P. J.

1976   *A Study of the Huarpa Ceramic Style of the Andean Early Intermediate Period*. M.A. thesis, SUNY–Binghamton.

Kohl, P. L.

1978   The Balance of Trade in Southwestern Asia in the Mid-Third Millennium BC. *Current Anthropology* 19(3):463–92.

1996   The Ancient Economy, Transferable Technologies, and the Bronze Age World-system: A View from the Northeastern Frontier of the Ancient Near East. Pp.

143–64 in R. W. Preucel and I. Hodder, eds., *Contemporary Archaeology in Theory*. Cambridge and Oxford: Blackwell.

Kolata, A.

1985   El papel de la agricultura intensiva en la economía política del estado Tiwanaku. *Diálogo Andino* 4:11–38.

1986   Agricultural Foundations of the Tiwanaku State: A View from the Heartland. *American Antiquity* 51(4):748–62.

1993   *The Tiwanaku: Portrait of an Andean Civilization*. Cambridge: Blackwell.

2003a   The Proyecto Wila Jawira Research Program. Pp. 3–17 in A. L. Kolata, ed., *Tiwanaku and Its Hinterland: Archaeology and Paleoecology of an Andean Civilization*, vol. 2: *Urban and Rural Archaeology*. Washington, D.C.: Smithsonian Institution Press.

2003b   The Social Production of Tiwanaku: Political Economy and Authority in a Native Andean State. Pp. 449–72 in A. L. Kolata, ed., *Tiwanaku and Its Hinterland: Archaeology and Paleoecology of an Andean Civilization*, vol. 2: *Urban and Rural Archaeology*. Washington, D.C.: Smithsonian Institution Press.

Kolata, A., ed.

1996   *Tiwanaku and Its Hinterland: Archaeology and Paleoecology of an Andean Civilization*, vol. 1: *Agroecology*. Washington, D.C.: Smithsonian Institution Press.

2003   *Tiwanaku and Its Hinterland: Archaeology and Paleoecology of an Andean Civilization*, vol. 2: *Urban and Rural Archaeology*. Washington, D.C.: Smithsonian Institution Press.

Kopytoff, I.

1986   The Cultural Biography of Things: Commoditization as Process. Pp. 64–91 in A. Appadurai, ed., *The Social Life of Things*. Cambridge: Cambridge University Press.

Kristiansen, K.

1998   *Europe before History*. Cambridge: Cambridge University Press.

Kuhrt, A.

1995   *The Ancient Near East c. 3000–330 BC.* 2 vols. New York: Routledge.

Kulke, H.

1978   *The Devarāja Cult.* Data Paper 108. Ithaca, N.Y.: Cornell University Southeast Asia Program.

1990   Indian Colonies, Indianization, or Cultural Convergence? Reflections on the Changing Image of India's Role in South-east Asia. Pp. 8–32 in H. S. Nordholt, ed., *Onderzoek in Zuidoost-Azië*. Leiden: Vakgroep Talen en Culture van Zuidoost-Azië en Oceanië, Rijksuniversiteit te Leiden.

Laffineur, R., ed.

1999   *Polemos: Le context guerrier en Égée à l'âge du Bronze*. Aegaeum 19. Liège: Université de Liège.

Laffineur, R., and P. Betancourt, eds.

1997   *Technê: Craftsmen, Craftswomen, and Craftsmanship in the Aegaean Bronze Age*. Aegaeum 16. Liège: Université de Liège.

Laffineur, R., and W.-D. Niemeyer, eds.

1995   *Politeia, Society, and State in the Aegean Bronze Age*. Aegaeum 12. Liège: Université de Liège.

Landa, Diego de

1941 *Relaciones de las Cosas de Yucatan.* Alfred M. Tozzer, ed. and trans. Papers of the Peabody Museum of American Archaeology and Ethnology, vol. 18. Cambridge: Harvard University Press.

Lanning, E. P.

1967 *Peru before the Incas.* Englewood Cliffs, N.J.: Prentice-Hall.

Laporte, J. P.

1996 *Organizacion territorial y politica prehispanica en el sureste de Peten.* Atlas arqueologico de Guatemala no. 4, Escuela de Historia. Guatemala City: Universidad de San Carlos.

Laporte, J. P., and H. E. Mejia

2002 Ucanal: Una ciudad del rio Mopan en Peten, Guatemala. *Utz'ib: Serie reportes* 1(2):1–71. Asociacion Tikal.

Lavy, P.

2003 As in Heaven, So on Earth: The Politics of Visnu, Shiva, and Harihara Images in Preangkorian Khmer Civilisation. *Journal of Southeast Asian Studies* 34(1):21–39.

Lewis, N.

1987 *Nomads and Settlers in Syria and Jordan, 1800–1980.* Cambridge: Cambridge University Press.

Lichtheim, M.

1973 *Ancient Egyptian Literature I: The Old and Middle Kingdoms.* Berkeley: University of California Press.

Liu, Li, and Xingcan Chen

2003 *State Formation in Early China.* London: Duckworth.

Loding, D.

1974 *A Craft Archive from Ur.* Ph.D. dissertation, University of Pennsylvania.

Lorton, D.

1995 Legal and Social Institutions of Pharaonic Egypt. Pp. 190–202 in J. Sasson et al., eds., *Civilizations of the Ancient Near East I.* New York: Charles Scribner's Sons.

Love, M.

2002 Domination, Resistance, and Political Cycling in Formative Period Pacific Guatemala. Pp. 214–37 in M. O'Donovan, ed., *The Dynamics of Power.* Center for Archaeological Investigations, Occasional Paper no. 30. Carbondale: Southern Illinois Press.

Lowe, J.W.G.

1985 *The Dynamics of Apocalypse: A Systems Simulation of the Classic Maya Collapse.* Albuquerque: University of New Mexico Press.

Lozada, M. C., and J. E. Buikstra

2002 *El senorio de Chiribaya en la costa sur del Peru.* Lima: Instituto de Estudios Peruanos.

Lucero, L. J.

2002 The Collapse of the Classic Maya: A Case for the Role of Water Control. *American Anthropologist* 104:814–26.

Luke, J. T.

1965 *Pastoralism and Politics in the Mari Period: A Reexamination of the Character and Political Significance of the Major West Semitic Tribal Groups on the Middle Euphrates, ca. 1828–1758 BC.* Ph.D. dissertation, University of Michigan.

Lumbreras, L. G.

1974   *The Peoples and Cultures of Ancient Peru.* Betty J. Meggers, trans. Washington, D.C.: Smithsonian Institution Press.

Mabbett, I. W.

1977   The "Indianization" of Southeast Asia. *Journal of Southeast Asian Studies* 8(2):429–42.

1997   The Indianization of Mainland Southeast Asia: A Reappraisal. Pp. 342–55 in N. Eilenberg, M. C. Subhadradis Diskul, and R. Brown, eds., *Living a Life in Accord with Dhamma: Papers in Honor of Professor Jean Boisselier on His Eightieth Birthday.* Bangkok: Silpakorn Press.

Machule, D., M. Benter, R. Czichon, M. Luciani, M. Miftah, W. Pape, and P. Werner

1993   Ausgrabungen in Tall Munbaqa/Ekalte 1991. *Mitteilungen der deutschen Orient-Gesellschaft* 125:69–101.

Malek, J.

2000   The Old Kingdom (c. 2686–2125 BC). Pp. 89–117 in I. Shaw, ed., *The Oxford History of Ancient Egypt.* New York: Oxford University Press.

Malleret, L.

1959   *L'archéologie du delta du Mékong,* part 1: *L'exploration archéologique et les Fouilles d'Oc-Èo.* Paris: École Française d'Extrême-Orient.

1962   *L'archéologie du delta du Mékong,* part 3: *La culture du Fou-Nan,* 2 vols. Paris: École Française d'Extrême-Orient.

Mallet, J.

1989   Ras Shamra-Ougarit (Syrie) stratigraphie des vestiges du Bronze Moyen II exhumés de 1979 à 1988 (39e, 40e, 41e, 43e et 48e campagnes). *Syria: Revue d'art oriental et d'archéologie* 67:43–101.

2002   Ras Shamra-Ougarit (Syrie), 62e campagne, 2002: L'exploration des niveaux du Bronze Moyen II (Ire moitié du IIe millénaire au J.-C.) sous le palais nord. *Ugarit-Forschungen* 34:527–50.

Manguin, P.-Y.

1996   Southeast Asian Shipping in the Indian Ocean during the First Millennium AD. Pp. 181–96 in H. P. Ray and J.-F. Salles, eds. *Tradition and Archaeology: Early Maritime Contacts in the Indian Ocean.* New Delhi and Lyon: Manohar.

2002   The Amorphous Nature of Coastal Polities in Insular Southeast Asia: Restricted Centers, Extended Peripheries. *Moussons* 5:73–99.

2004   The Archaeology of Early Maritime Polities of Southeast Asia. Pp. 282–313 in P. Bellwood and I. Glover, eds., *A Cultural History of Southeast Asia: From Earliest Times to the Indic Civilizations.* New York: RoutledgeCurzon.

Manguin, P.-Y., and Vo Si Khai

2000   Excavations at the Ba The/Oc Eo Complex (Viet Nam): A Preliminary Report on the 1998 Campaign. Pp. 107–21 in W. Lobo and S. Reimann, eds., *Southeast Asian Archaeology 1998.* Hull, U.K.: University of Hull.

Marcus, J.

1989   From Centralized Systems to City-States: Possible Models for the Epiclassic. Pp. 201–8 in R. Diehl and J. C. Berlo, eds., *Mesoamerica after the Decline of Teotihuacan, AD 700–900.* Washington, D.C.: Dumbarton Oaks.

1992   Dynamic Cycles of Mesoamerican States. *National Geographic Research and Exploration* 8:392–411.

1993   Ancient Maya Political Organization. Pp. 111–84 in J. A. Sabloff and J. Henderson, eds., *Lowland Maya Civilization in the Eighth Century AD.* Washington, D.C.: Dumbarton Oaks.

1998   The Peaks and Valleys of Ancient States: An Extension of the Dynamic Model. Pp. 59–94 in G. Feinman and J. Marcus, eds., *Archaic States.* Santa Fe: School of American Research.

2001   La Zona Maya en el Clásico Terminal. Pp. 303–46 in L. Manzanilla and L. López Luján, eds., *Historia antigua de México,* vol. 2. Mexico City: INAH.

Marfoe, L.

1979   The Integrative Transformation: Patterns of Sociopolitical Organization in Southern Syria. *Bulletin of the American Schools of Oriental Research* 234:1–42.

Martin, S., and N. Grube

1995   Maya Superstates. *Archaeology* 48(6):41–46.

2000   *The Chronicles of Maya Kings and Queens.* London: Thames and Hudson.

Masson, M. A.

1997   Cultural Transformations at the Maya Postclassic Community of Laguna de On, Belize. *Latin American Antiquity* 8(4):293–316.

2000   *In the Realm of Nachan Kan: Postclassic Maya Archaeology at Laguna de On, Belize.* Boulder: University of Colorado Press.

2001   Changing Patterns of Ceramic Stylistic Diversity in the Pre-Hispanic Maya Lowlands. *Acta Archaeologica* 17:1–30.

2002   Community Economy and the Mercantile Transformation in Postclassic Northeastern Belize. Pp. 335–364 in M. Masson and D. Freidel, eds., *Ancient Maya Political Economies.* Walnut Creek, Calif.: Altamira Press.

2003   Economic Patterns in Northern Belize. Pp. 269–81 in M. E. Smith and F. F. Berdan, eds., *The Postclassic Mesoamerican World.* Salt Lake City: University of Utah Press.

Masson, M. A., and H. Chaya

2000   Obsidian Trade Connections at the Postclassic Maya Site of Laguna de On, Belize. *Lithic Technology* 25:135–44.

Masson, M. A., and S. B. Mock

2004   Maya Cultural Adaptations from the Terminal Classic to Postclassic Period at Lagoon Sites in Northern Belize as Reflected in Changing Ceramic Industries. Pp. 367–401 in D. S. Rice, P. M. Rice, and A. A. Demarest, eds., *The Terminal Classic in the Maya Lowlands: Collapse, Transition, and Transformation.* Boulder: University of Colorado Press.

Masson, M. A., and C. Peraza Lope

2004   Nuevas investigaciones en tres unidades residenciales fuera de la monumental zona de Mayapán. Paper presented at the XIV Encuentro Internacional: Los Investigadores de la Cultura Maya, Campeche, Mexico, November 12.

Mathews, P.

1991   Classic Maya Emblem Glyphs. Pp. 19–29 in T. P. Culbert, ed., *Classic Maya Political History.* Cambridge: Cambridge University Press.

Matthiae, P.

1980   Du-ub^{ki} di Mardikh IIB1 = Tu-ba^{ki} di Alalakh VII. *Studi Eblaiti* 1:115–18.

Ma Tuan-lin

1883   *Ethnographie des peuples étranges à la Chine: Ouvrage composé au XIIIe siècle de notre ère.* Marquis d'Hervey de Saint-Denys, trans. Geneva: H. George.

Mazar, A.

1997   Iron Age Chronology: A Reply to I. Finkelstein. *Levant* 29:157–67.

Mazarakis Ainian, A.

1997   *From Rulers' Dwellings to Temples.* Studies in Mediterranean Archaeology 121. Jonsered: Paul Åströms Förlag.

McAnany, P. A.

1994   Operation 2033: Horizontal Exposure of a Terminal Classic Platform. Pp. 79–89 in T. R. Hester, H. J. Shafer, and J. D. Eaton, eds., *Continuing Archaeology at Colha, Belize.* Austin: Texas Archeological Research Laboratory.

1995   *Living with the Ancestors: Kinship and Kingship in Ancient Maya Society.* Austin: University of Texas Press.

2001   Cosmology and the Institutionalization of Hierarchy in the Maya Region. Pp. 125–48 in J. Haas, ed., *From Leaders to Rulers.* New York: Kluwer Academic/Plenum.

McClellan, T.

1999   Urbanism on the Upper Syrian Euphrates. Pp. 413–25 in G. del Olmo Lete and J.-L. Montero Fenóllos, eds., *Archaeology of the Upper Syrian Euphrates—The Tishrin Dam Area: Proceedings of the International Symposium Held at Barcelona, Jan. 28th–30th, 1998.* Barcelona: Editorial Ausa.

McCormick, M.

2001   *Origins of the European Economy: Communications and Commerce AD 300–900.* Cambridge: Cambridge University Press.

McEwan, G. F.

1987   *The Middle Horizon in the Valley of Cuzco, Peru: The Impact of the Wari Occupation of Pikillacta in the Lucre Basin.* BAR International Series S-372. Oxford: BAR.

1991   Investigations at the Pikillacta Site: A Provincial Huari Center in the Valley of Cuzco. Pp. 93–120 in W. H. Isbell and G. McEwan, eds., *Huari Administrative Structure: Prehistoric Monumental Architecture and State Government.* Washington, D.C.: Dumbarton Oaks.

1996   Archaeological Investigations at Pikillacta, a Wari Site in Peru. *Journal of Field Archaeology* 23(2):169–86.

1998   The Function of Niched Halls in Wari Architecture. *Latin American Antiquity* 9(1):68–86.

McEwan, G. F., ed.

2005   *Pikillacta: The Wari Empire in Cuzco.* Iowa City: University of Iowa Press.

McEwan, G. F., M. Chatfield, and A. Gibaja

2002   The Archaeology of Inca Origins. Pp. 287–302 in W. Isbell and H. Silverman, eds., *Andean Archaeology 1: Variations in Sociopolitical Organization.* New York: Kluwer Academic/Plenum.

McGuire, R. H.

1983   Breaking Down Cultural Complexity: Inequality and Heterogeneity. *Advances in Archaeological Method and Theory* 6:91–143.

Meijer, D.

1986   *A Survey in Northeastern Syria.* Leiden: Nederlands Archeologisch-Historisch Instituut te Istanbul.

1996   Tell Hammam Al-Turkman: Preliminary Report on the Seventh Campaign, May–July 1995. *Anatolica* 22:181–93.

Menzel, D.

1959   The Inca Occupation of the South Coast of Peru. *Southwestern Journal of Anthropology* 15(2):125–42.

1964   Style and Time in the Middle Horizon. *Ñawpa Pacha* 2:66–105.

Milbrath, S., and C. Peraza Lope

2003   Revisiting Mayapán: Mexico's Last Maya Capital. *Ancient Mesoamerica* 14:1–46.

Miller, A. G.

1982   *On the Edge of the Sea: Mural Painting at Tancah-Tulum, Quintana Roo, Mexico.* Washington, D.C.: Dumbarton Oaks.

Miller, M.

2000   Understanding the Murals of Bonampak. Pp. 234–43 in N. Grube, ed., *Maya: Divine Kings of the Rainforest.* Cologne: Konemann Verlagsgesellschaft.

Moholy-Nagy, H.

1997   Middens, Construction Fill, and Offerings: Evidence for the Organization of Classic Period Craft Production at Tikal, Guatemala. *Journal of Field Archaeology* 24:293–313.

1999   Mexican Obsidian at Tikal, Guatemala. *Latin American Antiquity* 10(3):300–313.

Morris, I.

1987   *Burial and Ancient Society.* Cambridge: Cambridge University Press.

1991   The Early Polis as City and State. Pp. 24–57 in J. Rich and A. Wallace-Hadrill, eds., *City and Country in the Ancient World.* London: Routledge.

1997   An Archaeology of Equalities? The Greek City-States. Pp. 97–195 in T. Charlton and D. Nichols, eds., *The Archaeology of City-States: Cross-Cultural Approaches.* Washington, D.C.: Smithsonian Institution Press.

1998   Archaeology and Archaic Greek History. Pp. 1–91 in N. Fisher and H. van Wees, *Archaic Greece: New Approaches and New Evidence.* London: Duckworth.

2000   *Archaeology as Cultural History: Words and Things in Iron Age Greece.* Malden: Blackwell.

2001   The Use and Abuse of Homer. Pp. 57–91 in D. Cairns, ed., *Oxford Readings in Homer's Iliad.* Oxford: Oxford University Press.

2003   Mediterraneanization. *Mediterranean Historical Review* 18:30–55.

2004   Economic Growth in Ancient Greece. *Journal of Institutional and Theoretical Economics* 160:709–742.

2005a   The Growth of Greek Cities in the First Millennium BC. *In* G. Storey, ed., *Urbanism in the Preindustrial World.* Tuscaloosa: University of Alabama Press.

2005b   Archaeology, Standards of Living, and Greek Economic History. Pp. 91–126 in J. Manning and I. Morris, eds., *The Ancient Economy: Evidence and Models.* Stanford: Stanford University Press.

2006   Early Iron Age Greece. Chapter 9 in W. Scheidel, I. Morris, and R. Saller, eds., *The Cambridge Economic History of the Greco-Roman World.* Cambridge: Cambridge University Press. (in press)

Morris, S. P.

1992a   *Daidalos and the Origins of Greek Art.* Princeton: Princeton University Press.

1992b   Introduction. Pp. xiii–xviii in G. Kopcke and I. Tokumaru, eds., *Greece between East and West, 10th–8th Centuries BC.* Mainz: Philipp von Zabern.

Moseley, M. E.

1992   *The Incas and Their Ancestors.* New York: Thames and Hudson.

Moseley, M., R. A. Feldman, P. S. Goldstein, and L. Watanabe

1991   Colonies and Conquest: Tiwanaku and Huari in Moquegua. Pp. 121–40 in W. H. Isbell and G. McEwan, eds., *Huari Administrative Structure: Prehistoric and Monumental Architecture and State Government.* Washington, D.C.: Dumbarton Oaks.

Mujica, E.

1985   Altiplano-Coast Relationships in the South-central Andes: From Indirect to Direct Complementarity. Pp. 103–40 in S. Mazuda, I. Shimada, and C. Morris, eds., *Andean Ecology and Civilization.* Tokyo: Tokyo University Press.

Murra, J. V.

1962   An Archaeological "Restudy" of an Andean Ethnohistorical Account. *American Antiquity* 28(1):1–4.

1964   Una apreciación etnológica de la visita. Pp. 421–44 in W. Espinoza Soriano, ed., *Visita hecha a la provincia de Chucuito por Garci Diez de San Miguel.* Lima: Ediciones de la Casa de la Cultura de Perú.

1972   El "control vertical" de un maximo de pisos ecologicos en la economia de las sociedades Andinas. Pp. 427–76 in J. V. Murra, ed., *Visita del la Provincia de Leon de Huanuco en 1562,* vol. 2. Documentos para la historia y etnologia de Huanuco y la Selva Central. Huanuco: Universidad Nacional Hermilio Valdizan.

1975   El traffico en mullu en la costa del Pacifico. Pp. 255–67 in J. V. Murra, ed., *Formaciones económicas y políticas del mundo andino.* Lima: Instituto de Estudios Peruanos.

Nash, D.

1996   *Cerro Petroglifo: Settlement Pattern and Social Organization of a Residential Wari Community.* M.A. thesis, University of Florida.

2002   *The Archaeology of Space: Places of Power in the Wari Empire.* Ph.D. dissertation, University of Florida.

Naveh, J.

1973   Some Semitic Epigraphical Considerations on the Antiquity of the Greek Alphabet. *American Journal of Archaeology* 77:1–8.

Nelson, M. C.

2000   Abandonment: Conceptualization, Representation, and Social Change. Pp. 52–62 in M. Schiffer, ed., *Social Theory in Archaeology.* Salt Lake City: University of Utah Press.

Nelson, W.

1973   *Fact or Fiction: The Dilemma of the Renaissance Storyteller.* Cambridge, Mass.: Harvard University Press.

Nichols, J.

2004   *Amorite Agro-pastoralism and the Early to Middle Bronze Age Transition in Syria.* Ph.D. dissertation, Johns Hopkins University.

Nicholson, H. B.

1982   The Mixteca-Puebla Concept Revisited. Pp. 227–54 in E. Boone, ed., *The Art and Ico-nography of Late Post-Classic Central Mexico*. Washington, D.C.: Dumbarton Oaks.

Oates, D., J. Oates, and H. McDonald

2001   *Excavations at Tell Brak,* vol. 2: *Nagar in the Third Millennium* BC. Cambridge and London: McDonald Institute for Archaeological Research and the British School of Archaeology in Iraq.

Obeyesekere, G.

1992   *The Apotheosis of Captain Cook: European Mythmaking in the Pacific.* Princeton: Princeton University Press.

O'Connor, D.

1972   A Regional Population in Egypt to circa 600 BC. Pp. 78–100 in B. Spooner, ed., *Population Growth: Anthropological Implications.* Cambridge: M.I.T. Press.

Orthmann, W.

1981   *Halawa, 1977–1979.* Bonn: Rudolf Habelt.

1989   *Halawa, 1980–1986.* Bonn: Rudolf Habelt.

Orthmann, W., and H. Kühne

1974   Mumbaqat 1973: Vorläufiger Bericht über die von der deutschen Orient-Gesell-schaft mit Mitteln der Stiftung Volkswagenwerk unternommenen Ausgrabungen. *Mitteilungen der deutschen Orient-Gesellschaft* 106:53–97.

Ortloff, C. R., and A. L. Kolata

1993   Climate and Collapse: Agro-ecological Perspectives on the Decline of the Tiwa-naku State. *Journal of Archaeological Science* 20:195–221.

Osborne, R.

1995   *Greece in the Making, 1200–479 BC.* London: Routledge.

1996   Pots and Trade in Archaic Greece. *Antiquity* 70:31–44.

1998   *Archaic and Classical Greek Art.* Oxford: Oxford University Press.

Owen, B.

1993   *A Model of Multiethnicity: State Collapse, Competition, and Social Complexity from Tiwanaku to Chiribaya in the Osmore Valley, Peru.* Ph.D. dissertation, University of California at Los Angeles.

1996   *Inventario arqueológico del drenaje superior del Río Osmore: Informe del campo e informe final.* Lima/Moquegua: Instituto Nacional de la Cultura del Perú.

1999   *Proyecto vecinos de Cerro Baúl 1997: Informe de campo y final presentado al Instituto Nacional de Cultura.* Lima/Moquegua: Instituto Nacional de Cultura del Perú.

Owen, B., and P. Goldstein

2001   Tiwanaku en Moquegua: Intèracciones regionales y colapso. Pp. 169–88 in P. Kaulicke and W. H. Isbell, eds., *Boletín de arqueología,* vol. 5. Lima: Pontificia Universidad Católica del Perú.

Owen, B., and R. Menaut

2002   Visión preliminar de la prehistoria de la región Carumas Calacoa. Pp. 24–25 in *Integración: Prensa para el desarrollo,* vol. 2. Ilo: Southern Peru Copper.

Palumbo, G.

2001   The Early Bronze Age IV. Pp. 233–69 in B. MacDonald, R. Adams, and P. Bien-kowski, eds., *The Archaeology of Jordan.* Sheffield: Sheffield Academic Press.

Papadopoulos, J.

1993 To Kill a Cemetery: The Athenian Kerameikos and the Early Iron Age in the Aegean. *Journal of Mediterranean Archaeology* 6:175–206.

Parker Pearson, M.

1982 Mortuary Practices, Society, and Ideology: An Ethnoarchaeological Study. Pp. 99–113 in I. Hodder, ed., *Symbolic and Structural Archaeology.* Cambridge: Cambridge University Press.

Pauketat, T. R.

2003 Resettled Farmers and the Making of a Mississippian Polity. *American Antiquity* 68(1):39–66.

Pearson, R.

1997 The Chuzan Kingdom of Okinawa as a City-State. Pp. 119–34 in D. Nichols and T. Charlton, eds., *The Archaeology of City-States: Cross-Cultural Approaches.* Washington, D.C.: Smithsonian Institution Press.

Pelliot, P.

1903 Le Fou-nan. *Bulletin de l'École Française de l'Extrême Orient* 3:248–303.

Peltenburg, E.

1999 Tell Jerablus Tahtani, 1992–1996: A Summary. Pp. 97–105 in G. del Olmo Lete and J.-L. Montero Fenollós, eds., *Archaeology of the Upper Syrian Euphrates— The Tishrin Dam Area: Proceedings of the International Symposium Held at Barcelona, Jan. 28th–30th, 1998.* Barcelona: Editorial Ausa.

2000 From Nucleation to Dispersal: Late Third Millennium BC Settlement Pattern Transformations in the Near East and Aegean. Pp. 163–86 in O. Rouault and M. Wäfler, eds., *La Djéziré et l'Euphrate syriens de la protohistoire à la fin du IIe millénaire av. J.-C.: Tendances dans l'interprétation historique des données nouvelles.* Turnhout: Brepols.

Peltenburg, E., S. Campbell, S. Carter, F.M.K. Stephen, and R. Tipping

1997 Jerablus-Tahtani, Syria, 1996: Preliminary Report. *Levant* 29:1–18.

Peltenburg, E., S. Campbell, P. Croft, D. Lunt, M. A. Murray, and M. E. Watt

1995 Jerablus-Tahtani, Syria, 1992–4: Preliminary Report. *Levant* 27:1–28.

Pendergast, D. M.

1984 The Hunchback Tomb: A Major Archaeological Discovery in Central America. *Rotunda* 16(4):5–11.

1986 Stability through Change: Lamanai, Belize, from the Ninth to the Seventeenth Century. Pp. 223–50 in J. A. Sabloff and E. W. Andrews, eds., *Late Lowland Maya Civilization: Classic to Postclassic.* Albuquerque: University of New Mexico Press.

1992 Noblesse Oblige: The Elites of Altun Ha and Lamanai, Belize. Pp. 61–79 in D. Chase and A. Chase, eds., *Mesoamerican Elites.* Norman: University of Oklahoma Press.

Peraza Lope, C.

1998 Mayapán: Ciudad-capital del Postclásico. *Arqueología Mexicana* 2:48–53.

Peraza Lope, C., P. Delgado Kú, and B. Escamilla Ojeda

2002 *Trabajo de mantenimiento y conservacíon arquitectonica en Mayapán, Yucatán, informe de la Tercera Temporada 1998.* Informe de actividades al Consejo de Arqueología del Instituto Nacional de Antropología e Historia. Merida: INAH–Centro Yucatán.

Peraza Lope, C., and M. A. Masson

n.d. The Late Postclassic Chronology of Mayapán. Manuscript submitted to *Ancient Mesoamerica.*

Phillips, D. A., Jr.

1979   *Material Culture and Trade of the Postclassic Maya.* Ph.D. dissertation, University of Arizona.

Pillsbury, J.

1996   The Thorny Oyster and the Origins of Empire: Implications of Recently Uncovered *Spondylus* Imagery from Chan Chan, Peru. *Latin American Antiquity* 7(4):313–40.

Piña Chan, R.

1978   Commerce in the Yucatec Peninsula: The Conquest and Colonial Period. Pp. 37–48 in T. A. Lee and C. Navarrete, eds., *Mesoamerican Communication Routes and Culture Contacts.* Papers of the New World Archaeological Foundation 40. Provo, Utah: Brigham Young Press.

Pirenne, H.

1925   *Medieval Cities: Their Origins and the Revival of Trade.* Princeton: Princeton University Press.

1939   *Mohammed and Charlemagne.* New York: W. W. Norton.

Podzorski, P.

1999   Naga ed-Deir. Pp. 551–54 in K. Bard, ed., *Encyclopedia of the Archaeology of Ancient Egypt.* New York: Routledge.

Pollock, H.E.D.

1962   Introduction. Pp. 1–24 in H.E.D. Pollock, R. L. Roys, T. Proskouriakoff, and A. L. Smith, eds., *Mayapan, Yucatan, Mexico.* Carnegie Institute of Washington Publication no. 619. Washington, D.C.: Carnegie Institute.

Pollock, H.E.D., R. L. Roys, T. Proskouriakoff, and A. L. Smith

1962   *Mayapan, Yucatan, Mexico.* Carnegie Institute of Washington Publication no. 619. Washington, D.C.: Carnegie Institute.

Pons, N.

2001   La potérie de Tell Amarna (Syrie) au BA IV et au BM I. *Akkadica* 121:23–76.

Popham, M., P. Calligas, and H. Sackett

1993   *Lefkandi,* vol. 2, part 2. Athens: British School of Archaeology at Athens.

Porter, A.

1995a   The Third Millennium Settlement Complex at Tell Banat: Tell Kabir. *Damaszener Mitteilungen* 8:125–63.

1995b   Tell Banat—Tomb 1. *Damaszener Mitteilungen* 8:1–50.

2002a   The Dynamics of Death: Ancestors, Pastoralism, and the Origins of a Third-millennium City in Syria. *Bulletin of the American Schools of Oriental Research* 325:1–36.

2002b   Communities in Conflict: Death and the Contest for Social Order in the Euphrates River Valley. *Near Eastern Archaeology* 65:156–73.

Porter, A., and T. McClellan

1998   The Third Millennium Settlement Complex at Tell Banat: Results of the 1994 Excavations. *Damaszener Mitteilungen* 10:11–63.

Possehl, G.

1997   Climate and the Eclipse of the Ancient Cities of the Indus. Pp. 193–244 in H. N. Dalfes, G. Kukla, and H. Weiss, eds., *Third Millennium BC Climate Change and Old World Collapse.* Berlin: Springer-Verlag.

Postgate, J. N.

1986   The Equids of Sumer, Again. Pp. 194–206 in R. H. Meadow and H. P. Uerpmann, eds., *Equids in the Ancient World.* Wiesbaden: Ludwig Reichert.

1992   *Early Mesopotamia: Society and Economy at the Dawn of History.* New York: Routledge.

Pottier, C.

1999   *Carte archéologique de la région d'Angkor, zone sud.* 3 vols. Ph.D. thesis, Université Paris III–Sorbonne Nouvelle, UFR Orient et Monde Arabe.

Powell, B.

1991   *Homer and the Origin of the Greek Alphabet.* Cambridge: Cambridge University Press.

Powis, T. G., F. Valdez Jr., T. R. Hester, W. J. Hurst, and S. M. Tarka Jr.

2002   Spouted Vessels and Cacao Use among the Preclassic Maya. *Latin American Antiquity* 13:85–106.

Price, B.

1977   Secondary State Formation: An Explanatory Model. Pp. 161–86 in R. Cohen and E. Service, eds., *Origins of the State: The Anthropology of Political Evolution.* Philadelphia: Institute for the Study of Human Issues.

Proskouriakoff, T.

1950   *A Study of Classic Maya Sculpture.* Publication no. 593. Washington, D.C.: Carnegie Institution.

1962   Civic and Religious Structures of Mayapan. Pp. 87–164 in H.E.D. Pollock, R. Roys, T. Proskouriakoff, and A. L. Smith, eds., *Mayapan, Yucatan, Mexico.* Publication no. 619. Washington, D.C.: Carnegie Institution.

Pugh, T. W.

2001   Flood Reptiles, Serpent Temples, and the Quadripartite Universe: The *Imago Mundi* of Late Postclassic Mayapan. *Ancient Mesoamerica* 12:247–58.

Ray, H. P.

1989   Early Maritime Contacts between South and Southeast Asia. *Journal of Southeast Asian Studies* 10(1):42–54.

1994   *The Winds of Change: Buddhism and the Maritime Links of Early South Asia.* Delhi: Oxford University Press.

Redford, D. B.

1992   *Egypt, Canaan, and Israel in Ancient Times.* Princeton: Princeton University Press.

Reed, R.

1972   *Ancient Skins, Parchments, and Leathers.* New York: Seminar Press.

Reents-Budet, D.

1994   *Painting the Maya Universe: Royal Ceramics of the Classic Period.* Durham, N.C.: Duke University Press.

Rees, M.

2001   Historical Science or Silence? Toward a Historical Anthropology of the Mississippian Political Culture. Pp. 121–40 in T. Pauketat, ed., *The Archaeology of Traditions.* Gainesville: University Press of Florida.

Rehak, P., ed.

1995   *The Role of the Ruler in the Prehistoric Aegean.* Aegaeum 11. Liège: Université de Liège.

Reindel, M., and J. A. Isla Cuadrado

1998   *Proyecto Arqueológico PALPA, informe final.* Lima: Instituto Nacional de Cultura del Perú.

Rempel, J., and N. Yoffee

1999   The End of the Cycle? Assessing the Impact of Hellenization on Mesopotamian Civilization. Pp. 385–98 in B. Böck, E. Cancik-Kirschbaum, and T. Richter, eds., *Munscula Mesopotamica: Festschrift für Johannes Renger*. Münster: Ugarit-Verlag, 1999.

Renfrew, C.

1972   *The Emergence of Civilisation.* London: Methuen.

1979   Systems Collapse as Social Transformation: Catastrophe and Anastrophe in Early State Societies. Pp. 481–506 in C. Renfrew and K. Cooke, eds., *Transformations: Mathematical Approaches to Culture Change.* New York: Academic Press.

Renfrew, C., and J. Cherry, eds.

1986   *Peer Polity Interaction and Socio-political Change.* Cambridge: Cambridge University Press.

Restall, M.

1997   *The Maya World.* Stanford: Stanford University Press.

Rice, D. S.

1989   Osmore Drainage, Peru: The Ecological Setting. Pp. 17–33 in D. S. Rice, C. Stanish, and P. R. Scarr, eds., *Ecology, Settlement and History in the Osmore Drainage, Peru.* BAR International Series 545. Oxford: BAR.

Rice, D. S., C. Stanish, and P. R. Scarr, eds.

1989   *Ecology, Settlement, and History in the Osmore Drainage, Peru.* BAR International Series 545. Oxford: BAR.

Rice, P. M.

1984   Obsidian Procurement in the Central Peten Lakes Region, Guatemala. *Journal of Field Archaeology* 11:181–94.

1987   Economic Change in the Lowland Maya Late Classic Period. Pp. 76–85 in E. M. Brumfiel and T. K. Earle, eds. *Specialization, Exchange, and Complex Societies.* Cambridge: Cambridge University Press.

1989   *Pottery Analysis: A Sourcebook.* Chicago: Chicago Press.

Rice, P. M., and D. S. Rice

2004   Late Classic to Postclassic Transformations in the Petén Lakes Region, Guatemala. Pp. 125–39 in A. A. Demarest, P. M. Rice, and D. S. Rice, eds., *The Terminal Classic in the Maya Lowlands: Collapse, Transition, and Transformation.* Boulder: University of Colorado Press.

Richard, S.

1987   The Early Bronze Age: The Rise and Collapse of Urbanism. *Biblical Archaeologist* 50:22–43.

Richards, J.

1997   Ancient Egyptian Mortuary Practice and the Study of Socioeconomic Differentiation. Pp. 33–42 in J. Lustig, ed., *Anthropology and Egyptology: A Developing Dialogue.* Sheffield, U.K.: Sheffield Academic Press.

2000   Modified Order, Responsive Legitimacy, Redistributed Wealth: Egypt 2260–1650 BC. Pp. 36–45 in J. Richards and M. Van Buren, eds., *Order, Legitimacy, and Wealth in Ancient States.* New York: Cambridge University Press.

2002   Text and Context in Late Old Kingdom Egypt: The Archaeology and Historiography of Weni the Elder. *Journal of the American Research Center in Egypt* 39:75–102.

Ricklefs, M. C.

1966   Land and the Law in the Epigraphy of Tenth-century Cambodia. *Journal of Asian Studies* 26(3):411–20.

Ringle, W. M.

2004   On the Political Organization of Chichen Itzá. *Ancient Mesoamerica* 15:167–218.

Ringle, W. M., and G. J. Bey III

2001   Post-Classic and Terminal Classic Courts of the Northern Maya Lowlands. Pp. 266–307 in T. Inomata and S. D. Houston, eds., *Royal Courts of the Maya*, vol. 2: *Data and Case Studies.* Boulder, Colo.: Westview Press.

Ringle, W. M., T. Gallareta Negron, and G. J. Bey III

1998   The Return of Quetzalcoatl: Evidence for the Spread of a World Religion during the Epiclassic period. *Ancient Mesoamerica* 9:183–232.

Robertson, D.

1970   The Tulum Murals: The International Style of the Late Post-Classic. *Verhandlungen des XXXVIII Internationalen Amerikanistenkongresses* 2:77–88.

Robles, F. Castellanos, and A. P. Andrews

1986   A Review and Synthesis of Recent Postclassic Archaeology in Northern Yucatan. Pp. 53–98 in J. A. Sabloff and E. Wyllys Andrews, eds., *The Late Lowland Maya Civilization: Classic to Postclassic.* Albuquerque: University of New Mexico Press.

Roobaert, A., and G. Bunnens

1999   Excavations at Tell Ahmar–Til Barsib. Pp. 163–78 in G. del Olmo Lete and J.-L. Montero Fenollós, eds., *Archaeology of the Upper Syrian Euphrates—The Tishrin Dam Area: Proceedings of the International Symposium Held at Barcelona, Jan. 28th–30th, 1998.* Barcelona: Editorial Ausa.

Rostworowski de Diez Canseco, M.

1999   *History of the Inca Realm.* Harry B. Iceland, trans. Cambridge: Cambridge University Press.

Rowe, J. H.

1944   *An Introduction to the Archaeology of Cuzco.* Papers of the Peabody Museum of American Archaeology and Ethnology, 27(2). Cambridge, Mass.: Harvard University Press.

1946   Inca Culture at the Time of the Spanish Conquest. Pp. 183–330 in J. H. Steward, ed., *Handbook of South American Indians.* Bulletin 143, vol. 2. Washington, D.C.: Bureau of American Ethnology.

1962   Stages and Periods in Archaeological Interpretation. *Southwestern Journal of Anthropology* 18(1):40–54.

Roys, R. L.

1943   *The Indian Background of Colonial Yucatan.* Carnegie Institution of Washington, Publication 548. Washington, D.C.: Carnegie Institution.

1957   *The Political Geography of the Yucatan Maya.* Publication 613. Washington, D.C.: Carnegie Institution.

1962   Literary Sources for the History of Mayapan. Pp. 25–86 in H.E.D. Pollock, R. L. Roys, T. Proskouriakoff, and A. L. Smith, eds. *Mayapan, Yucatan, Mexico.* Publication 619. Washington, D.C.: Carnegie Institution.

Ruppert, K.

1950   Gallery Patio Type Structures at Chichen Itza. Pp. 249–58 in *For the Dean: Essays in Anthropology in Honor of Byron Cummings on his 89th Birthday, September 20, 1950.* Tucson: Hohokam Museums Association.

1952 *Chichen Itza Architectural Notes and Plans.* Publication 595. Washington, D.C.: Carnegie Institute.

Russell, B. W., and T. Ormsby

2003 Esfuerzos de exploracíon fuera de la muralla de la ciudad de Mayapán, Yucatán, México: Temporada de campo 2002. Pp. 229–372 in M. A. Masson, C. Peraza Lope, and T. S. Hare, eds., *Los fundamentos del poder económico de Mayapan, Proyecto Mayapan–temporada 2002.* Informe para el Consejo de Arqueología de México. Albany: SUNY, and Merida: INAH–Centro Yucatán.

Sabloff, J. A.

1973 Continuity and Disruption during Terminal Late Classic Times at Seibal: Ceramic and Other Evidence. Pp. 107–31 in T. P. Culbert, ed., *The Classic Maya Collapse.* Albuquerque: University of New Mexico Press.

Sabloff, J. A., and J. S. Henderson

1993 *Lowland Maya Civilization in the Eighth Century AD.* Washington, D.C.: Dumbarton Oaks.

Sabloff, J. A., and W. L. Rathje

1975 The Rise of a Maya Merchant Class. *Scientific American* 233:72–82.

Sahlins, M. D.

1972 *Stone Age Economics.* New York: Aldine.

1981 *Historical Metaphors and Mythical Realities: Structure in the Early History of the Sandwich Islands Kingdom.* Association for Social Anthropology in Oceania Special Publication no. 1. Ann Arbor: University of Michigan Press.

1995 *How "Natives" Think: About Captain Cook, For Example.* Chicago: University of Chicago Press.

2004 *Apologies to Thucydides: Understanding History as Culture and Vice Versa.* Chicago: University of Chicago Press.

Saignes, T.

1986 The Ethnic Groups in the Valleys of Larecaja: From Descent to Residence. Pp. 311–41 in J. V. Murra, N. Wachtel, and J. Revel, eds., *Anthropological History of Andean Polities.* Cambridge: Cambridge University Press.

Sanders, W. T., and D. Webster

1988 The Mesoamerican Urban Tradition. *American Anthropologist* 90(3):521–46.

Savage, S. H.

1997 Descent Group Competition and Economic Strategies in Predynastic Egypt. *Journal of Anthropological Archaeology* 16:226–68.

Schaedel, R. P.

1951 Mochica Murals at Pañamarca. *Archaeology* 4(3):145–54.

1966 Incipient Urbanization and Secularization in Tiahuanacoid Peru. *American Antiquity* 31(3):338–44.

Scheidel, W.

2001 *Death on the Nile.* Leiden: E. J. Brill.

2006 Demography. Chapter 2 in W. Scheidel, I. Morris, and R. Saller, eds., *The Cambridge Economic History of the Greco-Roman World.* Cambridge: Cambridge University Press. (in press)

Schele, L., and D. Freidel

1990   *A Forest of Kings: The Untold Story of the Ancient Maya.* New York: William Morrow.

Schele, L., and P. Mathews

1998   *The Code of Kings.* New York: Scribner.

Schloen, J. D.

2001   *The House of the Father in Fact and Symbol: Patrimonialism in Ugarit and the Ancient Near East.* Studies in the Archaeology and History of the Levant 2. Winona Lake, Ind.: Eisenbrauns.

Schreiber, K. J.

1984   Prehistoric Roads in the Carahuarazo Valley, Peru. Pp. 75–94 in A. Kendall, ed., *Current Archaeological Projects in the Central Andes: Some Approaches and Results.* BAR International Series 210. Oxford: BAR.

1992   *Wari Imperialism in Middle Horizon Peru.* Anthropological Papers no. 87. Ann Arbor: University of Michigan Museum of Anthropology.

1999   Regional Approaches to the Study of Prehistoric Empires: Examples from Ayacucho and Nasca, Peru. Pp. 160–71 in B. R. Billman and G. M. Feinman, eds., *Settlement Pattern Studies in the Americas: Fifty Years since Virú.* Washington, D.C.: Smithsonian Institution Press.

2001   The Wari Empire of Middle Horizon Peru: The Epistemological Challenge of Documenting an Empire without Documentary Evidence. Pp. 70–92 in S. E. Alcock, T. N. D'Altroy, K. D. Morrison, and C. M. Sinopoli, eds., *Empires: Perspectives from Archaeology and History.* Cambridge: Cambridge University Press.

Schreiber, K. J., and J. Lancho Rojas

1995   The Puquios of Nasca. *Latin American Antiquity* 6(3):229–54.

2003   *Irrigation and Society in the Peruvian Desert: The Puquios of Nasca.* Lanham, Md.: Lexington Books.

Schwartz, G. M., H. H. Curvers, S. Dunham, and B. Stuart

2003   A Third-millennium BC Elite Tomb and Other New Evidence from Tell Umm el-Marra, Syria. *American Journal of Archaeology* 107(3):325–61.

Schwartz, G. M., H. H. Curvers, F. A. Gerritsen, J. MacCormack, N. F. Miller, and J. A. Weber

2000   Excavation and Survey in the Jabbul Plain: The Umm el-Marra Project, 1996–7. *American Journal of Archaeology* 104:419–62.

Schwartz, G., H. H. Curvers, and B. Stuart

2000   A Third Millennium BC Elite Tomb from Tell Umm el-Marra, Syria. *Antiquity* 74:771–72.

Sedov, L. A.

1978   Angkor: Society and State. Pp. 111–30 in H.J.M. Claessen and P. Skalník, eds., *The Early State.* New Babylon Studies in the Social Sciences 32. New York: Mouton.

Seidlmayer, S.

1990   *Gräberfelder aus dem Übergang vom Alten zum Mittleren Reich: Studien zur Archäologie der Ersten Zwischenzeit.* Heidelberg: Heidelberger Orientverlag.

2000   The First Intermediate Period (c. 2160–2055 BC). Pp. 118–47 in I. Shaw, ed., *The Oxford History of Ancient Egypt.* New York: Oxford University Press.

Serjeantson, D.

1989a   Introduction. Pp. 1–12 in D. Serjeantson, ed., *Diet and Crafts in Towns: The Evidence of Animal Remains from the Roman to the Post-Medieval Periods.* Oxford: BAR.

1989b   Animal Remains and the Tanning Trade. Pp. 129–46 in D. Serjeantson, ed., *Diet and Crafts in Towns: The Evidence of Animal Remains from the Roman to the Post-Medieval Periods.* Oxford: BAR.

Service, E. R.

1960   The Law of Evolutionary Potential. Pp. 93–122 in M. D. Sahlins and E. R. Service, eds., *Evolution and Culture.* Ann Arbor: University of Michigan Press.

Shafer, H. J., and T. R. Hester

1983   Ancient Maya Chert Workshops in Northern Belize, Central America. *American Antiquity* 48(3):519–43.

Sharer, R. J.

1994   *The Ancient Maya.* 5th ed. Stanford: Stanford University Press.

Shaw, J.

1989   Phoenicians in Southern Crete. *American Journal of Archaeology* 93:165–83.

2003   Climate Change and Deforestation: Implications for the Maya Collapse. *Ancient Mesoamerica* 14:157–67.

Sherratt, A., and S. Sherratt

1993   The Growth of the Mediterranean Economy in the Early First Millennium BC. *World Archaeology* 24:361–78.

Shook, E. M.

1954   Three Temples and Their Associated Structures at Mayapan. *Current Reports no. 14,* pp. 254–91. Washington, D.C.: Carnegie Institute Department of Archaeology.

Sigrist, M.

1981   Le travail des cuirs et peaux à Umma sous la dynastie d'Ur III. *Journal of Cuneiform Studies* 33:141–90.

Silverman, H.

1993   *Cahuachi in the Ancient Nasca World.* Iowa City: University of Iowa Press.

2002   *Ancient Nasca Settlement and Society.* Iowa City: University of Iowa Press.

Silverman, H., and D. A. Proulx

2002   *The Nasca.* Malden, U.K.: Blackwell.

Simon, H.

1965   The Architecture of Complexity. *Yearbook of the Society for General Systems Research* 10:63–76.

1973   The Organization of Complex Systems. Pp. 3–27 in H. H. Pattee, ed., *Hierarchy Theory: The Challenge of Complex Systems.* New York: G. Braziller.

Sinopoli, C. M., and K. D. Morrison

1995   Dimensions of Imperial Control: The Vijayanagara Capital. *American Anthropologist* 97(1):83–96.

Smith, C. A.

1976   Exchange Systems and the Spatial Distribution of Elites: The Organization of Stratification in Agrarian Societies. Pp. 309–74 in C. Smith, ed., *Regional Analysis: Social Systems,* vol. 2. New York: Academic Press.

Smith, M. E.

1999   "Indianization" from the Indian Point of View: Trade and Cultural Contacts with Southeast Asia in the Early First Millennium CE. *Journal of the Economic and Social History of the Orient* 42(1):1–26.

2005   City Size in Postclassic Mesoamerica. *Journal of Urban History* 31:918–21.

Smith, M. E., and F. F. Berdan

2003a   Postclassic Mesoamerica. Pp. 1–13 in M. E. Smith and F. F. Berdan, eds., *The Postclassic Mesoamerican World*. Salt Lake City: University of Utah Press.

2003b   *The Postclassic Mesoamerican World*. Salt Lake City: University of Utah Press.

Smith, M. E., and C. Heath-Smith

1994   Rural Economy in Late Postclassic Morelos. Pp. 349–76 in M. G. Hodge and M. E. Smith, eds., *Economies and Polities in the Aztec Realm*. Institute for Mesoamerican Studies, Studies on Culture and Society vol. 6. Albany: SUNY Institute for Mesoamerican Studies.

Snodgrass, A. M.

1971   *The Dark Age of Greece*. Edinburgh: Edinburgh University Press.

1980   *Archaic Greece: The Age of Experiment*. London: J. M. Dent.

Spence, M. W.

1996   Commodity or Gift: Teotihuacán Obsidian in the Maya Region. *Latin American Antiquity* 7:21–40.

Spengler, O.

1918–22   *The Decline of the West*. C. F. Atkinson, trans. New York: Alfred Knopf.

Spickard, L. E.

1983   The Development of Huari Administrative Architecture. Pp. 136–60 in D. H. Sandweiss, ed., *Investigations of the Andean Past*. Ithaca, N.Y.: Cornell University Press.

Stanish, C.

1989   Household Archaeology: Testing Models of Zoning Complementarity in South Central Andes. *American Anthropologist* 91(1):7–25.

1992   *Ancient Andean Political Economy*. Austin: University of Texas Press.

Stark, M. T.

1998   The Transition to History in the Mekong Delta: A View from Cambodia. *International Journal of Historical Archaeology* 2(3):175–204.

2003   Angkor Borei and the Archaeology of Cambodia's Mekong Delta. Pp. 87–106 in J. Koo, ed., *Art and Archaeology of Fu Nan: Pre-Khmer Kingdom of the Lower Mekong Valley*. Bangkok: Orchid Books.

2004   Pre-Angkorian and Angkorian Cambodia. Pp. 89–119 in P. Bellwood and I. Glover, eds., *A Cultural History of Southeast Asia: From Earliest Times to the Indic Civilizations*. New York: RoutledgeCurzon.

Stark, M. T., and S. J. Allen

1998   The Transition to History in Southeast Asia: An Introduction. *International Journal of Historical Archaeology* 2(3):163–75.

Stark, M. T., and Bong Sovath

2001   Recent Research on the Emergence of Early Historic States in Cambodia's Lower Mekong. *Bulletin of the Indo-Pacific Prehistory Association* 19:85–98.

2004   Pre–Angkorian Settlement Organization in Cambodia's Mekong Delta: A Preliminary Report. Presented at the New Trends in Khmer Studies Conference, Center for Khmer Studies, Wat Damnak, Siem Reap, Cambodia, January 8–9, 2004.

Stark, M. T., P. B. Griffin, Chuch Phoeurn, J. Ledgerwood, M. Dega, C. Mortland Dowling, J. M. Bayman, Bong Sovath, Tea Van, Chhan Chamroeun, and D. K. Latinis

1999   Results of the 1995–1996 Field Investigations at Angkor Borei, Cambodia. *Asian Perspectives* 38(1):7–36.

Steckel, R., and J. Rose, eds.
2002   *The Backbone of History.* Cambridge: Cambridge University Press.

Stein, G.
1998   Heterogeneity, Power, and Political Economy: Some Current Research Issues in the Archaeology of Old World Complex Societies. *Journal of Archaeological Research* 6:1–44.
1999   *Rethinking World-Systems: Diasporas, Colonies, and Interaction in Uruk Mesopotamia.* Tucson: University of Arizona Press.
2002   From Passive Periphery to Active Agents: Emerging Perspectives in the Archaeology of Interregional Interaction. *American Anthropologist* 103:903–16.

Stissi, V.
1999   Production, Circulation, and Consumption of Archaic Greek Pottery (Sixth and Early Fifth Century BC). Pp. 83–113 in J.-P. Crielaard, V. Stissi, and G. van Wijngaarden, eds., *The Complex Past of Pottery.* Amsterdam: J. C. Gieben.

Stol, M.
1983   Leder (Industrie). *Reallexikon der Assyriologie* 6:527–43.

Stone, E. C.
1977   Economic Crisis and Social Upheaval in Old Babylonian Nippur. Pp. 267–89 in T. C. Young Jr. and L. Levine, eds., *Mountains and Lowlands: Essays in the Archaeology of Greater Mesopotamia.* Bibliotheca Mesopotamica 7. Malibu, Calif.: Undena.
1987   *Nippur Neighborhoods.* Chicago: Oriental Institute.

Stone, T.
1999   The Chaos of Collapse: Disintegration and Reintegration of Inter-regional Systems. *Antiquity* 73:110–18.

Streck, M. P.
2000   *Das amurritische Onomastikon der altbabylonischen Zeit.* Alter Orient und Altes Testament, Band 271(1). Münster: Ugarit-Verlag.

Stuart, D.
1988   The Río Azul Cacao Pot: Epigraphic Observations on the Function of a Maya Ceramic Vessel. *Antiquity* 62:153–57.

Sutter, R. C.
2000   Prehistoric Genetic and Culture Change: A Bioarchaeological Search for Pre-Inka Altiplano C Colonies in the Coastal Valleys of Moquegua, Peru, and Azapa, Chile. *Latin American Antiquity* 11(1):43–70.

Sznycer, M.
1979   L'inscription phénicienne de Tekke, près de Cnossos. *Kadmos* 18:89–93.

Tainter, J. A.
1988   *The Collapse of Complex Societies.* Cambridge: Cambridge University Press.

Tambiah, S.
1976   *World Conqueror and World Renouncer.* Cambridge: Cambridge University Press.
1977   The Galactic Polity: The Structure of Traditional Kingdoms in Southeast Asia. *Annals of the New York Academy of Sciences* 293:69–97.

Taschek, J. T.
1994   *The Artifacts of Dzibilchaltun, Yucatan, Mexico: Shell, Polished Stone, Bone, Wood, and Ceramics.* Publication 50. New Orleans: Tulane University Middle American Research Institute.

Taube, K. A.

1992   *The Major Gods of Yucatan.* Studies in Pre-Columbian Art and Archaeology no. 32. Washington, D.C.: Dumbarton Oaks.

Tefnin, R.

1980   Exploration archéologique au Nord du lac de Djabboul (Syrie): Une campagne de sondages sur le site d'Oumm el-Marra, 1978. *Annuaire de l'Institut de Philologie et d'Histoire Orientales et Slaves* 23:71–94.

Thompson, E. H.

1938   *The High Priest's Grave, Chichen Itza, Yucatan, Mexico.* Anthropological Series, Publication 412, Field Museum of Natural History, 27(1). Chicago: Field Museum.

Thompson, J.

1957   *Deities Portrayed on Censers at Mayapan.* Department of Archaeology Current Reports no. 40. Washington, D.C.: Carnegie Institute.

Thompson, L. G., E. Mosley-Thompson, J. F. Bolzan, and B. R. Koci

1985   A 1500-Year Record of Tropical Precipitation in Ice Cores from the Quelccaya Ice Cap, Peru. *Science* 229:971–73.

Thurston, T. L.

2001   *Landscapes of Power, Landscapes of Conflict: State Formation in the South Scandinavian Iron Age.* New York: Kluwer Academic/Plenum.

Tomka, S. A., and M. G. Stevenson

1993   Understanding Abandonment Processes: Summary and Remaining Concerns. Pp. 191–95 in C. M. Cameron and S. A. Tomka, eds., *Abandonment of Settlements and Regions: Ethnoarchaeological and Archaeological Approaches.* Cambridge: Cambridge University Press.

Tourtellot, G., III

1988   *Peripheral Survey and Excavation: Settlement and Community Pattern, Excavations at Seibal, Department of Peten, Guatemala.* Memoirs of the Peabody Museum of Archaeology and Ethnology 16. Cambridge: Harvard University Press.

Tourtellot, G., III, and J. A. Sabloff

1994   Community Structure at Sayil: A Case Study of Puuc Settlement. Pp. 71–92 in H. J. Prem, ed., *Hidden among the Hills: Maya Archaeology of the Northwest Yucatan Peninsula.* Acta Mesoamericana 7. Markt Schwaben: Anton Saurwein.

Toynbee, A.

1933–43   *A Study of History.* [Vol. 1 (1946): abridgment of vols. 1–6; vol. 2 (1957): abridgment of vols. 7–10 (D. C. Somervell).] Oxford: Oxford University Press.

Tozzer, A. M., ed. and trans.

1941   Notes to *Landa's Relaciones de las Cosas de Yucatan.* Papers of the Peabody Museum of American Archaeology and Ethnology 18. Cambridge, Mass.: Harvard University Press.

Trigger, B.

2003   *Understanding Early Civilizations: A Comparative Study.* Cambridge: Cambridge University Press.

Trinh Thi Hoà

1996   Réflexions sur le vestiges de la culture d'Óc Eo. *Etudes Vietnamiennes* 50(120):111–23.

Tunca, Ö.

1999   Tell Amarna: Présentation sommaire de sept campagnes de fouilles (1991–1997).

Pp. 129–36 in G. del Olmo Lete and J.-L. Montero Fenollós, eds., *Archaeology of the Upper Syrian Euphrates—The Tishrin Dam Area: Proceedings of the International Symposium Held at Barcelona, Jan. 28th–30th, 1998.* Barcelona: Editorial Ausa.

Urton, G.

1990   *The History of a Myth: Pacariqtambo and the Origin of the Incas.* Austin: University of Texas Press.

Vagnetti, L.

1999   Mycenaean Pottery in the Central Mediterranean. Pp. 137–61 in J.-P. Crielaard, V. Stissi, and G. van Wijngaarden, eds., *The Complex Past of Pottery.* Amsterdam: J. C. Gieben.

Valdés, J. A.

1997   Tamarindito: Archaeology and Regional Politics in the Petexbatun Region. *Ancient Mesoamerica* 8:321–35.

Valdés Pereiro, C.

1999   Tell Qara Quzaq: A Summary of the First Results. Pp. 117–27 in G. del Olmo Lete and J.-L. Montero Fenollós, eds., *Archaeology of the Upper Syrian Euphrates— The Tishrin Dam Area: Proceedings of the International Symposium Held at Barcelona, Jan. 28th–30th, 1998.* Barcelona: Editorial Ausa.

2001   La cerámica de Tell Qara Quzaq, Campañas 1992–1994. Pp. 119–254 in G. del Olmo Lete, J.-L. Montero Fenollós, et al., eds., *Tell Qara Quzaq, II: Campañas IV–VI (1992–1994).* Barcelona: Editorial Ausa.

Valdez, L. M.

1994   Cahuachi: New Evidence for an Early Nasca Ceremonial Role. *Current Anthropology* 35(5):675–79.

Valencia, Z., and A. Gibaja

1991   *Marcavalle: El rostro oculto del Cuzco.* Cuzco: Instituto Nacional de Cultura, Region Inka.

Van Buren, M.

1996   Rethinking the Vertical Archipelago: Ethnicity, Exchange, and History in the South Central Andes. *American Anthropologist* 98(2):338–51.

2000   Political Fragmentation and Ideological Continuity in the Andean Highlands. Pp. 77–87 in J. Richards and M. Van Buren, eds., *Order, Legitimacy, and Wealth in Ancient States.* Cambridge: Cambridge University Press.

Van De Mieroop, M.

1987   *Crafts in the Early Isin Period: A Study of the Isin Craft Archive from the Reigns of Išbi-Erra and Šu-Ilišu.* Leuven: Department Orientalistiek.

2004   *A History of the Ancient Near East.* Oxford: Oxford University Press.

van Ess, M.

1991   Keramik: Akkad- bis der altbabylonischer Zeit. P. 91 in U. Finkbeiner, ed., *Uruk— Kampagne 35–37, 1982–84: Die archäologische Oberflächenuntersuchung (Survey).* Ausgrabungen in Uruk-Warka Endberichte 4. Mainz: Philipp von Zabern.

van Lerberghe

1996   The Livestock. *Administrative Documents from Tell Beydar: Subartu II,* pp. 107–17.

van Liere, W. J.

1980   Traditional Water Management in the Lower Mekong Basin. *World Archaeology* 11(3):265–80.

van Loon, M. N., ed.

2001   *Selenkahiye.* Leiden: Nederlands Historisch-Archaeologisch Instituut te Istanbul.

van Wees, H.

1997   Homeric Warfare. Pp. 668–93 in I. Morris and B. Powell, eds., *A New Companion to Homer.* Leiden: E. J. Brill.

2004   *Greek Warfare.* London: Duckworth.

van Wijngaarden, G.

1999   Production, Circulation, and Consumption of Mycenaean Pottery (Sixteenth to Twelfth Century BC). Pp. 21–47 in J.-P. Crielaard, V. Stissi, and G. van Wijngaarden, eds., *The Complex Past of Pottery.* Amsterdam: J. C. Gieben.

Vaughn, K.

2000   *Archaeological Investigations at Marcaya: A Village Approach to Nasca Economic and Sociopolitical Organization.* Ph.D. dissertation, University of California, Santa Barbara.

2002   Craft Economies and the Development and Limitations of Power in Early Intermediate Period Nasca. Paper presented at the American Anthropological Association, 101st Annual Meeting, New Orleans.

2005   Crafts and the Materialization of Chiefly Power in Nasca. Pp. 113–30 in K. Vaughn, D. Ogburn, and C. A. Conlee, eds., *The Foundations of Power in the Prehispanic Andes.* Archaeological Papers of the American Anthropological Association no. 14. Berkeley: University of California Press.

Vaughn, K., H. Neff, C. Conlee, and K. Schreiber

2002   Compositional Analysis of Nasca Polychrome Paints: Implications for Nasca Craft Economies. Paper presented at the Society for American Archaeology, 67th Annual Meeting, Denver.

Vickery, M.

1985   The Reign of Sûryavarman I and Royal Factionalism at Angkor. *Journal of Southeast Asian Studies* 16(2):226–44.

1986   Some Remarks on Early State Formation in Cambodia. Pp. 95–115 in D. G. Marr and A. C. Milner, eds., *Southeast Asia in the 9th to 14th Centuries.* Singapore: Institute of Southeast Asian Studies.

1994   What and Where Was Chenla? Pp. 197–212 in F. Bizot, ed., *Recherches nouvelles sur le Cambodia.* Paris: École Française d'Extrême-Orient.

1998   *Society, Economics, and Politics in Pre-Angkor Cambodia: The 7th–8th Centuries.* Tokyo: Center for East Asian Cultural Studies for UNESCO, Toyo Bunko.

Vo Si Khai

1998   Plans architecturaux des anciens monuments du delta du Mékong du 1er au 10e siècles AD. Pp. 207–14 in P.-Y. Manguin, ed., *Southeast Asian Archaeology 1994,* vol. 1. Hull, U.K.: Hull Centre for Southeast Asian Studies.

2003   The Kingdom of Funan and the Culture of Oc Eo. Pp. 35–86 in J. M. Khoo, ed., *Art and Archaeology of Fu Nan: Pre-Khmer Kingdom of the Lower Mekong Valley.* Bangkok: Orchid Press.

Wallerstein, I.

1974   *The Modern World-System,* vol. 1. New York: Academic Press.

Wallinga, H. T.

1993   *Ships and Sea Power before the Great Persian War.* Leiden: E. J. Brill.

Warmenbol, E.
1980   Oumm el-Marra à l'époque des royaumes d'Ebla et de Iamkhad. *Akkadica*
        19:58–59.

Watanabe, L.
1989   Cerro Baúl: Un santuario de filiación Wari en Moquegua. Pp. 257–67 in R. Don,
        C. Stanish, and P. R. Scarr, eds., *Ecology, Settlement, and History in the Osmore
        Drainage, Peru.* BAR International Series 545. Oxford: BAR.

Wattenmaker, P.
1994   Political Fluctuations and Local Exchange Systems in the Ancient Near East:
        Evidence from the Early Bronze Age Settlements at Kurban Höyük. Pp. 193–208
        in G. Stein and M. Rothman, eds., *Chiefdoms and Early States in the Near East:
        The Organizational Dynamics of Complexity.* Madison, Wisc.: Prehistory Press.

Webster, D.
2002   *The Fall of the Ancient Maya: Solving the Mystery of the Maya Collapse.* London:
        Thames and Hudson.

Webster, D. L., A. C. Freter, and D. Rue
1993   The Obsidian Hydration Project at Copan: A Regional Approach and Why It
        Works. *Latin American Antiquity* 4:303–24.

Weiss, H.
1997   Late Third Millennium Abrupt Climate Change and Social Collapse in West
        Asia and Egypt. Pp. 711–23 in N. Dalfes, G. Kukla, and H. Weiss, eds., *Third Mil-
        lennium Abrupt Climate Change and Old World Social Collapse.* NATO ASI Ser.
        I, 49. Heidelberg: Springer-Verlag.

Weiss, H., and Courty, M.-A.
1993   The Genesis and Collapse of the Akkadian Empire: The Accidental Refraction
        of Historical Law. Pp. 131–55 in M. Liverani, ed., *Akkad, the First World Empire.*
        Padua: Sargon.

Weiss, H., M.-A. Courty, W. Wetterstrom, F. Guichard, L. Senior, R. Meadow, and A.
        Curnow
1993   The Genesis and Collapse of Third Millennium North Mesopotamian Civiliza-
        tion. *Science* 261:995–1004.

Welch, D. J.
1989   Late Prehistoric and Early Historic Exchange Patterns in the Phimai Region,
        Thailand. *Journal of Southeast Asian Studies* 10(1):11–26.
1998   Archaeology of Northeast Thailand in Relation to the Pre-Khmer and Khmer
        Historical Records. *International Journal of Historical Archaeology* 2(3):205–
        34.

Werner, P.
1998   *Tall Munbaqa: Bronzezeit in Syrien.* Neumünster: Wachholtz.

West, G.
2002   Ceramic Exchange in the Late Classic and Postclassic Maya Lowlands: A Dia-
        chronic Approach. Pp. 140–96 in M. A. Masson and D. A. Freidel, eds., *Ancient
        Maya Political Economies.* Walnut Creek, Calif.: Altamira Press.

Wheatley, P.
1961   *The Golden Khersonese: Studies in the Historical Geography of the Malay Penin-
        sula Before AD 1500.* Kuala Lumpur: University of Malaya Press.
1975   Satyānṛta in Suvarṇadvīpa: From Reciprocity to Redistribution in Ancient

Southeast Asia. Pp. 227–84 in J. Sabloff and C. C. Lamberg-Karlovsky, eds., *Ancient Civilization and Trade.* Albuquerque: University of New Mexico Press.

1983   *Nagara and Commandery: Origins of the Southeast Asian Urban Traditions.* Research Papers nos. 207–8. Chicago: University of Chicago Department of Geography.

White, J.

1995   Incorporating Heterarchy into Theory on Socio-political Development: The Case from Southeast Asia. Pp. 101–23 in R. M. Ehrenreich, C. L. Crumley, and J. E. Levy, eds., *Heterarchy and the Analysis of Complex Societies.* Arlington, Va.: American Anthropological Association.

White, J., and V. Pigott

1996   From Community Craft to Regional Specialization: Intensification of Copper Production in Prestate Thailand. Pp. 151–75 in B. Wailes, ed., *Craft Specialization and Social Evolution: In Memory of V. Gordon Childe.* Philadelphia: University Museum.

White, L., Jr.

1962   *Medieval Technology and Social Change.* Oxford: Clarendon Press.

Whitelaw, T.

2001a   From Sites to Communities: Defining the Human Dimensions of Minoan Urbanism. Pp. 15–37 in K. Branigan, ed., *Urbanism in the Aegean Bronze Age.* Sheffield: Sheffield Academic Press.

2001b   Reading between the Tablets: Assessing Mycenaean Palatial Involvement in Ceramic Production and Consumption. Pp. 51–79 in S. Voutsaki and J. Killen, eds., *Economy and Politics in the Mycenaean Palace States.* Proceedings of the Cambridge Philological Society, supp. vol. 27. Cambridge.

Whitley, J.

1991   *Style and Society in Dark Age Greece.* Cambridge: Cambridge University Press.

Wilkinson, E.

2000   *Chinese History: A Manual.* Rev. ed., Asia Center for the Harvard-Yenching Institute. Cambridge: Harvard University Press.

Wilkinson, T.

1996   *State Formation in Egypt: Chronology and Society.* Cambridge Monographs in African Archaeology 40. Oxford: Tempus Reparatum.

Wilkinson, T. J.

1994   The Structure and Dynamics of Dry-farming States in Upper Mesopotamia. *Current Anthropology* 35:483–520.

1997   Environmental Fluctuations, Agricultural Production, and Collapse: A View from Bronze Age Upper Mesopotamia. Pp. 67–106 in H. Dalfes, G. Kukla, and H. Weiss, eds., *Third Millennium BC Climate Change and Old World Collapse.* Berlin: Springer-Verlag.

2004   *On the Margin of the Euphrates: Settlement and Land Use at Tell es-Sweyhat and in the Upper Tabqa Area, Syria.* OIP 124. Chicago: Oriental Institute of the University of Chicago.

Willey, G. R., W. R. Bullard Jr., and J. B. Glass

1955   The Maya Community of Prehistoric Times. *Archaeology* 8(1):8–25.

Willey, G. R., W. R. Bullard Jr., J. B. Glass, and J. C. Gifford

1965   *Prehistoric Maya Settlements in the Belize Valley.* Papers of the Peabody Museum of Archaeology and Ethnology 54. Cambridge: Harvard University Press.

Williams, P. R.

1997   *The Role of Disaster in the Evolution of Agriculture and the Development of Social Complexity in the South Central Andean Sierra.* Ph.D. dissertation, University of Florida.

2001   Cerro Baúl: A Wari Administrative Center on the Tiwanaku Frontier. *Latin American Antiquity* 12(1):67–83.

2002   Rethinking Disaster-induced Collapse in the Demise of the Andean Highland States: Wari and Tiwanaku. *World Archaeology* 33(3):361–74.

Williams, P. R., and D. Nash

2002   Imperial Interaction in the Andes: Huari and Tiwanaku at Cerro Baúl. Pp. 243–65 in W. H. Isbell and H. Silverman, eds., *Andean Archaeology: Variations in Sociopolitical Organization,* vol. I. New York: Kluwer Academic/Plenum Publishers.

Williams, P. R., and K. Sims

1998   Archaeological Population Estimates and Agrarian Productivity. 97th Annual Meeting of the American Anthropological Association, Philadelphia.

Wolters, O. W.

1973   Jayavarman II's Military Power: The Territorial Foundation of the Angkor Empire. *Journal of the Royal Asiatic Society of Great Britain and Ireland* 17:21–30.

1974   North-western Cambodia in the Seventh Century. *Bulletin of the School of Oriental and African Studies* 37(2):355–84.

1979   Khmer "Hinduism" in the Seventh Century. Pp. 427–42 in R. B. Smith and W. Watson, eds., *Early South East Asia.* New York: Oxford University Press.

1999   *History, Culture, and Region in Southeast Asian Perspectives.* Rev. ed. Ithaca, N.Y.: Cornell University Southeast Asia Program.

Wong, G.

1979   A Comment on the Tributary Trade between China and Southeast Asia, and the Place of Porcelain in This Trade, during the Period of the Song Dynasty in China. Pp. 73–100 in Singapore Southeast Asian Ceramic Society, comp., *Chinese Celadons and Other Related Wares in Southeast Asia.* Singapore: Arts Orientalis.

Woolley, C. L.

1934   *The Royal Cemetery: Ur Excavations,* vol. 2. London: Trustees of the British Museum and of the Museum of the University of Pennsylvania.

Yoffee, N.

1979   The Decline and Rise of Mesopotamian Civilization: An Ethnoarchaeological Perspective on the Evolution of Social Complexity. *American Antiquity* 44:5–35.

1988a   The Collapse of Ancient Mesopotamian States and Civilization. Pp. 44–68 in N. Yoffee and G. Cowgill, eds., *The Collapse of Ancient States and Civilizations.* Tucson: University of Arizona Press.

1988b   Orienting Collapse. Pp. 1–19 in N. Yoffee and G. Cowgill, eds., *The Collapse of Ancient States and Civilizations.* Tucson: University of Arizona Press.

1993   Too Many Chiefs? (or, Safe Texts for the 90s). Pp. 60–78 in N. Yoffee and A. Sherratt, eds., *Archaeological Theory: Who Sets the Agenda?* Cambridge: Cambridge University Press.

1995   Political Economy in Early Mesopotamian States. *Annual Review of Anthropology* 24:281–311.

2005   *Myths of the Archaic State: Evolution of the Earliest Cities, States, and Civilizations.* Cambridge: Cambridge University Press.

Yoffee, N., and G. Cowgill, eds.
1988   *The Collapse of Ancient States and Civilizations.* Tucson: University of Arizona Press.

Zapata, J.
1990   Una estructura funeraria Huari en Batan Urqo, Cusco. *Saqsaywaman* 1(3):39–54.
1992   Proyecto Arqueologico Huaro. Report to the National Geographic Society.

Zarins, J.
1986   Equids Associated with Human Burials in Third Millennium BC Mesopotamia: Two Complementary Facets. Pp. 194–206 in R. H. Meadow and H.-P. Uerpmann, eds., *Equids in the Ancient World.* Wiesbaden: Reichert.

Zettler, R. L., (with) J. A. Armstrong, A. Bell, M. Braithwaite, M. D. Danti, N. F. Miller, P. N. Peregrine, and J. A. Weber
1997   *Subsistence and Settlement in a Marginal Environment: Tell es-Sweyhat, 1989–1995 Preliminary Report.* MASCA Research Papers in Science and Archaeology, vol. 14. Philadelphia: Museum of Applied Science for Archaeology.

About the Editors

Glenn M. Schwartz is Whiting Professor of Archaeology at the Johns Hopkins University. His research focuses on the emergence and early history of complex societies in Syria and Mesopotamia, and his current field project at Tell Umm el-Marra in western Syria concentrates on the origins, collapse, and regeneration of an early urban center. Schwartz's previous fieldwork was based at the third millennium BC village of Tell al-Raqa'i in northeastern Syria, in a project focused on the role of small rural communities in early urban societies. The issue of rural archaeology was addressed in *Archaeological Views from the Countryside: Village Communities in Early Complex Societies* (1994, edited with Steven E. Falconer). Schwartz is author, co-author, and co-editor of several additional books, including, most recently, *The Archaeology of Syria: From Complex Hunter-Gatherers to Early Urban Societies, ca. 16,000–300 BC*, co-authored with Peter Akkermans.

John J. Nichols received his Ph.D. from the Johns Hopkins University in Near Eastern archaeology in 2004. He has participated in archaeological fieldwork in Syria, Egypt, and the United States, and his Ph.D. dissertation concerns the transition from the Early to the Middle Bronze Age in western Syria and the problem of Amorite ethnicity.

About the Contributors

Bennet Bronson is a curator of Asian archaeology and ethnology in the Department of Anthropology of the Field Museum. Bronson received his Ph.D. from the University of Pennsylvania in 1976. He specializes in the economic and social evolution of human society, with special reference to early technology and trade. He has worked in close collaboration with other specialists in ancient metallurgy, ceramics, and textiles. Since 1988, he has also been an adjunct professor in the Anthropology Department of the University of Illinois at Chicago. He is a co-author of *Pearls: A Natural History* (2001).

Arlen F. Chase is a professor of anthropology at the University of Central Florida. Chase received his B.A. in 1975 and his Ph.D. in 1983 in anthropology from the University of Pennsylvania. His research interests focus on archaeological method and theory in the Maya area with particular emphasis on contextual, settlement, and ceramic analysis and secondary interests on urbanism, ethnicity, and epigraphic interpretation. For the past two decades, Chase has co-directed excavations at Caracol, Belize; before that, he worked on a seven-year project at Santa Rita Corozal in the same country. He is the author or co-author of more than 100 publications, as well as co-editor of numerous others, including *Lowland Maya Postclassic* (1985; edited with P. M. Rice) and, more recently, *Mesoamerican Elites: An Archaeological Assessment* (1992; edited with D. Z. Chase). He is currently working on a book being co-authored with Diane Z. Chase called *Maya Archaeology: Reconstructing an Ancient Civilization*.

Diane Z. Chase is Pegasus Professor and a professor of anthropology at the University of Central Florida. She currently serves as interim assistant vice president for international and interdisciplinary studies in academic affairs. Chase received her B.A. in 1975 and her Ph.D. in 1982 in anthropology from the University of Pennsylvania. Her research interests focus on archaeological method and theory in the Maya area with a particular emphasis on the rise and fall of complex societies, osteological and mortuary analysis, and ethnohistory. For the past two decades, Chase has co-directed excavations at Caracol, Belize; before that, she directed a seven-year project at Santa Rita Corozal in the same country. She is the author or co-author of more than 100 publications, as well as co-editor of several others, including *Mesoamerican Elites: An Archaeological Assessment* (1992; edited with A. F. Chase). She is currently working on a book being co-authored with A. F. Chase called *Maya Archaeology: Reconstructing an Ancient Civilization*.

Christina A. Conlee is an assistant professor of anthropology at Texas State University–San Marcos. She received her B.A. in anthropology from the University of California–Santa Cruz and her M.A. and Ph.D. in anthropology from the University of California–Santa Barbara. Her research interests include the foundation and relations of power, ethnicity, rural society, and the effects of state collapse. She has conducted archaeological work in Peru and coastal California and has participated in projects in northern Mexico and Germany. Currently, Conlee is directing a multiyear archaeological project at the site of La Tiza in the Nasca region on the south coast of Peru.

Lisa Cooper obtained her Ph.D. in 1997 at the University of Toronto, where she studied Near Eastern history and archaeology. Since 1999, she has been an assistant professor in the Department of Classical, Near Eastern, and Religious Studies at the University of British Columbia in Vancouver. Cooper has participated in several archaeological projects in Iraq, Turkey, and Syria. At present, she is the assistant director of the Canadian archaeological mission to Tell ʿAcharneh in western Syria. She has also just completed a book manuscript entitled *Early Urbanism on the Syrian Euphrates* (Routledge, in press).

Timothy S. Hare is an assistant professor of anthropology in the Institute for Regional Analysis and Public Policy and is affiliated with the Geography Department at Morehead State University. He specializes in the use of quantitative techniques for spatial and regional analysis to investigate issues of political economy and public health. Hare's research interests include social theory, political economy, gender, health, and quantitative geography. He has directed and participated in several archaeological and ethnohistorical projects in Mexico and Belize aimed at reconstructing the transformation of political and economic systems in ancient Aztec and Mayan societies. In addition, he is developing software tools to facilitate quantitative geographic analysis and the comparison of multivariate spatial distributions. Hare's current research focuses on unraveling the social, political, economic, and cultural factors influencing regional patterns of public health in Appalachia, including morbidity, mortality, and health care service utilization. His prior work has appeared in *Anthropos*, *Ancient Mesoamerica*, and the *Papers of the Applied Geography Conference*.

Alan L. Kolata (Ph.D., Harvard University, 1978) is the Neukom Family Distinguished Service Professor in the Department of Anthropology at the University of Chicago. He directs ongoing, interdisciplinary research projects funded by multiple grants from the National Science Foundation and the National Oceanic and Atmospheric Agency analyzing human-environment interactions in Peru, Thailand, and most recently Cambodia. His current theoretical and empirical interests focus on issues of political economy, historical ecology, human dimensions of global environmental change, and sustainable development. Recent publications include a two-volume research monograph, *Tiwanaku and Its Hinterland* (1996, 2003), along with several other single authored and edited books and articles in journals including *Nature, Proceedings of the National Academy of Sciences, Quaternary Research, The Holocene*, and *Journal of Anthropological Archaeology*.

Marilyn A. Masson is an associate professor in Mesoamerican archaeology at the University at Albany–SUNY. She is co-director of the Economic Foundations of Mayapán Project, a research program focused on reconstructing the social and economic organization of

Mayapán's vast settlement zone outside of the monumental center. She has concentrated on Postclassic Maya archaeology since 1991 and also directs the Belize Postclassic Project that investigates the long-term social transformations of lagoon settlements at Laguna de On and Progresso Lagoon. She has published three books: *In the Realm of Nachan Kan: Postclassic Maya Archaeology at Laguna de On, Belize* (2000), *Ancient Civilizations of Mesoamerica* (2000; co-edited with Michael Smith), and *Ancient Maya Political Economies* (2002; co-edited with David Freidel). Her current book project, with Carlos Peraza Lope, is entitled *Kukulkan's Realm: The Postclassic Maya City of Mayapán.*

Gordon F. McEwan is a professor of anthropology at Wagner College. He received his Ph.D. in anthropology from the University of Texas at Austin. McEwan has done fieldwork in Cuzco, Peru, since 1978, concentrating his excavations in the eastern end of the valley of Cuzco, on the archaeological sites of Pikillacta and Chokepukio. He is the author of several volumes and numerous scientific papers on the Wari empire, its occupation of Cuzco, and its impact on the formation of the Inca empire. McEwan is currently excavating the Chokepukio site in Cuzco, where he has worked for the past thirteen years.

Ellen Morris is currently an adjunct assistant professor in the Anthropology Department at Columbia University. She has taught courses that seek to integrate anthropological theory and Egyptian data at the University of Michigan, the University of Chicago, and the University of Wales–Swansea. Morris is the author of, most recently, *The Architecture of Imperialism: Military Bases and the Evolution of Foreign Policy in Egypt's New Kingdom* (2005) and an explicitly anthropologically oriented investigation of ancient Egyptian empires entitled *Egyptian Imperialism* (forthcoming). In addition to writing and teaching, Morris has excavated at Abydos, Mendes, and Thebes, as well as in the American Southwest.

Ian Morris is the Jean and Rebecca Willard Professor of Classics and a professor of history at Stanford University, where he has served as chair of the Classics Department, associate dean of humanities and sciences, director of the Social Science History Institute, and director of the Archaeology Center. His most recent books are *The Greeks: History, Society, and Culture* (2005; with Barry Powell), *The Ancient Economy: Evidence and Models* (2005; co-edited with Joe Manning), and *The Cambridge Economic History of the Greco-Roman World* (2006; co-edited with Walter Scheidel and Richard Saller). His current research is on economic growth in the ancient Mediterranean. With political scientist Barry Weingast he edited a special section on this theme in the *Journal of Institutional and Theoretical Economics* 160 (2004). Since 2000, Morris has directed Stanford University's excavations at Monte Polizzo, an Iron Age and medieval site in Sicily.

Carlos Peraza Lope is an archaeologist with the Instituto Nacional de Antropología e Historia regional office in Mérida, Yucatán, Mexico. Since 1996 he has directed the INAH–Mayapán Project, which has investigated and restored much of the monumental center of Mayapán for tourism. He is also co-director of the Economic Foundations of Mayapán Project, an international collaborative research program with the University of Albany–SUNY. He has also performed research at hundreds of other sites in the northern Maya lowlands, including Kulubá and Cozumel. He has recently authored two major articles on Mayapán in the journals *Arqueología Mexicana* and *Ancient Mesoamerica*. His two-volume monograph on the ceramics of Cozumel, *Estudio y secuencia del material cerámico de San Gervasio, Cozumel* (1993), is a seminal work on Postclassic Maya pottery. He is currently working on a book about Mayapán, entitled *Kukulkan's Realm: The Postclassic Maya City of Mayapán*, with Marilyn Masson.

Kenny Sims received his B.A. from the University of Florida, where he worked with Michael Moseley and others. At present, Sims is a doctoral student in the Department of Anthropology at the University of Michigan, Ann Arbor. In 1998, he became a member of the Proyecto Arqueológico de Cerro Baúl in the Moquegua Valley of southern Peru. Although he has been contributing to other fieldwork projects in Peru, Panama, and the United States, he has steadily pursued his own dissertation research in the Moquegua Valley of Peru. This dissertation project assesses how household archaeology can be used to investigate local, regional, and state interaction; the effects of political and economic decline on local societies; and the relationship between political economy and ethnic identity.

Miriam T. Stark is an associate professor in the Department of Anthropology at the University of Hawaii, Manoa. She has worked in Southeast Asia since 1987 and also has experience in North American and Near Eastern archaeology. Stark has co-directed the Lower Mekong Archaeological Project in Cambodia's Mekong delta since 1996 in collaboration with His Excellency Chuch Phoeurn (Ministry of Culture and Fine Arts, Kingdom of Cambodia). She has published numerous articles on her Philippines and Cambodian research; her most recent edited volume is entitled *Archaeology of Asia* (2005).

Jill A. Weber received her B.A. in anthropology from Northwestern University and expects to receive her Ph.D. in anthropology from the University of Pennsylvania in 2006. She has thirteen years of experience working at archaeological sites in Turkey and Syria and is currently responsible for the analysis of animal remains from four projects in northern Syria. Her research interests are focused broadly on complex societies of the ancient Near East, with a focus on the ways in which animals were integrated into the political and economic systems of ancient societies. At present, she is examining the economic, symbolic, and ritual uses of donkeys, onagers, and their hybrids.

Her publications include articles in *American Journal of Archaeology, Iraq, Expedition,* and chapters in the edited volumes *Treasures from the Royal Tombs of Ur* (R. L. Zettler and L. Horne, eds.), *Excavations at Tell Brak 2* (D. Oates, J. Oates, and H. McDonald, eds.), and *Subsistence and Settlement in a Marginal Environment: Excavations at Tell es-Sweyhat (Syria), 1989–1995* (R. L. Zettler, ed.).

Norman Yoffee is a professor in the Department of Near Eastern Studies and in the Department of Anthropology, University of Michigan. He studies ancient Mesopotamian history and archaeology, primarily working on social organization and politics in the Old Babylonian period. Yoffee has published two volumes with co-authors on texts from the city of Kish in the Old Babylonian period and intends to write a history of the city of Kish. Yoffee also writes on social evolutionary theory, especially the rise and collapse of ancient states and civilizations. His recent book *Myths of the Archaic State: Evolution of the Earliest Cities, States, and Civilizations* was published in 2005.

Index

(Page references to maps and figures are in *italics*.)

"administrative underdevelopment," principle of, 119, 134

"Admonitions of Ipuwer," 66–67

agrarian economy, 31, 160, 165, 204

agriculture: Khmer wet-rice, 160, 218; maximization of in Bronze Age Syria, 18–20; Maya slash-and-burn plots, 203; Nasca, 102, 106; specialization in Middle Bronze Age Palestine, 19–20; surpluses, 6, 10–11; Tiwanaku/Wari hydraulic, 92, 124

agro-pastoralism, in Middle Bronze Age Syria, 56

Akkadian empire, 18, 30, 40–41

Akragas, Greece, *74*, 76, 80

alliance(s): in First Intermediate Period Egypt, 68–69; marriage in Bronze Age Syria, 40, 42; Maya, 180, 182, 224; Nasca, 111–112; political, 209; underlying social complexity, 8, 10

altars, Maya stone, 168–169, 172, 180

Amorite ethnic group(s), 12–13, 35, 41–42, 47, 51–56. *See also* ethnic group(s)

ancestor veneration, 155, 178, 181, 184–186

Andahuaylillas, Peru, 89, 93

Angkor Borei (Funan capital), Cambodia, 151–152, 160

Angkorian polity, 146, *157*, *158*, 162

annals, Chinese dynastic, 144, 146, 149, 151, 153, 162

architecture, monumental: Lucre-style, 94; Maya, 171, 173, 176–177, 179–181, 185–186; Tiwanaku, 122–123, 125, 127–128, 134; Wari administrative, 89, 94, 105, 125

army, 69, 79, 83, 164, 226–227

art programs, Maya, 177, 190, 193–195

assembly: of elders in Middle Bronze Age Syria, 32–33; Maya multiple, 189–190; Middle Kingdom Egyptian, 71

Assyrian: army, 83, 226–227; state, 16, 83–84, 226

Athens, Greece, *74*, 78, 80

axes, Maya, 199, 203

Ayacucho, Peru, 89, 92, 104, 123–124

Babylonia, Mesopotamian state of, 16, 35, 226–227

ballcourts, Mayapán, 190, *191*, 206

barbarians, 7, 86, 139

Batan Urqo cemetery, Peru, 88, 91

beer, Inca corn (*chicha*), 92, 109

Bhavavarman, pre-Angkor Cambodia, 153

boundaries, 6, 31, 59, 68, 71, 101, 149, 164, 182, 203

Buddhism, Cambodian adoption of, 155, 159, 164

bureaucracy: Chinese imperial, 217, 225; concept of, 210; in Early Bronze Age Syria, 18; Maya ruling, 193

burial(s), human: Batan Urqo, Peru, 88, 91; Dark Age Greek, 76, 79; Egyptian First Intermediate Period, 62–63, 66; Inca, 85, 88, 94-95; Maya, 172, 177, 179–181, *191*, 206; Nasca, 105; Syrian Bronze Age, 22–23, 26, 32, 44–46, 52–53, 62; Tiwanaku, 122, 131; Wari, 91

cacao beans, Maya trade in, 198, 200, 207

cache figures, Maya trade in, 177, 182

caching, Maya, 180-181, 184–186
calendrical ritual, 166, 181–182, 185–186, 193
canals: Cambodian, 149; Inca, 89;
    Tumilaca state, 132–133; Wari, 123–124,
    127–129
Cape Gelidonya, Turkey, *74*, 77
Caracol, Belize, 15, 168–170, 174, 176–180,
    198
Carchemish, Turkey, *21*, 29
Caye Coco, Belize, 200, *202*, 203
Cerro Baúl, Peru, 106, *115*, 116, 123–135
Cerro Mejia, Peru, 124–125, 129
Cerro San Miguel, Peru, *115*, 134
Chancas ethnic group(s), 106, 224
Chao Phraya region, Southeast Asia, 144,
    149, 164
Chen Chen, Peru, *115*, 122–123, 125, 127–128
Chenla polity, Cambodia, 152–153, *154*–155
Chichen Itza, 16, 88, 115, 188–195, *189*, *190*,
    191, 197, 199, 206
Chinese dynastic annals, 144–146, 149, 151,
    153, 162
Chokepukio (Cuzco), Peru, 86, 88–89, 91,
    93–96
cities, conceptions of, 28, 40, 210–211
city-state(s): Bronze Age Near Eastern, 8,
    19, 25, 30, 56; Classic Maya, 224; early
    Greek (*poleis*), 9, 75, 79–80, 83–84
"civilizing mission" in colonial ideology,
    210, 216
climate change, 6, 11, 14, 19, 30, 41, 83–84,
    91–92, 106, 220
cloth, 92, 161, 199–200
collapse: concept of multidirectional, 223;
    defined, 5–6; studies of, 3–4, 222–224
colonizing state, concept of, 210–211
colonnaded halls, Maya, 178, *190*, *191*, 194
commercial economy: early Southeast
    Asian, 151; European, 7–8; Mayan,
    198–199; Middle Bronze Age Syrian,
    25, 36, 42, 50–51, 55–56; Phoenician, 83
commodities exchange: as element of
    statehood, 209; Maya, 203; Middle
    Bronze Age Syria, 13, 50, 54; sixth-
    century Greek, 78
complex society: defined, 17n1; in early
    Greece, 72–73; study of, 3

confederacy, 31, 35, 153, 193, 205, 224
consciousness, historical, 211, 214–216,
    218–220
conspicuous consumption, 45, 210
copper, 77, 167, 167n4, 177, 199
"core" areas, regional, 8, 13, 80, 83, 160, 224
corporate political strategy, 12, 31–33, 53,
    62, 183
corvée service, 156, 205
cosmological ideology, 155, 180
cotton goods, 111, 199–201, 207
craft production, 28, 54, 78–79, 112, 199,
    205
cross-cultural examination, 5, 13, 17, 193
"cultural matrix," 145, 159
currency, 54, 161, 200–201, 227
Cuzco, Peru, 14, 85–86, 89–90, *90*, 91–96, 98
Cyrus the Great, 226–227

Dark Age Greece, 76
"dark ages," 7, 30, 208
decentralization, concept of, 11, 13
democracy, 9, 178–179
devaraja, at Angkor, 156, 163
diet, as Maya status marker, 178, 185
dog, 48, 188, 199
donkey, 46, 48, 50, 53
Dos Pilas, 169, 205
doxology, state, 214–215
dress, 96, 169–170
dyeing, 47–48, 201
Dzibilchaltun (Chunchucmil), Yucatan,
    200, 204–206

Ebla, Syria, 28, 32, 40–42, 44–45, 52
ecology, political, 165, 209–210
economy: diversified subsistence, 13, 15,
    19, 29, 35; flexible, 30, 34, 56; Maya
    market, 224; Tiwanaku domestic, 118;
    Wari state, 118
education, 65, 80–81
effigy censers, Maya, 193, 197, 206
egalitarianism, symbolic, 9, 15, 178–183,
    185–187
Emar, Syria, 22–23, 26, *29*, 32–33
emblem glyph, Maya, 176–177, 183, 186
environmental degradation, 11, 41, 168

equid hunting and processing, 43–51, *44*, 53, 56–57
Estuquiña culture, 116, *117*, 135
ethnic group(s): Amorite, 12–13, 35, 41–42, 51–56; Chancas, 106; Inca, 94–95; legitimizing aspect of, 42, 47, 139; Nasca, 109, 112; Tiwanaku, 128; Wari, 112
"exclusionary" strategies, 31–32

families, Maya noble, 195–197, 205–206
faunal analysis, 29–30, 41–44, *44*, 47–48, 199
feasting: early Egyptian, 63; Inca ritual, 93–96; Nasca, 14, 111–112
finance, 10, 54, 75, 165
First Intermediate Period Egypt, 9, 14, 19, 56, 58–70, 219, 223
fish, in Maya tribute and trade, 199, 201
flexibility, strategies of, 11, 13, 38, 56, 60, 221
foddering, intensive, 51, 153–155, 198
fortifications, 26–27, 33, 47, 51, 211
frame analysis, 15, 168, 173, *174*, 175–187
Front Face Deity, 123, *126*, 128, 131
Funan, 146, *150*, 151–152

gallery patio architecture, Maya, 190, *191*, 206
gazelle, 30, 49–50
genetic data: Moquegua and Altiplano, Peru, 122
gifting, Maya, 199, 207
gold: Egyptian jewelry of, 67; Inca jewelry of, 95; Khmer exchange in, 161, 167n4; Maya trade in, 177
"golden ages," concept of, 4
Gordion (Persian-period Turkey), false regeneration at, 137
governance, Maya shared, 185–186

Habuba Kabira, Syria, *22–23*, 26
Halawa, Syria, 21, *22–23*, 26, 33
Han-period China, 148, 225
hegemony and sovereignty, strategy of, 16, 165, 209–216
hegemony without sovereignty, 16, 105, 210–221n1
heterarchical organization, 12, 33–34, 112, 138, 152, 176, 183

Hinduism, Cambodian adoption of, 155, 163
historical consciousness, 211, 214–216, 218–220
historical memory, 16, 206
Homer, 75–76, 78–79
Hopewell culture, non-regeneration of, 143
household: functional units, Maya standardization in, 177–178; *plazuela* groups, 176, 178–181; production and distribution, Maya, 176–177, 182, 198, 201; Tiwanaku, 130
house(s): in Bronze Age Syria, 21, 24, 26, 33, 44–45, 48, 52–53; early Greek, 76, 78, 80–81; Maya, 197, 199, 204–206, 224; Nasca, 107, 109–110, 112; Tumilaca, 118, 121–122, 131–135. *See also* household
huacas (Wari religious sites), 91, 96
Huaracane (prestate Moquegua Valley inhabitants), 130
Huaro (Wari), Peru, 86, 88–91, 93, 96
hunting, 13, 49, 54, 56, 132
hydraulic systems, 89–90, 96, 106

ibn Khaldun, 7, 12
iconography: Maya, 170, 180–181; Nasca/Wari, 91, 93, 102, 104, 109; Southeast Asian Vishnu, 148, 163
ideology: Inca imperial, 96; Indic, 145; pluralizing, 219
Inca: cult of the sun god, 9; map of empire, *97*; origins of, 55, 85–86, 89, 92, 96, *104*, 116, *117*, 218
incense burners (Maya *incensarios*), 181–182
India, 137, 148, 151, 160, 225
"Indianization," in Southeast Asia, 152
Indic: çaka system, 166–167n2; ideology, 145, 155, 159–160, 163–164
Indus civilization, 3
innovation, technological, 41
"international style," Maya Late Postclassic, 183
inversion of social order, 56, 67, 219
irrigation agriculture: canal, 89, 123–124, 127–129, 132–134, 149; introduction in Peru, 102; Khmer, 160; terrace, 105, 109, 123–124, 129, 176

Isanavarman, first king of Chenla (Cambodia), 155

Jabbul Plain, Syria, 13, 38–39, 40–47, 54–56
Jayavarman I–II, pre-Angkor Cambodia, 151, 153, 155–156
Jayavarman VII, king of Angkor, 159–162
Jerablus Tahtani, Syria, 20–21, *21*, 22–23, 32
jewelry, 67, 95, 122, 177
Jincamocco, Peru, 105, 124
Jurchen, in Northeast Asia, 139–140

Khabur Plains, Syria, 18, 20, 29–30, 40
Khmer: attached specialists, 160; civilization, 144–146; chronology, 146, *147*; polities, 15; "template," 218–219, 225
knives, Maya stone bifacial, 203
Knossos, Crete, 74–77, *74*
kurakas (Inca traditional leaders), 120

labor system, Tumilaca reciprocal, 134
Laguna de On, Belize, 200, 202–203, *202*
Lake Titicaca, Bolivia, 86, 88–89, 92, 103, 106
Lamanai, Belize, 169, 177–179
La Tiza, Peru, 103, 108–110, 112, 124
"Law of Evolutionary Potential," 119
leather production, 13, 43, 49–51, 54, 57
Lefkandi, Greece, *74*, 76, 82
leisure, 80–81, 212
Linear B tablets, 75, 77–80
literacy, in early China, 140–141
literature, 66, 79, 164, 223
lithic debris, at Tikal, 202–203
llamas, 109, 122
long-count dates, Maya, 173, 190
Lucre: basin, Peru, 90–91; as style, 93–95

maat, 14, 58
maize, 89–90, 122, 199
Malaysia, false regeneration in, 138
Manchu state, Northeast Asia, 139
Marcavalle, Cuzco (Peru), 86–88
Mari, 28–29, 31–32, 36, 40, 42, 50–53
market systems, Maya, 185, 198, 200–201
Mayapán, Yucatan, 15, 188, *189*, *190*, *194*
memory, historical, 15–16, 138, 192, 206

Mentuhotep II, 59, 69–70
mercantilism, Maya, 168–169, 177, 184, 195
merchants, 16, 36, 61, 195–197, 206–207
metals, 20, 36, 41, 44, 52, 77–78, 149
"middling ideology," 9, 77
military: establishment, 226; force as instrument of social control, 70, 73, 79, 83–84, 140–141, 156, 162, 200, 205, 210–212; hereditary Angkorian, 162; power, Assyrian, 83; service, Maya, 204–205. *See also* army
mining, Wari/Tiwanaku, 127, 129
mobility, social, 9, 14, 219, 223
Mongol Yuan dynasty, China, 139–140
monuments: funerary, 20, 32, 64; Maya stone, 169, 178, 180–181; South Asian brick, 148, 161, 163–164
Moquegua River Valley, Peru, 14, 114–115, *115*, *117*
morbidity and mortality, in early Greece, 80–81
mortuary: center, 20, 32; complex, 44–45, 50, 53; cult, 61–65, 68; differentiation, 64, 122; monuments, 163, 172; studies, 60, 63; temples, 61–62, 163, 172, 181, 186. *See also* burial(s), human
multepal (Maya joint leadership), 179, 194
Munbaqa, Syria, 22–23, 26–27, 33, 37n2
Mycenae, Greece, 14, 72–74, *74*, 75–81

Nagada II–III Egypt, 63–64, 68
Nasca drainage, Peru, 102–103, *103*
Nasca lines (geoglyphs), 102
Nohmul, Belize, 168, 177, 182
nomadism, pastoral, 19, 31
Nubia, 63, 69

obsidian: Maya green, 202; Maya household access to, 176; Maya trade in, 111, 124–125, 127, 177–178, 199, 201, 206; sites in Belize and Mayapán, 202–203, *202*; studies, 169, 202
Oc Eo, Vietnam, 149, 152
Omo, Peru, *115*, 122–123, 125, 127–128
onager, 13, 30, 43, 46, 49, 56
organizational studies, 3, 142, 173

orthodoxy, 16, 212–216, 218, 220
orthopraxy, 16, 212, 215–216, 218, 220
"overbounded systems," 179

Pacheco, Peru, 104–105
Pajonal Alto, Peru, *103*, 108, 110–111
palace(s): Bronze Age Greece and Crete,
    14, 72, 75–76, 78–79, 84; Chinese
    wooden, 149; as element of orthodoxy,
    211, 213; Maya multiple-room, 169,
    176–183; patio-group, 125
Palestine, 19, 29–30, 34, 222
pastoralism, 19, 29, 42, 56
patio groups, Wari, 103–105, 125
peasant revolt(s), 106, 168, 178
peer polity interaction, 10
peripheries, regeneration at, 14, 65, 83, 96,
    100, 116, 140, 223
Petén region, Guatemala, 172, 196, 198,
    202, 223
Petexbatun polities, of Maya Classic
    period, 205
Philippines, southern (false generation
    in), 138
Pikillacta, Peru, 86, 89, 91–94, 96, 98
Pithekoussai, *74*
platform: Akapana temple, 122–123;
    Egyptian mortuary, 68; Maya,
    171; Omo ritual, 128–129; Syrian
    monumental, 46, 48, 50
plaza(s), 110–111, 125, 213. *See also*
    household: *plazuela* groups
pottery, Bronze Age Syria, 22–23, 27–28,
    37n1, 51–52
pottery, Dark Age Greece, 78
pottery: Chanapata, 88; K'illke, 94–95;
    Lucre, 93–96; Marcavalle, 87–88; Maya,
    95, 170, 177–178, 180–181, 193, 197;
    Mollo, 95; Mycenaean, 77–78; Nasca,
    102–103, 108, 111; Tiwanaku, 96, 122,
    126, 128–130; Tumilaca, *126*, 131–132;
    Wari, 91, 93, 105, 110, 125, 127
prestige economy, Maya, 207
priesthood, Maya, 195–197, 206–207
"primate" settlement, Maya, 193, 199
pristine state formation, 10, 69
production, Maya standardization in, 176

Puma Head, 123, 128, 131
Pylos, Greece, 73–*74*, 80
pyramid(s): Angkor temple, 156; Giza, 69;
    Maya epicentral, 181; Nasca mound,
    102; Egyptian Third and Fourth
    Dynasties, 61, 65, 69

Qara Quzaq, Syria, 22–23, 26, 33, 37n2
quarries, Wari-controlled, 125, 127

ranked confederacy, Maya, 193, 195, 205
regeneration: defined, 7–12; "false," 15,
    137–138, 224; "genuine," 72; "negative,"
    15; "stimulus," 15, 138–140, 218, 224;
    "template," 15, 55, 70, 85, 140, 159,
    192, 206, 216–218, 224–225. *See also*
    peripheries, regeneration at
"regression," societal, 38
religion, "democratization" of, 67, 71;
    state, as element of orthodoxy, 212–213
religious ideology, 103–104, 112, 144–145,
    163, 166
resilience, 9, 16; in Cambodia, 165–166;
    strategies of in Middle Bronze Age
    Syria, 26, 29, 30, 34, 51, 54, 56, 138, 221
revolts, Maya peasant, 168, 218
rice, Khmer, 161, 218
ritual: altiplano, 122; brick architecture
    in Mekong region, 152; community-
    based, 110, 184–185; concept of
    public, 13; Maya calendric, 185–186;
    Maya state-sponsored, 224; Nasca
    community/exclusive, 111–112
ritualization, Khmer, 162–163
Roman empire, 7, 11, 72, 141–142, 148, 151
ruling council (*multepal*), Maya, 179, 194–195
Rudravarman, king of Funan, 151

Saivism, Southeast Asian adoption of,
    155–156, 163
salt, 88, 199, 201, 205, 207
Sanskrit, use by Khmer, 153, 217–218,
    144–145, 148–149
Santa Rita Corozal, Belize, 168, 177–184,
    193, 203
Santa Rita, Peru, *115*, 132
sculpture(s), 76, 148, 155, 164

secondary elites, 16, 223–224
second-generation states, examples of,
10, 73, 83–84, 114, 116. *See also* state(s),
concept of
Selenkahiye, Syria, 20–21, *21*, 22–23, 27, 33
Selinous, Sicily, *74*, 76
settlement hierarchy: Bronze Age Syria, 41,
44, 47; Maya, 176; Middle Bronze Age
Palestine, 19; Nasca, 108; Wari colonial
multitier, 124–125
Shamshi-Adad, 42, 50
shared rule, of Classic Maya model, 15, 183
shell beads, Maya trade in, 201
shrines, 211, 213; Angkor Borei brick, 152,
155–163; Inca Sacsayhuaman, 96;
Levantine, at Kommos, 78; Maya,
177–178, 180–183, 186; state, as element of
orthodoxy, 213; Tell Hadidi, Syria, 22–23;
Tiwanaku, 96; Wari huacas, 91, 96
Shubat-Enlil (modern Leilan), Syria, 42
silver: Athenian, 79; Khmer exchange in,
161, 167n4; Wari, 95
slaves: Archaic Greek, 75; Khmer exchange
in, 161; Mayapán, 207; Muslim world
demand for, 8
snake symbolism, Maya, 181, 190, *191*, 197
social order: ancient Egyptian inversion
of, 59, 67; at Middle Bronze Age
Umm el-Marra (Syria), 52, 56; pre-
Angkorian, 164; three dimensions of,
120
Sondondo Valley, 105, 124
Song state, China, 140, 161
Sparta, Greece, 74–75, *74*, 79–80
specialization: as aspect of frame
analysis, 175; in Bronze Age Syria, 13,
19–20; Greek craft, 73, 78. *See also*
standardization
spindle whorls, 132, 170–171, 200
Spondylus shell, 109, 111, 177, 201
Srivijaya, trading empire, 152, 166
standardization: in Bronze Age Syria,
47, 50–51; in commercial currency
(Khmer), 161; early Chinese, 217; Inca,
93. *See also* specialization
staple finance, concept of, 10
state emblems, Tumilaca, 128

state formation, pristine, 63, 139, 144, 217,
226
state religion: Cambodian establishment
of, 156; as element of state orthodoxy,
212–213
state(s), concept of: primary, 3; second-
generation, 4, 10
state systems, high risk–high return, 33,
59–60, 71, 220
statuary, Indic, 148, 152, 163
status differentiation, Maya, 170–171
stelae: Khmer and/or Sanskrit inscribed,
144; Maya, 168–169, 185–186, 192–193,
206; Middle Kingdom Egyptian
votive, 71
stimulus regeneration, 15, 138–139, in Holy
Roman Empire, 139; in 1780s United
States, 139; in Zimbabwe, 139; and
Zulu empire, 139
"Stockholm syndrome," 211
stones: exotic, as tribute to Mayapán, 199;
Nasca elite polishing, 110–111; Near
Eastern Bronze Age precious, 35–36,
67; Wari precious, 124
"structural template," 218–219
stucco, Maya architectural, 171, 181, 192
subsistence economy: Bronze Age Syrian
diversified, 11–13, 19, 25, 29–31, 33,
35; Khmer, 15, 160; Mayapán local,
203–204
Sui dynasty, China, 140, 151, 153
Sumatra, 138, 152, 161, 166
Suryavarman I, Khmer ruler, 156, 164
symbolic egalitarianism, concept of, 9, 15,
178–187
Syria, Bronze Age, 8, 11–12, *21*, *39*, 40–57

Tang state, China, 140, 152–153, 161
tariffs, as instrument of social control,
36, 211
taxation: early Egyptian, 61, 65; early
Greek, 73, 75, 79; for social control,
210–212, 216; Khmer, 156–159;
Mycenaean, 75
Tayasal, Guatemala, 168–169, 171
Tell Ahmar, Syria, *21–22*, 26, 32, 37n2
Tell Banat, Syria, 20, *21–22*, 32–33

Tell es-Sweyhat, Syria, *21–22*, 24, 26–29, 33

Tell Hadidi, Syria, *21–22*, 24, 26, 33

Tell Kabir, Syria, *21–22*, 26–28, 33

Tell Umm el-Marra, Syria, 4–5, 13, 38, *39*, 40, 42, *43*, 44–56

template regeneration: in Han state (China), 140; in Japan, 141; in Korea, 141; in Ming state (China), 140; in northwest Europe, 142; in Vietnam, 141

temple(s): in ancient Near East, 20, 22–23, 24, 27–28; Egyptian mortuary, 61, 69–70; as element of state orthodoxy, 213; estates (Khmer), 145, 155, 159–161, 165; Greek *hekatompeda*, 76; Lucre, 96; Maya, 180, 185, 189, *190*, *191*, 206; platform, 122–123; pyramids (Angkor), 156; "temple-in-antis," 21–23; Tiwanaku, 129; Wari, 91

temporal cycles, orthodox use of, 212–214

terraces, field: Maya, 176; Nasca, 109; Tiwanaku, 123; Wari, 105, 124, 128–129, 132–133

textiles: Chinese, 217; Maya, 199–200; Nasca, 102; Tiwanaku elite, 96, 122. *See also* cloth

Thebes, Egypt, 69, 70

Thebes, Greece, 73–74, *74*

Tikal, Guatemala, 169, 177, 202–204

tin, 77, 167n4

Tiryns, Greece, 73–74, *74*

Titicaca basin, Lake: Bolivia and Peru, 85–86, 88–90, 92, 103, 106

Tiwanaku: empire, 9, 14, 85, *90*, 103; pre–Middle Horizon spheres of influence, *87*

tomb(s): chamber, 24; monumental stone, 20, 22–23, 24, 26, 32, 37n1, 44, 64–67, 76–77, 127. *See also* burial(s), human

Tonle Sap polity, Cambodia, *150*, *154*, 155

trade network(s): Bronze Age Near Eastern, 36, 41, 50; early Southeast

Asian international maritime, 15, 148, 151–152, 159, 161, 166; Mediterranean, 7; Maya, 176

trans-Jordan, Early Bronze Age, 34

tribal society: in Bronze Age Syria, 12, 30–33, 35; Chenla, 153; resulting from devolution of complexity, tribute, 156, 167n4, 211

Troy, Aegean, 73–74, *74*

Tumilaca, 12, 14, 55, 114–115, *115*, 116, *117*, 118–135, 142

Ulu Burun, Turkey, *74*, 77

Umm el-Marra, Syria. *See* Tell Umm el-Marra, Syria

Urcos, Peru, 89–91, 93

vacant-terrain locales, 124, 171–172

Vaishnavism/Vaisnavism, Southeast Asian adoption of, 155, 163–164

Wari: Ayacucho (capital), 104–105, 123–124; empire, 14, 85, 89, 90–91, *90*, 93, 95, 99, 102–109, *115*; pre–Middle Horizon spheres of influence, *87*

Wat Phu (Chenla capital), Laos, 153

wood, trade in, 151, 167, 201

wool, trade in, 75, 122

workshop(s): Bronze Age Syrian, 20, 22–23, 28, 48–49, 54; Mayapán, 203; Mycenaean, 78

world-systems approaches, 12, 83, 198

worship: Dark Age Greek, 76; Maya privatized, 168–169; Nasca mountain and water, 109; pre-Angkorian ancestor, 155

Yamkhad, Bronze Age Syria, 28, 42, 47

Zimbabwe: non-regeneration of culture in, 143. *See also* stimulus regeneration